*THE JOHN HARVARD LIBRARY*

*Bernard Bailyn*
*Editor-in-Chief*

# *TRAVELS in NEW ENGLAND and NEW YORK*

*BY TIMOTHY DWIGHT*

*Edited by Barbara Miller Solomon*
*with the assistance of*
*Patricia M. King*

*VOLUME IV*

*The John Harvard Library*

JHL

*The Belknap Press of*
*Harvard University Press*
*Cambridge, Massachusetts*
*1969*

Distributed in Great Britain by Oxford University Press, London
Library of Congress Catalog Card Number: 69-12735
Printed in the United States of America

John Harvard Library books are edited at the Charles Warren Center for Studies in American History, Harvard University.

# *CONTENTS*

## *Volume IV*

# TRAVELS;

IN

# NEW-ENGLAND AND NEW-YORK:

BY


TIMOTHY DWIGHT, S. T. D. LL. D.

LATE PRESIDENT OF YALE COLLEGE;

AUTHOR OF

THEOLOGY EXPLAINED AND DEFENDED.


IN FOUR VOLUMES.

## VOL. IV.


NEW-HAVEN:
PUBLISHED BY TIMOTHY DWIGHT.

S. CONVERSE, PRINTER.

1822.

# CONTENTS

## JOURNEY TO NIAGARA

## *SECOND JOURNEY TO LAKE WINNIPESAUKEE OR WENTWORTH*



## *JOURNEY TO UTICA*



## *THE IROQUOIS*



## *REMARKS ON EUROPEAN TRAVELERS IN AMERICA*

## *LANGUAGE OF NEW ENGLAND*



## *LEARNING, MORALS, ETC. OF NEW ENGLAND*

## *RELIGION OF NEW ENGLAND*

## *MASSACHUSETTS*

### LETTER I



### LETTER II



## *PROSPECTS OF THE UNITED STATES*

### LETTER I



### LETTER II

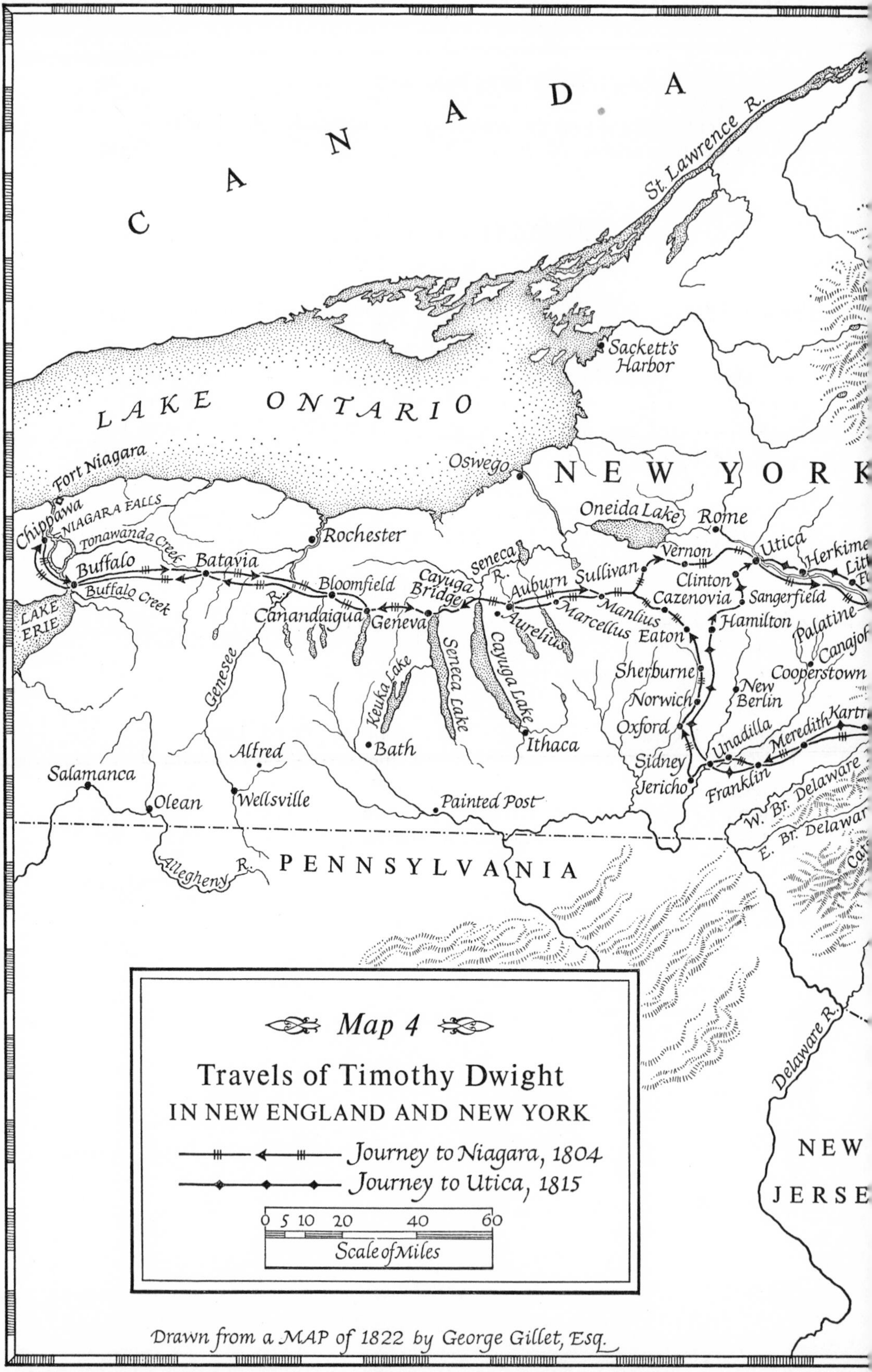
C A N A D A
St. Lawrence R.
Sackett's Harbor
LAKE ONTARIO
Fort Niagara
Oswego
NEW YORK
Chippawa
NIAGARA FALLS
Tonawanda Creek
Rochester
Oneida Lake
Rome
Vernon
Utica
Herkimer
Buffalo
Batavia
Buffalo Creek
LAKE ERIE
Bloomfield
Canandaigua
Geneva
Cayuga Bridge
Seneca R.
Auburn
Sullivan
Clinton
Cazenovia
Sangerfield
Manlius
Marcellus
Aurelius
Eaton
Hamilton
Palatine
Canajoharie
Cooperstown
Sherburne
Norwich
New Berlin
Oxford
Unadilla
Meredith
Sidney
Jericho
Franklin
Genesee R.
Keuka Lake
Seneca Lake
Cayuga Lake
Ithaca
Bath
Alfred
Salamanca
Olean
Wellsville
Painted Post
W. Br. Delaware
E. Br. Delaware
Allegheny R.
PENNSYLVANIA
Delaware R.
NEW JERSEY
Map 4
Travels of Timothy Dwight
IN NEW ENGLAND AND NEW YORK
Journey to Niagara, 1804
Journey to Utica, 1815
0 5 10 20 40 60
Scale of Miles
Drawn from a MAP of 1822 by George Gillet, Esq.

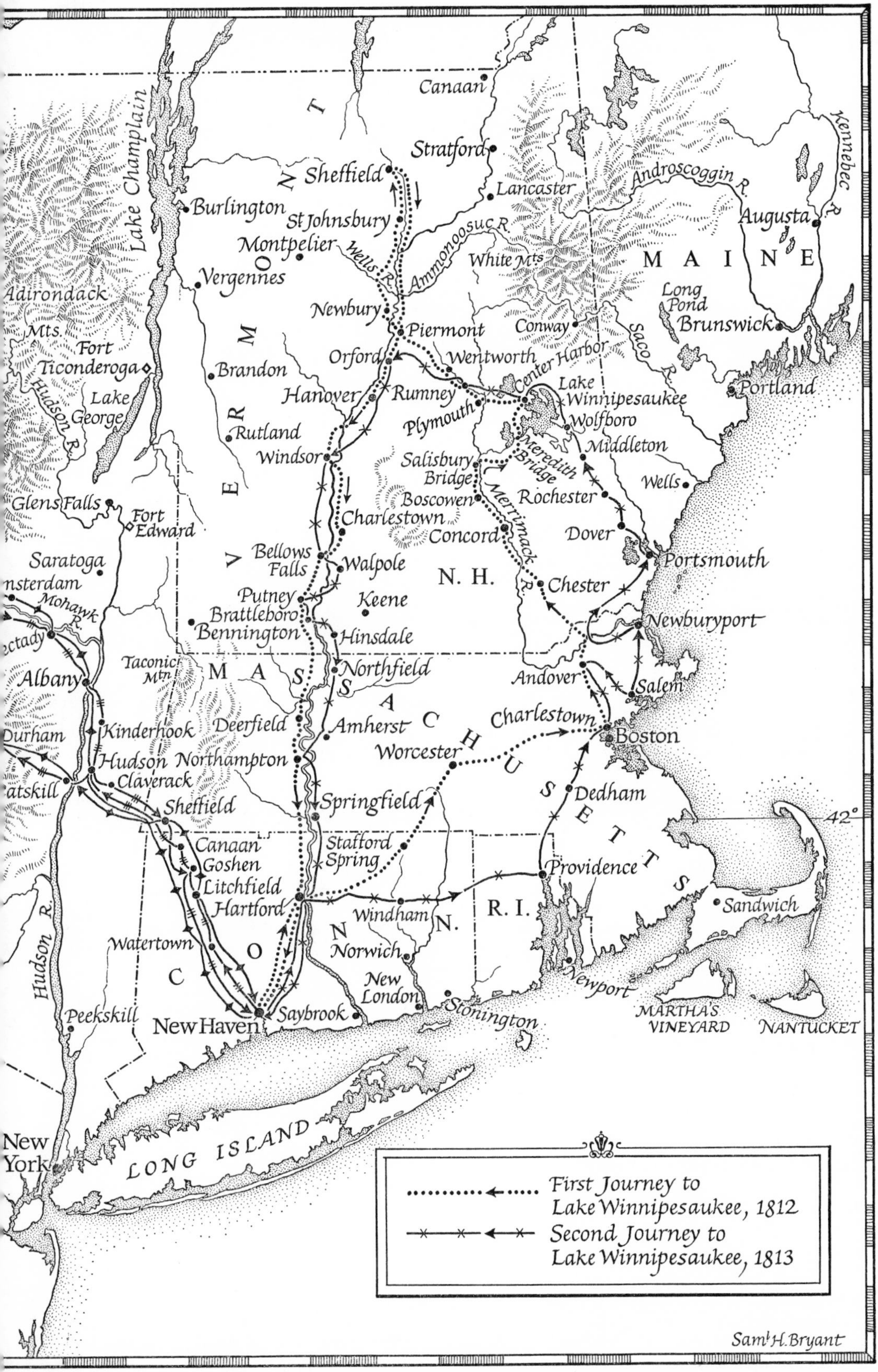

First Journey to Lake Winnipesaukee, 1812
Second Journey to Lake Winnipesaukee, 1813
VERMONT
MAINE
N. H.
MASSACHUSETTS
CONN.
R. I.
LONG ISLAND
Lake Champlain
Burlington
Vergennes
Montpelier
St Johnsbury
Sheffield
Canaan
Stratford
Lancaster
Newbury
Piermont
Orford
Hanover
Wentworth
Rumney
Plymouth
Center Harbor
Lake Winnipesaukee
Wolfboro
Middleton
Rochester
Dover
Portsmouth
Newburyport
Salem
Andover
Boston
Charlestown
Worcester
Dedham
Providence
Newport
Sandwich
MARTHA'S VINEYARD
NANTUCKET
Augusta
Brunswick
Portland
Long Pond
Wells
Conway
White Mts
Androscoggin R.
Kennebec R.
Saco R.
Ammonoosuc R.
Wells R.
Merrimack R.
Meredith Bridge
Salisbury Bridge
Boscowen
Concord
Chester
Windsor
Charlestown
Bellows Falls
Walpole
Keene
Putney
Brattleboro
Hinsdale
Northfield
Amherst
Deerfield
Northampton
Springfield
Stafford Spring
Hartford
Windham
Norwich
New London
Stonington
Saybrook
New Haven
Watertown
Litchfield
Goshen
Canaan
Sheffield
Claverack
Hudson
Kinderhook
Albany
Catskill
Durham
Schenectady
Amsterdam
Mohawk R.
Saratoga
Glens Falls
Fort Edward
Lake George
Fort Ticonderoga
Adirondack Mts.
Hudson R.
Brandon
Rutland
Bennington
Taconic Mtn
Peekskill
New York
42°
Sam^l H. Bryant

# JOURNEY TO NIAGARA

## LETTER I

*Journey to Sheffield—White marble—Rapid descent of the streams which fall into the Hudson and into the Housatonic—Egremont—Manor of Livingston—Claverack—Character of first settlers in little landing places—Catskill—Canton—Durham—Catskill Mountains—Bristol—Blenheim—Stamford—Harpersfield—Meredith—White pine tree—Franklin—Sidney—Miserable inns—Troublesome innkeeper—Unadilla—Oxford—Norwich—Jericho—Chenango River and Valley—Sherburne—Hamilton—Cazenovia*

*Dear Sir,*

On Wednesday, September 19, 1804, I began a journey to the falls of Niagara. I was detained by rain until three o'clock in the afternoon, and then rode to Watertown: twenty-six miles. The next day I proceeded to Sheffield: forty-one miles. At Litchfield, and afterwards at Canaan, I had expected to find my destined companions in this excursion, but missed of them in both places. At the latter, after a solitary ride of between fifty and sixty miles, I found some gentlemen going to Sheffield, whose company made the remainder of the way very agreeable. The day was remarkably cold for the season and was followed by a severe frost: the ice at Sheffield being the next morning about the thickness of a dollar, and the tender vegetables generally destroyed. During the preceding nine years there has not in those parts of the country where I have journeyed been a frost sufficiently intense to destroy vegetables of this class until about the middle of October.

At Sheffield, I found two gentlemen designing to set out for Catskill,* and with them I proceeded very pleasantly on the journey. The road turns directly west from Sheffield, and enters the state of New York in the township of Hillsdale. The part of it which is in Massachusetts is alternately a forest and a collection of solitary settlements.

About a mile and a half from Sheffield we passed by a number of workmen employed in sawing, grinding, and polishing marble. Immense quarries of this mineral are found in the range of hills at the foot of which their works were erected. It is white and generally of the same texture with that at West Stockbridge. The workmen, however, showed us some speci-

* The name of this town was originally spelled *Kaatskill,* but has since been altered by the legislature to *Catskill.* PUB.

mens of a much finer quality, and very beautiful. The business is here in its infancy; but, if pursued with industry and prudence, can scarcely fail of being profitable.

The ascent of the Taconic Range on the eastern side is gradual and easy; on the western, the declivity is longer and steeper. From the bottom of this range the tributary streams of the Hudson run through a country twenty miles in breadth, with a rapidity not less than that with which those of the Housatonic run five miles. Both the valley and the bed of the Hudson, therefore, are much nearer the level of the ocean in this latitude than those of the Housatonic. This conclusion is obvious also from an attention to the current of these rivers. That of the Housatonic from Canaan to Derby is almost universally rapid, and is interrupted by several falls and rifts. The whole perpendicular descent of these must be more than two hundred feet; and that of the general current, much more. From Canaan to the Sound, the length of the river as measured on the road is seventy-two miles; and this distance, although the road follows the course of the river in a remarkable degree, is yet short of the truth. Almost all this distance is a continued ripple. Three hundred feet will be a moderate allowance for such a descent throughout such a distance. In the Hudson there is not even a rapid below Troy.

The first township through which we passed after leaving Sheffield was Egremont in Massachusetts, bordering upon the western line of the state and lying on the summit and eastern declivity of Taconic. The soil of this township is generally good. The settlement is comparatively recent. The inhabitants live on scattered plantations, and suffer the usual inconveniences, both moral and physical, of such settlements. Their number in 1790 was 759; in 1800, 835; and in 1810, 790.

From the ridge of this mountain there is a handsome view of the Green Mountain Range, and a noble one of the Catskill Mountains.

The stone found on Taconic, so far as we had an opportunity to observe it, is principally blue, shining schist, like that formerly mentioned on Saddle Mountain.

After we began to descend from the ridge, we saw on the left between two steep declivities a small and very beautiful valley, of a rich soil and verdure, so narrow and so deep as to be styled without impropriety a ravine. In this retired spot stood a few humble dwellings, which appeared as if every storm, both of the natural and the political world, would pass over them without disturbing their peaceful inhabitants. No spot has presented to my eye more forcibly the idea of being sequestered from intrusion and bustle. It was a valley of Switzerland, and I felt as if it would be easy to find in this little cluster the cottage of Venoni.

When we had passed the line which divides Massachusetts from New York, the appearance of the country in many respects was changed in an instant. The houses became ordinary and ill repaired. A great number of them were taverns; generally, however, of so wretched an appearance as must, one would think, prevent the entrance of any traveler. Not a church, nor a schoolhouse was visible till we reached Claverack, at the distance of sixteen or eighteen miles. About the taverns, early as it was, were gathered a number of persons from the neighborhood, idling and drinking away their time, rude in their appearance, and clownish in their manners.

From the ridge to Claverack the whole country is slate ground, the soil tolerably good, and the surface an alternation of hills and valleys. There is so much sameness in the succession as to make the whole prospect tame and dull, without anything picturesque, or even sprightly. The houses also are generally indifferent, and the agriculture on a humble scale. I ought to add that this tract is extensively cultivated by tenants, and belongs to one branch of the family of Livingston.

We dined at a very good inn in Claverack, a pleasant and very ancient Dutch settlement. This town is about four miles from Hudson, and contains sixty or seventy substantial houses built in the Dutch manner; two churches, a Dutch and an Episcopal; a courthouse, and a jail, all of them ordinary buildings. The site of Claverack is a handsome elevation near a sprightly millstream, which is bordered with intervals.

Agriculture in this neighborhood seems to be at a stand. Neither improvement, nor enterprise meets the eye; and everything, except the passing of a great number of wagons, wears the appearance of stillness and seclusion.

Claverack is the shire town of the county of Columbia. In 1790, it contained 3,262 inhabitants; in 1800, 4,414; and in 1810, 3,593.

On the Hudson, there are many clusters of houses and stores, which are gathered at the end of every considerable road terminating at the bank in what is called a landing. Trade is the motive which at the first settlement summons to these places adventurers of every sort from every quarter. Together with a collection of discreet and virtuous people, there is sometimes an unhappy proportion of loose, lazy, shiftless, and unprincipled inhabitants. They are of the clan which I have heretofore mentioned under the name of foresters.

It is a peculiar characteristic of the ignorant and vicious part of such aggregations to feel that their settlement intimately resembles great trading towns. To exhibit this resemblance to each other, and to strangers, is always a favorite object of their attention. Too ignorant, however, to discern in what the real respectability of such towns principally consists, and too vicious willingly to adopt what is excellent in their character, they employ themselves in copying the fashions, follies, and vices of cities. To be first, and excessive, in fashions; to make a parade in the midst of poverty; to be pert; to gamble; to haunt taverns; to drink; to swear; to read newspapers;

to talk on political subjects; to manage the affairs of the nation and neglect their own; to profess themselves infidels; to seem to know everything and plainly to care nothing about religion; to array themselves against its ministers, its friends, and its interests; and to be *wiser in their own conceit than seven men who can render a reason* [1] are strong features of the character of such men.

Another peculiar characteristic found in many of the inhabitants in such settlements is a bold spirit of commercial adventure. They chiefly come together for the purposes of trade; and generally have neither the capital, skill, experience, nor caution which are indispensable to success in business of this nature. With a full conviction of their competency, they contract debts, and trust their property to persons whom they have never seen, without fear, and almost without thought. They, therefore, bargain with everybody who will bargain with them. Their darling object is to have the reputation of doing a great deal of business, and the question whether it is done with advantage or not seems to give them little anxiety. You will not wonder that many of them speedily become bankrupts.

Another trait in the character of such settlers is expensiveness. To be like the inhabitants of great cities, they feel that they must in some measure resemble them in show. This spirit displays itself in dress, buildings, furniture, and modes of living, and is often the gulf which swallows up the property and ruins the family.

The road from Claverack to Catskill is disagreeable, wandering through a solitary country composed chiefly of rough and barren hills, and containing a very few indifferent houses.

At the ferry we were obliged to wait a long time; and, what was worse, were compelled during this time to hear two men, mere brutes, professedly talking, and actually swearing and cursing, about politics and religion. Of these subjects neither of them knew anything except a few words to which each attached no other signification except that some of these were the words of his own party, or sect, and the remainder, words of that which he opposed. Our passage was in other respects safe and pleasant.

Catskill is a town built on a creek, or millstream, of the same name. It contains about one hundred houses, almost all built on a single street near and parallel with the creek, and in a direction from southeast to northwest. Several of the houses are built of brick. These, and some others which are of wood, are good buildings. A high and steep hill rises in the northeast at a small distance, leaving an easy slope at the bottom, of sufficient breadth for this street and its appendages. The soil is clay, in wet seasons very muddy; and in dry, very dusty. Naturally it is cold and barren, but capable with good husbandry of producing plentiful crops. Many of the grounds, heretofore enclosed, are now suffered to lie waste, a decisive proof that they are of little value.

The business done at Catskill is considerable, consisting principally in the importation of foreign commodities from New York and elsewhere, and in the exportation of wheat, flour, and lumber. Much of this business is done in the way of barter,† and is attended with all the evils incident to those modes of exchanging property in which there is no settled standard of dealing. One of the chief benefits of money is that it furnishes the parties in all contracts with a known rule of estimation, by which they can determine the value and price of their commodities, and understand perfectly the nature of their bargains.

Catskill, that is, the creek which bears this name, is navigable into the heart of the town for vessels drawing nine or ten feet of water. The channel of the Hudson is here one third of a mile distant from this shore. An island bordering upon the channel, formed probably by the slime of the creek, is connected with the shore by a beach formed in the same manner. On this beach the inhabitants have begun to build a causey, which is to unite the island with the main, and to give them access to the channel of the Hudson. This work, an honorable proof of enterprise in these inhabitants, has since been completed, and an opening made from Catskill to the ocean for mercantile vessels of any burden.

Catskill contains two congregations: an Episcopal and a Presbyterian. The Episcopalians, aided by the funds of Trinity Church in the city of New York, have erected a neat church. The Presbyterians meet in the courthouse.‡ There are here a few Baptists, and a smaller number of Methodists. There are in the township also two Dutch churches: one, five miles north, and the other, four miles west of the town.

There are two academies in this town, one of them incorporated.

The prospects from the high grounds near the village, all present two very interesting objects: the Hudson and the Catskill Mountains. Otherwise they are dull and discouraging, destitute of the fine scenes of nature and the pleasing traces of art.

Catskill is the shire town of the county of Greene, which contains also the townships of Coxsackie, Greenville, Freehold, Canton, Durham, New Baltimore, and Windham. The Catskill Mountains, so far as they are entitled to any distinction, have their whole course in this county. The number of its inhabitants in 1800 was 12,584. It then contained four townships. In 1810, its inhabitants amounted to 19,536. The township of Catskill contained in the year 1790, 1,980 inhabitants; in the year 1800, 2,408; and in 1810, 4,245.

I found my expected companion, Professor D[ay], of Yale College, and Mr. D[wight], of New Haven, at Catskill. Here we spent our time very agreeably in a circle of good friends till Monday, September 24th; when we

† 1804.

‡ They have since built a handsome church.

rode to Bristol, in the county of Schoharie, through the townships of Canton and Freehold, as they were then named. You will observe that the local divisions of this state are continually changing, especially in the more recent settlements. It is impossible for a traveler, therefore, to follow these changes, unless he were to have frequent recourse to the records of the state.

Our journey proceeded in a turnpike road, a branch of the Greenwoods turnpike from Hartford to Albany, commencing at Canaan, in Connecticut, and passing to Wattles' ferry on the Susquehanna. Thence it is proposed to extend it to the county of Trumbull of the southern shore of Lake Erie. The road is well made. After leaving Catskill we passed by two hamlets built on the creek, in one of which is the best mill seat that I have met with. The dam is formed by a ledge of limestone, the front of which is perpendicular, and so high as to be on a level with the floor of the fourth story of the mill. This building stands on the side of the creek, in a spot perfectly safe; the water wheels are overshot; and the whole expense laid out upon the dam is incurred by placing a single stick of timber upon the brow of the ledge, and by forming a flume, perhaps four or five feet in length. It cannot, I think, have exceeded ten dollars. The stream is abundant and never failing. The interior furnishes immense quantities of wheat. Navigable water is scarcely four miles distant. More than thirty thousand barrels of flour are, or may easily be, manufactured here in a season.

Between these hamlets and near the bank of the creek, there is a cave, said to extend in a winding direction thirty rods in length. The account must, I think, be conjectural, for the entrance is so ragged as to discourage effectually all investigation.

The country from Catskill through the township of Canton is a dull, dreary region. The ground is clay; the soil, lean and filled with slate; the forests, low and unthrifty; the houses, few and miserable; and the cultivation, wretched. Such of the inhabitants as we saw corresponded in their appearance with all the particulars of this description. Few spots within my knowledge wear a more forbidding aspect. The dullness of the scene was however relieved by fine views of the Catskill Mountains.

Canton, which since this journey has changed its name to Cairo, is a counterpart of the region already described. Its surface appeared to my eye as if it had been anciently and frequently burnt over by the Indians, and not unfrequently by those who succeeded them. The settlements which we saw were few, recent, and wretched.

From Canton we entered Freehold, passing through a settlement called New Durham, and since incorporated into a township by the name of Durham. Here the face of the country changed in an instant. The surface became a succession of long, easy declivities on the northeastern margin of the Catskill Range, together with beautiful, open valleys lying between them. The soil, a mixture of loam and clay, is rich and abundantly productive of both grass and wheat. The inhabitants have availed themselves of their advantages. This settlement, when we were on the ground, was of little more than twenty years' standing; yet it was thoroughly cleared, well cultivated, and divided by good enclosures into beautiful farms. Indeed everything here wears the appearance of prosperity. Almost all the inhabitants are emigrants from Connecticut, and have preserved the habits of their native country. Of this we saw sufficient proof in their schoolhouses and their church. The congregation consists of two hundred families. Among them there has lately prevailed an extensive revival of religion, a rich reward for their efforts to establish the worship of God.

From Durham the road rises by a very easy and regular ascent to the ridge of the Catskill Mountains, here divided into two arms at the distance of more than twenty miles from the northernmost of the three principal summits. From the ridge at this place are seen the valley of the Hudson, Saddle Mountain, and the Taconic and Green Mountain ranges. This valley is here at least forty miles wide. Its extent northward and northeastward is vast, exhibiting a remarkable specimen of the grandeur produced by amplitude; but is not ornamented, nor even relieved by variegations of natural or artificial beauty. To the west, nothing was visible but huge piles of mountains, separated by deep and narrow valleys.

Into this valley our road descended very gradually along the declivity of the northern ridge. Here we found a few lonely plantations recently begun upon the road. The southern ridge, or rather the southwestern, is a rude and lofty mountain. At the bottom runs a sprightly millstream, winding in several places through rich intervals, a small number of them cleared and covered with flourishing verdure. Occasionally we passed a cottage, and heard the distant sound of an ax and of a human voice. All else was grandeur, gloom, and solitude. The mountains on either hand seemed to shut out the few inhabitants of the valley from the rest of mankind. If I can conjecture the feelings of a Swiss, and the habits which he must be supposed to derive from the circumstances of his native country, I should believe that in this spot he might easily imagine himself to be still in Switzerland.

We reached our destined inn soon after sunset. It was kept by a plain, but very friendly and obliging Dutchman named Rechtmeyer, who had been planted here a considerable time, and had an excellent farm under good cultivation. One of his sons was the first uneducated Dutchman whom I have heard speak English so perfectly that I should not have suspected him to have been of Dutch extraction.

The latter part of our journey lay in the township of Bristol, and the county of Schoharie. It was incorporated in 1797; and contained in 1800, 1,078 inhabitants.

In the morning, September 25th, we proceeded on our route through a part of Blenheim, a part of Jefferson, a corner of Stamford, and through the townships of Harpersfield and Kortright to Meredith: thirty-seven miles. The first part of our way lay in the valley already described. The northern ridge receded gradually toward the northwest; the southern continued its former western direction, and increased its height and rudeness until it terminated on Schoharie Creek, eight miles from Rechtmeyer's. When we arrived at the creek, we found the bridge swept away by a late flood. This stream rises in the neighborhood of Kingston, and runs directly north to the Mohawk, about eighty miles. Its bed is deep and rocky, its course rapid, and its waters during every considerable rain swollen instantaneously by torrents from the mountains into a deluge. Its banks for a great distance are formed by the ends of these eminences, rising on both sides in a long succession, and abutting upon the river in the form of huge promontories. The appearance of these heights, and of the whole neighboring region, is singularly shaggy, wild, and horrid; nor is the prospect cheered by a smiling object.

We were necessitated to ford the river. Happily we found a wagoner on the spot, who directed us to a place where we crossed it without much difficulty. On the opposite bank, however, we were compelled to make our horses climb up a rocky precipice, scarcely practicable, and attended with no small danger.

From the Schoharie we entered Blenheim, ascending a mountainous acclivity near three miles in length. This township, so far as it was visible from the road, we found an almost absolute forest, as we afterwards did those of Jefferson and Stamford. I can scarcely conceive that an agreeable residence will ever be found in either of these places.

Blenheim was incorporated since the year 1790, and Jefferson since the year 1800. The former contained in 1800, 783 inhabitants; and in 1810, 1,319; and the latter, in 1810, 1,740. Stamford was incorporated in 1792; and contained in 1800, 924 inhabitants; and in 1810, 1,658. It lies in the county of Delaware. In this part of our road we crossed two of the headwaters [of] the river which bears that name, and found them mere millbrooks.

Harpersfield, which is in the same county, is a settlement of some standing. The surface is irregular; the hills are sudden; and the valleys are narrow. The face of the country is much inferior in beauty and the soil in fertility to Durham. The houses are comfortable; and the inhabitants have built themselves a decent church, added to it a steeple, in this region a singularity, and settled a clergyman. When I speak of a clergyman with any qualification in the phraseology, I always intend a man regularly educated for the ministry, and regularly inducted into that office.

In the year 1790, Harpersfield contained 1,726 inhabitants. It was then an extensive tract of country, and belonged to the county of Montgomery. The present Harpersfield contained in 1800, 1,007 inhabitants; and in 1810, 1,691. It is now in the county of Delaware, which has been formed since the Census of 1790.

All the hills and mountains in this region run from southeast to northwest, in the same direction with the Catskill Range; some of them, however, inclining more toward the north, and others toward the west. It is observed by Evans, in the memoir accompanying his Map of the British Colonies, that the Catskill Mountains are the termination of the Allegheny Range; and that the country westward of them is a continued plain, of the same elevation with these mountains.[2] These assertions, which originally excited in my mind no small astonishment, have been extensively believed, as well as often repeated. Nothing, however, can be farther from the truth.

The Catskill Mountains are a range of lofty eminences, of no great breadth, the most elevated summits of which are far higher than any other land in the state. Westward of them the country throughout a considerable extent is a rude collection of hills and of interjacent valleys, often so narrow and deep as strongly to resemble ravines. The loftiest of these eminences is a mere hillock compared with the height of the Catskills. All of them, so far as I had opportunity to observe, run in a northwestern direction, at right angles with that of the Allegheny Range. The Allegheny Range terminates near the headwaters of the Genesee River, and is visible from the great western road to Niagara. The space between the Catskill and its dependencies, and the Allegheny Range, or that occupied by the headwaters of the Susquehanna, is filled up with hills and valleys, running in a great variety of directions, so great that to the eye on elevated ground the whole region appears to be a mere mass of confusion.

From Harpersfield we entered Kortright. The settlements on the road in this township are less numerous than in Harpersfield. The principal of them is formed in a pleasant valley and on the bordering hills, which are handsomely arched. In such objects we felt not a little interested, as having been for some time strangers to them. The soil and the houses of Kortright differ little from those in Harpersfield. We saw neither church, nor schoolhouse. In 1800, Kortright contained 1,513 inhabitants; and in 1810, 2,993.

From Kortright we entered Meredith. This township, as to its surface, is entirely distinguished from every other on this road, being formed of smooth, easy, elegant rising grounds, and of valleys of corresponding beauty. Durham can boast of finer prospects and of a handsome surface, but the surface in Meredith is far more inviting to the eye than that of Durham.

From the house of Mr. Law, a handsome mansion in the center of the town, the prospect stretches to the south over a valley ultimately bounded by mountains at the distance of thirty miles, and to the north over another valley which extends ten miles.[3] The hill which limits the northern prospect is covered with a magnificent growth of white pines; one of which, having fallen down, was measured by Mr. Law, and was found to be 247 feet in length. This cluster is the only considerable one composed of full grown trees of this kind which I have seen. A few years since, such trees were in great numbers along the northern parts of Connecticut River; but they are now very generally destroyed. It is not improbable that the next generation may never see a white pine of the full size, and may regard an exact account of this noble vegetable production as a mere fable.

The soil of this township is rich, being the same with that mentioned heretofore in the description of Hartford. We saw oats here six feet in length, and were informed by Mr. Law that they frequently grew to seven.

The central parts of this township labor under a singular, as well as very great inconvenience: the want of water for domestic uses. Wells have been dug to very great depths, but without any success.§

The central square mile in Meredith is laid out in lots of a moderate size for the accommodation of merchants, mechanics, and others not employed in farming. The turnpike road which passes through the middle of this plat is here crossed by another road passing through the middle of it, also from north to south. Around the point of intersection is laid a public square, intended to be the site of a church, an academy, townhouse, schoolhouses, etc. The ground is naturally handsome, and the situation very pleasant. It is not improbable, therefore, that on this spot may be hereafter added the beauties of art to those which it derives from nature. For these advantages, and many more important ones which will seriously contribute to their future prosperity, the inhabitants of this township will be indebted to the taste, good sense, and good principles of Mr. Law, almost the only person, I am sorry to say, who in directing the concerns of a new settlement has, within my knowledge, furnished occasion for remarks of this nature.

Meredith is in the fullest sense a new settlement. In the year 1800, it contained only 213 inhabitants; and in the year 1810, 726. Peculiar efforts have been made by Mr. Law to introduce into this township sober, industrious, virtuous settlers. In this manner he has probably secured its prosperity, both moral and physical, for a century. Since the date of my journal the inhabitants have built an academy, in which they assemble for public worship.

§ One has been dug since, which yields a tolerable supply of water.

In the morning we left Meredith, and passed through Franklin and a corner of Sidney to Unadilla: twenty-eight miles. The first part of our road through Meredith and the eastern part of Franklin was almost wholly a forest. As soon as we left Meredith the hills began to be steep and rough, and the country to lose its beauty. From this forbidding tract we entered a settlement on the Ouleout, a handsome millstream which is a branch of the Susquehanna. The valley through which it runs extends from east to west a considerable distance. The borders of the Ouleout are in a long succession formed by rich intervals, divided into meadow and arable, and covered alternately with a lively verdure and good crops of maize and other species of corn: the river winding through them with a course elegant and delightful. The settlement is for some miles a thinly built village composed of neat, tidy houses. The inhabitants are Baptists and Presbyterians. One of these classes had raised and was building a church. Everything on this spot indicated prosperity. From Meredith to this settlement the road descended with a disagreeable rapidity. Here we found it very pleasant. When we left this village, it became again disagreeable. The rapid declension was renewed. The country wore a forbidding aspect. The hills were steep and shaggy; and the valleys, narrow, rude, and lean. The houses also were thinly scattered, and many of them denoted great poverty. Both Franklin and Sidney are in the county of Delaware. In the year 1800, Franklin contained 1,390 inhabitants; and in the year 1810, 1,708. Sidney, in the year 1810, contained 1,388.

When we arrived at the Susquehanna, we found the only innkeeper on the eastern side of the river unable to furnish us a dinner. To obtain this indispensable article, we were obliged, therefore, to cross the river. The ferryboat was gone. The inhabitants had been some time employed in building a bridge, but it was unfinished and impassable. There was nothing left us, therefore, but to cross a deep and rapid ford. Happily, the bottom was free from rocks and stones, and the passage from the danger which we encountered in fording the Lower Ammonoosuc: a stream of about the same breadth and depth as the Susquehanna at this place.

About four miles from the ferry we came to an inn kept by a Scotchman named Hanna. Within this distance we called at several others, none of which could furnish us a dinner. I call them inns because this name is given to them by the laws of the state, and because each of them hung out a sign challenging this title. But the law has nicknamed them, and the signs are liars. It is said, and I suppose truly, that in this state any man who will pay for an innkeeper's license obtains one of course. In consequence of this practice, the number of houses which bear the appellation is already enormous. Too many of them are mere dramshops, of no other use than to deceive, disappoint, and vex travelers, and to spread little circles of drunkenness throughout the state. The government probably derives from them a small pecuniary benefit, but the purpose for which the license is given is frustrated. No inquiries, if I am correctly informed, are made concerning the character of those to whom they are distributed. Not a question is asked, whether they are able or unable to entertain travelers; whether they are men of fair reputation, or of none. No system is formed; no restrictions are prescribed. The object is left to chance; and the licenses are offered for sale as goods, wares, and merchandise. The effects of this negligence in the government of the state are deplorable. A traveler, after passing from inn to inn in a tedious succession, finds that he can get nothing for his horse, and nothing for himself. At the same time he is molested by night and by day by a collection of dram drinkers, who offend his eye by their drunkenness and his ear with their profaneness and obscenity, while they prevent or disturb his sleep by the noise and riot of their intoxication. In many parts of this state, whether the object of the traveler be food or lodging, he must diligently inquire at a sufficient previous distance for a comfortable place of entertainment, and must shorten or lengthen his journey so as to suit these indispensable purposes.

If these evils resulted merely from the recent settlement of the country, they certainly ought to be borne without a complaint. Partially this is the cause. But they are chiefly owing to the multiplication of these houses, and to a criminal neglect of requiring the proper qualifications as an indispensable prerequisite to giving the license. Were only one inn permitted where there are now five or six, proper houses might usually be selected, sufficient custom secured to enable the innkeeper to furnish the requisite accommodations, and the traveler find a supper and a lodging where now he can obtain neither food, nor sleep.

We at length procured a dinner, and finding no house at a proper distance where we could be lodged, concluded to stay where we were. Our fare was indeed bad enough, but we were sheltered from the weather. Our innkeeper, besides furnishing us with such other accommodations as his house afforded, added to it the pleasures of his company; and plainly considered himself as doing us no small favor. In that peculiar situation in which the tongue vibrates with its utmost ease and celerity, he repeated to us a series of anecdotes, dull and vulgar in the extreme. Yet they all contained a seasoning which was exquisite, for himself was in every case the hero of the tale: and the merum sal of Athens could not have been more delightful. To add to our amusement, he called for the poems of Allan Ramsay; and read several of them to us in what he declared to be the true Scottish pronunciation, laughing incessantly and with great self-complacency as he proceeded.[4] For his ability to read in this manner, I found he valued himself more than for any other characteristic; and he often declared to us that he had found but one man in America who could read the Scottish dialect as well as himself. The man, it seems, is a native American, and for this attainment only was held by our landlord in extravagant estimation. I never before saw a Scotchman who did not possess a strong attachment to his native country. But our host appeared to value Scotland for no other reason than because it had given birth to so respectable a personage as himself.

The road on which we had traveled since we left Catskill is called the Susquehanna turnpike. It commences at Catskill and terminates at Wattles' ferry, is well made, but passes over ground too uneven to be pleasant. A new turnpike road is begun from the ferry, and intended to join the great western road from Utica, either at Cayuga Bridge or Canandaigua. This route will furnish a nearer journey to Niagara than that which is used at present.

The township of Sidney terminates at the river. That in which we now were is named Unadilla, and lies in the county of Otsego. It is composed of rough hills and valleys, with a handsome collection of intervals along the Susquehanna. On the remarkably ragged eminence immediately northwest of the river, we saw the first oaks and chestnuts after leaving the neighborhood of Catskill. The intervening forests were beech, maple, etc. The houses in Unadilla were scattered along the road which runs parallel with the river. The settlement is new, and appears like most others of a similar date. Rafts, containing each from twenty to twenty-five thousand feet of boards, are from this township floated down the Susquehanna to Baltimore. Unadilla contained in 1800, 828 inhabitants; and in 1810, 1,430.

Thursday, September 27th, we left our inn, and rode through Oxford township, and No. 15 in Norwich, to the north line of No. 10 in the same township; I presume also we must have crossed a corner of Jericho before we entered Oxford; but, as I am ignorant of the dividing line between these townships, may easily have mistaken this fact. The whole distance was thirty-one miles.

The first two miles of our road along the Susquehanna were tolerably good, and with a little labor capable of being excellent. We then crossed the Unadilla, a river somewhat smaller, but considerably longer than the Susquehanna proper, quite as deep, and as difficult to be forded. Our course to this river was southwest. We then turned directly north along the banks of the Unadilla; and, traveling over a ragged hill, passed through a noble cluster of white pines, some of which, though not more than three feet in diameter, were, as I judged, not less than two hundred feet in height. No object in the vegetable world can be compared with this.

The way which we were advised to take was an obscure path, crossing a tract which lay in an acute angle formed by the common road. We were assured that we should save five miles out of ten of our distance. About five miles of our way, we had no other than a horse track, with the aid of which we crossed two deep valleys and two lofty hills, the last of them a mountainous height. Our path was alternately miry, rocky, and steep, so steep at times as to oblige us to lead our horses. To add to our trouble, we were several times at a loss concerning our road; and, the country being an absolute forest, were unable to inquire.

After descending the last of these hills, we found the common road on the margin of the river Chenango. Here we soon left the township of Oxford and entered that of Norwich. In this part of our journey we passed through a corner of Jericho and the whole breadth of Oxford, both of them in the county of Chenango. I have already exhibited the appearance of these townships in the parts through which we passed. The town of Oxford is built on the Chenango, four or five miles west of our course. It is said to be a pretty, flourishing village of considerable size and business.

Oxford contained in 1800, 1,405 inhabitants; and in 1810, 2,983. Jericho [Bainbridge] contained in 1800, 939 inhabitants; and in 1810, 1,608.

Oxford is the shire town of this county.* The soil of the township appeared generally to be good.

The remainder of our journey lay within the township of Norwich. A township in this state, you will remember, is a very different thing from what the same word indicates in New England. There it denotes a tract, often less, and not very frequently more than six miles square. Here a township is most commonly a considerable extent of country. Windham, for instance, contains more than one third of the county of Greene; and Batavia, almost the whole county of Genesee, a tract little less than the state of Connecticut. To this mode of division the present state of population gives birth. As inhabitants of townships, the people of this state are entitled to a great part of the privileges and subjected to a great part of the duties which belong to its citizens. For this reason, whenever a sufficient number of persons have planted themselves in a given tract, of such extent that they can act without serious inconvenience in the proper business of a township, such a tract is incorporated for this purpose. When you read, therefore, in these letters that a township in this state contains several thousand inhabitants, you will remember that the ground occupied by them is in most instances of sufficient extent to form several such townships as those in Connecticut or Massachusetts.

Norwich, through which lay the remainder of our journey this day, contains six squares, and a large gore, or irregular tract, equal in the whole to seven New England townships. The parts through which we traveled were Nos. 15 and 10. Our road passed wholly along the river Chenango, partly on intervals, and partly on the rising grounds by which they were bordered. The surface was agreeable, and the road good.

This river is little less than the Susquehanna before its junction with the Unadilla, and of considerably greater length. It rises in Cazenovia; and,

* Norwich is now the shire town. (1815.)

running a southeastern, southern, and southwestern course, unites, after receiving the Tioughnioga, with the Susquehanna between the townships of Chenango and Union. It is a beautiful stream. Two ranges of hills run parallel with its course for a great distance. Between them spreads an expansion composed partly of declivities and partly of intervals, extending, after we entered it, more than thirty miles in length, and from half a mile to two or three miles in breadth. Down the river it extends many miles farther. The part of this valley through which we passed, particularly the first twenty miles, is much more beautiful than any other spot which we saw in our journey except the valley of the Mohawk. The intervals especially are possessed of all the elegance and fertility found in those which lie far up Connecticut River. These fine grounds are devoted to the several objects of cultivation suited to the climate, and bountifully reward the labors of the husbandman. By the hills, which are of considerable height, handsomely varied in their summits, and in several places finely tufted with groves of white pine, this region is, to the eye, sequestered from the world. Like the vale of Kashmir, it seems capable of yielding within itself ample means of happiness to a great number of virtuous inhabitants. At a future period, when the population of these states shall be far advanced, men of intelligence and virtue may perhaps seek a retreat from the folly, bustle, and vice which haunt the residence of wealth and splendor in the beautiful vale of Chenango.

We fared this day much better than the preceding.

Norwich was incorporated in 1793. In 1800, the number of its inhabitants was 2,219; in 1810, that part of it which still retained the name, contained 2,550.

Tuesday morning, September 28th, we left Norwich, and rode to Cazenovia, through the townships of Sherburne and Hamilton, pursuing our course along the Chenango to its headwaters, about sixteen miles. The settlements here seemed to have been little more than begun, and terminated soon after we left the Chenango in an absolute forest.

Before we left the valley, we crossed a tract of muddy road, such as I formerly described in the account of Littleton. After we ascended the hills in which the Chenango finds its springs, we struggled through six or eight miles more: the mire being deep and encumbered with roots and stones. These hills lie partly in Hamilton and partly in Cazenovia. They are rough and unpleasant. The soil, however, is good. The settlements are absolutely new, and the inhabitants are laboring under all the inconveniences and hardships attendant upon the difficult task of clearing a wilderness.

Sherburne contained in 1800, 1,282; and in 1810, 2,428 inhabitants. Hamilton contained in 1800, 2,363 [2,673]; and in 1810, 2,220 inhabitants.

Both these townships have, I suppose, been divided since the year 1800;

and both, in tracts farther eastward, have considerable settlements. The county of Chenango also has been divided; and the northern division, including these townships, is named the county of Madison.

Within a few miles of the town of Cazenovia, the face of the country was suddenly changed. The steep hills and narrow valleys gave place to a succession of easy rising grounds and open expansions. To us this change was peculiarly pleasant. We were wearied by laboring down rapid descents and climbing steep acclivities; and our eyes, long straightened in their excursions, and tired by a confinement to the same disagreeable objects, were delighted with being able to expatiate over an extensive region. We also found the road better, and a chain of settlements continued to the town of Cazenovia. We arrived at sunset.

The time was peculiarly unfortunate. A regiment of militia collected from the surrounding country had just been dismissed after a review. Many of the officers and soldiers had come from such a distance that it was too late for them to return home. They had, therefore, taken lodgings here for the night. Tumult and disorder are incident to occasions of this nature; here they were increased by peculiar circumstances. The officers lately commanding the regiment were men of worth and reputation. They possessed also a considerable share of military skill, spirit, and ambition. Under their discipline the regiment had become distinguished for peculiar improvements in every part of the military character, and had prided itself not a little on this distinction. When these officers were displaced by the government of the state, all the noncommissioned officers in the regiment, as a testimony of their disgust, resigned their places; but their resignation was not accepted.

The newly appointed officers were of opposite politics, and as opposite characters. They were, as we were informed, destitute of all military knowledge, and ignorant even of the most ordinary exercise. When they first appeared upon the parade, the soldiers professed to be wholly unacquainted with their duty, and intentionally performed every maneuver in the most awkward and improper manner. At length, the officers, mortified beyond expression, besought them in terms of very humble supplication to do their duty. The soldiers replied that if the officers would be so good as to teach them how it should be done, they would readily obey their instructions. This, however, the soldiers well knew they were unable to do. The evil was, therefore, without remedy.

The troop attached to this regiment, a fine, volunteer company of young men, dressed in a handsome uniform, well accoutered and well mounted, refused absolutely to obey the new officers; and compelled the government of the state either to disband them, or continue their former officers in command. The latter part of the alternative the government chose as the less evil, not improbably because it would hazard the loss of the fewest votes. These men, therefore, still held their commissions, except perhaps the captain. At this house the troop had this day engaged a dinner. But, when they found that the field officers of the regiment were to dine at the same table, and to take precedency of their own officers, they withdrew to a man.

This little tale exhibits in a clear light the depraving efficacy of ambition on the minds of those who are seized by the love of place and power. Nothing could more forcibly display the groveling tendency of this character than the measures adopted by the government of the state on this occasion.

Such expedients as these rend asunder the sinews of government. Subjects cannot fail to discern in them the selfishness, injustice, and folly of their rulers. The law loses its dominion; and the government, its utility. The contempt and reprobation directed immediately to those who are appointed are instinctively transferred to those who appoint; and from the officer, to the law under which he acts. Besides, the concessions here made by the magistrate were made to revolt, and can terminate in nothing but the encouragement of disobedience. The government which thus yields will soon be obliged to yield regularly, and at no great distance of time will be a government in name only.

I shall not now descant on the morality and policy of rewarding with offices of trust and profit those who are of our party, merely because they are of *our party;* or those who support our political advancement, merely because they support it. This subject I may perhaps resume at another time. At present, I shall only observe that it is a prostitution alike of principle and decency, and that within a moderate period it may subvert the freedom of any country.

We arrived when the confusion to which I have alluded was at its height, and found the only inns in the town preoccupied. Mr. B——, a respectable inhabitant of this town, having become acquainted with our situation, very politely invited us to his house, where we found every proof of refined hospitality and spent the evening in the company of intelligent, friendly, and well-bred gentlemen.

The town of Cazenovia is a pretty settlement built on the southeastern quarter of a small lake bearing the same name. This beautiful piece of water is about four miles in length from north to south, and from half to perhaps three quarters of a mile in breadth. A millstream enters it at the southern end; and, passing through it, carries its waters onward to the Oneida Lake. It is principally supplied by subjacent springs. Its temperature is, therefore, cool, and its waters are salubrious.

The houses in this town are chiefly built on a single street, running from east to west. Generally they are decent, and some of them, neat. Colonel Lincklaen, a native of Holland, and agent of what is here called the Holland Company, has built a handsome seat with pretty appendages on the eastern border of the lake.[5]

By this gentleman, I was informed that a considerable part of the lands which had been sold under his agency had already gone through the hands of several successive proprietors. What is true of these lands is extensively true of the whole of what is called the western country of this state. The persons by whom these lands are purchased have in many instances been of the class which I have mentioned before as pioneers or foresters. The character of these people, and the manner in which they conduct the business of forming plantations in the wilderness, I have heretofore exhibited. To that exhibition I shall add nothing here except that, when they have sold their first farm, they purchase and sell in the same manner a second, a third, and sometimes a fourth; and that their progress from east to west removes, and has already removed them, from New England to New York, from New York to the state of Ohio, and from the state of Ohio to Louisiana. In this manner the strong columns of civilized men regularly push before them these Arabian troops, and will at no great distance of time follow them too to the Pacific Ocean.

I am, Sir, yours, etc.

## LETTER II

*Holland Company—Face of the country from Sullivan to Canandaigua—Manlius—Varieties of names given to townships—Onondaga—Salt springs—Marcellus—Early fall of snow—Skaneateles Lake—Aurelius—Cayuga Bridge—Account of lakes in this region—Junius—Geneva—Seneca Lake*

*Dear Sir,*

The Holland Company originally purchased in this vicinity sixty thousand acres of land, a large tract in the neighborhood of Whitesboro, lying about fifty miles northeastward from Cazenovia; and almost the whole county of Genesee at the western end of this state. I have already mentioned that they have also made a considerable purchase in the western parts of Pennsylvania. Their whole possessions in these two states are considerably more extensive than Connecticut.

Saturday, September 29th, we left our hospitable friends at Cazenovia, and proceeded through the townships of Manlius and Onondaga to Marcellus: thirty-one miles. For three miles our road lay along the beautiful lake which I have mentioned, and was very pleasant. It ought to be remarked that the fever and ague is here unknown, and that the soil of this neighborhood is rich.

The Cazenovia road joins the Western Turnpike, as it is here called (that is, the great road from Utica to Canandaigua) at the distance of four miles, and in the center of a pretty settlement in the township of Manlius. Here our traveling inconveniences chiefly vanished. The road was excellent; the surface, smooth; and the settlement, though nearly of the same date, was much farther advanced. The houses were better, and were surrounded with more conveniences. Fruit trees also abounded, and among them the peach, growing and bearing with the utmost luxuriance. Indeed from Cazenovia onward the appearance of the country differed less from that of the ancient settlements in New England than from that of the country through which we had lately passed. Still there are intermingled many proofs that it had been recently settled.

The houses visible from this road generally stand on its sides, and have been built within the last fifteen years, most of them indeed within ten. The changes made here during this period are greater than any person who has not been an eyewitness of them will believe; and greater, I suspect, than any which have taken place in the United States during an equal length of time. I think it may be fairly questioned whether they have ever been paralleled in the world.

As this country differs materially from any other through which I have passed, it will be necessary to exhibit it in a general description, particularly because an extensive sameness spreads over it, and few of those distinctive features which divide other tracts into minuter portions are found here.

The surface from Sullivan to the western limit of Canandaigua (beyond which a sensible alteration begins) is made up of hills, valleys, and plains.* In this description, I include about twenty miles on each side of the road, so far as that extent was visible on our route. Throughout the whole tract I do not remember a single mountain, except two or three of a moderate height at the distance of fifteen or twenty miles on the south. None of the hills are high, nor are they, except in very few instances, of a rapid ascent. Each hill may be conceived of in the following manner. When you ascend from a valley to the top, you behold a vast plain spread before you and on both hands, where the view is uninterrupted except by forests. These plains are not indeed without inequalities, but they are such as make little impression on the eye. The traveler passes over them with sensations differing very little from those which are excited by a surface absolutely level, and they often extend from six or eight to twelve or fourteen miles. Descending

* Sullivan is immediately north of Cazenovia and east of Manlius.

into a valley he finds a long-continued hollow, reaching in length a great distance, and in its appearance semicylindrical, except that it is flattened at the bottom. The heights of the hills on either side are limited by a line nearly horizontal, exactly resemble each other, and stretch many miles north and south of the road. As he passes onward day after day, he will find the streams, the lakes, and the villages to be almost the only variations from this picture. Not an interval except in two spots, not an arched or pointed summit, a round or conical hill, a cliff, or a precipice was visible from Utica to Buffalo Creek, a distance of two hundred miles, except a small tract of undulating country in Bloomfield and Charleston, to be mentioned hereafter. The traveler can, therefore, find no difficulties presented by the surface, nor the farmer any serious hindrances to his cultivation. But the man of taste will find those varieties wanting which have delighted his eye in other regions; and the poet and the painter will seek in vain for those objects which they have been accustomed to behold under the influence of fascination, and to depict with enthusiasm and rapture. The phrase *beautiful country,* as used here, means appropriately and almost only lands suited to the purposes of husbandry, and has scarcely a remote reference to beauty of landscape. When we first entered this region after having escaped from the rude hills which surround the headwaters of the Chenango, we were not a little gratified; but before we had traveled in it a single day, it became dull and wearisome.

Of the progress which has been made in settling this country, you may form tolerably correct apprehensions from the following account. There are a few instances in which the forests extend on the road four, five, and six miles. On the Seneca River we found one spreading perhaps seven or eight. Frequently they occupy small distances. The settlements are either villages, hamlets, or long-continued lines of farmhouses distant from each other an eighth, a fourth, a half, and sometimes three fourths of a mile. The villages are few; the hamlets are more numerous; but the extent is chiefly occupied by these lines of farmhouses. There is nothing which can be called a town except Geneva and Canandaigua.

The houses throughout this tract are almost universally of wood, many of one and many of two stories. A great number of them are decent buildings; many are neat; and some are handsome. Taken together, they exceeded my most sanguine expectations.

On the borders of a millstream, and around the mill erected upon it, there is regularly a small cluster of houses. Three such streams water the township of Manlius. The road is lined with farms and houses throughout. The soil is good, and the fields are in a good state of cultivation.

Manlius was incorporated in 1794, and is the first township in this quarter belonging to the county of Onondaga, and in this quarter also the first of those called the military townships. These, composing the three counties of Onondaga, Cayuga, and Seneca, contain a million and a half of acres; and were given, after the close of the Revolutionary War, to the officers and soldiers belonging to the state of New York. The number of these townships is twenty-five, and each contains sixty thousand acres. Within them, however, are two considerable reservations: one belonging to the Onondaga and the other to the Cayuga Indians. This tract, generally considered, is one of the best in the western country.

There is something singular, and I think ludicrous, in the names given to townships in different parts of this country. In the tract under consideration, they are chiefly derived from ancient heroes. This may be considered as characteristical of the nature of the grant, and the spirit of those to whom it was made. To exhibit their love of learning and wisdom, they have added to these the names of Solon, Tully, Locke, Cato, Cicero, and Galen; and, to evince their taste for poetry, they have annexed those of Homer, Vergil, Ovid, Milton, and Dryden. In the county of Tioga, which lies directly south of the military tract, we are presented with a new set of names, such as Oghquaga, Chenango, Tioga, Owego, Chemung, etc. In the county of Oneida, we find the names of Arcadia, Hybla, Penelope, Lucretia, Pomona, Flora, and Rurabella; and in the county of Herkimer, immediately east of that, we have Unanimity, Frugality, Perseverance, Sobriety, Enterprise, Industry, Economy, and Regularity. In the county of St. Lawrence, north of these, we find another set: Kilkenny, Killarney, Killdare, Ballybeen, Ennis, St. Patrick, and Crumack. In another spot still, we have the following cluster: Coeymans, Guilderland, Watervliet, Boght, Coxsackie, Cobbleshill, and Schoharie.[1] I think you will agree with me that all these could not have come together by any common means, nor in the exercise of that ingenuity which falls to the share of ordinary men.

Manlius contained in the year 1800, 989 inhabitants; and in 1810, 3,121.

The township of Onondaga is composed of a remarkable valley, called *Onondaga Hollow,* and the flat hills on both sides. On the eastern elevation the soil is inferior to that of Manlius; and, what we had not seen since we left Unadilla, is covered with a forest of oaks.

Onondaga Hollow is a deep valley, or, to describe it more exactly, a plain sunk far below the level of the bordering country. The limit at the base of the hills on each side is almost absolutely straight, and therefore remote from beauty. The bottom is a level, nearly perfect, and was originally a lean, shrub oak plain. Its breadth is more than three fourths of a mile. On the south it has a boundary of distant hills; on the north it is unlimited. Through the middle of it runs Onondaga Creek, which empties its waters into a lake bearing the same name, and is here crossed on a good bridge. What is singular in this country, it is bordered for a considerable distance by two narrow, ribbonlike intervals.

Within this township are the celebrated springs called the Onondaga Salt Springs, scarcely rivaled in the world, if they are at all rivaled, in their utility to mankind. These springs rise in a marsh at the head of Onondaga Lake, sometimes called from them the Salt Lake.† This piece of water is about seven miles long, and, where widest, three broad. It is very deep. The water on the surface is perfectly fresh, but at a moderate distance beneath is salt. The cause of this fact is obvious. The lake receives its waters from both fresh and salt sources, and the salt water being specifically heavier subsides. According to Dr. DeWitt's estimate, taking the specific gravity of rain water at 1.00, that of these springs is from 1.078 to 1.110. The temperature is from 50° to 53°, and that of the lightest and the heaviest was the same.

The water of these springs is remarkably impregnated with salt. Fifty gallons yield by boiling a bushel of salt weighing fifty-six pounds. It contains a considerable quantity of lime.

The head of the lake is surrounded for some distance by marshy ground, interspersed with a few trees and bushes, and abounding in flags and wild grass. The salt springs issue chiefly from the marsh, near the banks by which it is enclosed, and at various distances from the waters of the lake. The principal springs which are most highly impregnated with salt, and which supply the greater number of the manufactories at present established, issue from the marsh in a group at the foot of the declivity commonly called the Salt Point, near the spot where the Onondaga Creek joins the lake. On this point is built the village of Salina. There are many other salt springs in different parts of the marsh, some along the shores of the lake several miles farther down, and others at a considerable distance up the creek. All these are not, however, equally replenished with this mineral.

These springs issue perpendicularly from the marsh through small orifices. The water is conveyed into cisterns, and thence into potash kettles, containing generally about eighty gallons, and placed over furnaces. When they are filled, they are made to boil briskly until the lime is deposited and removed. The salt then begins to crystallize, and the boiling is suffered to proceed gently until the water is chiefly evaporated. The salt is then taken out and drained dry.

Dr. DeWitt obtained from half a pint of this water, 1¼ oz. avoirdupois of salt, and 26 gr. of calcareous earth. A gallon of the water, therefore, contains 8,816 gr. or 20 oz. and 76 gr. of salt, and 416 gr. of calcareous earth. Accord-

† This account of the salt springs I have derived from a memoir of Benjamin DeWitt, Esq., M.D., and from the verbal information of Mr. Byington, of the company of Wood and Byington, principal occupants of the saltworks at this time. (1804.) [Benjamin DeWitt, *A Memoir on the Onondaga Salt Springs and Salt Manufactories in the Western Part of New York; . . .* (Albany, 1798) .]

ing to this experiment, this water contains more than one sixth of its own weight in salt. It also includes carbonic acid gas, and a small quantity of the sulphuric acid.

Mr. Byington informed me that the customary estimate of the salt actually obtained in the works was 56 pounds of salt from 50 gallons of water. This is believed to be the strongest natural brine hitherto found in the world. Dr. DeWitt supposed the water to be impregnated almost to saturation. Mr. Byington told me that salt could not be dissolved in it except in exceedingly small quantities.

The latter of these gentlemen also informed me that the quantity of salt made in the year 1803 amounted to ninety-six thousand bushels; and that in 1804, it would extend to one hundred thousand. A duty of four cents on the bushel is paid to the state.

This salt is forbidden by law to be sold for more than sixty cents per bushel. Notwithstanding the expense of transportation, therefore, it is obtained on very moderate terms by all the inhabitants of the western country, even at the greatest distance. Nor is this all. The regions round the Lakes Ontario, Erie, and Huron are supplied with salt from these springs. Even this is not all. Messrs. Wood and Byington have contracted to furnish the merchants in Pittsburgh, Pennsylvania, with four thousand barrels containing five bushels each in the years 1805, 1806, and 1807. This is to be delivered by the contractors at Oswego, near the southeastern corner of Lake Ontario. The transportation from the springs to this place is wholly by water, except twenty yards. At Oswego it will be shipped for Queenston; and thence conveyed by land eight miles to Chippawa. There it will be shipped again for Presque Isle on the southeastern shore of Lake Erie. Thence it will be transported by land to Le Boeuf by a portage of fifteen miles, and thence by French Creek and Allegheny River to Pittsburgh. From Pittsburgh it will be conveyed as far as the falls of the Ohio, for the general supply of the inhabitants on both sides of that river.

From these facts you will learn the importance of these springs, and will naturally ask whether they are so copious as to supply such an extent of country, especially when it shall be generally inhabited. I answer without hesitation that the quantity of water is sufficient for the whole of the tract to which I have referred. The deficiency, if it exist, will not be found in the quantity of water, but in the difficulty of manufacturing it into salt. This is accomplished by boiling, and demands, even on the present scale, a very great quantity of fuel. The wood in the vicinity is already consumed, and must even now be transported from a distance which very seriously enhances the expense of the process. Should the same mode be pursued, therefore, for any great length of time, the price of the salt itself must be materially increased.

I proposed to Mr. Byington to adopt the process in use on the peninsula of

Cape Cod, and formerly described in these letters. After I had explained it, he was so well satisfied of its expediency that he determined to put it in practice. Whether the attempt has been made, I am ignorant. The only obstacle to its success within my knowledge is the occasional wetness of the seasons in this region. But, allowing to this consideration all the importance which it could claim, I am convinced that it will prove much more convenient, salubrious, and less expensive than the present mode.

One of the greatest evils attending this business is the unhealthiness of the tract bordering on the springs. One period of the year is proverbially styled here, *the sickly season,* at which a considerable number of the workmen die annually. The evil is attended, and probably increased, by another: viz., the consumption of ardent spirits by the workmen. From a conviction that these furnish the greatest security against the dangers of the climate, these unhappy people use them so licentiously as in considerable numbers to become drunkards.

The sickliness of this spot is rationally believed to flow from the putrefaction of the waters in the marsh. These are salt water diluted by fresh: a compound which in the hot season becomes more suddenly and entirely putrid than either of them would be if unmixed. The smell in the warm season is extremely offensive, and fills the atmosphere of the vicinity. The diseases which prevail here are the fever and ague in the spring, and the bilious remittent in the autumn. It is a melancholy reflection that so much vice, and so great a waste of human life, should be incident to the acquisition of this necessary article. Should the other process be adopted, a sixth part of the hands now employed, and a sixth part of the time even of these, would probably compass the object. On both accounts the exposure would be proportionally less, and the vice would undoubtedly be lessened with the exposure.

The mines from which these springs derive their salt must, I think, be near; otherwise they would be more diluted with the fresh water of other subterranean streams. The attempts made to explore them have, however, furnished no prospect of obtaining the salt in mass.

Other salt springs of considerable importance have been discovered in different parts of this state, viz., in the counties of Cayuga, Seneca, Ontario, and Genesee. The quantity of salt furnished by all these sources in 1811 was the following.

| | Bushels |
|---|---|
| Onondaga | 453,840 |
| Cayuga | 54,000 |
| Seneca | 25,000 |
| Ontario | 8,760 |
| Genesee | 1,400 |
| | 543,000 |

This quantity, allowing three bushels to each, will furnish salt for 181,000 families; or, supposing six persons in each family, for 1,086,000 persons.

The tract surrounding the Onondaga Salt Springs is now formed into a township called Salina, which contained in 1810, 1,299 inhabitants.

We found a small number of houses in Onondaga Hollow.

The hill on the west of the valley is higher and steeper than any between Albany and the falls of Niagara. The soil on the height is clay, and is said to yield wheat better than the rich loam so generally found throughout this country. Here a little north of the road stands the courthouse of this county. It was designed to be a pretty building; but, being unfinished and standing in a solitary situation, has a gloomy aspect. The brow of the hill presents to the view of the traveler Onondaga and Oneida Lakes, and the country by which they are surrounded.

Onondaga is said to have been the principal settlement of the Iroquois, and to have been considered by them as a kind of metropolis.

The township of Onondaga contained in 1800, 893 inhabitants; and the present township, in 1810, 3,755. The whole township, including Salina, contained at the latter date, 5,054.

Marcellus, the next township, exhibits little to the eye of the traveler to distinguish it from the country in its neighborhood. The land here is however superior to most in this region, and produces all the grains and grasses of the climate in abundance. Wheat has yielded forty-five bushels an acre; maize, from seventy to eighty; and oats, seventy. Oats on an average grow to the height of five feet, and yield fifty bushels. The central settlement on this road is thrifty and handsome. The inhabitants have erected a well-appearing Presbyterian church, and are laboring with a commendable spirit to obtain a minister. On the morning of September 20th, we were not a little surprised to find the ground entirely covered with snow to the depth of an inch where it was least dissolved, and the shower still falling. This was a sight which no person in the township had ever seen at the same season of the year. We attended public worship, and suffered from the cold more than on most Sabbaths in the winter. The congregation were decent to an edifying degree; and, it seems, assemble every Sabbath, whether a preacher be present or not: some of the graver members of the church in the latter case making the prayers and reading a sermon. This, though very common in New England, was hardly expected by us here; but is one desirable proof among many of the happy influence of the institutions under which they have been educated. A general spirit of decency, sobriety, and good order is here very plainly characteristical. Religion is reverenced; and the Sabbath regarded as a day consecrated to God.

Around the church there is a prosperous settlement, formed in a valley which is watered by a sprightly millstream called Nine Mile Creek. This stream conveys the waters of Otisco Lake, in the southeastern corner of Marcellus, into that of Onondaga, and furnishes a considerable number of valuable mill seats.

In the year 1800, Marcellus contained 909 inhabitants; and in the year 1810, 4,735.

On Monday, October 1st, we left our inn very well pleased with our entertainment, and rode through the remaining part of Marcellus, and through Aurelius and Junius to Geneva: thirty miles. The country exhibited a similar face to that through which we had lately passed. The hills and valleys, however, returned more frequently; and the declivities were longer and steeper before than we found them on this day's journey. In the western part of Marcellus there is a beautiful lake named Skaneateles, commencing in the township of Tully, crossing the corner of Sempronius, and reaching through a considerable part of Marcellus. Its length is fifteen miles, and its breadth from one to two. At the outlet of this fine piece of water, sprightly and vigorous, running between high and rough banks, and without any of those marshy encumbrances which spread deformity and disease around the outlets of so many lakes in this region, there is a small settlement which I thought peculiarly pretty. It is built upon the north end of the lake and upon a handsome, clean margin. The lake is in full view, and interested me more than any other on this road. The shores on both sides are elegant, arched slopes; the eastern, already handsomely cultivated. The soil is excellent, and the fields were covered with a glowing verdure. At the south end of the lake the prospect is limited by distant mountains, in this region uncommon and therefore peculiarly gratifying objects.

The township of Aurelius, which lies immediately west of Marcellus, wears the same general appearance. The inhabitants are visibly prosperous; and, what is uncommon here, have settled a clergyman. This gentleman will not, I think, die for want of exercise. His cure comprehends probably seventy or eighty thousand acres, and he preaches successively at four different stations.‡

We dined at Cayuga Bridge, where there is a hamlet consisting of three very good and eight or ten indifferent houses. Its situation is pleasant, commanding a fine view of Cayuga Lake and the country on its borders.

The bridge over this lake, considering the recency of the settlements, may be justly styled a stupendous erection, and is probably the longest work of the kind in the United States, the planking being no less than a mile in length.§ It is built on wooden trestles, in the plainest and most or-

‡ The large and flourishing village of Auburn has been wholly built since the date of this journey. It is within the limits of what was then Aurelius. PUB.

§ The new Boston Bridge is commonly said to be longer, but the appellation of bridge is there given to two bridges, and as many causeys.

dinary manner, and exhibits nothing to strike the eye except its length. It is said to have cost $20,000, and to be the property of a Mr. Swartwout, of New York.[2] The toll is a quarter of a dollar for man and horse, the highest, I believe, in the United States, if we consider the amount of the capital and the quantum of traveling.

The appearance of Cayuga Lake, except that there is no current, is exactly that of a great river. Its length is thirty-eight miles; and, if we include its windings, not far from forty. The water is clean. The banks are of a moderate height, sloping, and, so far as the eye can reach, wholly covered, except at this little settlement, by a forest.

I have already mentioned several of these lakes. You may possibly wish to have a general account of them. The whole number in the western country is nineteen, of which fifteen empty their waters into the Great Lake, Ontario. Two of the others, viz., Otsego and Canadarago, are the headwaters of the Susquehanna proper. A third, Mud Lake, is one of the sources of the Tioga. A fourth, Chautauqua, is the principal source of Conewango Creek, one of the headwaters of the Allegheny. The first fifteen, beginning with the easternmost and proceeding onward to the westernmost, are the following.

| | Names | Length | Breadth |
|---|---|---|---|
| 1 | Oneida | 20 miles | 6 miles |
| 2 | Cazenovia | 4 " | 3/4 " |
| 3 | Onondaga | 7 " | 3 " |
| 4 | Otisco | 4 " | 1 1/2 " |
| 5 | Skaneateles | 15 " | 2 " |
| 6 | Cross | 5 " | 3 " |
| 7 | Owasco | 11 " | 2 " |
| 8 | Cayuga | 38 " | 4 " |
| 9 | Seneca | 35 " | 4 " |
| 10 | Crooked [Keuka] | 20 " | 2 " |
| 11 | Canandaigua | 15 " | 2 " |
| 12 | Hanyaya, or Honeoye | 6 " | 2 " |
| 13 | Little [Waneta] | 3 " | 1 " |
| 14 | Hemlock | 7 " | 3 " |
| 15 | Conesus | 8 " | 3 " |
| 16 | Otsego | 10 " | 3 " |
| 17 | Canadarago | 5 " | 2 " |
| 18 | Chautauqua | 15 " | 2 1/2 " |
| 19 | Mud | 5 " | 1 " |

To these, if we add Long Lake (of which, however, I know nothing but the name, and that it is said to lie in the county of Ontario), the number will be twenty. You will observe, I have given the greatest length and breadth of each. The first fifteen empty their waters into Lake Ontario by two channels. Of these the first eleven find a common passage in Oswego River; the remaining four, by the Genesee. Crooked Lake enters the Seneca by a small stream. The Seneca River carries their united waters into Cayuga River just at the outlet. The Canandaigua meets it farther down, as do the Owasco and Skaneateles, still further. Cross Lake is a basin formed by the common stream below the junction of the Skaneateles. The Onondaga unites with it about twenty miles still lower; and the Oneida, after receiving the waters of the Cazenovia, ten miles lower still. All these waters are considered here as received by the Seneca River until their junction with the Onondaga. After this the common stream is known by the name of Onondaga or Oswego River, which is navigable for boats about seventy miles. At a future day, it is probable that through this channel a considerable commerce will be carried on down Lake Ontario and the St. Lawrence with Montreal, whenever that city shall become the seat of regular and extensive business. Canandaigua, Seneca, Cayuga, and Oneida are already useful channels of internal intercourse to the inhabitants on their shores, particularly for the transportation of lumber and wheat.

These lakes are important additions to the beauty of the country. All those which I have seen are handsome. How far they contribute to health or disease, it is difficult to determine. The lakes themselves, I suspect, are salubrious. Several of their outlets are, however, evidently noxious.

This is certainly true of the Cayuga outlet, which, together with some others, is marshy and disagreeable to the eye. The families at the bridge, though living on high and clean grounds, are between the middle of August and the middle of October exposed, as they informed me, to fevers, especially to bilious remittents. We found some of them very ill at our arrival. As the settlement lies southeastward of this marshy ground, I was surprised to find this mentioned as the cause of the evil. In Connecticut, persons living at a small distance on the southern side of stagnant waters are rarely injured by them; while those who live at considerably greater distances on the northern side, particularly the northeastern, are apt to be sickly at this season of the year. The reason is, the southern winds, particularly the southwestern, blow in that state with little interruption throughout the summer half of the year. My surprise ceased when I was informed that the northwestern winds blow almost continually throughout the same season in this region, and therefore waft the miasmata of the marsh directly to this cluster of houses.

In the township of Aurelius, there were in 1800, 3,312 inhabitants; and in 1810, 4,642.

The lake Owasco lies almost equally in this township and Scipio.

After we had crossed the bridge we entered the township of Junius; and, traveling through a thinly settled and uninviting country about three miles, came to the Seneca River, a large, sprightly millstream of remarkably pure, transparent water. Here we found a small and poor settlement. The remaining distance to Geneva, about seven or eight miles, is a forest.

The soil is a hard clay, producing scattered and stinted oaks. Here also, we found in two or three spots the only white pines since we left the Chenango. The whole tract is dull and forbidding.

Two or three miles east from Geneva, we left the turnpike, and directed our course to the Seneca Lake. On the north end of this beautiful water, strongly resembling Lake George in its elegant, pellucid appearance, the waves agitated by the south wind have thrown up a hard beach, consisting wholly of small pebbles, about six feet in height and two rods in breadth. A better road and a pleasanter ride can scarcely be imagined, that is, in a country so destitute of cultivation. The outlet of the lake, which is the commencement of Seneca River, is bordered by a low, marshy, dismal ground, a copy of one of those concerning which Ossian says that their mist is "the dart of death." [3]

Geneva stands at the northwest corner of the Seneca Lake. The town is partly built on the acclivity by which it is entered from the east, and partly on a single street running north and south along the summit of the hill: the most beautiful eminence, I think, for the site of a town which I ever beheld. The street is about a mile in length, and from 150 to 200 feet in breadth. The surface is an easy, obtuse, elegant arch, and at the highest point elevated about 200 feet above the lake. The houses are chiefly built on the western side, the lands on the eastern being devoted to gardens, declining to the water, and forming a very ornamental part of the landscape. The houses on the acclivity and at its foot are generally very indifferent, as are also a number of those on the hill. There are a few pretty buildings, a considerable number of decent ones; and, what is remarkable as the town is scarcely of sixteen years' standing, a number well advanced in decay. This fact is partly accounted for by the negligence of the proprietors, and still more by the slight, imperfect manner of building which to a great extent prevails throughout this region. The prospect from the street is more attractive than any other in this part of the state. The lake is the most beautiful piece of water west of the Hudson. The shores on both sides are handsome rising grounds, covered, like those of the Cayuga, with a rich forest. The southeastern view is terminated at a great distance by a mountain of considerable length and moderate height, which, though exhibiting a straight, uniform summit, adds here an interesting variety to the landscape. The whole aspect is remarkably cheerful and pleasant, and is warmly commended by every traveler. Fortunately, the disagreeable buildings and marshy grounds which I have mentioned are chiefly out of sight.

Geneva is a settlement formed by Major Williamson.[4] The spot was pitched upon both as an object of taste and a theater of business. Hitherto, the latter part of the design has, however, failed. There are several stores and mechanics' shops, and a considerable distillery in the list of its buildings. But the general aspect of business is dull and lifeless.

A respectable clergyman is settled here, who preaches half the time to the inhabitants, and is employed the other half as a missionary in the surrounding country by the General Assembly of the Presbyterian Church.[5]

There are about seventy houses in this village. It lies in the township of Seneca, which in the year 1800 contained 1,522 inhabitants; and in 1810, 3,431.

I am, Sir, yours, etc.

# LETTER III

*Easton—Canandaigua—Bloomfield—Charleston—Hartford—Genesee River—Genesee flats—Oak plains—Their peculiar appearance, owing to fires kindled by the Indians—Their soil productive—County of Genesee—Buffalo—View of the lake, etc.—Beautiful collection of clouds*

*Dear Sir,*

Tuesday, October 2nd, we left Geneva in the morning, and rode to Bloomfield through Easton [Gorham] and Canandagua [Canandaigua]: twenty-one miles. In Easton we saw nothing remarkable, except that the forests to a considerable extent were composed of oaks. This township contained in the year 1800, 476 inhabitants.

The township of Canandaigua lies chiefly on the western side of the lake heretofore mentioned as bearing this name, and in the center of the county of Ontario.

The town of Canandaigua * is built chiefly on a single street formed along the great road. Its site is partly an easy, handsome acclivity, and partly an elevated level at its termination. The situation is inferior in beauty to that of Geneva. The town itself is greatly superior. The houses are remarkably good, in a better style than that of most older settlements, and at the same time are not defaced by any appearances of decay. The inhabitants are without a church, but have settled a respectable clergyman. A good building is erected here for an academy on a very pleasant elevation. It is not yet completed, but so far advanced that it is intended to establish a school in it the ensuing winter. This building was erected by several pub-

* This name was formerly written Canandargue, and is now commonly written Canandaigua. Both modes are erroneous. The Iroquois have in no other case used the diphthong *ai*.

lic-spirited individuals, who have endowed the institution with funds consisting chiefly of lands continually increasing in their value, and, as is said, already worth $40,000. It is under the management of a board of trustees.

The stores in this town are more numerous and the mercantile business more extensive than in any other west of Utica. At present it is the resort of the whole surrounding country. How long it will retain this advantage cannot be foreseen. Trade, everywhere fluctuating in some degree, is in a newly settled country always ready to shift its residence. The inhabitants of Canandaigua have availed themselves of their present advantages. A general spirit of industry and activity is everywhere visible, and the whole town wears a very cheerful appearance of thrift and prosperity.

The state of society is in several respects superior to what is found in any part of this country west of Whitesboro. The disadvantages attendant upon recency of settlement undoubtedly exist, but in a less degree than in any other place which we had visited on this journey.

The soil also is excellent, and yields abundantly the various produce of the climate. I never saw fruit trees more luxuriant. The late peaches were not gathered; and of many trees which I examined in the garden of Dr. Williams, there was not one, the boughs of which were not either bent quite to the ground, or broken by the load of fruit.[1] Plums, apricots, and apples, all prosper with a similar luxuriance. Some of the peaches which I tasted were finely flavored. General Taylor, an inhabitant of this town, was supposed to have in his orchard 1,100 bushels of peaches. Some persons have begun to distill the juice of this fruit into brandy.

The enemies which attack these fruits in many of the ancient settlements, such as the peach worm, the cankerworm, the rose bug, and the caterpillar, together with several sorts of flies, some of which sting the fruit and others the twigs of the more delicate fruit trees, have not yet made their appearance. Accordingly they all, even the nectarine, are cultivated with entire success. It is to be regretted that these enemies, which make a regular progress wherever man provides them with food, will at no great distance of time ravage the gardens and orchards of this region as they have long done those of others.

Canandaigua is the shire town of this county. In the courthouse, a decent building, the inhabitants hold their public worship.

Canandaigua Lake is a fine piece of water. At the north end, it is deformed by a marshy outlet and a margin of bulrushes; but it generally has a sprightly, beautiful aspect. The shores resemble those of the Seneca, but are furnished with the advantage of having several points on both sides which project handsomely into the water. The southern limit is pleasantly formed by distant mountains. In the year 1800, this township contained 1,153 inhabitants; and in 1810, 2,392.

Bloomfield, the next township to Canandaigua, is large, containing four squares, through the two southernmost of which passed our road. This tract is generally a collection of hills and valleys, resembling in a good degree those in Connecticut: not lying in long continuations or ranges like all the preceding country from Manlius to this township, but assuming many varieties of form and, therefore, to us at least, particularly pleasant. In these hills the inhabitants are furnished with the important article of stone for building and fencing. The soil, a mixture of loam with gravel, is excellent and produces everything suited to the climate.

The forests of Bloomfield are composed of oak, and in some instances of chestnut and hickory, together with maple, beech, bass, etc.: this tract yielding all the variety of timber found in the southern parts of New England. The oak which grows here, and which is the most valuable production of the forest, is straight, tall, and easily riven. A great part of the fields are enclosed with rails made of this timber, and the inhabitants believe it will not fall very far short of the chestnut in resisting the injuries of the weather. Of this, however, they cannot be competent judges because their experience has extended only through the short period of ten or twelve years. Even if they should be disappointed in their expectations, many of them will be able to form their enclosures of stone. In both respects they are distinguished from most of the people of this region.

Lands in this township have yielded fifty bushels of wheat an acre.

Bloomfield is also not less distinguished from all the preceding country by a succession of brooks and springs, watering the farms of the inhabitants as in New England. A stream called Mud Creek, on which there are several pretty intervals, waters the whole of the eastern side of this township. Another, which is the outlet of Hemlock, Little, and Honeoye Lakes, passes through both of the western divisions, and thence joins the Genesee River in the township of Hartford. A third rises in the center of Bloomfield; and, running northward through Northfield, discharges itself into Irondequoit Bay on the southern border of Lake Ontario. By these streams the inhabitants are very conveniently furnished with mill seats. A similar supply of water for the various purposes of life is not often found in the western counties of this state.

Bloomfield is wholly divided into farms, and contains three congregations. In two of these clergymen are settled. The third has lately built a beautiful church, the handsomest I met with westward of Albany.

A part of Bloomfield is the easternmost of those grounds which for reasons hereafter to be mentioned are denominated oak plains. Charleston and a part of Hartford are included in this tract.

In the year 1800, [East] Bloomfield contained 1,940 inhabitants; and in 1810, 4,425.

The next morning we left our friends at Bloomfield; and, being furnished with fresh horses, rode through the remaining part of this township,

Charleston, and Hartford to Genesee River, and beyond that river nineteen miles to Bemis' inn in the township of Southampton: thirty-eight miles. The Rev. Mr. F[ield], of Canandaigua, joined us at Bloomfield.[2]

Charleston and the uplands in Hartford generally resemble those in Bloomfield. The settlements in the former of these townships are of about the same standing, but the country is to my eye less pleasant and less fertile. The settlements in Hartford are more recent, so far as we saw them, than those in Charleston; and both the soil and the surface are visibly inferior.

Genesee River, by which Hartford is bounded on the west, rises in Pennsylvania a little south of its northern boundary, and near the middle point of its length from east to west. In the near neighborhood of its fountains rise the headwaters of the Allegheny River, the Tioga, and the Sinnemahoning, branches of the Susquehanna. The Genesee, after entering the state of New York, runs about thirty miles northwestward, and thence northeastward in a winding course about seventy more. After crossing the state of New York and separating the counties of Steuben and Ontario from the county of Genesee, it discharges its waters into Lake Ontario at a small distance westward of Irondequoit Bay. In its course it passes over three sets of falls, said to form a descent of one hundred and eighty feet in the whole. Where we crossed this river in Hartford, we found it about the size of the Susquehanna and Unadilla, and a dull, disagreeable stream.

On this river are the Genesee flats, large and very rich intervals, the boast of the inhabitants, and, in my opinion without reason, the envy of their neighbors. These lands are not unfrequently considered by the people of the western country as the best in the Atlantic states, and perhaps in the world. The quantity of land which they include, I am unable to ascertain; but it may amount perhaps to thirty thousand acres, a greater quantity than that on any other river of the same size within my knowledge.

The soil of these lands, where we crossed them, is the same with that of most other new grounds in this and other regions, viz., a black vegetable mold. Beneath this is a deep stratum formed by the finer particles of loam washed from the hills surrounding the headwaters of its tributaries, and floated down and deposited by the river in the manner formerly mentioned. The depth of this mass is said to be from one to ten or twelve feet. I presume the estimate is just, for it is no uncommon thing for intervals to exceed even twenty feet. The husbandry employed on these lands must at this early period be supposed to be very imperfect. Such as it is, the parts which are converted into meadow are said to yield annually three tons of good hay by the acre. It ought to be remembered that the vegetable mold with which they are covered is the best of all manure, that they are therefore in their highest state of productiveness; and that, if estimated according to their present fertility, they will be certainly overrated. The intervals on the Mohawk were within my remembrance not less celebrated than these. That these are still lands of an excellent quality is unquestionable.

Intervals have two advantages besides their inherent fertility. They are easily cultivated, and are annually manured with the slime brought down by the streams of which they are the borders. The Indians perfectly understood their value, and chose them for their own scanty husbandry with the same preference which their successors have discovered. Our road lay through a tract called the *Cannawagus Reservation,* on which were remaining a few ruined Indian wigwams, and the usual miserable relics of Indian agriculture.

These intervals yield wheat less successfully than other products, that which grows here weighing considerably less than that of the uplands. Hemp is cultivated with the greatest advantage, and it is said that more than fifty thousand dollars worth of this useful crop has been raised the present year. The opinion has long prevailed that hemp would grow successfully only on intervals, drained marshes, or other grounds of a peculiarly rich and deep soil. It seems not a little surprising that this opinion should ever have been taken up, and much more that it should have become general, especially in New England. For it grows here spontaneously to an enormous size around the houses of slovenly proprietors, and often in the highways. It is now become an object of the most successful cultivation in many places on uplands of no extraordinary fertility. Nor does it impoverish the land on which it grows beyond the average degree of other crops.

The intervals on the Genesee are eminently unhealthy, so unhealthy as to strip them of all their peculiar value.

At the distance of a mile and a half or two miles beyond the Genesee, we found a small inn. Here we dined on bread, butter, and cheese in the open air, our hostess being laudably employed in scrubbing the only room in the house, except two or three which might be called bed closets.

After dinner we soon entered the first of the oak plains on this side of the river. It extends about seven miles along the road.

The second begins about eight miles west of Batavia Village, or about thirty-three miles from the Genesee, and extends to a maple swamp, or low valley, about five miles.

The third begins immediately beyond this swamp and extends to Tonawanda Creek, about five miles more.

The fourth occupies most of the distance between Tonawanda and Murderers Creek, about three miles.

The fifth commences at Ransom's, fifty-one miles from the Genesee, and extends to Ellicott's Creek, or Eleven Mile Creek, about eight miles.

The sixth begins three miles from Ellicott's creek, sixty-three from the Genesee, and reaches to Four Mile Creek, four miles.

This account respects the old road only, and on this road all the distances are computed.

The first of these plains is in every respect less interesting than the others. Its surface is less beautiful, and the ground less open. Young trees and shrubs of a lean, forbidding appearance are everywhere springing up, which together with a few miserable settlements, looking as if they would long retain this character, left us little to be pleased with except the firmness of the road, in this country no contemptible gratification. On this plain, however, we found one interesting curiosity. A large part of the stones and rocks for some distance on the road, to the amount of one third or one fourth of the whole mass, was formed of marine shells. Among them we observed a great many of the oyster, mussel, and periwinkle. Some of these were petrified, or perhaps in better language, mineralized. Others were in their perfect, native state; and both retained their proper figure, unaltered by time or accident. The distance of this spot from the ocean is about 360 miles, and the elevation above its level probably not less than 800 feet.

From this plain we entered upon a tract of maple ground, extending about twenty-four miles on the road. At fifteen miles from the river we began our passage through a maple swamp, four miles in breadth. Here all the evils formerly mentioned as attendant upon a new road were experienced in the highest degree. The stumps and roots were innumerable, and singularly perplexing and dangerous. The mud throughout most of the distance was knee-deep, and often so stiff as to make it impossible for a horse to extricate himself without extreme labor. The sun was just set when we reached this ground. The road was a narrow passage, newly cut through a forest. The darkness soon became intense and palpable: the branches of the trees on the opposite sides of the road meeting over our heads and excluding the faint light of the stars, so that we were obliged to trust ourselves wholly to the guidance of our horses. A wolf, which I presume considered us as having sufficiently lost our wits to become his lawful prey, howled after us at a small distance; but, having preserved his own, perceived that we were too numerous to be attacked. These animals are frequent in this region, and often do mischief to sheep and other small cattle. They have not been known to attack men in the daytime. In the night companies of them have compelled individuals traveling alone to betake themselves to trees for safety, and confined them to this unpleasant lodging until morning.

After groping and struggling for three hours through this miserable tract of four miles, we arrived at nine o'clock at our destined inn. It was a log house, but we were very kindly and comfortably entertained.

The next morning, Thursday, October 24th, we left Bemis', and rode to Munger's: thirty-seven miles.

From Bemis' to Batavia the country is thinly and very recently settled. The village of Batavia is twenty-four miles from the Genesee, and stands on the Tonawanda Creek, which furnishes it with mill seats. The ground which it occupies is low, but toward the eastern end rises into a small elevation. It contains from twenty to thirty houses, a considerable number of them built of logs; the rest small, and chiefly of one story. The courthouse, a well-looking structure, has three stories, the second of which is the county jail.

A more untoward situation, both for pleasantness and health, is not often selected for a town. In the season when we were on the ground, so many persons were ill of the diseases common to this region that those who remained well were scarcely able to nurse the sick. The waters which had stagnated in the road were very loathsome, both in their appearance and smell.

Joseph Ellicott, Esq., agent for the Holland Company, resides in this village. This gentleman has published a valuable map of the county.[3]

From Batavia there are two roads to Buffalo Creek, and a third which passes directly to Queenston, seven miles below the falls of Niagara. The last is the nearest route to the falls; but, being lately and imperfectly made, and passing through a country scarcely at all inhabited, presents a traveler a disagreeable path and wretched accommodations.

The new road to Buffalo Creek is five miles shorter than the other, but is of recent date, and stretches out into no less than thirteen miles of mud before it becomes reunited.

The old road, which I suppose to have been the ancient military route, contains from eight to nine miles of mud out of twenty-three. We chose this by the advice of gentlemen acquainted with both, and soon entered upon the first of three miry expansions lying in this part of our journey. Here, however, we had the advantage of daylight; and the mire was less deep than on the preceding evening. Yet it was sufficiently tedious.

We dined at Dunham's, five miles beyond Batavia.

After leaving Dunham's, and passing through another maple swamp, we entered upon the second of the plains mentioned above. From the appellation, plains, usually given to these tracts, you will naturally think, as I did, that they are level grounds. This, however, is a mistake. They are generally elevated, and everywhere present a surface, winding easily, without any sudden declivity except on the borders of streams or swamps. The variations of surface are however continual, and some of the eminences rise considerably above the common level.

These grounds are also termed *openings,* as being in a great degree destitute of forests. The rest of the vegetation with which they are covered consists of grass, weeds, and shrubs of various kinds. The grass resembles a species sometimes seen on the intervals of the Connecticut, and named, perhaps locally, *thatch.* The stalk is single, from three to five feet in height, tinctured in various parts with a brown hue, and topped with a spreading ear, generally resembling that of spear grass. Besides the shrubs, which have nothing remarkable in them, there are on all these plains some, and on some of them many, young trees, particularly on that near the Genesee.

These grounds are of a singular and interesting appearance. The trees growing on them are almost universally oaks. They are of four sorts: two, white; the other two, the black and the yellow. One of the white is very common in New England; the other is of a species already mentioned in the account of Bloomfield. This tree is very tall. The stem is exactly straight, handsome, and without limbs to the height of fifty or sixty feet; and the crown is superior in beauty to that of every other species. In the low grounds bordering the second, third, and fourth of these plains, we saw many of these trees, remarkably elegant, and excelling every vegetable production except the white pine. The bark is of a very light hue, and separated into regular divisions resembling those of the rock maple, but much more beautiful. When this tree is full grown, its height exceeds one hundred feet.

On these grounds also grow the chestnut, the shagbark, or kiskatom, and several other trees.

The soil of these plains is loam, of a light brown hue, mingled with gravel, and covered by a very thin vegetable mold: the residuum chiefly of shrubs and herbage.

When one of these plains is seen at a little distance, a traveler emerging from the forest naturally concludes that it is the commencement of a settled country; and, as he advances toward it, is instinctively led to cast his eye forward to find the town or village of which it is the outskirt. From this impression his mind will be unable to free itself: for the thought, though given up, will recur again and again in spite of his absolute conviction that he is in the heart of an immense wilderness. At the same time, a sense of stillness and solitude, a feeling of absolute retirement from the world, deeper and more affecting than any which he has ever suspected before, will be forced upon him while he is roving over one of these sequestered regions. No passage out of them is presented to his eye. Yet though the tract around him is seemingly bounded everywhere, the boundary is everywhere obscure: being formed by trees, thinly dispersed, and retired beyond each other at such distances as that while in many places they actually limit the view, they appear rather to border dim, indistinct openings into other tracts of country. Thus he always feels the limit to be uncertain; and, until he is actually leaving one of these plains, will continually expect to find a part of the expansion still spreading beyond the reach of his eye. At every little distance, especially on the higher grounds, the view is widely, though indefinitely, extended along the surface; and a little above, where he looks through the stems of the trees, is bounded only by the horizon. On every side a multitude of chasms conduct his eye beyond the labyrinth by which he is surrounded, and present an imaginary passage back into the world from which he is withdrawn, bewildering him with expectation, continually awakened to be continually disappointed. Thus in a kind of wild, romantic rapture, he wanders over these plains with emotions similar to those with which, when a child, he roamed through the wildernesses created in Arabian tales, or the imaginary regions spread before him in a dream. He is not only separated from all human beings, but is every moment conscious of this separation. Whenever he ascends one of the superior elevations, he seems to stand above the rest of the globe. On every side he looks downward and beholds a prospect with many vistas opening indeed around him, but conducting his eye to no definite object, and losing it in confusion and obscurity. His view is confined neither by forests nor mountains: while yet trees in a thin dispersion partially interrupt it, but at the same time discover, through their various openings, that it has no other limitation than the skirts of the heavens.

While he wanders onward through this bewildering scenery, he cannot fail to remember that on these plains Indians have lived, and roved, and hunted, and fought, ever since their first arrival from the shores of Asia. Here, unless they molested each other, there was nothing to molest them. They were the sole lords, the undisturbed possessors of the country. Here, therefore, he will call up before his imagination the secret windings of the scout, the burst of the war whoop, the fury of an Indian onset, the triumphant display of scalps, and the horrors of the war dance before the tortured and expiring captive. Whether these thoughts will be excited in the mind of any future traveler, I know not; in my own, they sprang up instinctively.

The origin of the peculiar appearance of these grounds is probably this. The Indians annually, and sometimes oftener, burned such parts of the North American forests as they found sufficiently dry. In every such case the fuel consists chiefly of the fallen leaves, which are rarely dry enough for an extensive combustion except on uplands, and on these only when covered with a dry soil. Of this nature were always the oak and yellow pine grounds, which were therefore usually subjected to an annual conflagration. The beech and maple grounds were commonly too wet to be burned. Hence on these grounds the vegetable mold is from six inches to a foot in depth, having been rarely or never consumed by fire; while on the oak and pine grounds, it often does not exceed an inch. That this is the effect of fire only, and not of any diversity in the nature of the trees, is evident from the fact that in moist soils, where the fire cannot penetrate, the mold is as deep on the oak as on the maple grounds. This mold is combustible, and by an intense fire is wholly consumed.

The object of these conflagrations was to produce fresh and sweet pasture for the purpose of alluring the deer to the spots on which they had been kindled. Immediately after the fires, a species of grass springs up, sometimes called fire grass because it usually succeeds a conflagration. Whether it is a peculiar species of grass, I am unable to say, not having seen it since the days of childhood. Either from its nature, or from the efficacy of the fire, it is remarkably sweet, and eagerly sought by deer. All the underwood is at the same time consumed, so that these animals are easily discovered at considerable distances: a thing impracticable where the forests have not been burned. You will remember that to supply himself with timber for a wigwam and with wood for fuel was the only use which an Indian could make of a forest, and that the earth furnished him with nothing but a place for his residence, his garden, and his game. While, therefore, he destroyed both the forest and the soil, he converted them to the most profitable uses for himself.

When these grounds had been often burned, they were of course covered with grass. The seeds and nuts whence future trees would have germinated were extensively destroyed by successive fires. Few trees, therefore, could spring for want of seeds; and fewer still, because the surface was covered with grass: for wherever that vegetable has gained possession of the soil, forest trees will never spring. The small number scattered over these plains grew on spots which were less ravaged by the fire because they were moist, or because they were less covered with leaves.

Thus, in time, these plains were disforested to the degree in which we now see them, and were gradually converted into pasture grounds. It ought to be observed that they were in all probability burnt over for ages after they were disforested, I presume down to a very late period. In a dry season of autumn, the *grass* would furnish ample fuel for this purpose.

That this is the true cause of the singular appearance of these plains can scarcely be doubted when the following facts are compared.

That the Indians customarily burned, every year, such parts of the forests as were sufficiently dry to admit of conflagration:

That these were the only grounds which, except in rare cases, could be successfully burned:

That, wherever they have been for a considerable length of time free from fires, the young trees are now springing up in great numbers, and will soon change these open grounds into forests if left to the course of nature. Such particularly is the fact on the first of these plains near the Genesee River, and still more strikingly in Bloomfield and Charleston, where the fires have been longer intermitted.

That in various places the marks of the fire are now visible on the trunks of the remaining trees, particularly near the ground. These marks I suppose to have been impressed at a comparatively late period, and by fires kindled in the grass:

That on the borders of these very plains, trees of exactly the same species are now growing in great numbers, and in the usual regular succession of all ages and sizes, within the nearest neighborhood of those on the plains; and that this diversity, perfectly explicable on this supposition, is inexplicable on any other:

That there can be no account given why the vegetable mold should be so thinly spread over these plains except that it has been continually consumed by fire: since it exists in the usual quantity in the forests composed of the same trees on moister ground bordering these plains on every side:

And, that all the phenomena are, if I mistake not, explained by the cause alleged.

Should it be asked why there are no such grounds in New England, in which country also Indians lived and hunted, I answer:

Firstly. The New England oak and yellow pine forests have not been subjected to fire for many years.

Secondly. No accounts of their ancient appearance have come down to us.

Thirdly. The whole of southern New England, except the mountains and swamps, was almost wholly covered with oak and pine forests. All, therefore, being capable of an annual and easy conflagration, there was no inducement to burn any single part frequently. Yet, besides the well-known fact that the Indians kindled the forests yearly for the above-named purpose, there are now remaining many proofs of such fires.

Fourthly. That within my own remembrance there were in the township of Northampton spots desolated in a similar manner. These, although laid waste in an inferior degree, were yet so far destroyed as to be left in a great measure naked. Now they are completely covered with a thick forest. I suppose these grounds, however, to have been frequently burnt by the English inhabitants, who foolishly followed this Indian custom in order to provide feed for their cattle in the spring.

These plains have until very lately been considered as of little value when compared with the maple and beech land, which here is called, by way of distinction from them, timbered land. From numerous experiments made on them within a short time, it appears, however, that the wheat sown on them not only grows luxuriantly and yields a rich crop, but is heavier by several pounds in the bushel than that which grows on the maple lands. It is also whiter and better, and commands, therefore, a higher price. It is hardly necessary to observe that these facts have rapidly raised the plains in the public estimation.

On the third plain we found a singular mass of limestone gravel, consisting of pebbles about the size of a nutmeg and nearly the same shape. They were apparently formed of a partial dissolution of white lime rock, and were very nearly of one size. The mass extended over a considerable distance on the surface.

The second, third, and fourth of these plains lie between Dunham's, twenty-nine miles, and Van de Vender's, forty-seven miles from the Genesee River. In this extent there is but one house which is within one mile of Van de Vender's. Seventeen miles in this part of our journey, therefore, were destitute of a human habitation. There is, however, an Indian settlement called the Tonawanda Village, lying three or four miles north of the road on the creek of the same name. To this village benighted travelers not unfrequently betake themselves, and find hospitable entertainment.

We arrived at Van de Vender's, a log house, about sunset; but were unable to procure entertainment, the house having been preoccupied. After having traveled eight miles, four of them in a heavy rain, we gladly alighted about nine o'clock and placed ourselves at Munger's, a log house at a little distance from the road. Scarcely were we seated when we found ourselves in a state of very serious embarrassment. The house contained neither flour nor bread. We had rode thirty-seven miles, and were not in a very good humor to go to bed supperless. Nor were we willing to begin our journey the following day without a breakfast. In this quandary, a good-natured wagoner, who was removing his family into Upper Canada and carried his provisions along with him, kindly relieved our distress by offering to furnish the innkeeper with the necessary quantity of flour. With this supply our good landlady very expeditiously placed before us a cup of hyson tea, with loaf sugar, cream, and excellent hot biscuit, and butter. This supper, though found everywhere in decent inns and older settlements, was here unexpected and very highly relished. The house was not more than half-built. The region in which it stood was almost uninhabited; and we were wet and weary. It rained all night, and a part of our company were occasionally sprinkled. However, we slept soundly, and in the morning refreshed ourselves with an excellent breakfast.

We were detained till late the next morning by the rain. At length, perceiving it to slacken, we began our journey to Buffalo Creek, and arrived about two o'clock: fourteen or fifteen miles. We were twice stopped by the rain, and were fatigued by crossing a deep, maple swamp, three miles in breadth: a facsimile of that in the neighborhood of Bemis'.

The county of Genesee comprises the whole western end of the state of New York. It is bounded on the north by Lake Ontario, on the south by Pennsylvania, on the east by the counties of Steuben and Ontario, and on the west by the river Niagara, Lake Erie, and a line drawn from that lake (limiting, eastward, a small tract purchased of Congress by the state of Pennsylvania) until it intersects its north line. The greatest length of this county from north to south is ninety-two miles. On the south line it measures ninety-six miles. From Lake Erie to the county of Ontario, in a direct line, the distance is fifty-eight miles. This tract is commonly said to contain upwards of four millions of acres, being more than are included in the state of Connecticut. Its surface in the northern parts is remarkably level, not a single hill of any importance being found on the great road from Genesee River to Buffalo Creek, unless the descent and ascent to and from the swamps and millstreams should be called hills. Here, however, we only fall below the common level, and rise to it again. Nor is there, so far as I have been informed, any considerable hill between the road and Lake Ontario, if we except the brow of the limestone stratum, which, it is said, crosses the whole breadth of this tract, entering the county of Ontario on the east, and Upper Canada on the west.

The southern parts of this tract, including perhaps one third, and possibly two fifths of the whole, are said to be hilly, and even mountainous. From the number of considerable streams rising in this region and forming a part of the headwaters of the Allegheny and Genesee Rivers, the account appears to be true.

This county, throughout the northern half, is scantily furnished with springs and streams. All these of any size, except Allens Creek, a branch of the Genesee, and two or three smaller ones which empty their waters into Lake Ontario, have been already mentioned in the course of these letters. Smaller streams and springs are scarce. The soil of this country is principally of the two kinds already so often mentioned: that of the oak and that of the maple lands. As I shall have occasion to consider this subject more particularly hereafter, I shall only remark for the present that I consider this tract as inferior to several of those which lie farther east. Still it is a fertile country, and capable of producing plentifully all the vegetation of the climate.

The settlements in the county of Genesee are very few. On a farm in the neighborhood of the falls of Niagara, all the various kinds of fruit produced at Canandaigua have long flourished. Hereafter they will probably flourish throughout its whole extent. The only villages which it contains are Batavia and Buffalo Creek. The eastern part of this county, eleven miles in breadth on the south, and twenty-four on the north, is formed into three townships: Northampton on the north, Southampton in the middle, and Leicester, which is fifty-seven miles in length, on the south. The rest of the county, though everywhere divided by surveys, is included in the single township of Batavia, probably the largest which ever existed in the world.

From Buffalo Creek to Lake Ontario, a distance of thirty-seven miles, the state has reserved to itself one mile in breadth along the river Niagara, intending to control, without any interfering claims, the future navigation of this spot. Within the reservation is included the ground opposite to Black Rock, of which I shall have occasion to take notice hereafter. Independently of the two lakes, Erie and Ontario, the river Niagara, and the plains already described, I know nothing in the county which is particularly beautiful or magnificent. The uniformity of the surface must always be tedious to the eye.

The county of Genesee is, and during a considerable period will probably continue to be, unhealthy. The tracts on the Genesee River and on

Lake Ontario are particularly so. Buffalo Creek is also sickly. Batavia has been already mentioned. The oak plains appear to furnish a fairer promise of health than any other part of the northern half. In a flat country the streams during the summer half year will of course be noxious.

Almost all this extensive tract is the property of the Holland Company. These gentlemen, it is said, give very little encouragement to settlers. Too wealthy to feel any necessity of selling their lands, and knowing that they will of course increase in value, they propose, as I am informed, conditions of purchase which are not very alluring. The unsettled lands in other parts of the country will, therefore, be chiefly occupied before these are taken up. This is the more probable as the state of Ohio, the territories of Indiana and Illinois, and even that of Louisiana have already become inviting objects to emigrants.

Buffalo Creek, otherwise called New Amsterdam, is built on the northeastern border of a considerable millstream which bears the same name. A bar at the mouth prevents all vessels larger than boats from ascending its waters. For boats it is navigable about eight miles. Its appearance is more sprightly than that of some others in this region. The southwestern bank is here a peninsula, covered with a handsome grove. Through it several vistas might be cut with advantage, as they would open fine views of the lake, a beautiful object. The prospect which they would furnish toward the west and southwest would be boundless.

The village is built half a mile from the mouth of the creek, and consists of about twenty indifferent houses. The Holland Company own the soil. Hitherto they have declined to sell it; and, until very lately, to lease it. Most of the settlers have, therefore, taken up their ground without any title. The terms on which it is leased are that the lessee shall within nine months build a house, thirty feet in front, and two stories in height; and shall pay, if I mistake not, two dollars annually for each lot of half an acre. The streets are straight and cross each other at right angles, but are only forty feet wide. What could have induced this wretched limitation in a mere wilderness, I am unable to conceive. The spot is unhealthy, though of a sufficient elevation, and, so far as I have been informed, free from the vicinity of any stagnant waters. The diseases prevailing here are those which are common to all this country. The inhabitants † are a casual collection of adventurers, and have the usual character of such adventurers thus collected when remote from regular society, retaining but little sense of government or religion. We saw about as many Indians in this village as white people. The superintendent of Indian affairs for the Six Nations resides here.‡

† 1804.

‡ The village of Buffalo was burned down during the late war. Since that period it has been rebuilt, and is now a beautiful and flourishing town of one hundred and fifty houses. PUB. 1820.

New Amsterdam is at present the thoroughfare for all the commerce and traveling interchangeably going on between the eastern states (including New York and New Jersey) and the countries bordering on the great western lakes. The creek is frequently said to unite with the river Niagara. I should say, as I believe every other man would who spoke from his own inspection, that it unites with Lake Erie; and that the river Niagara begins two miles further north at, or rather just below, Black Rock. Here the first perceptible current commences; while at the mouth of the creek the waters, unless agitated by winds, are perfectly still, and have exactly the same appearance as other parts of the lake.

At Black Rock, a town which is a mile square is laid out by order of the state into house lots. The lots are to be disposed of at public sale in December of this year, upon terms with which I am unacquainted. Should they be equitable, the trade which I mentioned will soon center here. Between this rock and the shore is the only secure harbor on the American and a much better than any on the British side of the lake within a great distance. A road is already begun from this spot to Fort Niagara at the mouth of the river, and will not improbably be completed within a year.

The period is not distant when the commerce of this neighborhood will become a great national object, and involve no small part of the interests and happiness of millions. I shall consider it more particularly hereafter.

Since the date of this journey the county of Genesee has been formed into five: Genesee, Niagara, Allegany, Cattaraugus, and Chautauqua. The two first, Genesee on the east and Niagara on the west, are bounded on the north by Lake Ontario. The three last, Allegany on the east, Cattaraugus in the middle, and Chautauqua on the west, are all bounded on the south by the north line of Pennsylvania. In this division the distribution of the western country in the state of New York is probably completed.[4]

| | | | Townships | Inhabitants in 1810 |
|---|---|---|---|---|
| The present | Genesee | contains | 10 | 12,644 |
| | Niagara | " | 4 | 6,132 |
| | Allegany | " | 5 | 1,942 |
| | Cattaraugus | " | 1 | 458 |
| | Chautauqua | " | 2 | 2,381 |
| | | | 22 | 23,557 |

| | | | |
|---|---|---|---|
| The shire town of | Genesee | is | Batavia |
| | Niagara | " | Buffalo |
| | Allegany | " | Angelica |
| | Cattaraugus | " | Hamilton |
| | Chautauqua | " | Mayville |

From these facts it appears that the Holland Company have thought it proper to part with some of their lands on terms so reasonable as to allure a considerable number of purchasers; and that the population of this tract, although very gradual, has yet increased more rapidly than I had expected.

The prospect presented at Buffalo is now most attractive, notwithstanding the interruption mentioned above. Directly opposite, at the distance of two miles, but in full view, stands Fort Erie: a blockhouse accompanied by a suite of barracks and a hamlet. This collection of houses is built on a beautiful shore, wears less the appearance of a recent settlement, and exhibits a much greater degree of improvement than anything which we saw west of the Genesee River. Beyond this hamlet a handsome point stretches to the southwest, and furnishes an imperfect shelter to the vessels employed in the commerce of the lake. Seven of these vessels (five schooners, a sloop, and a pettiaugre [piragua]) lay in the harbor at this time, and presented to us an image of business and activity which, distant as we were from the ocean, was scarcely less impressive than that presented by the harbor of New York when crowded with almost as many hundred.

Behind this point another, much more remote, stretches out in the same direction, exhibiting a form of finished elegance, and seeming an exactly suitable limit for the sheet of water which fills the fine scoop between these arms. Still farther southward, the lake opens in boundless view, and presents in a perfect manner the blending of unlimited waters with the sky.

Over these points assembled, as if to feast our eyes at the commencement of the evening, after our arrival, one of the most beautiful collections of clouds ever seen by a votary of nature. They were of elegant forms, and of hues intense and refulgent. The richest crimson, fading into the tinges of the pink and the rose, adorned them on one side; and gold burnished into the highest brilliancy, on the other. Several strata of these splendors, extending over one tenth of the horizon, lay above each other, in the most fascinating variety of fantastical beauty; while others, single, in pairs, or in small groups, vied with the larger assemblages in contributing to the glory of the scene. Toward the southwest and northeast, two long ranges of leaden-colored clouds, with fleeces of mist hanging beneath them, reached round two thirds of the horizon. These at intervals were all along changed, sometimes gradually, and sometimes suddenly, into the gayest crimson and the most vivid purple, alternated in such a manner, as to defy the utmost efforts both of the pen and the pencil. The sky above, of that pure bright aspect which succeeds a storm when it becomes clear with a soft serenity, was varied from a glowing yellow, a brilliant straw color, and a willow green into a light, and finally into a darker, azure: the beautiful blue of autumn.

Beneath all this glory the lake, a boundless field of polished glass, glittered alternately with the variegated splendor of the clouds, and the hues of the sky, softening and improving the brilliancy of both with inimitable delicacy, and leaving on the mind the impression of enchantment rather than of reality. Not a breath was felt: not a leaf trembled; not a sound was heard: not a fluctuation disturbed the elegance of the surface. A lively imagination would easily have fancied that a paradise might be found beyond this charming expansion.

I am, Sir, yours, etc.

# LETTER IV

*Brief account of the Great Lakes which supply the river Niagara—Lake Superior—Its islands, rivers, etc.—River St. Marys—Its only outlet—Opinion that there are subterraneous outlets examined—Lake Huron—Lake Michigan—Island of Mackinac—Huron River—Lake St. Clair—Lake Erie—Evidence that the waters of these lakes are lower than they formerly were*

*Dear Sir,*

Before I commence my account of the river and falls of Niagara, it will not be amiss to describe summarily the great chain of lakes whose waters are conveyed to the ocean through this channel. Without a just apprehension of the extent of this singular collection of waters, it will not be easy for you to conceive, or even to admit, correct views of the importance and splendor of the river St. Lawrence.

The first and westernmost of these inland seas is Lake Superior. Carver, whose accounts so far as they have been examined have, notwithstanding the discredit at first attached to them, been found to be remarkably just and accurate, and who coasted the northeastern and northwestern shores of this lake near twelve hundred miles, informs us that its whole circuit measures more than sixteen hundred: an estimate somewhat larger than that of Mackenzie. It lies between 46° and 49° north latitude, and between 84° and 93° west longitude from London. So far as he had opportunities of examining, its shores are rough, rocky, and mountainous. The water is remarkably transparent, so that, in his language, over a depth of six fathoms his canoe, instead of appearing to rest on the water, seemed as if suspended in the air. In the summer it is warm at the surface, but at a small depth is very cold.

Lake Superior contains many islands, and among them five of a considerable size: Round, Pontchartrain, Philippeaux, Mirapau, and Royale: the last one hundred miles in length and forty in breadth. Neither of these islands has hitherto been explored. Some of them, regarded by the Indians as sacred places, are holden in high veneration.

About forty small rivers enter this lake, and three of a superior size: the Nipigon, the Michipicoten, and the St. Louis: the first on the northeastern, and the second on the northwestern side. The third, whose springs are the most remote waters of the St. Lawrence, discharges itself at the southwestern angle. To the eye this lake, except at the two angles, is an ocean: the view being literally boundless. Like the ocean also, it is frequently and furiously agitated by storms, which are in the highest degree dangerous to navigators.

Virgin copper is found in many places on the shore and on many of the small islands, particularly on those which are near the eastern coast.

A small river, a little eastward of the Nipigon, descends, just before its entrance into the lake, over a perpendicular precipice more than six hundred feet in height.

Lake Superior abounds in fish of various kinds, the principal of which are the trout, the whitefish, and the sturgeon.

The channel through which the waters of this vast reservoir are emptied into the Huron is the river St. Marys, which in one place is not more than six feet in depth. By Carver, and by others who have followed him, it is supposed that after making the utmost allowance for the quantity of water evaporated from its surface, the St. Marys is an insufficient channel for the conveyance of the superabundant waters of the lake, and that, therefore, they are drawn off by one or more subterraneous passages. Permit me to examine this opinion.

That subterraneous passages exist, which descend to the center or pass circuitously round the globe, or any considerable part of it, will hardly be imagined. If they terminate at any moderate distance beneath the surface, they must for thousands of years have been filled, and certainly can admit no more supplies from the lake. If they break through the surface, the effusion of water from the orifice must be too extraordinary to have escaped observation. If the passage terminates at the bottom of one of the neighboring lakes, say Huron or Michigan, the nearest, and therefore the most promising resorts in this investigation, the water above and around the opening would boil with a force which must detect the fact, since every part of these lakes is continually wandered over, both by the Indians and the whites. The only remaining supposition is that these conduits open in the bed of the St. Lawrence, where the effect would be still more visible than in either of the lakes, or in the ocean, above whose surface that of Lake Superior is elevated at least a thousand feet. The pressure of a column of this height to speak in very moderate terms would create such a disturbance of the surface of the ocean as must long since have been marked by many of the numberless vessels which ply continually in every part of the northern Atlantic. Such a phenomenon must have been universally known throughout the eighteenth century, and probably through the latter half of the seventeenth.

At the same time, such a subterranean stream proceeding from this lake would occasion a violent whirlpool on the surface, and this must have been observed by some or other of the numerous voyagers who pass over it every summer; but nothing of this nature has been seen. On the contrary, the waters in calm weather are perfectly smooth and quiescent.

That the river St. Marys is a sufficient outlet for these waters, sufficient I mean to carry off all its supplies except what are exhausted by evaporation, I have not a single doubt. In the year 1810, a lake in the township either of Glover or of Greensboro and county of Orleans, in the state of Vermont, broke through its barriers and emptied its waters into the Lake Memphremagog. The bed was left entirely vacant. Before this event a millstream ran out of it into the river Lamoille: a stream now runs from its bed into Barton River, furnished by the same springs which, originally subjacent, supplied the waters of the lake. The difference between these two streams is imperceptible. From this fact it appears that the little stream which formerly carried the waters of this lake into the Lamoille, apparently disproportioned to the quantity of water, conveyed off whatever was superfluous, or in other words whatever was supplied by the springs. This lake was about two miles and a half in length, a mile in breadth, and one hundred and ninety-seven feet in depth. The quantity of water which flowed into this bed and accumulated this mass, or in other words, the supplies necessary to form such an accumulation, was incomparably less than we have been accustomed to believe.*

* From the New England Palladium, Friday, June 22, 1810.

*Vermont, Montpelier, June* 9, 1810

On the 6th inst. the large pond, in the northeast part of Greensboro, which formed the head of the river Lamoille, burst its bounds, and emptied itself into Lake Memphremagog, distant about twenty-five miles. This pond which was about two and a half miles in length, one in breadth, and about one hundred feet in depth, was situated on the Green Mountain range, and was considerably higher than the surrounding country. At the distance of about forty rods was another smaller pond; on the outlet of which stood a number of mills. The perpendicular height of the former above the latter was about one hundred feet. It had long been contemplated to make a communication between them, in the expectation that it would greatly benefit the mills below the small pond. On the day above mentioned a number of the inhabitants of Wheelock, Sheffield, Glover, and Barton met for the purpose of digging a channel and commenced their operations on the brow of a descent a few rods from the large pond. They soon finished a channel five or six feet in depth. As this was filled, the ground, which was a kind of quicksand, began to sink; and the pressure soon produced a chasm of upwards of one hundred feet in depth, and eighteen or twenty rods in breadth. The water issued from the pond with such impetuosity that it was completely drained in one hour. The ground sunk so suddenly that the workmen had scarcely time to save themselves; and one of them sunk five or six feet, but was so fortunate as to escape by laying hold on the root of a tree. The water rushed into the lower pond, and thence proceeded through a forest

The whole mass of Connecticut River often runs during a part of the summer in a channel at Bellows Falls at times not more than twenty-five feet in breadth, and so far as I am able to judge, of not more than four or five feet in depth; and yet, at a small distance above and below, the river is forty rods in breadth, probably not less than six or eight in depth, and runs with a strong current. Not a man living would, I presume, believe it possible for such a mass of water to descend through this crevice, for it is little more, without being compelled by ocular demonstration.

All the supplies furnished by rivers to Lake Superior except those derived from subjacent springs amount to a quantity not very considerable. Not a small part of them must be drawn off by evaporation; for the remainder the St. Marys must, I think, be an ample channel, when I consider the facts mentioned above.

In this opinion I am confirmed by observing the drains of other lakes, few if any of which bear any such proportion as *a priori* we should expect to the body of waters which they contain. The Sorelle would be thought a less river than would be formed by the union of Otter Creek, Onion River, the Lamoille, the Misciscoui, Pulteney River, and the outlet at Lake George. Yet Lake Champlain receives a multitude of streams of a smaller size, besides what is furnished by springs. The outlet of Lake George also is a little stream. The same may be said of many, perhaps of almost all others. The Caspian has no outlet, although it receives the waters of the Volga, the Ural, the Kur [Kura], the Tedjon [Terek], and several other considerable rivers.

It is said that the surface of Lake Superior is evidently about six feet lower than it was at some former period. The proof alleged is the appearance of the rocks and other parts of the shore, which to this height bear evident marks of having been once covered by water. Aside from this evidence the opinion may be received without difficulty. The St. Marys is undoubtedly continually lowering its bed, insensibly indeed, but certainly. That in a long progress of years it should have worn it down the depth specified can excite no surprise.

Just at the head of the St. Marys, there is a remarkably rich prospect of the river, the lake, its islands, the points, and other parts of the neighboring shores.

---

of heavy timber six miles to Barton River, carrying with it everything in its way. It then took the course of Barton River, repeating the same devastation till it reached Lake Memphremagog. Farms which lay on the banks of this river, were covered ten or twelve feet deep; and two sawmills, a gristmill, and a blacksmith shop, five bridges, and a great number of sheep were swept into the lake.

The scene which it presented was awful. The valleys were filled up, and the hills were leveled. The earth trembled throughout a circuit of many miles. The noise, which was heard throughout a great distance, was at first supposed to be thunder; but, as the sky was unclouded, was speedily believed to be that of an earthquake. Happily no lives were lost.

Lake Huron, into which the St. Marys enters, is the second of this singular collection. It lies between 43° and 47° north latitude, and between 80° and 85° west longitude. Its circumference is eleven hundred miles; and its shape, triangular. A remarkable island, named *Manitoulin,* rises near the north shore, one hundred miles in length and eight only in breadth, and furnishes another object of religious reverence to the Indians. A large bay on the southwestern side, called Saganaum [Saginaw] Bay, about twenty miles in breadth, opens eighty miles into the interior. Halfway between this and the straights of Mackinac, on the same side, is another, known by the name of Thunder Bay. This is about nine miles in diameter, and as its name indicates is distinguished from all other temperate parts of North America by an almost perpetual succession of thunderstorms. French River on the north, the outlet of Lake Nepisingui [Nipissing], about seventy-five miles in length, is the only stream except the St. Marys received by this lake. Its shores are less uneven than those of Lake Superior, and are more sandy and barren.

Lake Huron receives the waters of Michigan, which is three hundred miles in length, and nine hundred and forty-five in circumference, lying between 41° and 46° north latitude, and 84° and 87° west longitude. Its greatest breadth is sixty miles. Its shores are extensively flat, and covered with an indifferent soil. In its northwestern corner opens a large inlet called Green Bay, not far from one hundred miles in length, and from fifteen to twenty in breadth. Fox River, a considerable stream which passes through the Winnebago and empties its waters into Green Bay, the St. Joseph, and the river Grand are the only streams of importance which terminate in this lake. It is wholly within the United States, and without any islands of consequence. One of the principal passages from the lakes to the Mississippi is up Green Bay and the Fox River and down the Wisconsin; and another, up the Michigan and down the Illinois.

Near the mouth of the straits which unite the Michigan with the Huron, and within the latter, is the island of Mackinac, long distinguished as a military post of no small importance in the contest between France and Great Britain, and a place highly advantageous for commerce with the Indians of the north and west. This island lies in the 46th degree of north latitude, is of a circular form, and seven miles and a half in circumference. Its distance from the shore is somewhat more than three miles. It is considerably higher than the main, and is a mere rock of limestone, covered with a good soil, and originally with a rich growth of timber. Its form resembles the back of a turtle, and thence it is said to have derived its name. The air is here fine, and the water excellent. Few places are healthier. Fish abound in the neighborhood, particularly the whitefish, esteemed a great delicacy; trout, weighing from fifteen to seventy-five pounds; and various others, particularly such as have been mentioned in the account of Lake Superior.

There is a small village † on this island, built around the harbor. The streets are narrow; the houses, chiefly of one story; and the number of inhabitants, about three hundred. A few of them are Americans, some of whom were heretofore wealthy; the rest are principally Canadian French, a miserable, unanimated race, without ambition or energy, without intelligence or taste, and during the winter almost without business or food. Their chief employment for six months is fishing and procuring fuel.

Mackinac is considered as the key of the northwestern country, and is the great depot of the fur trade. Hither the merchants of Montreal, and others from the United States, resort in the spring to receive furs and peltries from their agents, and furnish them supplies for renewing the business through the succeeding season. The navigation opens in May and closes in November.

From the fort, an indifferent edifice of little strength, commanded by high ground in the rear, there is a delightful prospect, unlimited in the east over Lake Huron, and in the west over Michigan. The fort itself is a very infirm structure as a place of defense, and its outworks are still worse. Like other public American possessions, it has been neglected; and, as a military post, forgotten.

The water of these lakes, like that of Superior, is transparent.

The river Huron is the channel through which this accumulated mass flows into Lake Erie. It is from half a mile to three miles in breadth. The current is moderate, and the depth sufficient for ships of considerable burden. On its banks stands the town of Detroit, nine miles below an expansion of the river about thirty miles in diameter named Lake St. Clair. The situation of this town is unhealthy. Heretofore it has contained about 260 houses, and 2,000 inhabitants.‡ This was the principal settlement of the French in the western country. The river Huron is ninety miles in length. Its banks have long been in a great measure covered with plantations.

Lake Erie lies between 41° and 43° north latitude, and 71° and 80° west longitude. Its length is more than 200 miles, according to Carver near 300; its breadth, forty. Its circumference is said to be 710 miles. Its water is remarkably clear and beautiful, though esteemed somewhat less so than those of the three which have been mentioned. It also furnishes not only the same kinds of fish, but several others. Those which were mentioned to me at Buffalo are the following: sturgeon, weighing sixty or seventy pounds, and yielding a great quantity of oil; white bass, large and very good; pike, three kinds, very good, and well sized; catfish, large; salmon trout, very good, not so large as those caught in Michigan. It also contains a great number of water snakes, which hide in a multitude of water lilies surrounding its islands.

† 1804.

‡ In the month of June 1805, Detroit was totally destroyed by fire.

The navigation of Lake Erie when agitated by a tempest is extremely dangerous, on account of a number of points which project into it a considerable distance. Near the Cayahoga River, which discharges itself on the south shore, a ridge of rocks, forming a magnificent promontory, shoots out several miles into the lake, and has often proved fatal to navigators. Perhaps no piece of water of the same extent has fewer safe harbors. On the southern side I know of but three: Black Rock, Presque Isle, and Sandusky Bay.

The shores of this lake are to a great extent unhealthy, not from the waters of the lake, but from the marshes which in several places line its border. To the eye surveying these shores at a distance, they are often beautiful.

Such are the fountains of that part of the St. Lawrence which is termed the river Niagara, a stream inferior in splendor to none perhaps in the world.

It ought to be observed that on the island of Mackinac, there are the most decisive proofs that the waters of Huron and Michigan are several feet lower than they once were. Proofs, equally decisive, are presented on its southern borders of a similar subsidence in Lake Erie. Of these facts I am amply assured by my friends, the Rev. Mr. Bacon, who resided at Mackinac as a missionary one season, Josiah Dunham, Esq., who commanded at that post six years, and John S. Edwards, Esq., who has personally examined the appearances on the southern borders of Lake Erie.[1] From the testimony of these gentlemen the general fact cannot be doubted. Nor is the cause at all difficult to be discovered. The river Niagara, at and above the falls, shows unquestionable proofs that its waters have worn their channel, particularly the rocky part of it, continually lower.

I am, Sir, yours, etc.

# LETTER V

*River Niagara—Properly called the St. Lawrence—Islands in the river—General appearance and character of this region—Cataract of Niagara*

*Dear Sir,*

Next morning, Saturday, October 6th, we commenced our journey to the falls. On the beach upon which the road lies from Buffalo to the ferry, we had a complete view of the lake. On the southern side the prospect was limited successively by three promontories: the first about eight or ten miles distant, the second at twice, and the third at three times that distance. Handsomer headlands can scarcely be imagined. They are all elegant declivities, descending with almost imperceptible gradation toward the water. The second and third are so lofty that they may be styled mountainous, and blend with their beauty a considerable degree of grandeur. The succession in which they are presented to the eye adds to their individual appearance a fine impression of symmetry.

After coasting the end of the lake two miles, we came to the great outlet of this world of waters, covering about ninety-six million acres, or one hundred and fifty thousand square miles. The stream which commences here is improperly called the river Niagara, that is, unless this name should be extended to every part of the current from its fountains to the ocean. It has been the misfortune of this magnificent river to be called by so many names as to leave on the mind the impression of numerous, disjointed parts, and not of one vast, continued stream. Hence the geographical reader, finding it in different instances styled the river St. Marys, Detroit, St. Clair, Niagara, Iroquois, Cataraqui, and St. Lawrence, becomes perplexed and lost amidst this confusion of appellations. Hence also the proper character and real greatness of the river are concealed; and its extent, importance, and place in the list of streams are unknown. The Rhone with the strictest propriety is called by this name equally before and after its entrance into the lake of Geneva; and the Rhine, before and after its entrance into that of Constance. In each case the stream is but one, and is as truly continued through the lake as between its own banks. For the same reason I pronounce the river St. Lawrence to be one, from its rise in the near neighborhood of the Mississippi to its junction with the ocean.

The St. Lawrence, considered in this, the only vindicable manner, is one of the noblest rivers in the world, and in several points of distinction superior to them all. Its length is about three thousand miles, and its mass of waters greater than that of any other stream, except perhaps the Amazon and the La Plata. The vast lakes or inland seas by which it is attended, and to whose waters it is the great channel of discharge, are nowhere rivaled in importance and grandeur. Nor is the navigation of this river, or its capability of being useful to man, a capability which within less than a century may perhaps be realized to its full extent, even approached by those of any other stream. This navigation is indeed interrupted in three places: the river of St. Marys, at the falls of Niagara, and the rapids of the river Iroquois. The river St. Marys is navigable by boats, but not by larger vessels. A portage of ten miles conveys merchandise around the falls of Niagara. Concerning the rapids of the river Iroquois or that part of the St. Lawrence which runs between Lake Ontario and Montreal, I am imperfectly informed. Whatever obstructions they present to transportation, they are of so little consequence that a barrel is now brought from Montreal to Queenston for a dollar. In the intervals between these interruptions the navigation is so convenient, and already so important, as to employ many of the smaller kinds of vessels used upon the ocean.

The St. Lawrence meets the tide four hundred miles from its mouth. To this distance fleets of men-of-war have ascended, and found ample room for a naval engagement. Merchant ships ascend to Montreal, near two hundred miles farther. In accordance with its interior grandeur, the mouth of this river is ninety miles wide. The cataract which it forms at Niagara is proverbially a wonder of the world. The astonishing grandeur with which the river Ottawa breaks up the ice of the St. Lawrence at Montreal in the spring, as described to me by a gentleman who was an eyewitness of this stupendous operation of nature, is at times more majestic than even the cataract itself. Upon the whole, if these facts are fairly considered, I shall hazard little in saying that the St. Lawrence is the most magnificent stream on the globe.

This character it displays strongly at its passage out of Lake Erie. At the ferry, one mile below, it is seven furlongs in breadth, and from twenty-five to thirty feet in depth. The current, at the lowest estimation, is five miles an hour, and in all probability six. Such a mass of fresh water rarely runs on this globe. Yet after passing Lake Ontario the quantity must be materially increased. The water is of a beautiful sea green, like that of Lake George formerly described, although somewhat less pure.

After we had crossed the ferry without inconvenience, though with much fatigue to our boatmen, we pursued our route toward the cataract. Throughout this distance, eighteen miles, the road scarcely leaves the bank at all, the surface of whch is almost a perfect level. In all this part of its progress the river is entirely free from that dull, canal-like appearance which frequently lessens the beauty of other streams. Its breadth at different places is, one, two, three, and three and a half miles; and its current in the highest degree sprightly and vigorous.

Throughout a considerable part of this distance it is, however, divided by several beautiful islands. Of these by far the largest is Grand Island, being six miles long, and from three to four broad. Navy Island, opposite to the northern point of Grand Island, is next in size, being about one mile in length. Three others lie against the mouths of Five Mile, Tonawanda, and Unnekugua Creeks, at twenty, twenty-six, and thirty-five miles from the influx of the river into Lake Ontario. These three islands are, I presume, the effects of alluvion. Goat Islands lie immediately above the falls. There are also two or three smaller ones. All which we saw were covered with a rich growth of wood, and formed very pleasing parts of the picture.

Against Grand Island the river is almost equally divided, and each division is a river of prodigious size. The eastern bank, like the western, is nearly level and almost entirely forested. We saw but two or three settlements upon it from the ferry to the falls.

On the western shore, houses, commencing at Fort Erie, are continued to the falls; and, I presume, to Lake Ontario. The houses which it contains are all, except three or four, built on the western side of the road, from ten rods to half a mile asunder. The ground behind them, a mere flat, is cleared from a furlong to one half of a mile; and is laid out in fields, imperfectly enclosed.

The soil is alternately a stiff loam and clay, and is very fertile. Under the loose culture which is now employed, it produces wheat, rye, grass, flax, maize, and oats in abundance. Apples, peaches, plums, and several other fruits loaded the trees, and all the fruits of southern New England would flourish here with the utmost luxuriance.

The forests are beech, maple, bass, etc., but are shorter and less thrifty than in the preceding parts of our journey: the cause of this fact I cannot assign. The climate is certainly as mild, and the soil apparently not inferior. Of the mildness of the climate during the present season, we had full proof. The tender plants, such as maize, potatoes, squashes, and pompions [pumpkins], were here generally uninjured by frost, and exhibited the freshest verdure. On the eastern side, from Sheffield to Buffalo Creek, these plants were destroyed in most places by the frost of September 20th.

The houses in this settlement are chiefly built of logs, and generally appear by the care bestowed on them to be designed for permanent habitations. Some of them are of two stories, and are built of squared timber. Others, probably the residence of indigent proprietors, are extremely wretched. The barns are generally of the same materials. Several of the houses are, however, framed; some are decent; and a few are neat.

In New England a log house is universally intended to be a temporary habitation, a mere retreat from the weather till the proprietor shall be able to build a better. Considered in this light, a traveler will easily regard such a building as a comfortable shelter for the family at the present time, and as a step, and a short one, toward their future convenience and prosperity. Throughout the earliest stages of cultivation in a country recently settled, such houses, built only with this design, will rather increase than diminish the cheerfulness of the prospect. But, when by peculiar pains employed in their construction, they seem designed for a lasting residence, the cheerfulness vanishes at once. In themselves, though capable of resisting the inclemency of seasons and of sheltering their tenants from rain and frost, these houses are uncomfortable dwellings. They are of course the haunts and the nurseries of vermin in great numbers, subjected to speedy decay, gloomy to the sight, offensive to the smell; and, unless continually repaired, are both cold and leaky. When the timber of which they are built is hewn, and the parts most easily dissoluble are removed, they will endure a greater length of time, but even then will barely last long enough for one generation. In the meantime these inconveniences must be suffered, and with continual augmentation.

The habitation has not a little influence on the mode of living; and the mode of living sensibly affects the taste, the manners, and even the morals of the inhabitants. If a poor man builds a poor house, without any design or hope of possessing a better, he will either originally, or within a short time, conform his aims and expectations to the style of his house. His dress, his food, his manners, his taste, his sentiments, his education of his children, and their character, as well as his own, will all be seriously affected by this single circumstance. The thoughts and conduct of the family will be reduced to a humble level, and a general aspect of lowliness and littleness will be seen on whatever they contrive or do. The common remark concerning their conduct will be, nothing more could be expected from their character.

The aims of the inhabitants planted along this river seem to accord with these observations. Around both them and their exertions, a barrier seems to be fixed by the state of their own minds, over which they have never thought of passing. A kind of peasantlike humbleness invests everything with which they are concerned. They appear, not merely contented and unambitious, but unacquainted with the objects which excite ambition. Life to them does not glide; it is stagnant. Such at least was the impression forced on my mind while I was passing by their habitations, and observing and conversing with such of the inhabitants as I saw. Their dress, their manners, their language, nay, their walk exhibited, with a small number of exceptions, a single character.

Independently of these things, they are very pleasantly settled, if their situation is healthy. The soil is rich, the climate mild, and the local position beautiful. Were the country filled with the enterprise and cultivation, the churches and schools, the manners, intelligence, and morals of New England, few places could boast a more numerous assemblage of delightful objects.

Eighteen miles from Buffalo is built on a large millstream bearing the same name the little village of Chippawa, containing from twelve to twenty houses, a few of them decent. Here is a small fortress, and a garrison destined, as I should imagine, to a life of stagnant indolence.

About four miles above the cataract we began to see the mist raised by the agitation of the water, ascending in the form of a large white cloud, and continually varying its aspect as it was blown by the wind into every fantastical shape. At times, it almost entirely disappeared; at others, it burst suddenly upon the sight; and, rising slowly with great solemnity and grandeur, dispersed its magnificent volumes into the atmosphere. Nothing could afford us more noble anticipations of the splendor of the scene to which we were approaching.

After dining at Chippawa, we proceeded to the cataract. About a mile from our inn, we were presented with one of the noblest prospects in the world, the more impressive as none of us had ever heard it mentioned. Here the immense bed of limestone which fills this country begins rapidly to decline. A number of shelves, parallel to each other, cross the river obliquely, almost to the American shore. They are however irregular, broken, and wild; formed into long and short ranges, sudden prominences, and pointed rocks. Over this ragged and finely varied surface, the river rolls its amazing mass of waters with a force and grandeur of which my own mind had never before formed a conception. The torrent is thrown up with immeasurable violence as it rushes down the vast declivity, between two and three miles in breadth, into a thousand eminences of foam. All the magnificence of water scenery shrunk in a moment into playthings of Lilliput.

When we came over against the cataract, we secured our horses and descended the ancient bank of the river, a steep of one hundred and fifty or two hundred feet. The footway which conducted us was of clay; and, having been wet by the preceding rain, was so slippery that we could hardly keep our footing. At the bottom we found a swamp, encumbered with trees, bushes, mire, and water. After stooping, struggling, and sliding near a quarter of a mile, we came to the Table Rock, a part of the stratum over which the river descends, and the edge of the precipice which at this place forms the British bank of the river. This rock is at a small distance from the cataract, and presents the spectator with as perfect a view as can be imagined.

The falls of Niagara have been often described. Some or other of these descriptions I may have read, but at so early a period of my life as not to remember even this fact. When I began to explore and describe this country, it was my determination to avoid reading any account of any part of it which was proposed as a scene of my own excursions. My reason was the wish to make my own observations, and to keep my own views unmixed with those of others. This scheme, it must be acknowledged, is not free from disadvantages; yet, it is certain that it has its advantages also. To me at least, it appeared very desirable to bring to every scene a mind, neither biased, nor perplexed by the views of others; and it seemed better to correct my own views afterwards by theirs, than by preoccupying my judgment and fancy to leave no room for original observation. I shall therefore exhibit to you this scene, as I have others, just as it struck my eye.

These falls are situated twenty-one miles, reckoned on the British, and twenty-three, reckoned on the American arm of the river (where it is divided by Grand Island), from Buffalo, two miles less from the outlet of Lake Erie, and fourteen miles from the entrance of the river into Lake Ontario between Newark and Fort Niagara. The river bends on the American side about twelve miles to the northwest, and on the British side, about four, immediately below Navy Island. It is here little less than four miles wide, and sufficiently deep for any navigation. It gradually becomes narrower as it approaches the falls, but immediately above them its breadth is not far from three miles. From one mile and three quarters above, or opposite to the Stedman farm, it begins to descend with a rapid and powerful current.[1] At the falls it turns instantly with a right angle to the northeast, and in a moment is contracted to three quarters of a mile.

Below the falls the river is not more, and in some places it is less, than half a mile in breadth. Its depth here is great, being said to exceed three hundred feet; and its current is violent, proportionally to this contraction.

The cataract is formed by the brow of that vast bed of limestone which is the base of all this country. Here its surface is perhaps 150 feet beneath the common surface of the earth; elsewhere it approaches nearer. The brow extends, as I am informed, into the county of Ontario on the east, and on the west into Upper Canada a distance which is unknown. The great falls of the Genesee are formed by the same brow. On the river Niagara it approaches near to Queenston, at the distance of seven miles below the cataract. The whole height of the ledge above Lake Ontario is estimated by Mr. Ellicott to be 410 feet.[2] At Lake Erie the common level of the shore is about twenty feet above its waters. This level continues to the falls, and probably to the neighborhood of Queenston, the river gradually declining till it arrives at the rapids mentioned in the preceding letter. Here, within the distance of one mile and three fourths, it declines fifty-seven feet.

The precipice over which the cataract descends is, according to Major Prescott's survey, 151 feet.[3] This vast descent is perpendicular, except that the rocks are hollowed underneath the surface, particularly on the western side. The length of the precipice is three fourths of a mile.

At the cataract the river is divided by an island, whose brow is perpendicular and nearly coincident with the common line of the precipice. It occupies about one fifth or one sixth of the whole breadth. This island, it is reported, was visited by General Putnam during the last Canadian war, or that which began in the year 1755. A wager it is said was laid that no man in that part of the army would dare to attempt a descent upon it. Putnam with his customary resolution undertook the enterprise. Having made fast a strong rope to a batteau, he proceeded a considerable distance up the stream. Then taking some stout skillful rowers, he put out into the river directly above the island. The rope in the meantime was holden firmly by several muscular soldiers on the shore. The batteau descended securely enough to the island; and, the enterprise being accomplished, was drawn again to the shore by his attendants.*

The quantity of water descending at this place in a given time may with considerable probability be estimated from the following data.

The river at the ferry is seven furlongs wide, and at an average twenty-five feet deep. The latter of these facts I received from an intelligent ferry-man. The same man stated the current at four miles an hour. I am satisfied that it moves six miles an hour. I allege the following reasons.

1. Notwithstanding the great depth of the water, and its absolute freedom from any obstrucions, the surface at the ferry is strongly rippled, resembling the water of a millstream where it is shallow, and runs rapidly over a bed of stones.

2. The surface is here so oblique as to present a striking obliquity to the eye.

3. The boats, as we crossed and recrossed the river with three stout oarsmen, fell down the stream one half of a mile. The boats were light and convenient; and the wind was not unfavorable.

4. We traveled on the banks of the river four miles an hour by the watch, and the rapidity of the current evidently exceeded our progress.

5. Mr. Lamson, an intelligent and respectable inhabitant of the county of St. Lawrence, who has examined this subject with attention, informed me that the current had been proved to be six miles an hour by a log thrown into the river at the ferry and floated down to the village of Chippawa. It is to be observed that at the ferry the rapidity is greater than at any place between that and the village.

6. An ocular comparison with other streams, too tedious to be mentioned here, will establish this estimate.

For these reasons, I am satisfied that the current of this river is six miles an hour. If we calculate the quantity of water which passes the ferry, and of course descends at this cataract, on the supposition that the current is five miles, it will in an hour amount to 85,078,125 tons avoirdupois; if at six, to 102,093,750. At five miles the mass will in a day be 2,041,875,000; at six miles, it will be 2,450,250,000. It is not to be supposed that all these data are precisely correct, yet they cannot be far from the truth.

You will easily believe that by the falling of such a mass of water from such a height the stream below must be intensely convulsed. The world, it is presumed, furnishes no example of similar agitation. The river does not, however, boil, in the common acceptation of that word, at all. The whole surface, and probably all beneath it, is a body of foam, differing essentially from what I have seen produced elsewhere, and much more strongly indicating the immense force of the current. The bubbles, of which it is uni-

* A bridge now connects the island with the American shore. 1819. PUB.

versally composed, are extremely small; and appear continually ascending, and spreading on the surface in millions of irregular circular areas. These are all limited by lines formed by chains of the larger bubbles, stretching between the several areas so as to mark distinctly the extent of each. The lines themselves fluctuate unceasingly; and, while they continually change their form, move along the surface also in every direction. Thus the whole river appears in one common convulsion, as if affected with a deep, paralytic tremor, reaching from shore to shore, as far down the stream as the eye can trace it, and apparently from the surface to the bottom. To give you the impression which it made on my mind, I think of no better method than to say that it seemed as if a vast volcanic struggle had commenced beneath this world of waters, whose incumbent weight hitherto prevented the approaching explosion.

The cause of this singular phenomenon may be thus understood. Immediately below the precipice, the bed of the river where it receives the falling sheet is of immense depth. Into this receptacle the mass of descending water, plunging from such a height, forces its way to the bottom. Here, forming a curve, it begins to ascend. The current is, however, checked in every stage of its progress by the immeasurable weight of the superincumbent water. The motion upward must therefore become slow, divided, and irregular. In these circumstances, instead of a current, there must obviously be a general agitation, universal heaving, such as might be expected from the throes of an earthquake. As the ascending current is thus broken and enervated before it reaches the surface, the surface is not billowy, but comparatively level. The wavy, tossed aspect of other streams immediately below their cataracts is the result of a force applied at the surface, or of a current descending only to a moderate depth. In the present case, as the ascending current comes from a depth so vast, it almost equally affects the whole mass, and cannot disturb the common level by the smallest fluctuations. The whole appearance, however, made an impression on the mind of an agitation incalculably greater, and a force far more astonishing, than that which produces the loftiest billows of the ocean. This was a scene which I was unprepared to expect, and an exhibition of the force of water which I had never before imagined.

Of the singular depth of the river at this place no spectator will ask for proof. To others it may be alleged that a deep stream, from two to three and a half miles wide, is here contracted at once to somewhat less than half a mile; that logs and other substances, after descending the precipice, continue buried a long time before they emerge; and that this immense mass of water, plunging from such a height, has been so long and so unceasingly excavating the bed below.

The noise of this cataract has often been the object of admiration, and the subject of loose and general description. We heard it distinctly when crossing the ferry at the distance of eighteen miles, the wind blowing from the northwest, almost at right angles with the direction of the sound. Two gentlemen who had lived some time at York on the north side of Lake Ontario, and who were my companions in the stage, informed me that it was not unfrequently heard there. The distance is fifty miles.

The note, or tone, if I may call it such, is the same with the hoarse roar of the ocean, being much more grave, or less shrill, than that which proceeds from other objects of the same nature. It is not only louder, but seems as if it were expanded to a singular extent, as if it filled the atmosphere and spread over all the surrounding country. The only variety which attends it is a continual undulation, resembling that of long musical chords when struck with a forcible impulse. These undulations succeed each other with great rapidity. When two persons stand very near to each other, they can mutually hear their ordinary conversation. When removed to a small distance, they are obliged to halloo; and, when removed a little farther, cannot be heard at all. Every other sound is drowned in the tempest of noise made by the water, and all else in the regions of nature appears to be dumb. This noise is a vast thunder, filling the heavens, shaking the earth, and leaving the mind, although perfectly conscious of safety, and affected with a sense of grandeur only, lost and astonished, swelling with emotions which engross all its faculties and mock the power of utterance.

The strength of this sound may be illustrated in the following manner: the roar of the ocean on the beach south of Long Island is sometimes heard in New Haven, at the distance of forty miles. The cataract of Niagara is heard ten miles farther.

All cataracts produce greater or less quantities of mist, a proof to the common eye that vapor may rise by mere agitation. The mist raised here is proportioned to the greatness of the cause. A large, majestic cloud, visible from an advantageous position for a great number of miles, rises without intermission from the whole breadth of the river below; and, ascending with a slow, solemn progress, partly spreads itself down the stream by an arching and wonderfully magnificent motion, and partly mounts toward heaven, blown into every wild and fantastical form; when, separating into smaller clouds, it successively floats away through the atmosphere.

Nearest to the shore a considerable quantity of this vapor impinges against the rock; and, continually accumulating, descends in a constant shower of drops and little streams. A person standing under the shelving part of these rocks would in a short time be wet to the skin.

In the mist produced by all cataracts, rainbows are ordinarily seen in a proper position when the sun shines; always, indeed, unless when the vapor is too rare. Twice while we were here, the sun broke through the clouds, and lighted up in a moment the most lucid rainbow which I ever beheld. In each instance the phenomenon continued a long time, and left us in perfect leisure to enjoy its splendors. It commenced near the precipice and extended, so far as I was able to judge, at least a mile down the river. In the latter instance, the sun was near the horizon; and the cusps of the bow were depressed as much beneath the horizontal level as the sun was above it. It was therefore a semicircle, and the vertex was half a mile above the base. In the former instance, the dimensions were somewhat smaller. Both were however interrupted. The southern part of that here principally insisted on, or the division next to the precipice, was continued from the base to the vertex, and was therefore a full quadrant. The northern part, commencing at the base, did not exceed one quarter of the other.

In one respect both these rainbows differed widely from all others which I had seen; and, so far as I remember, from those of which I have read. The red, orange, and yellow were so vivid as to excite in our whole company strong emotions of surprise and pleasure; while the green, blue, indigo, and violet were certainly not more brilliant than in those which are usually seen on the bosom of a shower. I thought them less bright, possibly because they were so faint compared with the other colors. The cause of this peculiarity I have not attempted to investigate. The fact was certain, and the phenomenon more glorious than any of the kind which I had ever seen, or than I am able to describe.†

When the eye was fixed upon any spot, commencing a few rods above the precipice, that is, where the cataract begins to be formed, the descending water assumes everywhere a circular figure from the place, where it begins to descend to that where it falls perpendicularly. The motion here remarkably resembles that of a wheel, rolling toward the spectator. The section is about one fifth or one sixth part of a circle, perhaps twelve rods in diameter. The effort of this motion of so vast a body of water, equally novel and singular, was exquisitely delightful. It was an object of inexpressible grandeur, united with intense beauty of figure: a beauty greatly heightened by the brilliant and most elegant sea green of the waters, fading imperceptibly into a perfect white at the brow of the precipice.

The emotions excited by the view of this stupendous scene are unutterable. When the spectator casts his eye over the long ranges of ragged cliffs which form the shores of this great river below the cataract, cliffs 150 feet in height, bordering it with lonely gloom and grandeur, and shrouded everywhere by shaggy forests; when he surveys the precipice above, stretching with so great an amplitude, rising to so great a height, and presenting in a single view its awful brow, with an impression not a little enhanced by the

† Exactly three years from this day, viz., October 6, 1807, as I was riding between Newburyport and Ipswich in Massachusetts, with Messrs. D[wight] and G[rimké], in returning from Maine, we saw a rainbow of the same remarkable appearance. The three glowing colors were eminently brilliant, like those mentioned in the text. This also was formed in a body of vapor, or an uniformly diffused cloud. From these facts taken together, it seems evident that vapor is more favorable than drops of rain to the exhibition of these three colors; or in other words, refracts them with a perfection nearer to that of a prism.

division which the island forms between the two great branches of the river; when he contemplates the enormous mass of water pouring from this astonishing height in sheets so vast and with a force so amazing; when, turning his eye to the flood beneath, he beholds the immense convulsion of the mighty mass, and listens to the majestic sound which fills the heavens, his mind is overwhelmed by thoughts too great and by impressions too powerful to permit the current of the intellect to flow with serenity. The disturbance of his mind resembles that of the waters beneath him. His bosom swells with emotions never felt; his thoughts labor in a manner never known before. The pleasure is exquisite but violent. The conceptions are clear and strong, but rapid and tumultuous. The struggle within is discovered by the fixedness of his position, the deep solemnity of his aspect, and the intense gaze of his eye. When he moves, his motions appear uncontrived. When he is spoken to, he is silent; or, if he speaks, his answers are short, wandering from the subject, and indicating that absence of mind which is the result of laboring contemplation.

All these impressions are heightened to a degree which cannot be conjectured by the slowly ascending volumes of mist, rolled and tossed into a thousand forms by the varying blast, and by the splendor of the rainbow, successively illuminating their bosom. At the same time, the spectator cannot but reflect that he is surveying the most remarkable object on the globe. Nor will he fail to remember that he stands upon a river, in most respects equal, and in several of high distinction superior, to every other; or that the inland seas which it empties, the mass of water which it conveys, the commercial advantages which it furnishes, and the grandeur of its disruption in the spring are all suitable accompaniments of so sublime and glorious a scene.

I am, Sir, yours, etc.

# LETTER VI

*A passage behind the sheet of water of the cataract practicable at some times and not at others—Explanation of this phenomenon—Retrogression of the cataract considered*

*Dear Sir,*

From Mr. B——, an English gentleman who was occasionally our companion during a part of this tour, I received the following information:

that the day on which we left him at Chippawa, October 7th, he visited the falls, descended the ladder which reaches from the summit of the bank to the river, and went up the stream so far as to go behind the sheet of descending water. That three or four days afterwards he visited the falls again, and found the river so much higher as to render it impracticable for him to repeat this attempt with success.

The second night after we left Chippawa we lodged at Bemis'. While we were conversing upon this subject, Mr. Bemis declared that he himself had visited them and gone behind the sheet. My companions had all descended the ladder, and had made every effort to reach the cataract, but found it impossible: the water spreading quite to the bank, where it was too steep to permit any passing. They firmly denied, therefore, the practicability of succeeding in any attempt of this nature. Mr. Bemis however, persisted in his declaration. Being questioned concerning the manner and circumstances of his procedure, he replied that he went into the river to bathe, and that he went partly in the water and partly on the shore. This explanation satisfied them.

I received this information from Mr. B. on the evening of Monday, October 15th, at Staniford's, in Manlius; and the next morning committed it to my notebook. The same contradictory accounts had been given by others whose reputation repelled every suspicion of disingenuousness. It became an object in my view very desirable to reconcile these accounts with truth; and to remove finally, if it could be done, every ground of mutual suspicion from those by whom they were given. I therefore determined to put together the several things which I had heard relative to this subject, and to discover, if I could, the cause of the disagreement. In this design, if I mistake not, I was successful.

Lake Erie is regularly raised at the eastern end by every wind blowing between the northwest and southwest. Of this we were eyewitnesses the morning when we left Buffalo for the falls in the rapid rise of the waters upon the beach. A strong westerly wind elevates the surface six feet above its ordinary level. The river must of course be proportionally elevated; and at the outlet must, when such a wind blows, be six feet higher than the general watermark. Of this also the proof is sufficient, if it can need proof, in the appearance of the banks, which bear evident marks of having been washed to a considerable height above the common surface of the stream. All parts of the river must of course partake of this elevation. At the cataract and at the entrance into Lake Ontario, it must be higher than usual, as well as at its efflux from Lake Erie. Immediately below the cataract the elevation must, I think, be at least six feet, for the river though more rapid is scarcely half so wide as at the efflux.

On the contrary, whenever the wind blows from the northeast, the only easterly wind which in this region is of any importance, the waters of Lake

Erie must recede of course, and fall considerably below their usual level. Whenever this is the fact, the river also will be necessarily lower than at any other time.

We visited the falls on the 6th of October. All that day, except very early in the morning, the wind had blown with considerable strength from the northwest; and, when we reached the falls, had continued six or seven hours. Lake Erie had begun to rise sensibly when we commenced our journey. At the time of our arrival the river was full, for the lake was at its usual level in the morning. It is not strange, therefore, that when my companions attempted to make their way to the sheet, they should have found it impracticable, because the water, being thus increased, covered the only possible passage.

On the evening of October 6th, a violent northeast storm began about nine o'clock, and continued till the next morning. A strong breeze between the northeast and north blew till one in the afternoon. At this time Mr. B—— went to the falls. The river was at its lowest ebb; and he had the best opportunity which is ever afforded of going up to the sheet, and found a practicable passage along the shore where my companions found none, and where Mr. Bemis was obliged to betake himself to the water.

The St. Lawrence is probably the only great river in the world which through two thousand miles of its course is subject to no other rise or fall of its waters except that which is occasioned by wind. The greatest drought does not lower it; the greatest rain and most abundant dissolution of snow have not been observed to raise it a single inch. The balance between the evaporation of the lakes and the supplies from streams and subjacent springs is apparently exact. The surplus is conveyed off in a mass which is uniformly the same at all seasons.*

* During the year 1815, the waters of Lake Erie rose several feet above their common level. Causes for this extraordinary, if not singular phenomenon, are various. Some persons have declared that the rise has been gradual through the last seven years. These suppose the cause to have been a succession of wet seasons. They have however mistaken the fact. The rise, I am assured, has all taken place the present year. A gentleman who made a journey along the southern shore of this lake in 1812, and another in 1815, informed me that he found the waters in the former of these excursions at their usual level; and in the latter, saw many places along the shore where he had before rode on a dry, firm beach covered several feet deep. The testimony of the inhabitants along the shore universally concurred with this statement.

Others have observed that the waters of the Mississippi have this year (1815) been raised to an unprecedented height by extraordinary rains, and have concluded that the rise of Lake Erie is derived from the same source. As no rain and no dissolution of snow have been ever known to raise this lake a single inch, it seems incredible that from this source should be derived a rise of several feet. Besides, there is ordinarily no uniform state of weather on this continent within the northern temperate zone spreading sufficiently far to affect in the same manner the great branches of the Mississippi and the headwaters of the St. Lawrence.

Others still suppose that there is an internal and unknown cause of this remarkable event. Of this I shall only say that it is alleged without any evidence.

When Mr. B—— arrived behind the sheet, he found a violent wind blowing directly in his face with such strength that respiration became difficult. The difficulty increased in every step of his progress, and soon obliged him to stop. At the same time, a strong, offensive smell of sulphur, which continued without intermission, added to the difficulty of breathing, and obliged him to retreat. While he was here, he observed that the precipice everywhere exhibited the most evident proofs of moldering, of having been worn away, and of having been long in a state of continual dissolution. The higher parts of the precipice, down to the Table Rock and somewhat below, shelved considerably over the lower parts. The lower parts, as high as he could reach, had moldered to such a degree as to be easily pulled to pieces by his hand, and were so loosened that when he struck or pushed any part of the strata forcibly a perceptible trembling followed the impact.

The wind perceived here by Mr. B—— undoubtedly resulted from the descent of the cataract and the configuration of the place, as it blew nearly at right angles with the wind above. In the bed of the river without the cataract, all was a perfect calm. The manner in which this phenomena is produced, I am unable to explain.

It has been often declared that the falls of Niagara were originally at the brow of the great precipice near Queenston, seven miles further down the river. By the asserters of this opinion the fact has been confidently adduced as a proof that the world existed before the date assigned to it by Moses. Others have denied the fact itself.

That these falls actually existed at some former period at the place specified, I have not a doubt. At the same time, there is nothing strange or perplexing in this position. I have examined with attention three falls of the Saco, three of the Connecticut, two of the Housatonic, two of Otter Creek, three of Onion River, two of the Hudson, two of the Mohawk, one of the Canjoharie, and one of the Passaic, besides several others which need not here be mentioned. In every one of these the same process of nature has taken place. The mode and the degree in which the phenomenon exists are

---

Probably it will be found upon examination that the bottom of the channel of the river St. Marys where it is entered by the waters of Lake Superior has been hollowed out several feet below its former level. In consequence of this fact the waters of Lake Superior must descend into Huron, Michigan, and Erie in a quantity prodigiously greater than at preceding periods, and in this manner must have raised the three lakes considerably above their common level. What renders this supposition the more probable is that Lake Erie has again subsided eight or ten inches, and is continually lowering its surface. This must necessarily be the fact in the case supposed, unless the channel of St. Marys should continue to grow deeper and deeper.

Whether the facts here imagined have taken place, I cannot determine. But should future intelligence prove that the waters of Huron and Michigan have been raised above their customary level, the cause of the rise in Erie must undoubtedly be sought for in an extraordinary effusion of the waters of Lake Superior.

different in them all. Where the stone is of a firmer texture, and therefore less liable to be worn, or from its nature is less exposed to decomposition by the weather; and wherever the stream is smaller and less rapid, this phenomenon is found in a less degree; and, wherever the contrary causes are combined, in a greater. The rocks over which the Connecticut falls are in each of the instances above referred to very hard, and by the ordinary operations of nature scarcely at all subject to decomposition. The falls, therefore, have receded very little. Glens Falls were originally in the neighborhood of Fort Edward; and have receded not far from five miles in a bed of blue limestone, partly worn away by the current of the Hudson, and partly decomposed by the efficacy of the atmosphere. I visited these falls in 1798, 1799, 1802, and 1812. Between the second and third of these dates, a period of three years only, they were changed so much as to disappoint and surprise me. In 1799, I took a rough sketch of these falls, which, from a comparison made on a spot, I thought tolerably exact. In the year 1802, all the smaller resemblances had vanished. Several new and considerable chasms were formed, and others were sensibly enlarged and altered in their figures. In 1812, the scene had become in a great measure new. The Cohoes have receded about a mile from their original position. The channel of the Mohawk has here been forced through a mass of black slate, easily worn, and continually decomposed.

The Canajoharie, a creek formerly described in these letters, and a tributary of the Mohawk, has in the same manner made a passage through a bed of the same slate, between banks in some places not less than 150 feet in height. During the process, the falls in this stream have gone backward not less than a mile.

The falls of Niagara are formed, as has before been observed, in an immense mass of limestone, horizontally stratified. On this mass lay originally a bed of earth, not far from two hundred feet in thickness. After this had been washed away, the river floated on the surface of the limestone, and began gradually to wear that also.

Suppose then, the brow of this vast stratum near Queenston united where it is now separated by the channel of the river, and the declivity continued across its breadth, what changes would its current produce in its bed during the period which has elapsed since the Deluge? The very same which the Hudson has produced at Glens Falls, and the Mohawk at the Cohoes, and differing only according to the difference of circumstances. The river here is probably not far from one hundred times larger than the Hudson and the Mohawk at the places specified. The limestone strongly resembles that at Glens Falls. The efficacy of the atmosphere is the same. That this river, as well as others, must wear away the rocks beneath it, and that the falls must in some degree recede, cannot admit of a doubt. The only question which can arise is, what has been the extent, and what the degree of this operation? These questions it is in many respects beyond my power to answer. In some places the stone is soft, ready to molder, and easily worn away. In seasons marked by sudden and great changes of temperature, the decomposition is rapid and extensive. In other seasons and places, the progress in both these respects will be comparatively slow. Regularity, therefore, is in no sense attributable to the process; nor will it, so far as I can see, admit of any very probable calculation.

A gentleman, who has lived in this neighborhood thirty years, informed Mr. B—— that since his residence here the cataract had receded one hundred rods. I will suppose that Mr. B—— misunderstood this gentleman, and that he said yards instead of rods. If it be admitted that an intelligent man with ample opportunity to observe supposed the cataract to have receded one hundred yards within this period, it must also be admitted that the recession has at least been very perceptible. As an illustration of this truth it may be observed that in the year following the date of this journey a large part of this precipice on the British side, and near the Table Rock, fell at once. This probably is one out of many hundreds of instances of the same nature, and is a part of that retrogression by which the river is gradually forcing this deep channel round the Goat Islands. If we suppose the progress diminished from one hundred rods to one hundred yards in thirty years, the degree of recession will be more than sufficient to have proceeded through the whole distance since the Deluge, even if we should compute according to the commonly received chronology.

At the same time no regular calculation can be applied to the subject, as there are no principles which can be resorted to for a basis of such a calculation. The moldering state of the stone at the bottom of the precipice is ample proof of its tendency to decay. The waste of the inferior parts is everywhere so much more rapid than of the superior as to occasion a wide shelf to project from the surface over all that is beneath. There is direct evidence that the continual sprinkling has no small influence in effectuating this decay. The attrition of such an immense mass of water must be powerfully operative. Limestone, particularly of this quality, is easily and extensively broken by alternations of heat and cold. That these causes have operated extensively cannot be doubted; but how rapidly, and how differently at different seasons, it is impossible to determine.

An inquisitive man considering the subject will naturally ask what will be the final result of this recession. The first answer to this question is that by a regular progress it will ultimately reach the waters of Lake Erie, and by depressing the outlet to the common level of the channel below the falls will empty the waters of this lake, perhaps suddenly, into Lake Ontario. Such, it is rationally concluded, must be the event whenever the last, or southernmost, part of the great mound, by which the waters of Lake Erie are kept at their present level shall give way. The surface of Lake Erie is not far from 450 feet, perpendicular above the surface of Lake Ontario. It is probable that in most places the bottom of Lake Erie is much above this level. Should this mound then be broken down, its waters chiefly would be emptied into Lake Ontario; and all the flat country surrounding this lake, together with that which extends from it along the St. Lawrence to the ocean, would be buried in the deluge. If we may credit the best remaining historical records, such an event took place when, by the breaking down of a similar mound in the Bosphorus, the Euxine emptied an immense mass of water into the Mediterranean; and, raising that sea above its usual height, forced a passage through the isthmus which antecedently had connected Europe and Africa between the pillars of Hercules.

On this subject, however, there is no reason for apprehension. Before the waters of Lake Erie can be sensibly affected by this recession, it must have passed through a distance at least three, probably four, times as great as that between Queenston and Niagara.† Should all the causes of decay then operate with equal efficacy as in times past, it would be more than 16,000 years before this event would take place.

I have remarked that this stratum is horizontal. The level, however, two miles above, is at least sixty feet higher than at the precipice. The river also is everywhere wider above and below, upon an average at least threefold. By both these causes the retrogressive progress of the falls will be retarded. The attrition will be less; the dissolution, slower; and the mass of stone to be destroyed will be greater. It is to be acknowledged, however, that many uncertainties accompany this inquiry, and that the result of it must be dubious for a variety of reasons.

Notwithstanding the interruption which this mass of limestone presents to the navigation of the St. Lawrence, it is a source of immeasurable benefit to that inland world which surrounds the Great Lakes lying westward in so magnificent a succession. The elevation of land above the ocean, and the distance of it from the shore, may together be assumed as a scale by which the temperature of any spot within a given climate may be measured. The countries which border these lakes are in the heart of a great continent, and remote from every part of the ocean; and, like all other central regions, are considerably elevated above its surface. Were the lakes then to disappear, these countries would be subject to intense cold in the winter, and to intense heat in the summer. In all probability also, they would suffer, like the central parts of Asia and Africa, the severest evils of drought. In all these important particulars their situation is now the reverse. The whole of this vast region is rather wet than dry, moderately heated, and very little, if at all, distressed by frost. Snow falls in the tract east of Lake

† The Hon. Timothy Pickering informed me that the captain of a vessel with whom he crossed this lake told him that he had often cast anchor several miles westward of Buffalo, and had invariably found this stratum of limestone at the bottom.[1]

Erie and south of Lake Ontario less than at Albany, and as little as in the south of New England.

I am, Sir, yours, etc.

# LETTER VII

*Severe storm—General observations upon the western part of New York—Excessive value placed upon lands covered with vegetable mold—Climate and prevalent winds of this region—Western district of New York unhealthy—Diseases—Fever and ague—Goiters—Pulmonary affections rare*

*Dear Sir,*

A little before it was dark, we mounted our horses and rode to Chippawa. In the country where we now were, there was no public worship; and in the inn every tendency toward religion had apparently been long since forgotten. The Sabbath here and in the neighborhood was not visibly distinguished even as a day of relaxation. At Queenston, or Newark, our situation would have been the same. So far as we could learn either by observation or inquiry, religion is as truly to be originated here as among the Six Nations. About nine o'clock there came on a violent storm from the northeast, accompanied by a heavy rain, which continued with but little intermission until ten o'clock the next day.

We proceeded without any accident to Buffalo; whence, after having waited three hours for our dinner, we rode to Munger's: thirty-two miles. Here our former misfortunes befell us again. The house contained neither bread nor flour, and we were obliged to sup upon *sipawn.* * In the morning, however, we were furnished with biscuit for our breakfast by the fortunate arrival of a boy from the mill at a late hour of the night.

The next day we rode to Bemis': thirty-seven miles. Here we were arrested again by a storm from the northeast, accompanied with heavy rain and a considerable flight of snow, which, however, dissolved as it fell. This tempest commenced at Bemis' about nine o'clock in the evening, and continued until one the next day. In the eastern parts of the United States it continued until the morning of the tenth. Throughout most of New England it did more mischief than any other which is remembered. In Vermont the snow fell on the Green Mountains two feet deep; at Charlestown

* Hasty pudding made of maize.

in New Hampshire and at Goshen in Connecticut, twelve inches; on Taconic and on the Catskill Mountains, eighteen inches. The quantity of timber blown down was probably never equaled.

Even in this vicinity at the distance of more than four hundred miles from Boston, the wind was so violent that it blew down eleven trees across the road between Bemis' and Bloomfield.

We mounted our horses at two o'clock, made the best of our way to Genesee River, and fared very comfortably at Hosmer's, half a mile east of the bridge.

The next morning we returned to our hospitable friends at Bloomfield, and continued with them until the next day. Then we proceeded to Canandaigua, and spent the afternoon and evening very pleasantly in an intelligent circle of gentlemen.

On the succeeding day, October 12th, we rode to Geneva before dinner in a heavy rain, and lodged the following night at Cayuga Bridge.

Sunday we attended public worship at Manlius with a considerable and very decent assembly.

Monday morning, my horse having been wounded by the saddle, I sent him forward with my companions, and set out in a wagon for Staniford's, five miles ahead, intending to wait the arrival of the stage. The wagoner's horses were miserably poor, and were exhausted by the fatigue of a laborious journey. The driver was a young Dutchman, whose mind had hardly begun to think, and who was therefore not a very amusing companion. The wagon was heavily loaded, and it soon began to rain. Our progress resembled not a little that of my uncle Toby: for we could hardly be said to advance at all.[1] I therefore left my portmanteau with the wagoner, and made the rest of the journey, a little more than three miles, on foot. Soon after I reached Staniford's, the rain began again for the day. Here, in the possession of a good room and the civilities of an obliging family, I devoted my time very pleasantly to the completion of my notebook. Mr. B—— arrived in the evening, as did several other agreeable travelers. The next morning until twelve o'clock, I pursued the business of the preceding day.

As I am now about to quit the western country of New York, I will endeavor to give you, in a collected view, the information which I have gained, and the observations which I have made concerning this interesting tract. It has been an object of great attention in many parts of the United States, and a subject of much conversation.

The soil is better than that of any other tract of equal extent with which I am acquainted. It consists almost entirely of two sorts, loam and clay, both of them rich. The loam is generally of the same kind and color with that heretofore described in the account given of Middletown, of a reddish brown mixed with clay and therefore stiff. The clay is of a Quaker brown, tempered with other earth, and without any great difficulty pulverized.

In estimating the quality of new lands in America, serious errors are very commonly entertained from the want of due attention to the following fact. Wherever the forests have been undisturbed by fire, they have accumulated by shedding their foliage through a long succession of ages, and by their own decay, a covering of vegetable mold, from six to twelve inches deep, and sometimes from eighteen to twenty-four. This mold is the best of all soils, and eminently friendly to every species of vegetation. It is indeed no other than a mere mass of manure, and that of the very best kind, converted into mold; and, so long as it remains in considerable quantities, all grounds produce plentifully. Unless a proper allowance be made, therefore, when we are forming an estimate of the quality of soils, for the efficacy of this mold, which, so far as my observation has extended, is not often done, those on which it abounds will be of course overrated. On the contrary, where it does not abound, the quality of the soil will in a comparative view be underrated. Hence all maple lands, which from their moisture are incapable of being burnt, are considered as more fertile than they ultimately prove; while oak and even pine lands are almost of course regarded as being less fertile. The maple lands in Ballston are found to produce wheat in smaller quantities and of a worse quality than the inhabitants, misled by the exuberance of their first crops, expected. Their pine lands on the contrary yield more and better wheat than till very lately they could be induced to believe. The same things severally are true, as I have already observed, of the oak and maple lands in the county of Ontario.

From this source it has arisen that all the unburnt, new lands in the northern, middle, southern, and western states have been, and still are, uniformly valued beyond their real worth. When the tract on the Green Mountains in Massachusetts was first settled, the same luxuriant fertility was attributed to it which has since characterized Kentucky. About the same time it was ascribed to the valley of the Housatonic in the county of Berkshire. From these tracts it was transferred to the lands in New Hampshire and Vermont on the Connecticut, and thence to those in Vermont on the western side of the Green Mountains. From these regions the paradise has traveled to the western parts of the state of New York, to new Connecticut, to Upper Canada, to the countries on the Ohio, to the southwestern territory, and is now making its progress over the Mississippi into the newly purchased regions of Louisiana. The accounts given of all these countries successively were extensively true, but the conclusions which were deduced from them were in a great measure erroneous. So long as this mold remains, the produce will regularly be great, and that with very imperfect cultivation; for the mold in its native state is so soft and light as scarcely to need the aid of the plow.

But this mold after a length of time will be dissipated. Where lands are continually plowed, it is soon lost; on those which are covered with grass from the beginning, it is preserved through a considerable period. At length, however, every appearance of its efficacy, and even of its existence, vanishes.

The true object of inquiry whenever the quality of a soil is to be estimated is *the nature of the earth immediately beneath the vegetable mold:* for this in every case will ultimately be the soil. If this is capable of being rendered by skillful cultivation regularly productive, the soil is good; if not, it is poor. With this object in view, I have formed the opinion expressed above concerning the country under discussion. Throughout most of this tract, the earth beneath the mold is an excellent soil. The mold itself will speedily be gone. It is wisely and kindly provided by the Creator to answer the immediate calls of the first settlers. These are of course few and poor, are embarrassed by many wants and difficulties, and need their time and labor to build their houses, barns, and enclosures, as well as to procure with extreme inconvenience many articles of necessity and comfort which are obtained in older settlements without labor or time. To them it is a complete and ample manure, on which whatever is sown springs with vigor, and produces, almost without toil or skill, a plentiful harvest. But it was not intended to be permanent. It is not even desirable that it should be. To interrupt or even to slacken the regular labor of man materially is to do him an injury. One of the prime blessings of temperate climates is this: that they yield amply to skillful labor, and without it yield little or nothing. Where such is the fact, energy and effort will follow, and all their inestimable consequences. Where countries are radically barren, man will despair. Where they are so fertile as to demand little exertion, he will be idle and vicious. In the island of Otaheite [Tahiti], where subsistence is furnished almost without human exertion, the inhabitants in proportion to their capacity have been probably the most profligate on the globe.

But the soil of this tract will be rich after the mold has disappeared; and will still yield, as I believe, abundantly, all the productions of the climate. That which it so strongly resembles in Connecticut has been proved by ample experience to be enduring, and to be capable of any improvement. From its color and texture, this will probably endure in the same manner.

You will not understand that the soil of this tract of country is uniform. Some parts, where all are good, are superior to others. Some are indifferent, and some are lean. Ordinary grounds, as I know partly from observation and partly from information, abound much more in the southern than in the middle and northern divisions.

The climate of this region differs in several respects from that of New England and that of New York along the Hudson, and in some parts of the region itself differs sensibly from that of others. What it will ultimately appear to be cannot be determined until a longer time shall have elapsed after the date of its first settlement, and more and more accurate observations shall have been made concerning the subject.

There is, so far as my observation has extended, a circuit of seasons in this country, and perhaps in many others, accomplished in periods of from ten to perhaps fifteen years. The period in which most of this tract has been settled, commencing in the year 1791, and terminating with the year 1804, has been distinguished by an almost regular succession of warm seasons. There were but three cold winters, viz., those of 1792, 1798, and 1799. The summers were all warm. What the state of the climate was here during the preceding cold period, from the year 1780 to the year 1790 inclusive, it is impossible to decide. In the Census of 1790, three townships only are mentioned west of the German Flats: Whitestown, Chemung, and Chenango; and these contained at that time but 4,327 inhabitants, although they included nearly every individual of European extraction. Half a century at least will be necessary to furnish the facts on which such a decision can be directly founded.

Still I am of opinion that the climate of this tract is milder than that of the eastern parts of New York and New England which lie in the same latitude. The cause of this peculiar mildness I suppose to be the Great Lakes, which, commencing in its vicinity, extend along its whole northern boundary and almost all its western, and thence in a western and northwestern direction almost to the middle of North America. That these lakes do not contribute to render this climate colder has, I trust, been heretofore satisfactorily evinced. That they make it hotter has never been supposed.

It has been extensively agreed by modern philosophers that the two great causes of a mild temperature are *nearness to the shore* and *proximity to the level of the ocean.* Those countries which border on the ocean, are almost without an exception warmer than central countries in the same latitude, and those, which are little raised above its surface are regularly warmer than such as have a considerable elevation. M. Volney, however, with that promptness of decision for which he has long been remarkable, found, as he believed, satisfactory evidence, that this opinion is groundless in the climate of the regions bordering on the Lakes Erie and Ontario.[2] This climate he asserts to be milder than that of the shore in the same latitude, where it is scarcely raised above the ocean. Yet the tract which enjoys this mild temperature is elevated and distant from the sea. The premises here assumed are undoubtedly true; but the consequence does not follow. The lakes have the same influence here which the ocean has elsewhere. The elevation above them is so small, and the distance from them so near, that the full influence of both advantages is completely felt. Among the proofs that this is a true explanation of the subject, it is only necessary to observe, that the southeastern parts of the county of Genesee, the counties of Steuben, Tioga, Delaware, and Greene are sensibly colder than those immediately south of Lake Ontario.

It ought perhaps to be observed here that countries on the eastern side of a continent are regularly colder in winter and hotter in summer than those on the western. The reason is obvious. In the temperate zones, at least in the northern, the prevailing winds are from the west. Eastern shores, therefore, have their winds chiefly from the land, and western shores enjoy the softer breezes of the ocean.

As the winters are mild in the tract under consideration, so are the summers. It is not often the fact that people are willing to sleep here without a blanket.

In New England, and in the eastern and southern parts of New York, and I presume in the northern, most of their rains, except thundershowers, are brought by easterly winds. A few come from the southwest, particularly near the coast. I know of no spot in these regions which furnishes a material exception to this remark, besides that mentioned in the account of Lancaster in New Hampshire. At Buffalo Creek, and for about twenty miles further east, northeast storms, though less frequent than on the coast, are not uncommon. The stream of air passing up the valley of the St. Lawrence crosses Lake Ontario, and thence proceeds over Lake Erie. Perhaps when the country is more generally cleared of its forests, its influence may be felt still more extensively.

From the limit mentioned above to Manlius, rains and snows are brought almost universally by northwest winds, and in a few instances come from the southwest. Some intelligent men at Van de Vender's informed me that two northeast storms which had blown there in the year 1804 were extraordinary occurrences.

At Manlius the rains and snows come from the east and from the west nearly equally; at Herkimer, more frequently from the east than from the west.

Both rains and snows are frequent in this region, sudden in their advent, and short in their duration. The weather is very variable, but varies very differently from that in New England. In New England the variations which are most disagreeable are from heat to cold, and from cold to heat. In New England, storms sometimes last several days; and often, when the wind has ceased from its violence at the end of the first or second day, which indeed is almost always the fact, the cloudy and wet weather continues for some time. In this country the rain or the snow, together with the blast which produces it, is soon over, and some part of almost every day is fair. A general uncertainty concerning the weather even of a single day is here prevalent. The signs of fair and foul weather which the inhabitants have learned in their native country are of little use to them here; and those with whom I conversed had not made observations through a length of time sufficient to render them useful substitutes. A perfectly bright evening or morning with a northwest wind was regarded as one of the surest indications of rain during some part of the succeeding day. This in New England is an almost certain prognostic of fair weather. To travelers these sudden variations from dry to wet are disagreeable; but the inhabitants already begin to prefer their own climate, and speak of our long storms with disgust, and of our settled weather and serene sky with indifference, observing that they like such weather as will permit them to go abroad every day. Of twenty days, beginning Thursday, September 27th, and ending October 16th, it rained, while we were making our progress through this country, thirteen; several of them, the whole day.

In New England, rains and snows are produced either by the opposition, or the oblique percussion, of different winds blowing at the same time. Here, as at Lancaster in New Hampshire, they are chiefly produced by the continual progress of the same wind. A more rapid blast following one less rapid brings with it a shower, condensed by means of the obstruction which is occasioned by the slower movement of the preceding blast. When the shower is past, a slower wind succeeds; and is followed by a swifter one, which brings a second shower. The same alternation is repeated until the vapor is spent, and the sky becomes clear by the still-continued influence of the same wind. Thus the same wind brings fair weather, then rain, and then fair weather again the same day. Of these facts I was several times a witness. In a few instances I have observed them in New England, and have mentioned one instance of them in my account of the peculiar weather at Lancaster.

Hitherto the snow has never been inconveniently deep in this quarter, unless for a very short time, and that not more than once or twice since the country was settled. The only complaint which I heard was that they rarely had sufficient snow to furnish them with convenient transportation. The winter half of the year seems, therefore, to be drier than the summer half. The summer of 1803, however, was a very dry season, but it was the only one of any importance which these people have known.

The snows as well as the rains usually fall in soft and moderate showers, yet there have been some exceptions. In November 1803, the snow fell in the country surrounding Van de Vender's three feet deep during a single storm which came from the northeast. It lay, however, but a few days.

The Seneca Lake has hitherto furnished a strong proof of the mildness of this climate. Though nowhere more than four miles wide, it has never been frozen over.

The spring usually begins here about the 20th of March, and the winter about the 20th of December. Gardens are commonly begun the last week in April and the first in May: from six to eight weeks later than at New Haven.

Cows are usually put in pasture about the 10th of May: ten days earlier.

Green peas were gathered in 1804 at Canandaigua about the middle of June: a week later than at New Haven the same year. The season was cold and backward.

Maize is usually planted in the first half of May: a month later. The green ears were first gathered this year the 16th of August: a month later.

Oats are sown in the beginning of May.

Flax is sown at the full moon in May.

The first hay is cut in the middle of June.

Wheat is in mid-harvest the last week in July and the first in August: three weeks and a month later. But the late sown wheat is not cut till the last week in August.

These facts will give a tolerably just idea of the seasons in this country. Both agriculture and gardening are, however, governed in no small degree by the character of the proprietor and the quality of the soil. Where both are favorable, the productions will be earlier. In the garden especially, the difference will be considerable.

The tract of country which I am now considering has thus far been unhealthy. How far this fact is owing to the present stage in the progress of its settlement, it is impossible to determine. Most regions on this side of the Atlantic have been subjected to some peculiarities of disease during the progress of population, of which many have vanished when they had reached the state of complete settlement. While the country is entirely forested, it is ordinarily healthy. While it is passing from this state into that of general cultivation, it is usually less healthy. This arises partly from the hardships suffered by the planters, and partly from the situation of the lands. These hardships I have summarily recounted in a former part of this work, and you have undoubtedly observed that they were amply sufficient to try in a very serious manner the firmest constitution. The peculiar situation of the land you will be able to conjecture from the following observations.

In the forested state all grounds, except during a short time comprising a part of the summer and a part of the autumn, are more or less moist. Maple grounds are almost literally always moist. The vegetable mold with which they are thickly covered imbibes and retains water like a sponge, while the earth below, which in this region is tenacious, prevents it from descending. Whenever the air is sufficiently warm, vapor in considerable quantities, and unfavorable to human health, must be exhaled from such a surface. The evenings and the mornings particularly will through a great part of the summer half year be damp, chilly, and productive of colds, together with the diseases which spring from them. From such exhalations continually repeated must arise also a gradual diminution of bodily energy, imperceptibly increasing. A chill, if I mistake not, always lessens the vigor of the system, at least for the time; and a perpetual or often repeated chilliness must induce a general and continual debility. These evils, however, appear to be in a considerable measure counteracted while the forested state continues by several known and probably by some unknown causes. As the surface is less warmed, the vapor is less exhaled; the temperature is more uniform; and the changes are less sudden, as well as less frequent. The air also expired by the leaves is eminently pure and healthy. At the same time wood being abundant, large culinary fires are generally burning; and the house, together with all which it contains, is chiefly kept dry.

All these, and probably all other causes of this nature, gradually vanish as cultivation advances. The ground is laid open to the sun. The heat of the day in the warm season becomes often intense, and the more so because the remaining forest precludes the free access of the wind. The moist grounds, particularly marshes, being exposed to the entire influence of the heat, become corrupt, offensive, and replenished with miasmata, loathsome to the senses, and noxious to health. Diseases at this period are apt to abound, and to continue until the country is completely cultivated and an artificial vegetation is substituted for that which is natural. As most tracts in the United States which are now healthy have passed through this succession of changes, there is reason to believe that this, which is now extensively in the second of these stages, may escape from its disadvantages and enjoy in a good degree the benefits of the third.

The diseases which principally prevail here are the fever and ague, intermittents without ague, and bilious remittents. Fever and ague may be considered as nearly universal, almost all the inhabitants being sooner or later seized by it within a few years after their immigration. This disease, from the violence of its affections, its long continuance, its return at the same season for several successive years, and the lasting impression which it often leaves on the constitution, is regarded by the people of New England with a kind of horror. The other two diseases, though common to most parts of the country, are yet much more predominant in particular places. Along the Genesee they all abound. They are frequent also, as I was informed, on the southern shores of Lake Ontario, and in spots around the outlets of most of the smaller lakes, and in various others. A tract around the Onondaga Salt Springs is still more sickly and fatal.

To the evils mentioned above, I ought to add the exposure of the recent settlers to walking and working a great part of their time in moist ground, the badness of their houses, the poorness of their fare, together with the difficulty of obtaining proper medicines, good nurses, and skillful physicians. Nor ought it to be forgotten that the streams are frequently choked, rendered sluggish, and raised in many places above their usual height by the timber which is cut down, or which, being girdled, is suffered to fall into their channels. In this manner they affect the atmosphere in as noxious a manner as millponds and other artificial accumulations of water.

There is another disease which is unquestionably owing to the nature of this country, and not merely to the recency of its settlement. This is what is called in Switzerland the *goiters*, or the *hernia gutturis*. By the Hon. Uriah Tracy, late a senator of the United States from Connecticut, I am informed that this disease is found to some extent throughout a great part of the regions lying north of the Ohio and west of the Allegheny Mountains. Mr. Tracy was employed by the American government on a mission of importance which required him to make a tour throughout a large extent of this country. Accordingly he passed through Pennsylvania by the way of Pittsburgh and Presque Isle; and thence, crossing Lake Erie, proceeded to Detroit. From this place he went to Mackinac, and thence to Lake Superior. From Mackinac he returned to Buffalo Creek, and took the great western road to Albany. In this excursion he found the goiters existing in the older settlements more, in the newer, less frequently, but actually existing at different distances throughout the whole region.[3] Several other gentlemen have confirmed the account of Mr. Tracy. That the disease exists from Utica to Buffalo is, I think, certain, probably not in every township, but in such a manner as to indicate that it is incident to the country at large, and has a foundation in its nature and circumstances. When I was at Paris in the year 1799, there were in the parish of Clinton but two families affected with it. In these families, however, and most others where it has been for a number of years, it seized on several of the members. At the north end of the bridge which crosses the Mohawk from Utica, there was in the year 1799, a family within the township of Deerfield, consisting of ten or eleven persons, every one of whom, as I was informed, had the goiters.

Persons afflicted with this disease have, as is well known, swellings of the neck, rising indifferently in front, or at the sides; and, when they become large, extending throughout the anterior half. These swellings are of all sizes, from the slightest protuberance to that of a quart bowl; and are attended with stiffness of the neck, a slight degree of continual pain, and frequently a depression of spirits. The sufferings of the patient are increased by a cold, and by almost every other infirmity. Women are more frequently and more severely afflicted with this disease than men; feeble, than vigorous persons; and children, than adults. In the higher degrees it becomes a painful deformity, not only as an unnatural protuberance, but by imparting a disagreeable cast to the features, particularly to the eyes. When the patient continues in the same place and in the same habits of living by which it was produced, it generally increases; but, if he removes to a part of the country where it is unknown, it not uncommonly decreases, and sometimes disappears.

The cause of this disease is by Mr. Coxe † supposed to be the calcareous matter, which in Switzerland is called *tuff,* and which he concludes is so completely dissolved as not to affect the transparency of the water.[4] In this state of minuteness, he supposes that it may be introduced by the circulation of the blood, or otherwise, into the glands of the throat; where by accumulation and concretion, particularly in the thyroid gland, in its structure favorable to the deposition and detention of such particles; they produce an irritation by means of which a viscid fluid, naturally contained in the cells of this gland, is secreted in unnatural quantities, and the gland itself unnaturally enlarged by the distention of these cells.

In support of this opinion Mr. Coxe alleges the following proofs.

Firstly. He observes that during his travels through Europe he always found that tuff abounded wherever goiters were common. The places which he specifies are the Valais, the Valtellina, Lucerne, Fribourg, Bern, the region near Aigle and Bex, several places of the Pays de Vaud, the region near Dresden, the valleys of Savoy and Piedmont, and tracts near Turin and Milan.

Secondly. One of the principal springs which supplies Fribourg with water has deposited large quantities of tuff on the rock from which it issues.

Thirdly. A gentleman of veracity informed Mr. Coxe that he had a small swelling on his throat which usually increased in the winter when he chiefly resided at Bern, and diminished in summer when he removed to other places.

Fourthly. The waters at Lucerne except one spring are all impregnated with tuff; and the natives who live near that spring are less subjected to goiters than the other inhabitants; and members of the same family who drank only from that spring were less subject to the goiters than others who were not thus exact.

Fifthly. Places contiguous to those in which goiters and tuff were frequent, and having precisely the same situation and climate, but destitute of tuff, were observed by Mr. Coxe to be free from goiters.

Sixthly. A surgeon whom he met at the baths of Leuk informed Mr. Coxe that he had repeatedly extracted concretions of tuff from goiters; particularly, from one which suppurated he took several flat pieces, each about half an inch long. The same substance he declared had been found in the stomachs of cows, and in the goitrous tumors to which the dogs of that country were subject. The same gentleman assured Mr. Coxe that he had diminished and cured the goiters of many young persons, particularly one of his own children who was born with a goiter as large as an egg, by emollient liquors and external applications. The principal method adopted by

† See Coxe's Travels in Switzerland, Letter 35. [William Coxe, *Travels in Switzerland* (2nd ed., London, 1791), I, 397–406.]

this gentleman to prevent them in future was to remove his patients from the places where the springs were impregnated with tuff; and, if that could not be contrived, to forbid them the use of water altogether. His own family he prohibited from tasting the spring waters in his neighborhood unless they were distilled or mixed with wine or vinegar, and thus preserved them from goiters, which were extremely common in the town where he lived.

This account of Mr. Coxe appears to me satisfactory. The whole country where this disease prevails in the American states is calcareous. The goiters found here exist in spots and particular families. It is incredible that they should be derived from *the mode of living,* because they are found among those who live in every mode between luxury and beggary. It is incredible that they should be derived from *climate,* because there are no such differences of climate in the tracts where they abound and where they are unknown as to furnish any explanation of the subject, and because a great multitude of families have them not, who are interspersed among those who have them. They cannot be derived from *limestone in its common form,* or *the carbonate of lime,* because this mineral abounds throughout most of New England west of the Green Mountains, as well as in the eastern parts of the state of New York: and yet in both these regions goiters are unknown. It is unnecessary to observe that they cannot be derived from snow water.

The remark of M. de Saussure, that foreigners established in Switzerland are never affected with these tumors, is inapplicable to this region.[5] The inhabitants here are universally foreigners, and almost all of them came from New England, or other countries where this disease is absolutely unknown. Yet many of the original settlers, as well as their children, are afflicted with this evil.

From the account of Mr. Coxe, if there be no error in it, we are furnished with one very important truth relative to this subject. It is this: that the surgeon mentioned above preserved his own family by invariably prohibiting them from drinking the spring waters unless when they had been distilled or mixed with wine or vinegar. To distill water for the drink of the inhabitants of a town or village must certainly be an expensive and tedious process. Still it will be less tedious than a general diffusion of goiters. By many families it might be done for their own use without any considerable difficulty. All families cannot afford to mix their water with wine, but most might procure vinegar sufficient for this purpose; and habit would easily reconcile them to the use of this liquid. Among many nations it has been a favorite beverage. Possibly the tuff may be precipitated by means hitherto undiscovered, and yet safe and pleasant. That tuff exists in this country is not known, probably because it has never been examined.

The existence of this disease throughout so great an extent of country is, I believe, unexampled in the world. Should it spread very generally among the inhabitants of this region, it must hereafter affect many millions of the human race. When we consider the magnitude of this fact, and remember that the disease in its higher stages is hitherto incurable, it becomes a very serious evil. It is to be hoped that the same good Providence which has so lately and so wonderfully dissipated the terrors of the smallpox by the discovery of the vaccine innoculation will also disclose a remedy for the melancholy disease under consideration.

Distressing, however, as this disorder seems to a stranger, the inhabitants appear already to regard it with abated apprehensions, and to be approximating in their views of it towards indifference. An intelligent and respectable lady in Pittsburgh was asked by Mr. Tracy whether it existed in her family; she said, she presumed it did not. The children were then called up and examined, and five of them were found to be affected with it.

Few of the other diseases common to the climate are rife in this country. From the pulmonary consumption, so frequent elsewhere, they are in a great measure exempted. Dr. W[illiams], of Canandaigua, a physician in extensive practice, informed me that during the ten years of his residence there only three persons within his knowledge, had died of the consumption in that township and its neighborhood. He also observed that most of the diseases found on the coast were unknown there, and that he believed the fever and ague to be not improbably the cause of this exemption. As I passed through Sheffield, I was informed, in a manner which could not be rationally questioned, that the consumption is also very rare in that town. Should there be no error in this account, it will deserve inquiry whether the infrequency of this disease in the southern states is not owing more to the fever and ague than to the warmth of the climate; or perhaps in better words, whether the tendencies to disease in the human frame do not in particular tracts flow chiefly in this single channel. Should the result of this inquiry be an affirmative answer, Canandaigua may hereafter become a more convenient retreat for persons subject to pulmonic affections than the southern states.

The same gentleman mentioned to me a remarkable instance of the efficacy of the fever and ague. A woman, who had a little before removed from New England into the neighborhood of Canandaigua, lost her reason. Sometime afterwards, she had the fever and ague. When it left her, she became immediately sane.

I have mentioned the climate of this country as unhealthy. I ought to add that several of the respectable inhabitants, both physicians and others, insist that the proportional number of deaths is not greater than in the healthy parts of New England. Some of them also observed to me that the bilious remittent of this region admits of a cure more easily and more certainly than in any other with which they were acquainted.

I am, Sir, yours, etc.

# LETTER VIII

*General observations upon the western part of New York continued—Want of stone for building and fencing—Defective supply and quality of its timber—Water impregnated with lime—Commerce—Different outlets for its commodities*

*Dear Sir,*

Among the disadvantages to which this western country is subject, the *want of good stone for building and fencing* must, I think, be a serious one. In considerable tracts this want is absolute; in others, stone is scarce and obtained with difficulty. In almost all, so far as my information extends, it is either lime, slate, or gypsum; neither of them capable of enduring fire, nor of such a texture as to be conveniently wrought for the purposes of building. The specimens which I saw were coarse, rough, and destitute of beauty. In many places enclosures may be formed of stone; but in many, I believe in most, it will be difficult, if not impossible, to build cellar walls, the foundations of houses, or fireplaces which will be either convenient or lasting.

This material defect the inhabitants have not hitherto been able to supply by the substitution of *good bricks.* The clay of this country is everywhere mixed with other earths, of such a quality as to render the bricks made of it easily dissoluble by weather and by fire. In some places they are indeed firmer than in others; and their texture is perhaps generally rendered unnecessarily loose, and therefore unnecessarily subject to decomposition, by the ignorance, or by the unfaithfulness, of workmen. In all, the bricks are bad. Whether there may be any remedy for this misfortune, time must discover.

The *timber* of this tract also is to a great extent of a consistence too frail and perishable to last for any great length of time, either in buildings or enclosures. In the county of Ontario, and some other parts of the country, there is a sufficient quantity of oak, and it is said of pine also, both for building and fencing. But there are large tracts which are destitute of every species of timber fitted to resist the encroachments of the weather. Future experiments may perhaps furnish a remedy. The oak and the chestnut, and perhaps the pine, may be planted with success. Hedges may possibly be formed which will resist the influence of the climate, and better clay may be discovered for the erection of their houses. It seems incredible that Providence should have made this region in most respects so desirable a residence for man; and that in this apparently, and in several others, it should to such an extent disappoint a purpose so carefully pursued.

Another evil suffered by these inhabitants, of a similar nature and even more discouraging, is this: *when the forests are cut down, they either do not at all spring again, or they spring very thinly and insufficiently.* This misfortune has been supposed to arise from the peculiar nature of the trees, or the peculiar nature of the soil. I strongly suspect that it is owing to neither. Maple, beech, and bass may not indeed as readily germinate from the roots after the trees are cut down as oak, chestnut, and hickory. Whether this be true or not, I am unable to determine. But that they will not in the proper circumstances spring in sufficient quantities and vigor from the seeds, I cannot believe. That the soil is favorable both to the germination and flourishing growth of these trees is unanswerably evident from the multitude and the size of those which are now on the ground. Besides, I have seen in a variety of places, some of them in this very tract, a vigorous growth of these kinds of timber in spots where the full-grown trees had been lately cut down.

Grass grows in this region easily and vigorously; and, wherever it grows, will extensively prevent the germination and check the growth of trees of almost every kind. Were these inhabitants, instead of cutting down their forests in the manner which is called cutting clean, to thin them only, and thus leave the ground so much shaded as would be sufficient to prevent the vegetation of grass, they would, I am satisfied, find the seeds of future trees springing in abundance. Should they also effectually exclude cattle from their forests, so as to prevent them from cropping the young stems, they would probably find this evil done away.

Another disadvantage under which this country labors is *a deficiency of water for some important purposes of life.* In Manlius millstreams are sufficiently numerous; but, from that township westward to Buffalo Creek, they are thinly dispersed. Throughout this country generally, springs and small brooks are rare. A great part of the farms must be ill supplied with water for their pastures. The obvious substitute for these sources is wells; and these may be furnished in most places without any peculiar difficulty, and at no inconvenient depth. But as the water of all this tract is impregnated with lime, it is unfit for washing and for several other domestic uses; and to water cattle from a well, when they are numerous, is a severe tax upon the time and labor of the farmer.

*The commerce of this country* has hitherto struggled, and for an indefinite period must continue to struggle with difficulties. The distance from Canandaigua to Albany is 205 miles; and from Buffalo, 300. The transportation of goods over the whole distance, except seventy-nine miles, must be by land. From Utica they may be conveyed to Schenectady on the Mohawk, but the navigation is so imperfect that merchants often choose to transport their commodities along its bank in wagons. Notwithstanding this inconvenience, Albany is the port to which they must now, and probably for a long time hereafter, resort. Now their trade is wholly carried on in this channel. Many, however, stop at Utica; and, as the trade of that place enlarges, it may become more and more an emporium for the business of the western country. The only material difference made by stopping at Utica, or even at Albany, is that they pay the expense and trouble of a longer journey instead of incurring it personally. In either case, the trouble and expense of conveying the produce to New York are always considerable; and, when the commodities are bulky, must ever amount to no small part of their price in the market. Thus grain of all kinds, their principal produce, can be carried to market only when it commands an extraordinary price. Thus also hemp, flax, and even wool lose much of their value before they reach New York. Beef, as it may be driven, will be less affected than most other articles.

The inhabitants situated near Lake Ontario can ascend the Oswego or Onondaga River; and, passing through the Oneida Lake, go up Wood Creek into the Mohawk. But the navigation of these streams is still more embarrassed than that of the Mohawk.

Another channel of transportation is opened to the southern parts of this country by the Susquehanna. I have already mentioned that boards to a great amount are floated yearly down this river to Baltimore. Wheat also is carried to market the same way, in vessels of a peculiar structure called *arks*. These, at times of such a size as to carry, it is said, no less than twelve hundred bushels of wheat, descend the Tioga and the Susquehanna proper to Tioga Point, and thence pass down their common channel to Baltimore. The navigation, however, is both uncertain and dangerous. It is uncertain because it can be pursued only during the time of a freshet, and that often will not suffice for more than one third or one fourth of the voyage. During the interval the ark is obliged to wait for another freshet, when it proceeds anew; and ultimately, if not wrecked, reaches Baltimore. The dangers of the navigation arise from the swiftness of its current, and the shoals and rapids in the river, which have sometimes proved fatal both to boats and rafts. In the spring the voyage is frequently made with success, and even without interruption. In the other seasons it is either precarious or impossible. When it succeeds best, the conveyance is cheap and expeditious. The arks are broken up and sold at Baltimore for as much or more than they cost.

When the cargo is disposed of, the boatmen are obliged to return by land. The inconvenience of such a journey needs no explanation.

Measures have been proposed by the legislatures of Maryland and Pennsylvania which possibly may terminate in improving the navigation of the Susquehanna and facilitating the intercourse of this country with Baltimore, and perhaps by the Schuylkill with Philadelphia.

Another great channel of commerce between the western country and the ocean is by Lake Ontario, down the St. Lawrence to Montreal. This has ever appeared to me the cheapest, safest, and most unembarrassed passage for the produce of all the countries which surround the great American lakes. The ordinary price for transporting a quarter cask from Montreal to Queenston is but a single dollar. Whenever a regular trade is established between these countries and Montreal, and a regular transportation round the Niagara Falls, the freight of a quarter-cask from Queenston to Chippawa will not be more, and probably less than one fourth of a dollar. Thence merchandise of all kinds may be conveyed in ships of any convenient size to the south end of Lake Michigan; and, with the exception of a short land carriage, to the western limit of Lake Superior. A tract, consisting of from 400,000 to 500,000 square miles will hereafter empty its produce upon the ocean through the river St. Lawrence.* Hitherto, the merchants of Montreal have been chiefly employed in a commerce of which

* Since these remarks were written, a canal, on a scale far surpassing anything which has hitherto been attempted in this country, has been commenced in the state of New York, by order of their legislature. By means of it, it is intended to connect the waters of Lake Erie with those of the Hudson, a distance of 353 miles.

In the year 1810, persons who had been appointed by the government of the state, explored the intervening country from the Hudson to Erie, and made a report; but though some acts were passed concerning the subject, yet nothing was effectually done until the spring of 1817, when commissioners were appointed by the legislature, "to cause a communication by means of a canal to be made between Lake Erie and the Hudson." Since that time, the canal has advanced with such rapidity as to surprise not only the people living on its borders, but the inhabitants of the United States.

The whole expense of the canal, as estimated by the commissioners, is 4,571,813 dollars. At the close of the year 1821, the western canal was so far finished, that Gov. Clinton, to whom perhaps the country is as much indebted for the success of this great enterprise as to any one individual, in his speech before the legislature, Jan. 2, 1822, says, "Upon a full and comprehensive view of the whole operation, we may confidently pronounce that before the termination of the year 1823, there will be a complete and uninterrupted navigation for boats conveying one hundred tons, from the navigable waters of Hudson River to Lake Erie."

When this immense work, which might with propriety have been a national one, shall be finished, it will open a communication with the ocean to the commerce of a great part of Ohio, and to the countries along the shores of Lakes Ontario, Erie, Huron, Michigan, and Superior, and to the inhabitants living on the borders of the rivers which empty into these inland seas. Could we take a survey of these countries as they may appear fifty years hence, when the enterprise of the hardy sons of our country shall have converted the wilderness into fruitful fields; when this immense region shall be filled with towns and cities, and the people, amounting probably to twenty millions, are living in a state of competence, we should be able in some measure to appreciate the immense utility of this Herculean labor. There can be no doubt that the people who will then reap the advantages of this great work will hold in respectful and affectionate remembrance those patriots who have devised, carried on, and completed a task which brings happiness to so mighty a mass of the human family. PUB.

furs and peltry have been the principal materials. But the period is at no great distance when they will devote their attention to general commerce. The settlement of the countries which border the Lakes Ontario and Erie is already far advanced, and in its progress outruns the most sanguine calculation. Adventurers have already begun to plant themselves on Huron and Michigan. Within a century, the shores of these waters will probably be filled with villages, towns, and cities. To the immense population of these vast regions the river St. Lawrence will be the common channel of trade, and a common bond of union. Some difficulties will always attend this commerce. The ice will obstruct it throughout a considerable part of the year, and the navigation of the Gulf of St. Lawrence will always be exposed to some degree of hazard. The effect of these inconveniences will be the necessity of employing a larger capital, the demand of interest on it for a longer period, and a somewhat higher price of insurance. The business also must all depend on two voyages across the Atlantic each year. But a moderate lapse of time will necessarily introduce into it such a degree of system as will reduce the inconveniences to trifles, and conform to the existing circumstances all the plans and measures of these people. Under greater inconveniences Russia has rapidly increased in commerce and wealth.

That the trade in question will flow into this channel ultimately is scarcely less than certain, because the inhabitants of these countries will find here more convenience, and more profit, than they can find elsewhere.

Gypsum abounds in the township of Camillus, in quantities sufficient, it is said, to supply an extensive tract with that valuable article.

The sulphur springs in the township of Phelps will probably furnish hereafter not only the necessary supplies for the region around them, but a vast quantity also for commerce. The largest of these springs is the property of Sir William Pulteney; the other two, if I mistake not, of the Hon. Oliver Phelps.[1] The water is perfectly clear, but both the taste and the smell as strong and very offensive. The temperature is cold. The water is used as a bath for the rheumatism; and, it is said, with success. The mass of sulphur deposited by them in the neighborhood was estimated to me at more than one hundred tons. No attempts have hitherto been made to purify it and prepare it for commercial purposes.

There is a sulphur spring in the township of Litchfield in the county of Herkimer, about ten miles from Utica. This also is resorted to for relief from the rheumatism, and from several other diseases.

Concerning the inhabitants of the western country, I shall make some observations hereafter, and am,

Sir, yours, etc.

# LETTER IX

*Return slowly along the Mohawk to Albany—Kinderhook—Hudson—Uncommon phenomena observed on Taconic Mountain*

*Dear Sir,*

I left Staniford's, Tuesday, October 15th, and rode to Vernon, about twenty miles, in the stage wagon. We started at twelve o'clock. It had rained most of the preceding day, the whole night, and the whole forenoon of this day. The road had become a mass of deep mire; and the horses were obliged to walk, or rather to wade, at the rate of two miles an hour. In the afternoon it rained again, but with less violence. We were seven passengers in a vehicle so small as to be crowded, and so crazy as to be threatened even by a slight accident with being broken down. We were also from very distant countries and of different nations. The day was sufficiently gloomy; and the country presented little to our view besides thick forests, interspersed here and there with log houses. In solitary instances some have a better appearance. In the township of Sullivan, a large tract lying immediately eastward of Manlius, we found, however, an exception. As we descended a hill of considerable height, we were presented with a delightful prospect of the Oneida Lake, and a noble view of the circumjacent country. When the trees shall be sufficiently cut down, this hill will furnish one of the most interesting views between Albany and Buffalo.

Another variety in our journey was the Oneida Village, built on the reservation belonging to that people, and lying immediately south of the lake. We saw this village by moonlight. The houses in it appeared to differ very little from the log houses already described, except that they are smaller, worse built, and less carefully repaired. Skenandoa, their chief, lives in a framed house which is painted and decent.[1] He is said to be in easy circumstances. A small church stands in the center of the village. On the character and situation of this people, I propose to make some observations in another place, and shall only add here that at Young's, an inn at which we stopped in Vernon, several of them, who were half drunk, disturbed us not a little by their contention and outcries.

We took supper at Young's; and all the passengers who were bound to Utica, except one, concluded to proceed in order to take the Albany stage the next morning. Accordingly we set out in a dense mist, which deprived us of the moonlight, and effectually chilled us during the remainder of our journey. Our progress was snail-like and sufficiently tedious, and our prospect scarcely extended to the horses. But our driver was careful and obliging; and we all determined to make the best of our circumstances, and to lessen with patience and good humor the disagreeableness of our situation. We stopped once at Laird's in Westmoreland about one o'clock. The family rose without murmuring, and obligingly furnished us such refreshments as we wished, and, what was peculiarly agreeable to us all, a good fire. After we had passed through New Hartford, we found a better road, and the coachman was able to drive his horses on a trot. Here, however, we met a light breeze from the north, which, with the aid of the fog, pierced us through; so that, when we arrived at Utica just before five, we were almost frozen. In very few instances have I suffered more from the severities of winter. From Young's to Utica the distance is nineteen miles; from Manlius to Young's, twenty-two. In traveling the whole distance we had spent seventeen hours.

My companions had reached Utica the preceding evening.

The country through which I had traveled from Manlius consisted of the townships of Sullivan, Vernon, Westmoreland, and Whitestown. Sullivan and Vernon are new settlements, much more recent than most of those which we had passed on the road. The land is good, and the number of inhabitants fast increasing. Westmoreland is much improved since my journey into this country in 1799. Dark as the night was, I saw several well-built houses.

The village of New Hartford is also greatly improved. Here the mist had lost much of its density, and permitted us to discern a considerable number of good buildings, surrounded by neat appendages.

Sullivan was formerly in the county of Chenango. By the late division of that county it is become a part of Madison. The other three townships are in the county of Oneida.

Sullivan contained in 1810, 1,974 inhabitants. Vernon contained in 1810, 1,519 inhabitants. Westmoreland contained in 1800, 1,542; and in 1810, 1,135 inhabitants.

Sullivan and Vernon are not mentioned in the Census of 1800. The latter I suppose to have been then included in the township of Westmoreland.

Utica is still more improved. In 1790, there were fifty houses in this village, many of them small and temporary buildings. In 1804, the number was 120. The number of stores also and mechanics' shops is very great in proportion to that of the houses. Utica now exhibits the appearance of a handsome town. Its trade has increased much faster than its buildings, and is greater than that of any other town in the state, New York, Albany, and Troy excepted. Its advantages for business are its situation on the Mohawk, the junction of several great roads here, and the start which it has gained of other places in the vicinity.

After breakfast I took a seat in the Albany stage, and rode through Deerfield, Schuyler, Herkimer, and Manheim to Palatine: thirty-seven miles. The road, as you may perhaps remember, lies along the north bank of the Mohawk, and is now very good. I found the country generally improved since my former journey through it: the forests more extensively gone, the number of houses increased, and those which had been lately built generally of a better appearance. Settlements were also numerously made on the sides of the hills bordering the intervals of the Mohawk, and in several places they had lost that disagreeable uniformity of which I then complained.

We dined at the Little Falls, near the eastern limit of Herkimer. From a variety of observations made in and about the spot, I am entirely satisfied that the mountains, which here ascend immediately from the banks of the river, were anciently united; and that the river above formed an extensive lake, gradually emptied by the wearing away of the earth and stones which originally filled the gap. On the rocks bordering the road, unequivocal marks of the efficacy of water are visible at different heights, to forty feet above the level of the road, and to fifty above the river.

In the list of improvements on this road ought to be mentioned the increase of the number of churches, and of a disposition to settle ministers.

We lodged at a Dutch inn, and the next day, Thursday, October 18th, rode through the remainder of Palatine, Johnstown, and Amsterdam to Schenectady: forty-seven miles.

There is nothing in Palatine particularly meriting attention. It is a Dutch settlement of some standing, and contained in the year 1790, 3,404 inhabitants; in 1800, 3,517; and in 1810, divided, I presume, 3,111.

The remarks which have been made concerning the country through which we passed the preceding day are applicable to this tract also. In Amsterdam I found the Mohawk winding in a greater degree and with more beauty, through wider and handsomer intervals, than in any other part of its progress. It rained both this day and the following.

Schenectady I found reluctantly improving.

We rode in the morning to Albany. This city is improving fast. Many of the old Dutch houses have been destroyed by fires; others have been pulled down; and new ones, built in the English manner, occupy their places. The number is also greatly increased. Several public buildings have been erected, and the whole appearance of the city is changed for the better.

After dinner we rode to the border of Kinderhook, the whole distance thirty-one miles. Between Greenbush and Kinderhook the country is chiefly a pine ground, and the soil indifferent. It is divided between the towns of Greenbush, Schodack, and Kinderhook. The surface is dull; the houses are thinly scattered and ordinary; and the inhabitants apparently are not in very thrifty circumstances.

The next morning my companions left me to proceed to Sheffield, while I pursued my route to the city of Hudson, and with no small satisfaction found the day serene and very pleasant. The distance was sixteen miles. The first part of it consists of a yellow pine plain; and the remainder, of an uneven and unpleasant tract of clay. The soil of the plain is principally sand, and that of both indifferent. The houses, except in the town of Kinderhook, are thinly scattered and ordinary in their appearance.

Kinderhook is an ancient Dutch settlement, built on a sprightly mill-stream called Kinderhook Creek. This stream presented to the original settlers three inducements to seat themselves in this place: the intervals by which it is bordered, the mill seats which it furnishes, and the landing at its mouth, where there are about twenty or thirty houses and stores built on the banks of the Hudson. With these advantages, particularly the trade to which the landing gave birth, some of the inhabitants have heretofore acquired considerable wealth. Since the rise of the city of Hudson this trade has declined, and will probably never regain its former importance. There are several good houses in this town. The streets are wider and more regular than those of most other towns in this country, and its whole aspect is pleasing. To the traveler it presents a strong image of silence and quiet. It is distant from Albany twenty-one miles; and from Hudson, twelve. Between Kinderhook and Hudson, there is nothing interesting.

The township of Kinderhook is large. In 1790, it contained 4,661 inhabitants, including, I suppose, a part or the whole of Chatham. In 1800, the number was 4,348; and in 1810, 3,709.

I arrived at Hudson about eleven o'clock, and was not a little pleased to find it much improved since the year 1792. Then I suspected that it had arisen to the utmost height of its prosperity, for it evidently appeared to be stationary, if not retrogressive. But in this interval many new and valuable houses have been built, together with a great number of stores and mechanics' shops. The still, settled aspect of the place had also been exchanged for animation and activity. Everything which I saw had the air of sprightliness and vigor, and awakened that satisfaction which is always excited in a mind, not malevolent, by the appearance of enterprise and prosperity.

This spot, then a naked waste, was purchased with an intention to make it the site of a future commercial town in the autumn of 1783 by Messrs. Seth and Thomas Jenkins, inhabitants of Providence in the state of Rhode Island.[2] These gentlemen united to themselves a considerable company of adventurers, with whom they liberally shared the advantages of the purchase. In the spring of 1784, they began to build, and within two years raised up in a perfect solitude 150 houses, besides stores, shops, wharves, manufactories, and various other buildings. Fifteen hundred persons, it is said, were assembled within that short period. For a considerable time after this, both the building and the business advanced slowly, and at length appeared to be stationary. Within a few years past the inhabitants, with a commendable spirit of exertion, have opened several turnpike roads into the states of Massachusetts and Connecticut, and have thus created an easy intercourse between their city and a considerable tract of fertile and well-inhabited country. At the same time they have taken their share of the benefit which has resulted from the wise commercial regulations formed under the presidency of Washington.

The number of houses in Hudson now is between five and six hundred. They are generally built of brick, and make a handsome appearance.

The river Hudson is navigable some distance above this city for a sixty-four gun ship, that is to say, 130 miles from New York, and 150 from Sandy Hook.

The position of Hudson is pleasant. The principal street runs from northeast to southwest, nearly at right angles with the river. It is wide, straight, more than a mile in length, and declines easily to the shore. The surrounding scenery is interesting. The neighboring hills are handsome. The river is a noble object, and not the less so for being bounded on the west by a rude shore. The Catskill Mountains, here seen in the best view imaginable, at distances extending from twenty to forty miles, are eminently sublime.

The inhabitants exhibit a general and very commendable spirit of industry, and are said to be justly distinguished for their temperance. They are composed of Presbyterians, Episcopalians, Quakers, and Methodists. The Quakers are the most and the Methodists the least numerous.

Hudson is under the government of a mayor, aldermen, and a common council.

Literature has hitherto not engrossed any great share of attention.

Their commerce is considerable, but I have no means of ascertaining its extent.*

In 1790, the township of Hudson contained 2,584 inhabitants; in 1800, 3,664; in 1810, 4,048.

The rain detained me at Hudson until Tuesday morning, when it slack-

* In the abstract of duties on imports and tonnage which I have obtained since the text was written, there is the following list of duties paid at the customhouse at Hudson.

| Years | Duties | Years | Duties |
|---|---|---|---|
| In 1801 | $1,981 | In 1806 | $6,577 |
| 1802 | 5,366 | 1807 | 5,315 |
| 1803 | 4,576 | 1808 | 1,857 |
| 1804 | 7,001 | 1809 | 2,034 |
| 1805 | 9,564 | 1810 | 1,641 |

But almost all the commerce of this city passes, I suppose, through the customhouse at New York.

ened so much that I left this city, having been joined here by Mr. D—— from Catskill, and proceeded to Sheffield. On my return through Claverack, I thought it a prettier village than I had conceived it to be on my journey out. Indeed, the whole country between Hudson and Sheffield struck my eye with more pleasure. In one respect it was really improved. The streams, in consequence of the rains which had lately fallen, had become both more numerous and more sprightly, and by their cheerful windings and continual murmurs added not a little to the pleasure of our progress. The township of Hillsdale, which occupies the space between Claverack and the Massachusetts line, contained in 1790, 4,556 inhabitants; in 1800, 4,702; and in 1810, 4,182: a part of it I suppose being taken off to form another township.

In the journey of this day I met with a phenomenon which to me was a novelty. In the morning, the wind blew with moderate strength from the southeast, and continued to do so till we came to the neighborhood of Taconic. When we arrived within four or five miles of the ridge of that mountain, we heard a loud and most majestic sound, resembling the noise of the ocean, coming from the higher regions of the mountain. The noise seemed vast and expansive, as if caused at once throughout a wide tract of the atmosphere; and loud, as if produced by a violent agitation. Above a height at five or six hundred feet from the common surface of the neighboring country, the mountain was enveloped in a thick cloud. When we arrived at the foot of the lower acclivities, we found an uncomfortable and furious blast, which continued during the whole time of our ascent: the distance being about a mile and a half, or two miles. After we had gone over this distance, the violence of the blast ceased, and was perceived by us no more, either on the sides, or on the ridge. Still the noise was undiminished, and seemed to fill the heavens with a stormy, tumultuous grandeur. This wind evidently was confined to a very narrow region, including only the summits and sides of the mountain. The direction of this range is from south to north, that of the wind was nearly coincident, but varied a little toward the northwest.

After we had crossed the ridge and begun to descend the declivity, we saw a little eastward of one of the loftiest summits, a bright spot, strongly resembling that which I had formerly observed in the neighborhood of Ascutney. Like that, it continued fixed in its relative position to the summit mentioned for several hours, notwithstanding the violence of the wind and the rapid movement of the clouds; nor did it disappear till it was gradually lost in the twilight. Whether this phenomenon has been observed by others I am ignorant. These are the only instances in which it has been seen by me. The cloud was everywhere else of an uniform density. From the rapidity of its motion, fifty or sixty miles of its extent must have passed over this spot. The spot was apparently fixed, and certainly varied its position very little.

It was continually bright, and at times so bright that we thought the sun shone for a few moments in each instance through the aperture. The position of the luminous area in every instance with respect to the mountains was the same. The density and aspect of the clouds were the same; the direction and strength of the wind were very nearly the same; and both cases happened in the same season of the year.

We arrived at Sheffield in the afternoon, and continued there till one o'clock the following day, being confined by a violent rain. From October 15th to October 24th, it rained more or less every day except two: the 20th and 21st. On the 24th, we rode to Goshen, twenty-four miles; and on the 25th, to New Haven, forty-two.

I am, Sir, yours, etc.

# FIRST JOURNEY TO LAKE WINNIPESAUKEE OR WENTWORTH

## LETTER I

*Journey to Andover—Atkinson—Hampstead—Chester—Pembroke—Concord—Boscawen—Salisbury—Sanbornton—Gilmantown—Meredith—Center Harbor—Winnipesaukee Lake—Its extent—Fed by subjacent springs—Its numerous and beautiful islands*

*Dear Sir,*

On Tuesday, September 15, 1812, I left New Haven and rode to Hartford to meet the American Board of Commissioners for Foreign Missions. On the Thursday following, I rode to Stafford Springs, the next morning to Worcester, and on Saturday arrived at Charlestown. On Tuesday, I rode to Andover, and the next day attended an examination of the theological students, highly honorable both to themselves and the professors. September 29th, in company with two young gentlemen, A. B., of Yale College, directing our journey toward the central parts of New Hampshire, we passed through the parish of North Andover, Bradford, Haverhill, Atkinson, and Hampstead, and reached Chester at the commencement of the evening: twenty-six miles. The road, though repaired only by statute labor, is generally good.

The surface of the country from Haverhill to Chester is a succession of handsome hills and valleys, everywhere arched. The soil is a light brown loam, moderately good, and universally cultivated, except where handsome groves, interspersed at very agreeable distances, form one fine feature in the landscape. Another still finer is made up of distant mountains, sometimes very noble, seen successively from the summits of the hills.

The houses and barns throughout this region are generally good; and, together with the outbuildings, enclosures, and fields, sufficiently indicate that the inhabitants are in comfortable circumstances.

Chester I have mentioned heretofore, and have nothing to add concerning it here. The town of Atkinson is less than that of Chester; and Hampstead, than Atkinson.

There is in Atkinson an academy, established in 1789 by the Hon. N. Peabody, who gave to it a thousand acres of land.[1] There is also a large meadow in which, when overflowed by water raised by a dam, a tract of six acres rises and floats as an island.

Atkinson contained in 1775, 575; in 1790, 479; in 1800, 474; and in 1810, 556 inhabitants. Hampstead contained in 1775, 768; in 1790, 724; in 1800, 790; and in 1810, 738 inhabitants.

A part of Atkinson was annexed to Haverhill when the line was finally run between New Hampshire and Massachusetts.

Atkinson was incorporated in 1767, and Hampstead in 1749.

On Wednesday we proceeded to Concord. The road for fifteen miles to Pembroke is a turnpike, lately formed through a tract almost absolutely uninhabited, and alternately covered with forests of maple, pine, and oak. The first is principally marsh; the second, an alternation of plains and rising grounds; the third, a succession of hills. All of them are dull and dismal, and the whole region is one of the most uninviting which I have met with. The road is good and direct.

Pembroke is built principally on a hill, declining easily toward the southwest. The houses are not unlike those which have been mentioned. All these towns have decent churches. The prospect from the hill in Pembroke is fine, and the soil like that which has already been described.

In the year 1775, Pembroke contained 744 inhabitants; in 1790, 956; in 1800, 982; in 1810, 1,153.

From Pembroke to Concord the road, which is generally firm and good, lies almost wholly on a pine plain. We, however, wandered out of the direct road and lost five miles by the error. A considerable part of this distance we found uninhabited.

Concord is pleasantly situated on both sides of the Merrimack. The town is built principally on the western side upon a single street, near two miles in length, and running parallel with the river. Its site is a handsome plain, limited westward by hills at the distance of perhaps half a mile, and eastward by an interval which is both pleasant and fertile. The prospect from this town up and down the river is extensive and interesting, and the scenery around it is cheerful. The intervals within the limits of the township amount to about one thousand acres, the current price of which, by the acre, is from sixty to one hundred and twenty dollars. The western part of the township, separated from the town by a pine ridge, is excellent land. The public buildings are the church, courthouse, a well-built schoolhouse, and the state prison. The church is a large and good building. The state prison is a noble edifice of beautiful granite, which abounds in the vicinity. It is a copy of the state prison at Charlestown, both in the materials and the structure. The center and one wing only are finished.

Concord contains between three and four hundred families, all united in one congregation, the largest in the state. The township was incorporated in the year 1765, and in 1775 contained 1,052 inhabitants; in 1790, 1,747; in 1800, 2,052; and in 1810, 2,393.

Since the Revolution, Concord, much more frequently than any other town in New Hampshire, has been the place where the legislature has held its sessions, and will probably be the permanent seat of government.

The next morning, Thursday, October 2nd, we rode to Meredith Bridge in the township of Guilford: thirty-two miles. The road for the first eighteen miles lay along the Merrimack, and was to a considerable extent sandy. The remaining fourteen passed through a region of hills and valleys.

The first township which we entered after leaving Concord is Boscawen. Like Concord it is built principally in a single street, parallel with the river, on a plain, less pleasant and less productive. The space between the brow of this plain and the Merrimack, is occupied by intervals of considerable value. The houses are much inferior to those of Concord.

Boscawen was incorporated in 1760. In 1775, it contained 585 inhabitants; in 1790, 1,108; in 1800, 1,414; in 1810, 1,829.

Salisbury lies immediately above Boscawen. Of this township we saw nothing but a skirt: the town being built in the interior. The part over which we traveled generally resembled Boscawen. The northern division of our road through it, was, however, particularly agreeable, as it passed over a rich and pleasant interval, divided into fine farms, and ornamented with several good houses.

Salisbury was incorporated in 1768, and contained in 1775, 498 inhabitants; in 1790, 1,372; in 1800, 1,767; in 1810, 1,913, included in one congregation.

From Salisbury we crossed on a bridge the Pemigewasset, the western head of the Merrimack; and after a short distance, the Aquedochton [Winnipesaukee River] the eastern, on a bridge also, at a small distance above their junction. Both are considerable rivers, and run with a rapid and powerful stream.

From Salisbury we entered the township of Sanbornton, the best in this part of the state, and inhabited by the best body of farmers. It lies on elevated and handsome ground, bordered for several miles by a beautiful lake called Sanbornton Bay; about ten miles in length and from two to perhaps four in breadth. This fine piece of water receives the Aquedochton, and discharges its own waters through the continuation of that river.

From Salisbury bridge, over which we passed the Pemigewasset at the distance of eighteen miles from Concord, to Union bridge over the Winnipesaukee at the foot of Sanbornton Lake, eight miles further, the country on the road is rough; and the road which runs along the southern skirt of Sanbornton and near the Aquedochton is in various places stony and disagreeable. It ought however to be observed to the honor of the inhabitants of this state that, although the population is sparse, they are making their roads universally very good. In the parts where they were originally the worst, they have already made them to a great extent excellent, in the manner of turnpikes, and better than some roads which wear this name. These parts they are proceeding as fast as may be to unite, by filling up the interstices according to the same plan. When the design is completed, New Hampshire will, to say the least, be behind none of its sister states in this important particular; and will have the merit, which I believe is singular, of accomplishing so difficult an object by statute labor.

Sanbornton contains the ruins of an Indian fortification, which is remarkable for being formed of five enclosures. In the neighboring fields the plow has turned up many specimens of Indian pottery.

Sanbornton was incorporated in 1770, and in 1775 contained 450 inhabitants; in 1790, 1,587; in 1800, 2,695; and in 1810, 2,884.

At Union bridge we entered Gilmantown on the eastern side of the Aquedochton. This also is a valuable township. Our road passed along its western skirt on the border of Sanbornton Bay. The hills here are easy, elegant slopes; and the farms, rich and beautiful. These two townships are in the county of Strafford; Concord, in that of Rockingham; and Boscawen and Salisbury, in that of Hillsboro. In Gilmantown the court of common pleas usually sits once in a year. It contains an academy, which has obtained a good degree of reputation.

It was incorporated in 1727, and in 1775 contained 775 inhabitants; in 1790, 2,613; in 1800, 3,752; in 1810, 4,388: having a more numerous population than any in the county, and, except Portsmouth, than any other in the state.

We left Meredith bridge in the morning, and rode to Center Harbor to dinner: thirteen miles. The village known by the former of these names contains not far from forty houses, several of them neatly built, surrounding a new church of a handsome structure. It is situated upon low and generally level ground on both sides of the Aquedochton. A number of mills are erected on this stream a little above the bridge; and, together with the mechanics' shops and several stores, give the spot a cheerful aspect of business.

The situation of this village is very pleasant. It lies in the township of Guilford, taken partly from Gilmantown and partly from Meredith, and was incorporated since the last census.

At this bridge the Aquedochton is a fine sprightly stream, as indeed it is everywhere else, running with a vigorous current over a clean, stony bed. It is about the size of the Lower Ammonoosuc at Bath. To the eye it is scarcely less here than below Sanbornton Lake. Its water is very pure.

Immediately west, or rather northwest, of the bridge, the township of Meredith is a continuation of easy and very elegant slopes, declining to the southeast. The soil is rich; the pastures, meadows, and orchards are luxuriant; and the groves, thrifty and vigorous. The views are also fine and very extensive. Sanbornton Lake on the south is in the most perfect view, a noble sheet of water, festooned by elegant scoops, separated by handsome points and promontories. Smith Lake also on the east, a much smaller but beautiful piece of water, forms a luminous spot in the landscape. The distant prospect is rich and magnificent. The country along the remainder of the road, though not without its advantages, is less inviting. We saw nothing of the Winnipesaukee, except a small inlet, until we arrived at the point where we were to take a view of its whole length.

After passing over several lofty hills we reached the house of Charles Little, Esq., at Center Harbor, between eleven and twelve, where we dined.[2] From this house the lake is seen with more advantage than from any other place in this quarter of the same elevation.

I have elsewhere mentioned the want of curiosity of the New England people concerning things which are their own, particularly concerning the fine objects of their own country. The fact that New England abounds with elegant pieces of water has not even made its appearance in the books either of geographers or travelers. At least I know not where it has appeared. Yet there is probably no country which is more frequently or more highly adorned with this exquisite beauty of landscape. Of this lake, which has been generally supposed to be the largest of all those whose waters are wholly included within the limits of New England, I have never heard, nor seen, a syllable, except a few slight geographical notices concerning its length, breadth, position, and capacity of being passed in the summer with boats, together with two or three other trifling circumstances. Indeed a few observations made to me concerning this subject by my father when I was a child were not improbably more than all that I have heard concerning it from that time to the present.

Winnipesaukee Lake lies between 71° 5′ and 71° 25′ west longitude from Greenwich and between 43° 29′ and 43° 44′ north latitude: not far from the center of the state of New Hampshire. Its form is very irregular. At the western end it is divided into three large bays. On the north side there is a fourth. On the eastern end there are three others. The general course of the lake is from northwest to southeast. Its length, as estimated on the spot, is twenty-three miles; and its greatest breadth, fourteen. This, however, must be understood only of an oblique direction. In a direction right angled to its length, it cannot, I believe, exceed ten. On its borders lie the townships of Moultonboro, Tuftonboro, and Wolfboro on the northeast; Center Harbor on the northwest; Meredith, Guilford and Gilmantown on the southwest; the township of Alton and a tract called the Gore on the southeast. Its waters are in some places unfathomable by any means in the possession of the inhabitants. They abound with fish.

The navigation of this lake is hitherto of no great importance, but will probably become, hereafter, of considerable value. Should the company which has lately obtained a grant for the purpose of rendering the waters of the Merrimack and Aquedochton navigable for boats succeed in this project, the lake will become an interesting channel of communication, at least for the townships by which it is surrounded. A number of boats are now employed in conveying merchandise over it during the summer. In the winter sleighs usually begin to cross it in the month of February. It is frozen in January, but is not often crossed on account of the depth and lightness of the snow.

Several large promontories intrude into this lake. The largest is called Moultonboro Neck, and includes a considerable part of that township. The next in size is that of Center Harbor, including almost all the township of that name. Another of considerable extent stretches out from the south part of Tuftonboro. There are also several others of inferior dimensions.

The waters of the Winnipesaukee are remarkably pure and, when taken from a sufficient depth to give them the proper temperature, are perfectly sweet and palatable. I am not sure that the water is equally fine with that of Lake George, but I was unable to discover any degree of inferiority in this respect. Like Lake George, it is supplied chiefly by subjacent springs. One millstream only empties its waters into it, and the Aquedochton conveys from it probably ten times the quantity of water derived from all its tributaries. This river, issuing from the southwestern arm of the Winnipesaukee, runs into a small lake, whose name I cannot find; touches the southeastern extremity of Smith Lake; and thence, pouring in a rapid current about eight miles, unites with the Pemigewasset opposite Salisbury. It passes through the township of Guilford, and washes on the northwest Meredith and Sanbornton, and on the southeast, Gilmantown and Canterbury.

The boats hitherto employed in navigating it carry only twenty tons. These, however, are sufficiently large for the business of which it is the channel.

From Dover to Merrymeeting Bay, the southeastern extremity of the Winnipesaukee, the distance is said to be twenty-three miles. It has been often proposed to turn the navigation of the lake in this direction. Both the Cocheco and Salmon Fall River approach with their western arms within a few miles of its southeastern skirt. Of the practicability of this proposed communication, I have no knowledge.

The Winnipesaukee contains a great multitude of islands. Like those in Lake George and in Casco Bay, and like the ponds in the township of Plymouth, they are here declared to be three hundred and sixty-five. Without supposing the number of days in the year to have been consulted on this subject, and each day to have been provided with three islands and one pond, we may rationally conclude that the number in each of the cases is considerable. Several of these islands are so large as to furnish farms of sufficient extent. One of them contains five hundred acres; and three or four others, somewhat less. That which has been longest cultivated, and which is near to the Gilmantown shore, is in the possession of a Mr. Davis. Having been once in danger from the ice as he was attempting to pass in a boat from the shore to the island, he determined to build a bridge across the strait which separated them, and executed his design the following season. The soil of this island is said to be excellent. Thirteen others, as I was informed, are sufficiently large to become good farms; and two or three of these have already begun to be cultivated.

The prospect of this lake and its environs is enchanting, and is seen with great advantage from the house of Mr. Little, but with more from the hill in the rear of his house, on the road toward Plymouth. The day was remarkably fine. Not a breath disturbed the leaves or ruffled the surface of the waters. The sky was serene and beautiful. The sun shone with a soft and elegant luster, such as seems peculiar to that delightful weather which from the 20th of September to the 20th of October so often elicits from the mouths of mankind the epithet of charming. Mildness tempered the heat, and serenity hushed the world into universal quiet. The Winnipesaukee was an immense field of glass, silvered by the luster which floated on its surface. Its borders, now in full view, now dimly retiring from the eye, were formed by those flowing lines, those masterly sweeps of nature, from which art has derived all its apprehensions of ease and grace; alternated at the same time by the intrusion of points, by turns rough and bold, or marked with the highest elegance of figure. In the center a noble channel spread twenty-three miles before the eye, uninterrupted even by a bush or a rock. On both sides of this avenue a train of islands arranged themselves, as if to adorn it with the finish which could be given only by their glowing verdure and graceful forms.

Nor is this lake less distinguished by its suite of hills and mountains. On the northwest ascends a remarkably beautiful eminence called the Red Mountain, limited everywhere by circular lines, and in the proper sense elegant in its figure beyond any other mountain among the multitude which I have examined. On the south ascends Mount Major, a ridge of a bolder aspect and loftier height. At a still greater distance in the southeast rises another mountain, whose name I could not learn, more obscure and misty; presenting its loftiest summit, of an exactly semicircular form, directly at the foot of the channel above mentioned, and terminating the watery vista between the islands by which it is bordered in a magnificent manner. On the northeast the great Ossipee raises its long chain of summits with a bold sublimity, and proudly looks down on all the surrounding region.

As we did not cross the Winnipesaukee, I am unable to determine in what manner an excursion on its waters might be compared with that which I made on Lake George. That the internal and successive beauties of the Winnipesaukee strongly resemble and nearly approach those of Lake George, I cannot entertain a doubt. That they exceed them seems scarcely credible. But the prospect from the hill at the head of Center Harbor is much superior to that from Fort George, a fact of which hardly anything could have convinced me except the testimony of my own eyes. The Winnipesaukee presents a field of at least twice the extent. The islands in view are more numerous and, except one, of finer forms and more happily arranged. The shores are not inferior. The expansion is far more magnificent and the grandeur of the mountains, particularly of the great Ossipee, can scarcely be rivaled. It cannot be remarked without some surprise that Lake George is annually visited by people from the coast of New England; and that the Winnipesaukee, notwithstanding all its accumulation of splendor and elegance, is almost as much unknown to the inhabitants of this country as if it lay on the eastern side of the Caspian.

I am, Sir, yours, etc.

## LETTER II

*Holderness—Squam Lake—Plymouth—Baker River—Rumney—Wentworth —Warren—Ryegate—Barnet—St. Johnsbury—Lyndon—Sheffield—Premature frosts—Lebanon Falls—Boating on Connecticut River—Governor Griswold*

*Dear Sir,*

After dinner we left the house of Mr. Little and rode to Plymouth, through a part of the townships of Meredith and Holderness: thirteen miles. The whole of this tract is a succession of hills and valleys. The hills in several instances are high and stony. The soil throughout a considerable part of the extent is good grazing ground; and the road, like that last described.

In this part of our journey we passed Squam Lake, of which we had several beautiful views, and one peculiarly so from a high ground in Holderness. This lake, notwithstanding its uncouth name, is a splendid sheet of water, finely indented by points, arched with beautiful coves, and studded with a succession of romantic islands. At its head rose the Red Mountain in its grandest attitude, and formed an appropriate background of the picture.

This lake is ten miles in length, and where widest not less than six in breadth. Its water, like that of the Winnipesaukee, is pure and cheerful. I counted ten islands of elegant figures in its bosom. We passed also several smaller lakes, each very handsome, and adding not a little to the gaiety of our journey. On the eminence just mentioned we had a spacious prospect of the surrounding region, composed of valleys, hills, and mountains. Some of the mountains were lofty. One particularly, ascending in the northeast, was distinguished by the form and sublimity of its summit.

We crossed the Pemigewasset in a boat, and reached Plymouth a little after sunset. The next morning, Saturday, October 3rd, we rode to the northeast corner of Piermont to dinner: twenty-six miles; through Rumney, Wentworth, and Warren. Our road was good.

Plymouth is a half-shire town of the county of Grafton. It is indifferently built, and many of the houses wear the appearance of negligence and decay. A few of them are, however, decent. The courthouse is an ordinary and the church a good building.

After we left Plymouth, we quitted the Pemigewasset and ascended Baker River, a large and beautiful millstream, which is one of its tributaries. The scenery in this part of our journey was formed by the valley, frequently ornamented by intervals at the bottom, and a succession of hills by which it was bordered, rising at times to a mountainous height. The houses, with a few exceptions, indicated nothing more than that the inhabitants were in comfortable circumstances. Everywhere at little distances we saw schoolhouses neatly built. We also passed by several churches, which from their situation and appearance I concluded belonged to Baptists. This tract will hardly change its aspect for the better until the inhabitants shall have adopted a superior husbandry, or employed themselves in manufacturing.

After we left Baker River we began gradually to ascend the Lyme Range. The acclivities were very easy, but the country was less populous; and as we approached the highest ground, the settlements became rare. The soil was evidently better than most of that which we had left.

We had continued our journey through a stage unusually long from the appearance of an approaching rain. The rain began to fall just as we reached the door of our intended inn, and continued from two o'clock in the afternoon until Monday morning.

The number of inhabitants in Rumney was in 1790, 411; in 1800, 624; and in 1810, 765; in Wentworth, in 1790, 241; in 1800, 448; and in 1810, 645; in Warren, in 1790, 206; in 1800, 336; and in 1810, 506.

We were well entertained at this house kept by a Mr. Tarleton; and, having several religious books in our possession, were able to pass through the Sabbath with decency and comfort. The next morning we proceeded to Newbury, eight miles, through Haverhill.

Tarleton's house is situated on a beautiful plain, at the highest elevation attained by this road. The hills on the northeast and southwest ascend perhaps two hundred feet above this ground, forming handsome limits in both directions. To the northwest and the southeast a passage is opened into the country below. The house stands on the north side of the road; and this part of the farm declines gradually into a valley, at the bottom of which is a lake, about a mile and a half in length and three quarters of a mile in breadth. The whole scene is an elegant solitude, not a house being in sight besides the neat building of Mr. Tarleton.

Here we saw the mountain ash, which grows abundantly in this neighborhood. Here also the clouds, which had so copiously shed their waters during the two preceding days, descending from the elevations on the north and west, and passing slowly along the surface of the plain, gave us experimental evidence that they differed in nothing from a dense mist.

Soon after we started, the weather became clear, and the country, as we descended into the Connecticut Valley, delightful. Finer scenery can scarcely be imagined than that which is spread throughout this region.

Haverhill has become a beautiful village. A number of good houses have been erected here since the year 1803, particularly around what is called the square, a neat ground about forty rods in length and thirty in breadth.

We crossed the Connecticut on a toll bridge about two miles below the church in Newbury. Another at the north end of this town was lately carried away by the river.

We left our vehicles at Newbury; and, having obtained a convenient wagon and a discreet young man to drive it, made an excursion into the interior of Vermont through the townships of Ryegate, Barnet, St. Johnsbury, and Lyndon into Sheffield. The first day, we rode twenty-three miles after dinner. The second, we labored hard to finish twenty-four. The third, we returned to Wells River: forty-two. The first twelve or fifteen, our journey lay along Connecticut River, and then as much more along the Posoomsuck [Passumpsic]; the remainder was a continual ascent and descent of lofty hills. The first two thirds of the road were pretty good; the last third, intolerably bad. The soil throughout this distance is generally productive. On the Passumpsic, as well as on the Connecticut, are many rich and handsome intervals. In St. Johnsbury is a plain about half a mile in diameter, remarkable for being the only spot of this nature throughout the whole distance. Ryegate and Barnet are chiefly Scotch settlements, the former colonized by a collection of inhabitants brought from Scotland by Dr. Witherspoon.[1] We found a good character everywhere given of these people for their industry, good order, and good morals; and, so far as we could judge, they were generally in comfortable circumstances. A reputable clergyman from Scotland is settled in each of these townships. The weather, although it was only so late as the 5th and 6th of October, we found intensely cold. It snowed and rained alternately on both days, and on the morning of Wednesday the ground was hard frozen. The maize had been chiefly destroyed by a succession of frosts during the preceding month; and, what I had never heard of at this season of the year before, the wheat had in several instances been killed by frost about the 20th of August.

The summer was the coldest which I ever knew. In grounds which were not warm and particularly favorable, the maize scarcely attained half its proper growth; and of that which grew well, not more than two thirds or three fourths arrived at maturity. The best and ripest which I saw during the season was in Haverhill, on a fine interval which I have elsewhere described.

Most of the summer and autumnal fruits were also shriveled and insipid. The peaches, cherries, etc. were chiefly destroyed, and those which were left were generally of little value. The pears and apples were shrunk in many instances to half their proper size, and defective in their flavor. The late apples were, however, generally good.

From Wells River, where we found a good hospitable inn, we returned on Thursday morning, October 8th, to Newbury, and thence proceeded to Dartmouth College: thirty-five miles.

The next day we set out for Windsor, and arrived about twelve o'clock. In Lebanon, the horse belonging to my companions was frightened by a wagon; and, running off a causey, overturned their chaise and left them at the bottom. Both of them and the horse, however, escaped without any serious injury.

On Saturday, my companions quitted Windsor for Washington, and thence proceeded down the river. I had come to Windsor by appointment, as a delegate from the General Association of Connecticut to a convention of clergymen which was to be held here on Wednesday the 21st, and was therefore necessitated to continue in this part of the country till that time. The interval, except two days spent with some friends at Charlestown, I passed very pleasantly in this town. Nothing which politeness could dictate or hospitality furnish was omitted by a circle of very respectable families to make my residence peculiarly agreeable, and to leave on my mind the best impressions of their character.

The convention met on the day appointed and finished all the important parts of their business. On Thursday, therefore, I left my good friends at Windsor, and proceeded to Charlestown to dinner; and in the evening arrived at Putney: forty miles. The next day I reached the southern part of Deerfield: thirty-eight miles; and on Saturday arrived at Northampton: thirteen. Hence on Monday I proceeded to Hartford: forty-three; and the following day arrived at New Haven without an accident.

I found the whole country improved, and many of the parts not a little. Orford is become a beautiful town. The village of Dartmouth has assumed a much better aspect.

In the account which I formerly gave of Connecticut River, I made the following observations.

"A little labor bestowed on the falls of Ottauqueechee, and locks and a small dam at those of Lebanon, would extend the navigation to the foot of the Fifteen Mile Falls, about 245 miles. Whenever the country above shall have become universally settled, these obstructions will undoubtedly be removed. At present the quantity of business is insufficient to justify the expense necessary for this purpose." [2]

These observations were made in the year 1803. My expectations have been anticipated by a period of many years. In 1807, the legislature of New Hampshire granted to Mills Olcott, Esq., under the style of "The White River Falls Company," the privilege of completing a lock navigation over these falls, more generally known by the name of Lebanon Falls, and of regulating the rate of toll, on the condition that he should not interfere with the passage round them by the old or customary road. Mr. Olcott, under this style, was empowered at his opinion to unite others with him or not in this design, but determined to undertake the accomplishment of it without any associates, and completed it in the year 1809. The falls are three in number. At the second a dam is thrown across the river, which renders the navigation safe and easy over the first. Another dam at the third extends the navigation back to the second. There are three locks at the upper, and two at the lower dam. Sawmills of superior value and extent are erected at these works. Some of them are formed in such a manner as to saw planks sixty-five feet in length, intended for the decks of vessels. The whole expense of these works amounted to somewhat more than 30,000 dollars. The net revenue which they yielded during the years 1810 and 1811 was 3,000 dollars a year, or ten per cent. The rate of toll hitherto has been one dollar per ton.

The falls at Ottauqueechee were made passable about the same time.

Thus is the navigation of this river already opened and rendered convenient for boats carrying twenty or twenty-five tons, not to the foot of Fifteen Mile Falls, as I formerly supposed might be done, but to about thirteen miles above Newbury, and 247 from its mouth at Saybrook. Wells River, five miles above Newbury, will, however, be for a considerable time the most northern station of any importance for this business. To this spot produce, particularly potash, has been brought from the settlements in Vermont thirty miles higher up; and in the opinion of Major Hale, a respectable inhabitant of this place, will hereafter be generally conveyed.[3] Foreign goods have also been carried from this place to Lancaster in New Hampshire, forty miles, and in one instance to Colebrook, seventy-five miles above. When, therefore, I asserted that the commerce of this country from twenty-five miles above Newbury would one day center in the city of Hartford, you will consider me as having limited the assertion by moderate bounds.

When I was at Wells River, there were fourteen boats at that landing destined to this business. The voyage thence to Hartford, including the return, is made in twenty-five days. It has been performed in twenty-two or twenty-three. Of course, nine voyages may be conveniently made in a season.

Each boat is manned by two men. The stream carries it down at the rate of from three to four miles an hour. On their return the boatmen avail themselves of the eddies, or back currents, which are often found on the borders of the river. Each boat also carries a large square sail, which is hoisted whenever the wind favors. Such boats are found at convenient distances throughout the whole length of the river to the point where the proximity of Hartford renders them unnecessary. This mode of transportation is continually increasing, and becoming more and more regular. The period is not distant when it will convey most, if not all, of the marketable produce and manufactures of this extensive region to the ocean.

Among the towns through which I passed in my way from Windsor, those which had most improved in their appearance were Charlestown and Greenfield, Northampton and Hartford.

At Hartford I received the melancholy news of the death of His Excellency, Roger Griswold, Esq., governor of Connecticut.[4]

To the memory of this gentleman I would willingly pay such a tribute of respect as his distinguished worth, the important services which he rendered to his country, and, may I be permitted to add, the numerous testimonies of his friendship to me so justly demand.

He was born at Lyme, May 21, 1762. His father was the late Governor Griswold, heretofore respectfully mentioned in these letters; and his mother, the daughter of the first Governor Wolcott, and sister of the second. He was educated at Yale College, where he took his first degree in 1780. In 1783, he was admitted to the bar; in 1794, he was chosen a representative of this state in Congress; in 1801, he was appointed by President Adams, secretary of war, but declined the office. In 1807, having resigned his seat in Congress, he was appointed a judge of the superior court in this state. In 1809, he was chosen lieutenant governor, and in 1811 was raised to the chief seat of magistracy. In this station he died, October 1812.

Governor Griswold possessed an uncommonly good person, was tall, well made, and vigorous. His complexion, countenance, and eye were remarkably fine, presenting to a spectator an almost singular combination of amiableness and dignity.

His mind was perfectly suited to such a form. It was a mind of the first class, combining an imagination, an understanding, and a memory rarely united. With these powers were joined sweetness of temper, unwarping probity, great candor, firmness which nothing could shake, and patriotism unquestioned even by the malignant spirit of party. To these high attributes he added a delicacy scarcely rivaled by our sex, and not often excelled by the other.

It will not appear surprising that with such qualities Governor Griswold should acquire high distinction in every employment which he assumed. At the bar and on the bench, he was considered as standing in the first rank of his compeers. In Congress, for several years, he was regarded by those of both political parties as the first man in the House of Representatives. His knowledge of the public affairs and true interests of this country for some years before he left Congress was probably not excelled by that of any individual member in that body. It was at once comprehensive and minute: embracing the great and general principles of sound American policy, and entering, in a sense intuitively, into those details of business which ultimately regulate all the practical concerns of a community, and without which those concerns can never be directed either with success or safety. Whenever he spoke, men of all parties listened with profound attention: for they all knew that he never spoke unless to propose new subjects of consideration or to place those which were under discussion in a new and important light. At the same time the exact decorum which he observed, the politeness and delicacy with which he treated his opponents, and the candor which he manifested on every subject, although they could not subdue the stubbornness of party, compelled the respect even of its champions for himself.

In the year 1807, while he was deeply engaged in arguing a cause of great moment before the superior court of Connecticut, he was arrested by a disease which ultimately terminated his life.

It is hardly necessary to say that such a man excelled in every private station, relation, and duty of life.

There are many reasons to hope that he died a Christian.

I am, Sir, yours, etc.

# SECOND JOURNEY TO LAKE WINNIPESAUKEE OR WENTWORTH

## LETTER I

*Journey to Andover through Providence—To Portsmouth through Newburyport—Rochester—Norway Plain—Middleton—Wolfboro—Governor Wentworth—Tuftonboro—Moultonboro—Prospect of the Lake Winnipesaukee or Wentworth from the Red Mountain—Squam or Sullivan's Lake—Return*

*Dear Sir,*

In the year 1813, I left New Haven, September 6th, the public commencement having been holden the preceding week on account of a national fast; and, proceeding through Hartford and Providence, arrived at Charlestown on the 10th. On the 21st, I rode to Andover. The 23rd, I proceeded to Salem; the 24th, to Newburyport. The 25th, I made an excursion along the banks of the Merrimack to Bradford, and from thence proceeded to Essex bridge, newly built upon strong iron chains, probably the best mode of building bridges hitherto adopted in this country when the water is deep and the channel not very wide. On the 27th, I reached Portsmouth. My companions in the journey to Charlestown were two young gentlemen, to whom were added at Charlestown two others, all of them A. B. in Yale College.

From Providence to Andover our road was the same which has been heretofore mentioned. Of this part of my journey I shall only observe that the American Board of Commissioners, with whom I met at this time, found their affairs prosperous, and were amply assured by the liberality with which their funds were increased that the disposition in their countrymen to diffuse the blessings of the Gospel was very honorably extending itself, and becoming more vigorous in places where it had been before manifested.

The theological seminary at Andover I found prospering. The number of students was fifty.

The country between Andover and Salem, except the township of Danvers, is dull and spiritless. Its surface is undulating, but without beauty. The soil, the enclosures, and the buildings are indifferent. Danvers is generally a rich and beautiful township, containing a succession of fine enclosures and good houses throughout every part of its limits on this road.

The country between Newburyport and Bradford, lying twelve miles along the Merrimack, is a succession of hills and valleys, both almost universally and elegantly arched, the concave of the latter being little else than a counterpart to the convex of the former. The soil also is excellent, and the prospects are beautiful.

It deserves to be mentioned as a fact not a little interesting that Mr. Bartlett, on a farm which he possesses at Methuen, and Captain Stannard, on the plantation formerly belonging to Tristram Dalton, Esq., in Newbury, have renewed the culture of wheat in this region, and with very good success. Captain Stannard raised on three acres one hundred bushels. I ate some of the bread made of the wheat from Mr. Bartlett's farm and found it excellent. For more than one hundred years, if I mistake not, it has been proverbially and universally asserted that wheat could not come to perfection throughout most of the eastern half of Massachusetts. The charm is now broken, and the authority of this gray-haired prejudice destroyed. To Mr. Bartlett the credit is, I believe, due of having first furnished decisive proof that it was without foundation.

On Tuesday, the 28th, we left Portsmouth and rode to Middleton, crossing Piscataqua Bridge, and passing through Dover and Rochester: thirty-four miles. The road lies on the north side of the Cocheco, and is tolerably good, except the last six or eight miles which are very bad. The part which was good was made under the direction of His Excellency John Wentworth, Esq., then governor of the province of New Hampshire.

I found Dover considerably improved and beautified since my last visit; and, what was not a little gratifying to me, furnished with a good minister of the Gospel. The lands immediately west of Dover, and within the limits of that township, generally appeared well on this road, and were ornamented with a number of good farmers' houses. After passing three or four miles, the country assumed a lean and unpromising appearance. The surface was composed of hills, rising with easy and long acclivities to a very considerable height, and open valleys between them. The soil was evidently poor, though probably of a worse appearance on account of a severe drought under which the country at this time labored. A few of the buildings looked well. The prospects were in several instances extensive, and in one, magnificent.

Norway plain, so called from the multitude of Norway pines growing upon it, contains a decent village of the same name. It is within the township of Rochester, and the only one between Dover and Wolfboro.

Four miles farther, or twenty-eight from Portsmouth, the road continued to be good. The remainder ascended and descended a succession of gradual acclivities, covered with rocks and stones to such a degree as to make traveling not only excessively inconvenient, but at times dangerous. The inhabitants, who are few and thinly dispersed, seem to have done everything in their power to lessen the evil; but, unless they are assisted from some other quarter, they must labor many years before excursions to Wolfboro will be invited by the road. The forests throughout the whole of this tract are oak.

We arrived at Middleton a little after sunset. The soil of this township is pretty good grazing land.

The next morning we rode to Wolfboro bridge, where there is a decent village, consisting of about twenty houses. The situation of this village is very pleasant. It stands on both sides of the outlet by which the waters of Smith Lake and another of a small size the name of which I did not learn are discharged into the Winnipesaukee. Just below the bridge commences a beautiful bay, six miles in length and two in breadth, strongly resembling that part of Lake George which is visible from the fort, but of less than half the extent, and not terminated to the eye, as that is, by a boundary of mountains. The view here is only beautiful. The winding of the shores is superior to what is seen there. The water is of the purest transparency; and the islands, and points of land, and the distant mountains are all very interesting objects.

The shore in this region is handsome, sufficiently varied, and sloping gracefully toward the water's edge. The soil also is rich; and, wherever it is tolerably cultivated, is covered with a fine verdure. The outlet is a large and sprightly millstream.

All the productions of the climate: the grains, the grass, the flax, the hortulan vegetables, and the fruits, flourish in this spot. Peach trees grow well, and resist the severity of the winter. Yet they die within a few years, from some cause unknown to the inhabitants, but not improbably the ravages of the peach worm. Fruits of every other kind are very prosperous. Early frosts in the autumn are rarely known, but the spring is often cold and backward: the atmosphere being chilled by the waters of the lake, which are kept cold for a considerable season by the ice.

Various kinds of fine fish are caught at the bridge and elsewhere in great abundance. Among them are the following: trout, weighing from one to twenty pounds; pike, one to four; perch, one to three; roach, one to two; cusk, one to four; pout, eels, etc.

Wolfboro, Middleton, Tuftonboro, and various other parts of the neighboring country are principally inhabited by Baptists, of the class vulgarly called *Freewillers,* who are generally extremely ignorant.

It is a very great evil to these settlements, and many others in New Hampshire, that they are, and for a considerable length of time have been, destitute of well-educated ministers of the Gospel. The last minister of Wolfboro died about fourteen years since, and the reluctance to be at the necessary expense has prevented the inhabitants from settling another. This is an extensive calamity in New Hampshire.

Five miles east of the bridge is the seat formerly belonging to His Excellency John Wentworth, Esq.[1] This gentleman was the greatest benefactor to the province of New Hampshire mentioned in its history. He was a man of sound understanding, refined taste, enlarged views, and a dignified spirit. His manners also were elegant, and his disposition enterprising. Agriculture in this province owed more to him than to any other man. He also originated the formation of new roads and the improvement of old ones. All these circumstances rendered him very popular; and he would probably have continued to increase his reputation, had he not been prevented by the controversy between Great Britain and the colonies. As the case was, he retired from the chair with an unimpeachable character, and with higher reputation than any other man who at that time held the same office in this country.

A specimen of his good taste, and a very striking one, was exhibited in the fact that he chose the border of this lake for his summer residence. It was not then, and even to the present time has not been, customary for the wealthy inhabitants of New England to fix their country seats upon the fine pieces of water with which at little distances it is everywhere adorned. When Governor Wentworth came to this country, the region surrounding the Winnipesaukee was almost absolutely a forest. Few men have those preconceptions of taste, if I may call them such, especially with respect to subjects to the contemplation of which the mind is led by conversation or practice, which anticipates beauty and elegance in a wilderness, and finds them hidden beneath the rude covering of nature. Governor Wentworth, however, found them here, and by building on this ground set an example which will one day be followed by multitudes of his countrymen. The time will come when it will not be thought necessary to place a country residence in the purlieus of a great city, or desirable to look for the pleasures of rural life in the neighborhood of the dwellings of market people and the stalls of butchers.

The house of Governor Wentworth fell, after he left the country, into the hands of persons who were unworthy to succeed him; and, as might be expected, has advanced far in decay and ruin. The ground on which it stands will probably invite at some future period a man of a similar disposition to revive what it has lost, and add to it new ornaments supplied by wealth and fashioned by genius and taste.

Wednesday night it blew a storm from the northeast and rained violently. The rain continued by turns during the following day. We set out, however, at two o'clock, and rode through Tuftonboro and Moultonboro to Center Harbor: twenty miles. The road was such that we were able to travel without inconvenience five miles an hour, and throughout most of the distance, very good. The forests are oak, etc.

The soil of Tuftonboro is alternately good and indifferent; and the surface, an interchange of rough and pleasant grounds. We saw nothing like a village. Most of the settlements appear to have been recently made.

There are several arms of the lake stretching far into this township, of which we had a succession of beautiful views.

Moultonboro is a softer, pleasanter township than Tuftonboro. The settlements have been longer made; the cultivation is better; and the inhabitants appear to be more prosperous than their neighbors.

Moultonboro includes a single congregation, at the head of which is a worthy minister. This fact, to an observer of human affairs, will easily explain the superiority of their character and their circumstances.

Rochester contained in 1790, 2,857; in 1800, 2,646; in 1810, 2,118 inhabitants. Middleton contained in 1790, 617; in 1800, 431; in 1810, 439 inhabitants. Wolfboro contained in 1790, 447; in 1800, 941; in 1810, 1,376 inhabitants. Tuftonboro contained in 1790, 109; in 1800, 357; in 1810, 709 inhabitants. Moultonboro contained in 1790, 565; in 1800, 857; in 1810, 994 inhabitants.

We reached Center Harbor in the evening, and lodged at the house of Mrs. Little. Mr. Little died the preceding spring, universally lamented as a benefactor to this part of the country.

The next morning we determined on an excursion to the summit of the Red Mountain, for the purpose of taking a complete view of the Winnipesaukee; or, as I shall henceforth call it, the *Wentworth*. Accordingly we set out on horseback at an early hour, and rode quite to the highest point. The ascent was often steep and difficult, but nowhere impracticable. When we had reached the summit, we found a prospect worth not only the trouble of the ascent, but that of our whole journey. We stood on the southeastern point of these mountains, which was posited with extreme felicity for our purpose, and commanded without obstruction a view of all the subjacent and surrounding country.

Southwestward, at the distance of seventy miles, appeared the conical summit of Monadnock, like a blue cloud in the skirt of the horizon, and looked down on every object in that part of the hemisphere. A succession of other mountains, of diversified forms and elevations, extended on either hand from this eminence till they reached and passed our parallel. Directly north of us rose the Sandwich Mountains, a magnificent range, proceeding in a northeastern direction, and terminating at the distance of thirty miles. Here a succession of finely varied summits, of the boldest figures, and wrapped in a mantle of misty azure, ascended far above all parts of the visible earth. Singly, they were in an eminent degree sublime; in their union, they broke upon the view with grandeur inexpressible.

I have already mentioned the appearance of the great Ossipee, Mount Major, Moose Mountain, and the mountain of Alton. I shall only add that they were seen from this point with an advantage so superior to what had appeared in the prospect taken by us in the preceding year as to be in a sense wholly new.

Immediately at the foot of the height on which we stood, and in the bottom of the immense valley below, spread southeastward the waters of the Wentworth in complete view, except that one or two of its arms were partially concealed by intervening peninsulas. A finer object of the same nature was perhaps never seen. The lakes which I had visited in my northern and western excursions were all of them *undivided masses,* bordered by shores comparatively straight. This was centrally a vast column, if I may be allowed the term, twenty-three miles in length, and from six to eight in breadth, shooting out with inimitable beauty a succession of arms, some of them not inferior in length to the whole breadth of the lake. These were fashioned with every elegance of figure, bordered with the most beautiful winding shores, and studded with a multitude of islands. Their relative positions also could scarcely be more happy.

Many of the islands in the lake are large, exquisitely fashioned, and arranged in a manner not less singular than pleasing. As they met the eye when surveyed from this summit, they were set in groups on both sides of the great channel, and left this vast field of water unoccupied between them. Their length was universally at right angles to that of the lake; and they appeared as if several chains of hills, originally crossing the country in that direction, had by some convulsion been merged in the water so low that no part of them was left visible except the oblong segments of their summits. Of those which by their size and situation were most conspicuous, I counted forty-five, without attempting to enumerate the smaller ones, or such as were obscured.

The points which intrude into this lake were widely different from those which were mentioned in the description of Lake George: bold, masculine bluffs, impinging directly upon the water. These in several instances were spacious peninsulas, fitted to become rich and delightful residences of man, often elevated into handsome hills and sloping gracefully into the lake.

On the west, also immediately beneath our feet, lay Squam Lake, which I shall take the liberty to call by the name of *Sullivan,* from Major General Sullivan, formerly president of this state. This sheet of water is inferior in beauty to no other; and is richly furnished with its suite of islands, points, and promontories, among the least of which was the mountain whence we gained our prospect. The separation between these lakes is formed by a narrow isthmus, capable, in the judgment of Mr. Little, of admitting a navigable communication between them at the expense of five hundred dollars. To us they appeared but one, a narrow part of which was naturally supposed to be hidden by the intervening forest.

Nothing could be more cheerful than the appearance of these fields of water, extending on both sides of the promontory where we stood between thirty and forty miles. The whole scene was made up of the most beautiful parts, and these were so arranged as to compose a finished whole. But the impression was immeasurably enhanced by the objects with which these waters were surrounded. The expansion was vast and noble. Several smaller and very beautiful lakes illumined in spots the dark ground of forests by which they were encircled. Subordinate hills and intervening valleys, with houses, enclosures, and other proofs of cultivation dispersed throughout the neighboring region, added, though in a less degree than we could have wished, a pleasing variety to the ruder scenery. As these objects receded and vanished, the distant mountains began to ascend in misty and awful grandeur, and raised an insurmountable barrier between us and the rest of the world; while to the eye of imagination, this vast array of magnificence was designed only to be the enclosure of the field of waters beneath our feet.

After we had feasted ourselves upon the prospect as long as our circumstances would permit, we descended the mountain and returned to Mrs. Little's. At three o'clock, bidding adieu to this worthy family, we resumed our journey. Passing through Holderness and Plymouth, we reached Rumney that evening. The next morning we rode to Tarleton's to dinner. In the afternoon my companions proceeded to Newbury, and thence to Bradford. My horse having become suddenly lame, I directed my course the shortest way to Orford in a rain which rendered the journey sufficiently disagreeable. The next morning, my companions rejoined me. On Monday we rode to Windsor, and on Tuesday to Walpole. Here they left me again for Keene; whilst I, passing through Westmoreland, crossed the Connecticut to Putney, and again from Brattleboro to Hinsdale, and proceeded thence to Northfield. The next day we reached Northampton; and, having parted with our Charlestown companions at Springfield, arrived at New Haven on Wednesday, the 13th of October.

I am, Sir, yours, etc.

# LETTER II

*General Remarks upon New Hampshire—Its population, soil, and agriculture—Form of government—Support of religion*

*Dear Sir,*

Permit me now to make a few general observations on New Hampshire. This state lies between 42° and 45° 11′ north latitude, and between 72°

40′ and 70° 28′ west longitude. I am, however, of opinion that, if the words of the treaty of peace which terminated the Revolutionary War were to be exactly followed, its northern point would be found not far from 45° 30′. This state is of a triangular figure, about 170 miles in length from north to south, perhaps more truly 190. At the southern extremity it is 90 miles in breadth; at the northern it comes almost to a point. Its area is 9,491 square miles, or 6,074,240 acres. On the north it abuts upon Lower Canada. On the west it is bounded by the western bank of the Connecticut, on the east by Massachusetts Bay, on the northeast by the District of Maine, and on the south by Massachusetts.

New Hampshire contains six counties.

| | Inhabitants in 1790 | Inhabitants in 1800 | Inhabitants in 1810 |
|---|---|---|---|
| Rockingham | 43,169 | 45,427 | 50,175 |
| Strafford | 23,601 | 32,614 | 41,595 |
| Hillsboro | 32,871 | 43,899 | 49,149 |
| Cheshire | 28,772 | 38,825 | 40,988 |
| Grafton | 12,590 | 20,199 | 28,462 |
| Coos | 882 | 2,692 | 3,991 |
| Total | 141,885 | 183,858 | 214,414 * |
| Increase during the first ten years | | | 41,973 |
| Increase during the second ten years | | | 30,556 |

It is difficult to distribute this state into obvious and yet accurate divisions. The country along the Connecticut until we ascend the mountains of Littleton resembles that in Massachusetts. The valley, however, is generally narrower. The next division is formed by the range of Mount Washington: the only collection of mountains in this state which, so far as I have observed, is of any great extent. The northern half, as will appear from observations heretofore made, is in the proper sense a mountainous country.

New Hampshire abounds in lakes. Umbagog, from such information as I have been able to obtain, is larger than the Wentworth; and there are several smaller ones not mentioned in these letters.

The soil is inferior to that of the other New England states, Rhode Island excepted. In many places it is rich; and, under a superior husbandry, would easily become rich in many others. Much of it is better fitted for grazing than for agriculture. The light and warm lands might easily be rendered productive by the use of gypsum. Those which border the Merrimack are extensively of this nature. The improvement of this navigation will easily and cheaply furnish the inhabitants on its borders as far up as Concord or Boscawen with this valuable manure; while, on the Connecticut, it may be conveyed to Bath. When the reluctance to alter their modes of husbandry so often and so unhappily prevalent in farmers shall have been overcome, and

* By the Census of 1820, New Hampshire contained 244,161 inhabitants. PUB.

the efficacy of gypsum shall be realized, such lands will possess a new value, and their produce be increased beyond what the proprietors could now be induced to believe.

A great multitude of neat cattle fed in the pastures of New Hampshire are annually driven to the markets on the eastern shore. To sheep a great part of the country is very well suited, and their numbers are fast increasing.

Few countries in the world are better furnished with millstreams and mill seats than New Hampshire. Manufactures are begun in various places, and ere long will be an object of primary attention to the inhabitants. Iron is already made on a large scale at Franconia.

The trade of New Hampshire is principally carried on with Boston, and to some extent with Hartford, Newburyport, Portsmouth, and Portland. Connecticut River furnishes almost one hundred miles of water conveyance to the inhabitants on the western border. The central parts are beginning to derive similar advantages from the Merrimack, aided by the Middlesex Canal. The people in the north have begun to send cattle to Quebec. In 1810 and 1811, a road from the St. Lawrence, opposite to that city, was opened to the United States near the place where the Connecticut crosses the 45th degree of north latitude. From Montreal to the same place the distance is less, but no road has hitherto been opened through the intervening wilderness. The trade of Portsmouth with the interior has hitherto fallen in a great measure into the hands of its rivals. Newburyport and Portland have engrossed a part, and Boston much more. Numerous turnpike roads have been cut from that capital in every direction, and particularly through a great part of the interior of New Hampshire. The trade from the country along the Connecticut below Bath has within a few years been turned toward Hartford, and the business done in this channel is increasing.

The agriculture of this state, particularly that in the central and eastern parts, is visibly inferior to that of their southern neighbors. The fruits requiring a warm climate either do not grow at all, or at least do not flourish. It is, however, doubtful whether sufficient efforts have been made to obtain them.

The manners of the inhabitants differ little from those of Massachusetts. The proper New England character is, I think, more evident than in Vermont. The political constitution is altogether better. The government is obviously more stable. The inhabitants discover less propensity to disorder, and men who are eagerly employed in seeking offices seem less willing to countenance it.

The government of New Hampshire is founded upon the constitution of that state established at Concord, September 5, 1792. To this constitution is prefixed a bill of rights, consisting of thirty-eight articles, and containing in substance the declarations which are found in most other American instruments of the same nature. To these are added, as you would conclude from their number, several others. In the sixth article, morality and piety, rightly grounded on evangelical principles, are declared to give the best and greatest security to government; and the legislature is accordingly empowered to authorize congregations to make adequate provision at their own expense for the maintenance of Protestant teachers of morality and religion. At the same time it is declared that no person of any particular religious denomination shall be compelled to pay toward the support of a teacher who is of a different one. It is also declared that every denomination of Christians demeaning themselves as good subjects of the state shall be equally under its protection and entitled to equal privileges, and that no sect shall ever be legally subordinated to another.

By the thirteenth article, persons conscientiously scrupulous about the lawfulness of bearing arms are exempted on condition of paying an equivalent.

In the twenty-sixth, it is declared that in all cases and at all times the military ought to be under strict subordination to and governed by the civil power.

In the twenty-seventh, it is declared that in time of peace no soldier shall be quartered in any house without the consent of the owner; nor in the time of war, but by the civil magistrate in a manner ordained by the legislature.

In the thirty-third, the magistracy is forbidden to demand excessive bail or sureties, impose excessive fines, or inflict cruel or unusual punishments.

In the nineteenth, general warrants are forbidden, and the right of the subject to be secure from all unreasonable searches and seizure of his person, houses, papers, and possessions [is established].

In the thirty-fifth, the independence of the judges of the Supreme Judicial Court, *quam diu bene se gesserint*, and honorable salaries established by standing laws are required.

In the thirty-sixth, pensions are forbidden, except in consideration of actual services; and grants for any pensions, except for more than one year at a time.

The legislature consists of a Senate and House of Representatives, chosen annually by ballot.

A representative must have been two years at least next preceding his election an inhabitant of the state; must have an estate within the district which he represents of the value of one hundred pounds, half of it freehold; must at the time of his election be an inhabitant of the place which he represents; must be of the Protestant religion; and with the ceasing of these qualifications ceases to be a representative.

Every senator and representative has a right to have his protest or dissent entered on the journal.

The Senate consists of twelve members.

Every senator must be of the Protestant religion, must possess a freehold estate of the value of two hundred pounds lying within the state, must be thirty years of age, must have been an inhabitant of the state seven years next preceding his election, and at the time an inhabitant of the district for which he is chosen.

The Senate tries impeachments made by the House of Representatives.

The governor, in addition to the qualifications of a senator, must have an estate of the value of five hundred pounds, the one half of it a freehold lying in the state.

The power of pardoning offenses, except in cases of impeachment by the House of Representatives, is in the governor and Council.

The Council is chosen in the same manner as the senators. Its duty is to advise the governor in the executive part of the government. The number of members is five.

All judicial officers hold their offices during good behavior, but may be removed by the governor and Council upon address of both houses of the legislature. Justices of the peace, however, hold their commissions but five years. Judges and sheriffs hold their offices only to the age of seventy. The legislators and magistrates are required to cherish the interests of learning and science, seminaries and public schools; and to give rewards and immunities for the promotion of agriculture, arts, sciences, commerce, trades, manufactures, and the natural history of the country. At the same time they are required to countenance and inculcate all the social virtues.

It is unnecessary to make any particular remarks on this constitution. It has its defects, but they are perhaps as few as can be found in most instruments of this nature. If it should be watchfully preserved and faithfully administered, there seems to be no reason why the inhabitants of New Hampshire may not for a long time enjoy their full share of civil freedom and happiness.

Had the constitution empowered the legislature to require, and not merely to authorize, all the inhabitants to contribute proportionally toward the maintenance of public worship, reserving at the same time the rights of conscience, it would have been happier. This truth is sufficiently illustrated by the present state of religion in New Hampshire. The existing laws on this subject are such upon the whole as to leave it extensively at loose ends.

Of all religious sects, those which owe their existence to the reluctance felt by every avaricious man to support the public worship of God are the worst in their character, and the most hopeless of reformation. Arguments to enforce the duty of opening the purse are addressed to a heart of stone and an intellect of lead. The very fact that a man has quitted on this ground a religion which he approved for one which he disapproved will make him an enemy to the former, and a zealot for the latter. Conviction and principle are here out of the question. The only inquiry, the only thought is concerning a sum of money so pitiful that the proprietor is ashamed of being even suspected of his real design. In itself it is a base fraud, and all the measures employed to carry it into execution partake of the same baseness. To preserve his pelf, the man belies his conscience and insults his Maker. To appease the one, and soothe the other, and at the same time preserve some appearance of character among his neighbors, he endeavors to make up in the show of zeal what he so evidently lacks of common honesty. Hence he becomes enthusiastic, bigoted, censorious, impervious to conviction, a wanderer after every straggling exhorter and every bewildered tenet; and thus veers from one folly and falsehood, to another, and another, throughout his life. This conduct is often challenged as a mere exercise of the rights of conscience, but conscience is equally a stranger to the conduct and the man.

The real consequence of this state of things is that disregard to moral obligation, that indifference to the Creator and his laws, to the soul and its future destiny, which is emphatically called nihilism. Men may be irreligious under a settled system of doctrines and duties; but, while life lasts, there is always a hope remaining that they may return to a better character; because there are means within their reach by which their return may possibly be accomplished. In the present case, duty to the soul, and its salvation are bartered for a sum of money, that is, for the purpose of saving a sum of money which cannot be grudged without meanness, nor mentioned without a blush.

One of the chief evils, under which New Hampshire labors is the want of union and concert in the management of public affairs. The sense of a common interest appears to be loosely felt by the inhabitants. Those in the eastern counties are apparently little connected with those in the western, and those in the middle of the state still less perhaps with either. Boston commands a great part of their trade. The efficacy of a commercial metropolis of the state, so often useful as a bond of union, is in New Hampshire almost absolutely unknown. Nor have any other means been hitherto found sufficient to unite men of influence in the different parts of the community in such a frequency of intercourse and in such a sympathy of interest as seem indispensable to the promotion of a common good. Twenty-three years have elapsed since this constitution was established, and they have not yet been able to fix upon a permanent seat of government.

In some states, and at times in those which are small, what may be called a state pride has produced that sense of a common interest which ought to be derived from an enlarged understanding and from higher motives. New Hampshire seems to be destitute even of this auxiliary. In other communities birth and education on the same ground have produced this effect. But a large part of the people of New Hampshire are, or lately were, immigrants from other states. Time, however, will remove the evils flowing from this source. If the public functionaries and other men of influence could be induced to unite in promoting with zeal and expansive views the public and private education of their countrymen, a superior agriculture, and such arts and manufactures as are suited to the circumstances of the country; could they harmonize in a wise and public-spirited system of government in defiance of party; could they with a single voice befriend the progress of religion, New Hampshire would ere long realize a higher reputation and more ample prosperity than the most sanguine of its citizens have hitherto expected.

I am, Sir, yours, etc.

# JOURNEY TO UTICA

*Description of the Catskill Mountains—Extensive prospect from the summit—Journey to Utica—Hamilton College—Cavities worn by the Mohawk in the rocks at Little Falls—Return*

*Dear Sir,*

On the 20th September, 1815, in company with Mr. D. I set out upon an excursion to the western parts of the state of New York. At Litchfield I was detained until the 26th by the violent equinoctial storm which ravaged in an unprecedented manner a considerable part of the eastern and southern coast of New England. On the 26th, I proceeded to Sheffield, and on the next day to Catskill, and found it not a little improved in the number and value of its buildings, and in the good order, morals, and religion of its inhabitants.

On the 28th, in company with several gentlemen of that village, I ascended the Catskill Mountains. The turnpike road, made some years since over these heights from Catskill to Windham, enabled us to gain the summit without any other difficulty except what arises from their great elevation. Wagons, and at times even chaises, though it must be confessed with many a hard struggle, climb this ascent. We gained it partly on horseback and partly on foot. On a height more than two thousand feet above the common surface, we found two lakes: the northern, dull and dreary, disfigured by a variety of gloomy aquatic plants, and encircled by a dismal border of swamp shrubbery; the southern, clean, handsome, and surrounded by a neat shore. Both together are about a mile in length. A brook issuing from the former discharges its waters into the latter. Across this stream lay our road. Soon after, we entered the forest on the south; and, after penetrating it about a mile, came to a scene which amply repaid us for our toil. On the rear of the great ridge stretched out before us two spurs of a vast height. Between them sunk a ravine, extending several miles in length, and in different places from a thousand to fifteen hundred feet in depth. The mountains on either side were steep, wild, and shaggy, covered almost everywhere with a dark forest, the lofty trees of which approached nearer and nearer to each other as the eye wandered toward the bottom. In some places their branches became united; in others, separated by a small distance, they left a line of absolute darkness, resembling in its dimensions a winding rivulet, here somewhat wider, there narrower, and appearing as if it were a solitary bypath to the nether world. All beneath seemed to be midnight, although the day was uncommonly bright and beautiful; and all above a dreary solitude, secluded from the world, and destined never to be wandered over by the feet of man. At the head of this valley stood a precipice, here descending perpendicularly, there overhanging with a stupendous and awful grandeur. Over a bed of stone beside our feet ran a millstream, which discharged the waters of the lakes, and from the brow of the precipice rushed in a perpendicular torrent perfectly white and glittering nearly three hundred feet in length. This magnificent current, after dashing upon a shelf, falls over a second precipice of one hundred feet, when it vanishes in the midnight beneath, and rolls over a succession of precipices until it finally escapes from the mountains and empties its waters into the river Catskill. A cloud of vapor, raised by the dashing of this stream on the successive shelves in its bed, rises above the forests which shroud the bottom of the valley, and winds beautifully away from the sight until it finally vanishes in the bewildered course of this immense chasm. On the bosom of this elegant volume of mist appears to the eye placed in a proper position a succession of rainbows, floating slowly and gracefully down the valley, and reluctantly yielding their place to others by which they are continually followed. No contrast can be more perfect than that of these circles of light to the rude scenery by which they are environed; and no object of this nature which I have seen awakens emotions of such grandeur as are here excited, except the falls of Niagara.

On the brow of this precipice we regaled ourselves with an excellent dinner, and then proceeded to the eastern front of the mountains. From a height of three thousand feet we beheld a part of the counties of Albany, Greene, Ulster, and Orange on the west side of the Hudson; a part of the county of Putnam, and the whole of Dutchess, Columbia, and Rensselaer on the east; together with a part of Berkshire in Massachusetts, and Litchfield in Connecticut, lying in full view beneath us. The whole area was more than one hundred miles in length, and not far from fifty in breadth. This vast field was chiefly formed by the great valley of the Hudson lying north of the Highlands. A more distinct and perfect view of a landscape cannot be imagined. On the western side, it is forested to a much greater extent than I had been prepared to expect: a fact owing, as I was told, to the reluctance with which the Dutch farmers consent to any alteration in the state of their possessions. On the eastern side, the counties of Dutchess, Columbia, and Rensselaer, everywhere settled and cultivated, were beautifully spotted with an alternation of farms and groves, diffused over the whole surface in such a manner that there seemed to be scarcely room left for a single additional farmer. At the bottom of this valley, the Hudson stretched in clear view over a length of fifty miles, and even here maintained the appearance of a magnificent river. On its waters were moving in various directions a multitude of vessels in the form of dim white spots. One of these with a telescope we discovered to be the steamboat, making a rapid progress under the shore of Rhinebeck. In this great field, a series of towns and villages met the eye, among which the town of Catskill and the city of Hudson, almost under us, were particularly conspicuous.

The eastern prospect was chiefly limited by the Taconic Range, in which the Taconic and Saddle Mountains ascended with great magnificence. In various places, summits in the range of the Green Mountains were visible.

On the west, nothing was seen but the heights and forests in the neighborhood.

The base of these mountains, so far as we had opportunity to observe it, is formed of brown argillaceous slate resting upon sandstone. This, at high elevations, is surmounted by a vast body of sandstone. The structure of these mountains as far westward as Meredith and not improbably much farther is the same, all the spurs, so far as I was able to obtain information, having the same character.

On the height whence we took our prospect, we found whortleberries in abundance and in perfection. Some of them were green, and very few which we saw indicated any decay. We ate of them freely, and found them very fine. The date of this excursion was about two months later than the time of their perfection at New Haven. On Friday, 1st of October, 1813, I found them in perfection on the Red Mountains at the head of Lake Wentworth in New Hampshire. This fact, in both instances, is a proof of the coolness of the atmosphere in the places where the fruit was found. Allowance is however to be made for the superior latitude of the Red Mountains in the one case, and for the superior elevation of the Catskill Mountains in the other.

We descended from these heights a little before sunset; and, after a disagreeable delay occasioned by breaking through a bridge where we had well nigh lost our horses, we reached Catskill a little after ten in the evening.

On Friday, I proceeded along the Susquehanna turnpike, through the townships formerly mentioned, and reached Meredith. On Monday, I left Meredith and proceeded to Easton, a township lately incorporated from the eastern side of Oxford. On Tuesday, October 3rd, I passed through Oxford and Norwich to Sherburne; and on Wednesday, through Madison and Sangerfield to Clinton, where I lodged with the Rev. Dr. Backus, president of Hamilton College.

On Thursday, in company with Dr. Backus, I visited Jesse Deane, Esq., an inhabitant of Westmoreland, who, in the most obliging manner, communicated to me much valuable information concerning the Iroquois.[1] On Friday, I proceeded to Utica, where I continued till Monday morning.

The road from Catskill to Oxford, I found generally bad, as having been long neglected. The first twenty miles were tolerable, the last twenty absolutely intolerable.

Catskill has become a considerable town, containing many valuable houses and stores, a courthouse and Presbyterian church, both new and handsome. Its moral aspect is also materially changed. Religion has spread, and is still spreading, extensively over this settlement. A Bible Society for the county of Greene was formed here on the day of my arrival, with a zeal and liberality very honorable to the gentlemen concerned.

Cairo, formerly Canton, which was little more than a wilderness in 1804, is now become a promising settlement, adorned with a neat village, surrounding a Presbyterian church of the same character.

New Durham is completely settled, all the farms being occupied and cultivated. Of this fine tract I had a delightful view from the ridge of the Catskill Mountains, lying on the west, and formerly mentioned in these letters. It wore the aspect of a country long inhabited, and with its fine surface, rich farms, and high groves exhibited a very beautiful landscape.

The valley beyond this ridge, which in 1804 was an almost absolute solitude, was now parceled out into farms and set with human habitations. A handsome bridge of one arch has been erected over the Schoharie.

In Blenheim, Jefferson, and Stamford, the alterations, though considerable, were not very striking. Stamford, however, contains a thriving village named Waterville, lying south of the road at the distance of five or six miles.

Harpersfield is completely occupied, and wears the appearance of an old settlement.

Kortright has increased its population, but has an unpromising aspect, and struck my eye as less pleasant than formerly.

Meredith is settled to a considerable extent, and shows the beauty of its surface with increased advantage.

The population of both Franklin and Sidney has considerably increased, and, in the former place, religion has extensively prevailed.

Unadilla is becoming a very pretty village. It is built on a delightful ground along the Susquehanna, and the number of houses, particularly of good ones, has much increased. A part of the country between this and Oxford is cultivated; a considerable part is still a wilderness. The country is rough and of a high elevation.

Oxford is a beautiful town, charmingly situated in the valley of the Chenango.

Norwich, the shire town of this county, is still more pleasantly posited. This village, which has chiefly come into existence since the year 1804, is built near the foot of a fine range of hills on the west, upon a slope declining to the river near a mile, with an uniform descent, and with an ease and elegance nowhere excelled. The village itself is handsome, and the scenery beautiful.

Sherburne and Hamilton are also handsome villages on the eastern branch of the Chenango, situated on a fine soil and in a region where everything appears to flourish. Indeed the valley of this river appeared to me even more desirable than when I passed through it in 1804.

Madison is on rougher ground, but has a rich soil, as has Sangerfield also, with a smoother and pleasanter surface. In the three last of these towns there are neat churches.

The surface of Clinton is beautiful, and the soil of the highest fertility. The inhabitants are industrious, sober, orderly, and prosperous. This parish and indeed the whole township of Paris is completely settled.

Hamilton College, although its charter is in several respects imperfect, is in a flourishing condition. The number of students, the present year, will not be far from one hundred. Two professorships are filled in it, and at least two others will soon be established. The system of government and instruction pursued in it is in substance the same with that of Yale College. Two collegiate buildings are already erected on a healthy eminence commanding a noble prospect. The new one is handsome, and built of stone covered with cement. A third will soon be erected of the same form and structure. The kitchen and dining room are better contrived than any which I have seen.

Utica is become a considerable town, containing more than three thousand inhabitants, engaged in an extensive and profitable commerce; and not far from four hundred houses, many of them valuable, and several of them elegant structures. A considerable number of the stores in this town are inferior in size and beauty to few in the state.

Religion has of late prevailed extensively in Utica, especially in families of the first consideration, and has had a happy influence on the manners of the inhabitants at large.

Monday, October 7th, I left Utica, and rode to the Little Falls on the eastern limit of Herkimer. On this and the four preceding days it rained copiously. The path was liquid mud, glassy, often deep, and not without danger. In 1804, most of the country throughout this distance was a forest. It was now universally settled, and the inhabitants appear to be in prosperous circumstances.

Herkimer is become a handsome town. There is a considerable village at the Little Falls. At this spot commences, in the language of the inhabitants, the western country of New York.

From Catskill round to Utica I found the stones extensively consisting of marine shells, some of them mere masses of such shells cemented together, most of them mineralized. Others are limestone; and others still, slate with greater or less collections of shells imbedded in them. Such are the facts at Claverack, Hudson, Catskill, in several branches of the Catskill Mountains, at Meredith, Norwich, Sherburne, Hamilton, Madison, Sangerfield, and Clinton. Such also are the facts at Cherry Valley, and in a spot about eight miles beyond the Genesee River on the great road. These shells were chiefly scallops and periwinkles. Oyster shells were rare so far as I had opportunity to observe them in this excursion.

Granite I observed in the western parts of the township of Herkimer, and it continued to appear as far as Schenectady. The base of the lower

Anthony's Nose is granite, while the higher regions are compact limestone. There are two mountains of this name in the neighborhood of each other.

The rocks at the Little Falls are gneiss, extremely hard. Tuesday morning, I went out to examine them, and was astonished to see the cavities formerly worn by the Mohawk. Several of them were more than one hundred feet above the level of its present surface. The largest which I saw was at least fifteen feet in diameter, and about eight in depth. From these dimensions they diminished by imperceptible gradations down to two feet. One of them, about a mile from the center of the settlement, as we were informed by our host, is fifteen feet in depth, but not more than five or six in diameter.

The number of these cavities is very great and very difficult to be ascertained, for they are spread over an extended surface, by the variation of which they are concealed from the eye of an observer who does not examine them with very minute inspection. To such an observer it scarcely seems credible that the only known causes should have been sufficiently efficacious to produce the extraordinary phenomena which he sees to have been produced. The rock is one of the hardest which is known. The river is not more than one third of the size of the Connecticut at Bellows Falls. Yet the largest of these cavities is five or six times more capacious than any at that place. Almost all the latter also are small, while many of the former are very large.

I have observed that the most elevated of these cavities is more than one hundred feet above the present level of the Mohawk. Here we are furnished with decisive proof that the river at some former period ran on this elevation. An inspection of this place will satisfy any attentive observer that the water once ran many feet still higher, since the rocks exhibit the fullest evidence of having been long washed by the current. Of course the waters of the Mohawk found a barrier at the Little Falls, more than one hundred feet in height, and were therefore certainly a lake extending far back into the interior. In one case then, we are furnished with demonstration, so far as reasoning from facts may be called such, that the waters of a river which has now washed away its barrier were anciently confined by the jutting of mountains so as to constitute a large lake, agreeably to the scheme mentioned in the account given of my second journey to Lake George. Fair analogy will convince an observing traveler that there were once lakes of the same class in all the places which I have specified, and in many others.

Here I had an opportunity of seeing again the mongrel cedar, and found, by a more thorough examination than I was able formerly to make, that this tree loses its leaves every autumn in the manner formerly suggested in these letters. The process is this: at little distances over the whole tree small twigs, the product of the existing or perhaps the preceding year, die together with their leaves. These, though differing somewhat in their size, may be considered generally as exhibiting a surface equal to that of a man's hand; and, being everywhere alternated with living twigs, and of a reddish brown approaching near to a pink, seem at a small distance not unlike roses. To botanists the plant may be familiar; to me it is new.

This is a very interesting and romantic spot. The scenery is wild and magnificent, and forms a fine contrast to the elegant intervals which border the Mohawk both above and below.

Tuesday, I proceeded to Palatine; the road, less wet, but at least as deep and dangerous as on the preceding day. The next day I reached Albany, with a road generally bad, but materially better than I had seen since I left Utica.

The intervals on both sides of the Mohawk are with scarcely an exception universally cleared, and have the appearance of complete cultivation. They are remarkably handsome grounds. The hills on both sides also are in many places in the same state; in many others they are partially cleared, and to a considerable extent are still covered with forests. Several of them are handsomer grounds than I supposed in my former journeys.

The village of Caughnawaga is considerably increased and improved in its appearance. Several hamlets are begun at different places, and several churches are erected. Many of the houses all along the road are good buildings.

Two new colleges are built at Schenectady on the ground mentioned in the former part of these letters. I saw them at a distance only, and thought them handsome buildings.

Albany is rapidly improving. Its population and the number of its buildings have greatly increased during the last four years. The new buildings are generally handsome. Among them is a large and elegant church of stone with a handsome steeple, built in Chapel Street by a new Presbyterian congregation. This is one out of many instances of enterprise and public spirit manifested by the inhabitants. Another is the establishment of an academy on a broad foundation, with the design of furnishing every degree of education short of that which is obtained at colleges. The corporation of the city, which is rich, liberally lend their aid to every useful public object, in a manner which is highly honorable to the character of its members. Both the morals and the manners of its inhabitants are also not a little improved.

On Monday, I left Albany; and, on the following Thursday, reached New Haven.

Four miles west of Albany, I was thrown out of my sulky by the fall of my horse; but, although in imminent danger, escaped with very little injury. I mention this, I hope, with some degree of gratitude to that good Providence which, through excursions amounting to but little less than eighteen thousand miles, has permitted no other accident to befall me or my companions.

I am, etc.

# THE IROQUOIS

## LETTER I

*Authorities consulted in the following account of the Iroquois—Their form of government—Their story relative to the creation of man—Their mythology as related by the Oneidas*

*Dear Sir,*

It would be a gross departure from the plan which I formerly pursued in giving an account of New England should I neglect to make some observations concerning the aboriginal inhabitants of the state of New York. All these, except the Iroquois, were in my view unquestionably Mahicans, and were called by the early Dutch colonists *Mohikanders*. From the rest of the tribes of that great nation to which they belonged, they differed as little in their language, customs and character as those tribes from each other. The Iroquois were an entirely different people, speaking a radically different language, and having in many other respects a materially different character.

A complete account of these people has never been given to the public, and probably was never within the reach of civilized men. Now at least it is beyond their power. Still, there are several valuable sketches both of their character and history which have been written by men of curiosity and intelligence. The late Dr. Colden, lieutenant governor of the province of New York, published a work which he entitled a "History of the Five Indian Nations of Canada which are dependent on the Province of New York in America." [1] The principal design of it was to awaken the attention of the British nation on both sides of the Atlantic to the situation and character of this people, and to the importance of cultivating their friendship, securing their trade, and engaging their efforts in favor of the British colonies. With a degree of wisdom, and let me add of integrity also, not very often found in political philosophers, he has founded all his opinions on facts; and, after giving us a short sketch of their customs and character, has recited such parts of their history as could be well authenticated. The important parts of their character and policy he has exhibited to us also in a numerous succession of speeches made on various occasions. In these, besides the accounts which they give of various parts of their history, we have their own views concerning a variety of their customs, rights, character, interests, and policy. Nothing can be more characteristical than these speeches; and, so far as they go, nothing can explain to us so well what these nations were—I say, *were,* for their character has undergone a very important change. Their heroism, their greatness, and their independence exist only in the tales of other times. To Dr. Colden more than to all other men are we indebted for our knowledge of what these nations *have been.*

The Hon. William Smith, an eminent lawyer in New York and afterwards chief justice of the province of Canada, published a valuable history of his native province.[2] In this work he has given a detailed account of the character and actions of these tribes, derived, however, in its most material parts from the work of Dr. Colden.

The Hon. De Witt Clinton, in a discourse delivered before the New York Historical Society at their anniversary meeting, December 6, 1811, has given the public a very able and comprehensive account of these nations.[3] In this account, the most complete which is extant, the author has probably assembled all the facts which have been heretofore published concerning the Iroquois, and has added to them a considerable number which he has collected from living testimony. To these writers permit me to refer you for more minute information than it would be proper for me to detail in these letters. At your pleasure you can add those of Charlevoix, Lahontan, Father Hennepin, and others.[4]

I have for many years taken pains to become acquainted with the history, character, and manners of the Iroquois. For this purpose I early applied to the late Rev. Dr. Edwards, president of Union College, to his brother, the Hon. Timothy Edwards, of Stockbridge, and to the Rev. Mr. Kirkland, then a missionary to the Oneidas. In September and October 1815, I made a journey to Westmoreland in the county of Oneida in order to obtain information on this subject from Jesse Deane, Esq., a respectable magistrate living in that township. This gentleman was sent by his parents into the country of these persons for the purpose of learning their language. Probably no white man is now, or ever was, equally versed in it, or acquainted with the character of the people by whom it is spoken, so far as that character has existed since the period when he undertook this mission. Mr. Deane very cheerfully gave me the information which I requested, and also furnished me with a manuscript account which he had written of their mythology as reported to him by themselves. In the following observations, I shall interweave such information received from these gentlemen as in my own opinion may contribute to illustrate their character.

The Iroquois were a confederated republic, consisting originally of five nations: the *Mohawks,* the *Oneidas,* the *Onondagas,* the *Cayugas,* and the *Senecas.* To these were added in the year 1722 the *Tuscaroras.* This tribe originally inhabited part of North Carolina; and, from similarity of language, were justly pronounced by the other five to be a branch of the same original stem. At their request, therefore, they were adopted into the confederacy. Before this event they were called by the English *the Five Nations;* and after it, *the Six Nations;* and not unfrequently, *the Mohawks,* from the principal tribe: that most probably by which the confederation was proposed and established. By the French they were styled *the Iroquois;* by themselves, *the Mingwe, the Aganuschione* or United People, and *Onquehonwe,* or "men surpassing all others." *

The Iroquois were not among the original inhabitants of this part of North America. Dr. Edwards informed me that the Mahicans universally considered themselves as the original inhabitants, and styled the Iroquois interlopers. He also added that the Iroquois themselves admitted this fact, and gloried in it, asserting that they had fought their way to their present possessions, and acquired their country by conquering all who had resisted them.

That this united declaration is just is amply supported by facts. The Mahicans were spread from the neighborhood of the Pacific Ocean to the eastern shore of New England, and remains of this nation are now to be found in small tribes dispersed over a great part of North America. This is proved unanswerably by their language. The Iroquois were planted in the midst of this widely extended nation, and appear to have had no other connection with them than what is involved in wars, conquests, and treaties, and nothing in common with them besides the savage character and its universal appendages. At the same time, they were almost invariably at war with some or other of the Mahican tribes. With this spirit and its necessary consequences, it is impossible that they should have made their way through the western branches of the Mahicans, or in other words, of enemies dispersed over a territory of near three thousand miles in extent, in any other manner than by conquest.

This, however, is far from being their own account of their origin.

From Mr. Kirkland I received the following story, formally delivered to him, as he told me, in a solemn assembly of the Oneida sachems and some others of their principal people.

Before man existed, there were three great and good spirits, of whom one was superior to the other two, and is emphatically called the Great Spirit and the Good Spirit. At a certain time this exalted being said to one of the others, "Make a man." He obeyed, and taking chalk formed a paste of it, and molding it into the human shape infused into it the animating principle, and brought it to the Great Spirit. He, after surveying it, said, "This is too white."

He then directed the other to make a trial of his skill. Accordingly taking charcoal, he pursued the same process, and brought the result to the Great Spirit, who, after surveying it, said, "It is too black."

* Colden. [Cadwallader Colden, *History of the Five Indian Nations of Canada* (3rd ed., London, 1755), I, 3.]

Then said the Great Spirit, "I will now try myself"; and taking red earth he formed a human being in the same manner, surveyed it, and said, "This is a proper (or perfect) man." These three, as you will naturally anticipate, were the original ancestors of all the white, black, and red men of our race.

It is hardly necessary to observe that the Iroquois, who had no knowledge of white men until the arrival of the European colonists, nor of a black man until many years afterwards, made this story in order to explain the origin of these different classes of men, and that it is of rather a philosophical than of an historical nature. Nor can it be denied that the philosophy is as rational as that of most other theorists. Still it is possible that it may be partially made up of traditionary history, and may in the same manner exhibit to us what were the original apprehensions of these people concerning the creation of man. The word "Adam" seems originally to have signified red earth.

The Iroquois, like the Hindus, made the earth ultimately rest upon the back of the turtle.

The account given by the Oneidas to Mr. Deane of their mythology is widely different from that which has been recited. It is truly *Indian* in all its parts. I will give you the substance of it, taking the liberty to abridge it in several places where the facts recorded are of minor importance, and would contribute little or nothing toward the elucidation of the scheme.

An unlimited expanse of water once filled the space now occupied by the world which we inhabit. Here was the abode of total darkness, which no ray of light had ever penetrated. At this time the human family dwelt in a country situated in the upper regions of the air, abounding in everything conducive to the comfort and convenience of life. The forests were full of game; the lakes and streams swarmed with fish and fowl, while the ground and fields spontaneously produced a constant profusion of vegetables for the use of man. An unclouded sun enlivened their days, and storms and tempests were unknown in that happy region. The inhabitants were strangers to death and its harbingers, pain and disease; while their minds were free from the corroding passions of jealousy, hatred, malice, and revenge, so that their state was made perfectly happy.

At length, however, an event occurred which interrupted their tranquillity, and introduced care and anxiety until then unknown. A certain youth was noticed to withdraw himself from the circle of their social amusements. The solitary recesses of the grove became his favorite walks. Care and chagrin were depicted in his countenance, and his body from long abstinence presented to the view of his friends the mere skeleton of a man. Anxious solicitude in vain explored the cause of his grief, until at length, debilitated both in body and mind, he yielded to the importunity of his associates, and promised to disclose the cause of his trouble, on condition that they would dig up by the roots a certain white pine tree, lay him on his blanket by the margin of the hole, and seat his wife by his side. In a moment all hands were ready. The fatal tree was taken up by the roots, in doing which the earth was perforated, and a passage opened into the abyss below. The blanket was spread by the hole, the youth laid thereon, and his wife then in a state of pregnancy took her seat by his side. The multitude, eager to learn the cause of such strange and unusual conduct, pressed around; when on a sudden, to their horror and astonishment, he seized upon the woman and precipitated her headlong into the regions of darkness below; then, rising from the ground, he informed the assembly that he had for some time suspected the chastity of his wife, and that, having now disposed of the cause of his trouble, he should soon recover his usual health and vivacity.

All those amphibious animals which now inhabit this world then roamed through the watery waste to which this woman in her fall was hastening. The loon first discovered her coming, and called a council in haste to prepare for her reception, observing that the animal which approached was a human being, and that earth was indispensably necessary for its accommodation. The first subject of deliberation was who should support the burden. The sea bear first presented himself for a trial of his strength. Instantly the other animals gathered round and scrambled up upon his back, while the bear unable to support the weight sunk beneath the surface of the water, and was by the whole assembly judged unequal to the task of supporting the earth. Several others in succession presented themselves as candidates for the honor, with similar success. Last of all the turtle modestly advanced, tendering his broad shell as the basis of the earth now about to be formed. The beasts then made trial of his strength to bear, heaping themselves upon his back; and, finding their united pressure unable to sink him below the surface, adjudged to him the honor of supporting the world.

A foundation being thus provided, the next subject of deliberation was how to procure earth. It was concluded that it must be obtained from the bottom of the sea. Several of the most expert divers went in quest of it, and uniformly floated up dead to the surface of the water. The mink at length undertook the dangerous plunge; and, after a long absence, arose dead. On a critical examination a small quantity of earth was discovered in one of his claws, which he had scratched from the bottom. This being carefully preserved was placed on the back of the turtle.

In the meantime the woman continued falling, and at length alighted on the turtle. The earth had already grown to the size of a man's foot, where she stood with one foot covering the other. Shortly she had room for both feet, and was soon able to sit down. The earth continued to expand and soon formed a small island, skirted with willow and other aquatic shrubbery; and at length stretched out into a widely extended plain, interspersed with rivers and smaller streams, which with gentle currents moved forward their tributary waters to the ocean. She repaired to the seashore, erected a habitation, and settled in her new abode.

Not long after, she was delivered of a daughter, and was supported by the spontaneous productions of the earth until the child arrived to adult years. She was then solicited in marriage by several animals changed into the forms of young men, but they were rejected successively by the mother, until the turtle offered himself as a suitor and was received. After she had laid herself down to sleep, the turtle placed two arrows on her body in the form of a cross, one headed with flint, the other with the rough bark of a tree. In due time she was delivered of two sons, but died in childbirth.

The grandmother, enraged at her daughter's death, resolved to destroy them; and, taking them both in her arms, threw them both into the sea. Scarcely had she reached her wigwam when the children overtook her at the door. The experiment was several times repeated, but in vain. Discouraged by this ill success, she concluded to let them live. Then dividing the corpse of her daughter into two parts, she threw them up toward the heavens, where one became the moon, and the other the sun. Then began the succession of day and night in our world.

The children speedily became men and expert archers. The elder, whose name was *Thauwiskalau* [Tawiskaron], had the arrow of the turtle which was pointed with the flint, and killed with it the largest beasts of the forest. The younger, whose name was *Taulonghyauwaugoon* [Teharonhiawagon], had the arrow headed with bark. The former was by his malignant disposition and his skill and success in hunting a favorite with his grandmother. They lived in the midst of plenty, but would not permit the younger brother, whose arrow was insufficient to destroy anything larger than birds, to share in their abundance.

As this young man was wandering one day along the shore, he saw a bird perched upon a bough projecting over the water. He attempted to kill it; but his arrow, till that time unerring, flew wide of the mark and sunk in the sea. He determined to recover it; and, swimming to the spot where it fell, plunged to the bottom. Here to his astonishment, he found himself in a small cottage. A venerable old man who was sitting in it received him with a smile of paternal complacency, and thus addressed him: "My son, I welcome you to the habitation of your father. To obtain this interview, I directed all the circumstances which have conspired to bring you hither. Here is your arrow, and here is an ear of corn, which you will find pleasant and wholesome food. I have watched the unkindness of both your grandmother and your brother. His disposition is malignant and cruel. While he lives, the world can never be peopled. You must therefore take his life. When you return home, you must traverse the whole earth, collect all the flints which you find into heaps, and hang up all the buckhorns. These are the only things of which your brother is afraid, or which can make any impression on his body, which is made of flint. They will furnish you with weapons always at hand, wherever he may direct his course."

Having received these and other instructions from his father, the young man took his leave; and, returning again to the world, began immediately to obey his father's directions.

After a series of adventures, which it is unnecessary here to repeat, the two brothers began a quarrel, in which the elder endeavored to destroy the younger, but failing of his purpose, was attacked in his turn. As he fled, the earth trembled. A verdant plain, bounded by the distant ocean, lay before him. Behind him the ground sunk in deep valleys and frightful chasms, or rose into lofty mountains and stupendous precipices. The streams ceased to roll in silence and, bursting their barriers, poured down the cliffs in cataracts, or foamed through their rocky channels toward the ocean.

The younger brother followed the fugitive with a vigorous step, and wounded him continually with his weapons. At length, in a far distant region beyond the savannas in the southwest, he breathed his last, and loaded the earth with his flinty form.†

The great enemy to the race of the turtle being destroyed, they came up out of the ground in the human form, and for some time multiplied in peace, and spread extensively over its surface.

The grandmother, roused to furious resentment for the loss of her darling son, resolved to be avenged. For many days successively she caused the rain to descend from the clouds in torrents, until the whole surface of the earth, and even the highest mountains were covered. The inhabitants fled to their canoes and escaped the impending destruction. The disappointed grandmother then caused the rains to cease and the waters to subside. The inhabitants returned to their former dwellings. She then determined to effect her purpose in another manner, and covered the earth with a deluge of snow. To escape this new evil they betook themselves to their snowshoes, and thus eluded her vengeance. Chagrined at length by these disap-

† Supposed to intend the lofty range, now called the "Rocky Mountains."

pointments, she gave up the hope of destroying the whole human race at once; and determined to wreak her revenge upon them in a manner, which, though less violent, should be more efficacious. Accordingly she has ever since been employed in gratifying her malignant disposition by inflicting upon mankind all the various evils which are suffered in the present world. *Teharonhiawagon,*‡ on the other hand, displays the infinite benevolence of his nature by bestowing on the human race the blessings which they enjoy, all of which flow from his bountiful providence.

This wonderful story also, you will perceive, is chiefly philosophical, and certainly approaches much nearer to the extravagance of the Hindu philosophy than to the more chastened spirit of the Greeks. It is however far behind the excessive excursions of the Hindu tales.

The Iroquois, and probably all the other Indians, attributed in their superstition, not only intelligence, but sanctity to at least many kinds of animals, probably to all. This also was the general apprehension of the Hindus, and, if I mistake not, of many other Asiatic nations, as it was also of the Egyptians. The sanctity of serpents, a doctrine remarkably prevalent among the North American Indians, was, as you know, a favorite scheme throughout the whole polytheistical world; and images of these animals were formed in great numbers both within and without the temples dedicated to idol worship.

The Iroquois professed to be descended from the turtle, the bear, and the wolf. This descent, however, was not reckoned from these beings as mere animals, but as intelligences endued with a portion of the divine, or at least a superior nature. The divinity ascribed by the Hindus to the cow, they attributed to the turtle pre-eminently, to the bear, the wolf, the snake, and many other animals.§ Nor is there anything more absurd in this than in the story of Jupiter's adventure with Europa, the birth of Alexander the Great, as announced by himself, or a multitude of other recitals presented to us in the Greek and Roman fable.

The Iroquois, as I have just observed, claimed their descent from the turtle, the bear, and the wolf. Possibly in a less rude state of society, they bore images of these animals on their standards; and the memory of this fact may have descended to us in this distorted fable. Of these ancestors, the turtle was deemed the most honorable. A method therefore must be devised for deriving their genealogy from this dignified source. With this scheme were obviously connected the dogmas of their religion, just as other nations have united their own with the origin of nations. The task in this place was certainly a difficult one, but the performance of it was indispensable. Some man among them, distinguished for wisdom and authority, was probably

‡ *Teharonhiawagon,* literally translated, is the "*Holder* or *Supporter of the Heavens.*" This is the being who in Indian speeches, by a corrupt translation, is called the Great Spirit or Good Spirit.

§ See a very curious account of the reverence and affection entertained for the bear by the Chippewas in "Henry's Travels in Upper Canada." [Chapter 17, "A Bear Hunt."]

induced to undertake it, and made up the mass out of the creed and traditionary tales of the nation. What these would not supply, he furnished from his own fancy.

It is not a mere effort of the imagination to find, even in this monstrous mixture, some remains of real history. The story of the chaos, and the darkness by which it was covered; of paradise, and the happiness with which it was replenished, is not ill told at the beginning of this narrative if we suppose an Indian to be the narrator. The existence of the Deluge is distinctly marked, and the deliverance of the human race from its devastation. A few other facts may also be distantly discerned by a critical examiner.

I will only add that the Oneidas pretend even now to point out the place where their ancestors emerged from the ground; and that they themselves at the present time assign a very different reason why they denominate different bodies of their tribe the clans of the turtle, bear, and wolf: viz., that, when they first emerged from the ground, they were a collection of savage, beastlike beings, and assumed these appellations, therefore, to exhibit their own views of their original character. You cannot but perceive, however, that this explanation is a complete contradiction to the whole spirit of this story, and to all that pride which is the predominant attribute of our nature in general, especially as it exists in savages. It is, therefore, only an attempt of Indian philosophy to explain what to them seemed otherwise inexplicable.

Mr. Deane informed me that the mythology of the Oneidas, that which has been here recited, is with some variation of circumstances the mythology of all the Six Nations.

I am, Sir, yours, etc.

# LETTER II

*Government of the Iroquois—Sachems—Customs and laws of the nation*

*Dear Sir,*

The government of each tribe of the Iroquois is lodged in the council of that tribe, consisting especially of the men whose years, exploits, wisdom, and eloquence have given them peculiar weight in the eyes of their brethren. Ordinarily this council regulated by their decisions the internal affairs of the tribe. But if the warriors refused to be governed by their determinations, the council had no coercive power to constrain obedience; and the matter in question took its own course.

In difficult cases, however, although the warriors refused to be governed by the decisions of their councilors, yet there was a remedy. The sachems requested the women of principal reputation to assemble in a council by themselves, and to advise the warriors to desist from such enterprises as they were preparing to undertake against the advice of the men. If the women opposed the enterprise, the warriors always gave it up, because the opposition of such a female council to any public undertaking was regarded as a bad omen.*

The sachems had no coercive power.

The sachemdom was hereditary, but the descent was always on the female side only. The son of a daughter, whenever there was one, succeeded to the title.

Influence in the tribe was always that of merit: the man of the greatest talents and efficiency being the most powerful man, whatever might be the family from which he derived his origin.

Hunting, fighting, eloquence, and prudence in council were the only means of personal consequence; and a descendant of the sachem blood has rarely been a man of much importance. In these respects the customs of the Iroquois differed entirely from those of the Mahicans, among whom the descent was reckoned on both sides, and the sachem as such had commonly more influence than any other man.

The daughters of sachems married plebeians without any hindrance or disgrace, and a young hunter of reputation was always regarded as a proper match for any woman.

Women in various instances have been no less distinguished for eloquence than men.

Witches and wizards were condemned by a public council, and were then publicly knocked on the head. After their execution they were sometimes burnt, and at other times buried. These were the only criminals who were publicly punished, nor were any other persons publicly tried.

Murderers were put to death by the avenger of blood, usually a near relation of the deceased.

* "Our ancestors considered it as a great offense to reject the counsels of their women, particularly of the female governesses. They were esteemed mistresses of the soil. Who, said our forefathers, bring us into being; who cultivate our lands, kindle our fires, and boil our pots, but the women?

"They intreat that the veneration of their ancestors in favor of women be not disregarded, and that they may not be despised. The Great Spirit is their maker.

"The female governesses beg leave to speak with that freedom allowed to women, and agreeably to the spirit of our ancestors. They entreat the great chief to put forth his strength, and preserve them in peace, for they are the life of the nation." *Discourse of the Hon. Mr. Clinton—App. No. 3, P.* 80, 81. [De Witt Clinton, *A Discourse Delivered before the New-York Historical Society . . . ,* in the New York Historical Society *Collections,* 2 (1814), 115.]

Incontinence and theft were never punished, yet they were not characteristically lewd.

Marriages were often contracted for children by their parents, but the intended husband might refuse to take the intended wife without any disgrace.

The age at which young men usually married was about twenty-eight.

Ordinarily they do not appear to have been much affected by the passion of love.

The husband usually built the wigwam and provided meat for the family. The wife furnished the vegetable food. The wife made baskets, and the husband the other domestic utensils. The men made also their canoes and weapons.

The men oppressed the women by forcing them to labor and to carry burdens.

Labor was despised by the men.

The separation of a married pair was not esteemed disgraceful, either to themselves or their children, if they had before openly lived together. If the woman had been before married, and had had children by her former husband, these children, in case of a separation, went with her.

The women discovered no fear of the men.

The Iroquois regularly professed friendship to each other, and everyone had those whom he called his friends.

They never quarreled with each other, unless when they were intoxicated; and at times became intoxicated that they might quarrel without any disgrace, it being considered as a scandalous thing for a man to quarrel when he was sober.

A drunken man was not regarded as responsible for his actions, or as being a moral agent.

They treated their old people, that is, such as had become incapable of doing the business of life, with very little respect, and neglected even their parents in their old age to an extreme degree. The daughters of Skenandoa, the present sachem of the Oneidas, are very dutiful to him. This is an uncommon, perhaps, a singular fact. His son is very undutiful.

They live at times to a great age. Skenandoa is supposed to be not far from 120 years old.†

Suicide is often committed by both sexes, particularly when they have been severely reproved by their parents. The same violence is done to them-

† The following account of the death of this chief, published in the Utica Patriot of March 19, 1816, cannot fail of being acceptable to my readers. In a few particulars it is abridged.

Died, at his residence near Oneida Castle, on Monday the 11th inst., Skenandoa, the celebrated Oneida chief, aged 110 years, well known in the wars which occurred while

selves also in consequence of domestic broils, and by women when forsaken by their husbands. The means of destruction are the root of the hemlock.

---

we were British colonies, and in the contest which issued in our independence, as the undeviating friend of the people of the United States. He was very savage, and addicted to drunkenness in his youth; but by his own reflections, and the benevolent instructions of the late Rev. Mr. Kirkland, missionary to his tribe, he lived a reformed man for more than sixty years, and died in Christian hope. [*To this sentence a note is appended:* "In the year 1755, Skenandoa was present at a treaty made in Albany. At night he was excessively drunk, and in the morning found himself in the street, stripped of all his ornaments, and every article of clothing. His pride revolted at his self-degradation, and he resolved that he would never again deliver himself over to the power of *strong water.*"]

From attachment to Mr. Kirkland he had always expressed a strong desire to be buried near his minister and father, that he might (to use his own expression) *"go up with him at the great Resurrection."* At the approach of death, after listening to the prayers which were read at his bedside by his great-granddaughter, he again repeated the request. Accordingly, the family of Mr. Kirkland having received information by a runner that Skenandoa was dead, in compliance with a previous promise, sent assistance to the Indians that the corpse might be conveyed to the village of Clinton for burial. Divine service was attended at the meetinghouse in Clinton, on Wednesday, at two o'clock, P.M. An address was made to the Indians by Rev. Dr. Backus, president of Hamilton College, which was interpreted by Judge Deane of Westmoreland. Prayer was then offered, and appropriate psalms sung. After service, the concourse which had assembled from respect to the deceased chief, or from the singularity of the occasion, moved to the grave in the following order:

Students of Hamilton College,
CORPSE,
Indians,
Mr. Kirkland and family,
Judge Deane, Rev. Dr. Norton, Rev. Mr. Ayre,
Officers of Hamilton College,
Citizens.

After interment, the only surviving son of the deceased, self-moved, returned thanks through Judge Deane as interpreter to the people for the respect shown to his father on the occasion, and to Mrs. Kirkland and family for their kind and friendly attention.

Skenandoa's person was tall, well made, and robust. His countenance was intelligent, and displayed all the peculiar dignity of an Indian chief. In his youth he was a brave and intrepid warrior, and in his riper years one of the ablest counselors among the North American tribes; possessed a vigorous mind, and was alike sagacious, active, and persevering. As an enemy he was terrible. As a friend and ally, he was mild and gentle in his disposition, and faithful to his engagements. His vigilance once preserved from massacre the inhabitants of the little settlement at German Flats. In the Revolutionary War, his influence induced the Oneidas to take up arms in favor of the Americans. Among the Indians he was distinguished by the appellation of the *"White man's friend."*

Although he could speak but little English, and in his extreme old age was blind, yet his company was sought. In conversation he was highly decorous, evincing that he had profited by seeing civilized and polished society, and by mingling with good company in his better days.

To a friend who called on him a short time since, he thus expressed himself by an interpreter: "I am an aged hemlock. The winds of an hundred winters have whistled through my branches; I am dead at the top. The generation to which I belonged have run away and left me; why I live, the Great Good Spirit only knows. Pray to my Jesus, that I may have patience to wait for my appointed time to die."

The Iroquois were anciently very hospitable to strangers. The house of the principal man of each village was distinguished by a long pole set up at the door. To this house all strangers resorted as a matter of right, and were entertained as long as they chose to stay. If they were numerous, the inhabitants of the village brought in provisions for their support. If not, they were furnished by the family. When the strangers withdrew, they never thanked their host for his kindness, the hospitality being considered by both parties as their due.

The women were peculiarly kind to strangers, and in their treatment of them discovered a great degree of cordiality and good will.

Family government consisted almost wholly in advice and persuasion. Some parents took much pains in advising their children, and inculcated on them useful lessons of morality.

They have had no other worship, within the knowledge of Mr. Deane, except the annual sacrifice of a dog to Teharonhiawagon, the "*Supporter of the heavens.*" At this sacrifice they eat the dog.

The dog is their most precious property.

Their mythology is regularly communicated by the old sachems to the young.

There is no trace among the Iroquois, within the knowledge of Mr. Deane, of any tradition of their advent from the western regions. When asked concerning their origin, they regularly answer that they came up out of the ground in the regions where they now live.

Such is the account which was given me of this extraordinary people by Mr. Deane.

I am, Sir, yours, etc.

---

Honored chief! His prayer was answered; he was cheerful and resigned to the last. For several years he kept his dress for the grave prepared. Once, and again, and again, he came to Clinton to die, longing that his soul might be with Christ, and his body in the narrow house near his beloved Christian teacher.

While the ambitious but vulgar great look principally to sculptured monuments and to riches in the temple of earthly fame, Skenandoa, in the spirit of the only real nobility, stood with his loins girded waiting the coming of the Lord. His Lord has come! and the day approaches when the green hillock that covers his dust will be more respected than the pyramids, the mausolea, and the pantheons of the proud and imperious. His simple turf and stone will be viewed with veneration, when their tawdry ornaments shall awaken only pity and disgust.

Indulge, my native land, indulge the tear,
That steals impassion'd o'er a nation's doom;
To me each twig from Adam's stock is near;
And sorrows fall upon an Indian's tomb.

*Clinton, March* 14, 1816

# LETTER III

*Origin of the Iroquois—Their warlike character—Their faithfulness in keeping treaties—Their eloquence and language—Mischiefs produced by ardent spirits—The effects of General Sullivan's march through their country—Feast or thanksgiving of the Senecas*

*Dear Sir,*

The Iroquois in my apprehension were, like all the other aborigines found by the Europeans in this part of North America, of Tartar origin; and, at some period of time unknown to themselves as well as to us, came to this continent across the Straits of Bering. By their language, which was radically different from those of most, if not of all other tribes, they were completely separated from the other Indians of this continent, and firmly united together. Their union must have been strengthened by the smallness of their numbers; for, if we should admit with Salmon that at the arrival of the European colonists they were able to raise ten thousand fighting men, a number not improbably double to the real one, they were still a mere handful compared with the Mahicans.[1] In all probability they fought their way to the place of their final settlement. This was the tradition of the Mahicans; and, as Dr. Edwards many years since informed me, was anciently declared by some of the Iroquois themselves. That it was true cannot I think be rationally doubted by anyone who considers their local position, and looks for a moment into their own history.

But whatever was their origin, they certainly were a very extraordinary people. So far as their history is distinctly known to us, they have, like the Romans and Arabians, done little besides extending their conquests over the nations within their reach. It is perhaps a singular phenomenon that this handful of people should have been able to extend their dominion over a territory comprising little less than a million of square miles. It may be said that the Romans were originally few, and yet subdued a much larger territory. It will be remembered, however, that the Romans themselves became speedily numerous, and at an early period employed the surrounding, and ultimately distant, nations in their armies, whereas the numbers of the Iroquois were probably never materially greater than when the Europeans landed in this country; nor can it be said that they possessed any important incidental advantages over those whom they subdued. All their advantages seem to have been personal. It was because they were, or made themselves, superior to their neighbors in wisdom and courage that they ultimately so far excelled them as a warlike nation. It was in this manner that they became so great a terror to all the Mahican tribes. It does not appear from their language that any other nations are of the Iroquois stock, except the *Tuscaroras* and the *Hurons,* both of them few in number; whereas the Mahican filled a great part of the continent.

According to the accounts of the French writers, the Five Nations, appropriately called Iroquois, lived originally in the northern parts of the state of New York and in the neighboring parts of the province of Canada. Possibly this story may be correct. To me it seems more probable, however, that they occasionally wandered thither; and that their principal settlements were where they now are, and where they say they came up out of the ground. The Mahicans of New England believed that they fought their way to this region from the west; and that, having driven out the original inhabitants, they planted themselves in their stead.* However this may be, they are said by the French writers to have made the planting of corn their business. The *Algonquians,* or *Adirondacks,* a hunting and warlike nation in the northern parts of Canada who despised the Iroquois, quarreled with them, and drove them from all their settlements between the St. Lawrence and Lake Champlain.

This event roused both the fears and the vengeance of the Iroquois. With new spirit they betook themselves to the use of arms, and, after a series of adventures, drove the Algonquians out of their country.

From this period they became terrible, not only to the Algonquians whom they chiefly destroyed, but to all the nations by whom they were encircled. Some of these they exterminated; some they drove into distant regions; some they made their tributaries; and to the rest, they were a source of continual terror.† The Indian women on the eastern coast of New England used, it is

* Dr. [Jonathan] Edwards.

† "When the Dutch began the settlement of this country, all the Indians on Long Island and the northern shore of the Sound, on the banks of Connecticut, Hudson, Delaware, and Susquehanna Rivers were in subjection to the Five Nations; and, within the memory of persons now living, acknowledged it by the payment of an annual tribute." *Smith, p.* 134. [William Smith, *The History of the Province of New-York . . .* (London, 1757), pp. 134–135.]

The Connecticut Legislature, in their answer to "Heads of Inquiry," give a different account of this subject. They say, "The original title to the lands on which the colony (of Connecticut) was first settled was, at the time the English came hither, in the Pequot nation of Indians, who were numerous and warlike. Their country extended from Narragansett to Hudson River, and over all Long Island. Sassacus, their great sagamore, had under him twenty-six sachems, and exercised despotic dominion over his subjects." ["The Heads of Inquiry, Relative to the Present State and Condition of His Majesty's Colony of Connecticut . . . with the Answers . . . October, 1774," M.H.S. *Collections,* 1st. ser., 7 (1801), 233.]

At this time it is impossible to determine with precision which of these accounts is cor-

said, to hush their crying children by telling them, *"The Mohawks are coming."*

At subsequent periods they were a severe and dreadful scourge to the French in the province of Canada, and at times brought them to the borders of extermination. A large body of them, led by Sir William Johnson to cooperate with General Amherst in the reduction of Canada, had the satisfaction of seeing the ancient enemies of that province, whom they mortally hated, surrender to the British Crown.

Feeble and nerveless as was the internal government of these nations, all their great external concerns seem to have been absolutely governed by their national councils. These seem definitely to have made war and to have made peace, nor does any tribe appear to have felt itself authorized to withdraw from a measure agreed upon in the national senate.

Between themselves their league was perpetual, nor is there a trace of defection on the part of either of their tribes in their whole remaining history. This league, apparently without any alteration, has lasted more, it is impossible to say how much more, than two hundred years. I recollect no instance of the same stability in any political union of nations entirely independent.

To their treaties with the English they adhered with a similar firmness, and it must be owned that their integrity in this respect frequently cast a shade upon the existing governments of several of the British colonies.

Their councils were conducted with the utmost decorum. The successive speakers were listened to in profound silence. An interruption was unknown, and would have been regarded with indignation. They have observed with too much truth that, when Indians are together, only one talks at a time; but, when white men are together, they all talk at once.

Their eloquence was certainly dignified and powerful. The speeches recorded by Dr. Colden contain strong sense, bold conceptions, and striking specimens of character. At times also, they are specimens of keen ridicule. For satisfaction I refer you to the book itself, since the speeches are too long to be quoted here.

While Mr. Kirkland was a missionary to the Oneidas, being unwell, he

---

rect, or whether they are not both equally true. In the deed by which Momauquin, sachem of Quinnipiac, and his people conveyed the lands bordering upon that river to the first colonists of New Haven, they mention the heavy taxes levied upon them by the *Pequots* and *Mohawks* as a principal inducement to this transaction. From this fact it is evident that these formidable nations extended their ravages, and at times their dominion, to this spot. It is not improbable that the Pequots claimed the whole territory mentioned by the legislature, and occasionally at least kept the inhabitants in a species of subjection by the terror of their arms; while there is sufficient evidence that the Iroquois intruded upon them in various instances.

It does not appear that the Pequots acknowledged themselves inferior in any respect to the Iroquois, or to any other people. On the contrary, they seem evidently to have thought themselves also *"Ongue-howe,"* and to have had all the pride of the Iroquois, and perhaps even more insolence.

was unable to preach on the afternoon of a certain Sabbath, and told Good Peter, one of the head men of the Oneidas that he must address the congregation. Peter modestly and reluctantly consented. After a few words of introduction, he began a discourse on the character of the Saviour. "What, my brethren," said he, "are the views which you form of the character of Jesus? You will answer perhaps that he was a man of singular benevolence. You will tell me that he proved this to be his character by the nature of the miracles which he wrought. All these you will say were kind in the extreme. He created bread to feed thousands who were ready to perish. He raised to life the son of a poor woman who was a widow, and to whom his labors were necessary for her support in old age. Are these then your only views of the Saviour? I tell you they are lame. When Jesus came into our world he threw his blanket around him, but the God was within." This I had from Mr. Kirkland himself.

The object to which these people sacrificed all others was the maintenance of their superiority over surrounding nations. Glory and dominion with them, as with the Romans, constituted their only aim. Hence their favorite title, *Ongue-Honwe, "men superior to all others."* Perhaps no example more strongly illustrates the efficacy of the human faculties employed for the accomplishment of a single end than the success of the Iroquois in accomplishing this lofty purpose.

The language of these people was melodious, as well as energetic. Of this, the names of persons and places which are known to us are no bad proof. The names of some of their sachems were *Garangula, Cheyra, Decanesora, Tahajedoris.* The governor of Canada, they called *Onondio.* A mountain they called *Shenandoa.* Among their rivers were *Allegheny, Monongahela, Miami, Susquehanna, Tioga, Chenango,* and *Unadilla.*

They valued themselves not a little on their pronunciation. The Oneidas are considered by them as speaking their language in a manner more graceful and mellifluous than the rest of the tribes. All of them use the guttural aspirate. The Tuscaroras terminate a great part of their words with this aspirate, and are laughed at by the rest of their countrymen for the harshness which this circumstance introduces into their pronunciation. The Oneidas say that the pronunciation of a Tuscarora is like the noise of the white man's wagon running down a stony hill.

You will naturally suppose that among such a people eloquence was cultivated with great care, and holden in the highest estimation. To be eloquent was among the Iroquois the next glory to that of a renowned warrior. By his tongue only, *Red Jacket* rose to the rank of a chief among the Senecas, without the aid either of birth or exploits. I have seen this man, whose proper name is *Sagoyewatha,* and conversed with him. There was nothing dignified in his appearance, nor in his character. He intoxicated himself whenever he could get ardent spirits, and was on this account regarded with contempt by his nation. This they freely confessed to the white people; yet they said, "He is necessary to us on account of his eloquence." Red Jacket, in the year 1804, was accused by the Seneca Prophet, brother of Cornplanter, of witchcraft. Red Jacket defended himself before the council of the nation in a speech of near three hours, and prevailed against his enemies. "Perhaps," says Mr. Clinton, "the annals of history cannot furnish a more conspicuous instance of the triumph and power of oratory in a barbarous nation devoted to superstition, and looking up to the accuser as a delegated minister of the Almighty." [2]

The language of the Iroquois has no labials. They observe, with not a little significance, "When white men speak, they shut their mouths; red men, when they speak, open their mouths."

In variety of particulars, their manners resembled those of the Mahicans already mentioned. The women labor in the same exclusive manner. Their amusements are running, wrestling, throwing the hatchet, shooting at a mark, and gambling. An Indian will gamble till he has lost all his property, his blanket, and sometimes even his gun.‡ When they are not employed in these or more serious pursuits, they lie down in any place which suits them, and doze away half or even the whole of the day. The Iroquois are tall and straight, have at times good features, and some of them a very dignified appearance. A Seneca chief named the *Great Tree* came with eleven men of distinction, chiefly Tuscaroras, to West Point while I resided their during the Revolutionary War. This man, in his shape, stature, features and deportment, was one of the most dignified and well-appearing men whom I have ever seen. He had a fine eye, a lofty demeanor, and an aspect marked with strong lines of intelligence. Indians, even those who are shrewd, have generally smooth, vacant faces. His was distinguished by that conformation of features which indicates intense and laborious thought. Another, whose name I do not now recollect, had eyes more strongly resembling those of a rattlesnake than I should have believed to be possible, but for the testimony of my own. This band of chiefs exhibited to us a war dance, such as has been often described, a war song, and the war whoop.

*"Nil admirari"* is much more strongly and universally a rule of action to the Iroquois than it could have been of Horace,[3] a rule to which they conformed in the most absolute manner.§ It was strongly exemplified on the occasion mentioned above. They permitted themselves in no instance to indicate that they thought any other persons equal to the *"Ongue-Honwe"*; or anything done or possessed by other nations to be equally excellent with what is done or possessed by themselves. Accordingly, whenever they were among the English, they appeared to take no notice of anything which they

‡ Mr. Kirkland. [Apparently another reference to Dwight's 1798 conversation with Samuel Kirkland; see also "Journey to Berwick," Letter XI.]

§ Mr. [Samuel] Kirkland.

saw or heard as extraordinary or meriting commendation, or especially as exciting their surprise. One of them, in the year 1776, came to Hartford as a spy, to discover whatever he could concerning the strength of the Americans. While he was present at the election, at which there are usually collected from six to ten thousand people, and such scenes of parade and splendor as were very remote from anything which he had ever seen or imagined, he apparently took little more notice of what he saw and heard than if he had been asleep; yet, when he returned, he told his countrymen that the people of Connecticut alone were as numerous as the leaves on the forest trees, and that it would be unsafe for the Six Nations, therefore, to enter into a war with the British colonists. At the same time if I remember right, he described minutely, and in strong language, everything which had passed while he was present. Their inattention and apparent stupidity are therefore chiefly affected.

In one thing, however, they acknowledge the white men to be superior to them. This, as they express it, is "*making the paper talk*." Among the proofs of inferiority on the part of the whites, they never fail to enumerate laboring and sleeping on beds.

The introduction of ardent spirits among this people, and indeed among all the Indian tribes, has done more mischief to them than both their diseases and their wars. Indeed a more profligate and pernicious class of men than a great part of those who are called Indian traders has perhaps never existed. They have been most abominable corrupters of the Indians, plundered them by the grossest frauds, and have been the chief means of preventing them from becoming Christians.

The most fatal disasters which they ever experienced were effectuated by General Sullivan, during his march through their country in the year 1779. After defeating them in a general engagement at a place now called Newtown in the county of Tioga, he marched through a considerable part of their country, and destroyed the villages, fields, and orchards which were in his course. From this blow they never recovered. The sachem, whom I have before mentioned under the name of the *Great Tree,* stood on a mountain and saw his own possessions destroyed. As this chief was a friend to the Americans, and had strenuously urged his countrymen to observe a strict neutrality between them and the British, and had himself observed it with great exactness, his countrymen said to him, "You see how the Americans treat their friends." Great Tree calmly replied, with much good sense, "What I see is only the common fortune of war. It cannot be supposed that the Americans could distinguish my possessions from yours, who are their enemies." This man was never known to violate his word, and did not, on account of this disaster, lessen at all his attachment to the Americans.

After this event the Iroquois never recovered their former lofty spirit. A part of the character of those whom I have heretofore called tame Indians is strongly visible in these people, at least in many of them as I had a painful opportunity of seeing at Buffalo in the year 1804. Most of their lands they have surrendered to the state of New York. Were they farmers, they have reserved enough to furnish them ample means of subsistence. The Senecas indeed might in this case be said to be rich, having reserved almost one hundred acres for each individual of their nation, man, woman, and child; and having owned more than one hundred thousand dollars in the stock of the late Bank of the United States. Cornplanter, the principal chief among the Senecas, has within the last twenty years labored earnestly to induce his nation to form their possessions into private property, and betake themselves industriously to farming.[4] He has also endeavored to put a stop to their drinking. It was probably at his instance that the Prophet, who was his brother, made all those exertions for this purpose which some years past occupied a considerable part of our newspapers. The impressions made by this man on the superstitious feelings of the Six Nations were considerable, and a part of them directed to valuable purposes; but among other things he undertook to purge the nation from witchcraft, and in this way became the cause of violent death to one or more women belonging to these tribes. This probably was one source of his final unpopularity. Whatever was the cause, he actually became unpopular. Cornplanter therefore failed of accomplishing his benevolent design. This chief is a respectable man, possesses a large estate, and seems well to understand the superiority of civilized to savage society. Of late he has discovered serious and favorable sentiments concerning the Christian religion. Mr. Deane informed me that the Six Nations entertain many thoughts of removing into the western wilderness. He observes that they cherish no good will toward the Americans. Individuals they regard with affection, but the people of the United States as a body, they consider as their enemies. The mischiefs brought upon their country by General Sullivan, they undoubtedly remember with the deepest chagrin and resentment. But the evil which is most keenly felt by them is their own degradation, and the vast superiority which the Americans have acquired over all the savage tribes. One of their countrymen was in the year 1804 arrested for the crime of murdering a white man, and confined in jail at Canandaigua. The Senecas very strenuously remonstrated against his imprisonment. They seemed to have no serious objections to his being put to death, but they insisted that imprisonment was proper only for a slave.

Upon the whole, the Iroquois have certainly been a very extraordinary people. Had they enjoyed the advantages possessed by the Greeks and Romans, there is no reason to believe that they would have been at all inferior to these celebrated nations. Their minds appear to have been equal to any efforts within the reach of man. Their conquests, if we consider their numbers and their circumstances, were little inferior to those of Rome itself. In their harmony, the unity of their operations, the energy of their character, the vastness, vigor, and success of their enterprises, and the strength and sublimity of their eloquence, they may be fairly contrasted with the Greeks. Both the Greeks and the Romans, before they began to rise into distinction, had already reached that state of society in which men are able to improve. The Iroquois had not. The Greeks and Romans had ample means for improvement. The Iroquois had none.

In the preceding letter, I mentioned from Mr. Deane the sacrifice of a dog, annually performed by the Six Nations. The following account of this subject, as it exists among the Senecas, was given me in August 1812 by the Rev. Thaddeus Osgood, who has spent several years as a missionary, partly in the United States and partly in Canada.[5] Mr. Osgood was present at one of these solemn festivals, and acquired additional information, such as he wished, from the national interpreter.

At the time when the Senecas return from hunting in January or February, they annually keep a feast seven days, the professed object of which is to render thanks to the Great Spirit for the benefits which they have received from him during the preceding year, and to solicit the continuance of them through the year to come. On the evening before the feast commences, they kill two dogs, and after painting them with various colors and dressing them with ornaments, suspend them in the center of the camp, or in some conspicuous place in the village.

The whole of this solemn season is spent in feasting and dancing. Two select bands, one of men and another of women, ornamented with a variety of trinkets, and furnished each with an ear of corn which is held in the right hand, begin the dance at the council house. Both choirs, the men leading the way, dance in a circle around the council fire which is kindled for the occasion, and regulate their steps by music. Hence they proceed to every house in the village, and in the same manner dance in a circle around each fire.

On one of the festival days they perform a peculiar religious ceremony for the purpose of driving away evil spirits from their habitations. Three men clothe themselves in the skins of wild beasts and cover their faces with masks of a hideous appearance, and their hands with the shell of the tortoise. In this garb they go from house to house, making a horrid noise, and in every house take the fuel from the fire and scatter the embers and ashes about the floor with their hands.

Toward the close of the festival they erect a funeral pile, place upon it the two dogs, and set it on fire. When they are partly consumed, one of them is taken off and put into a large kettle, with vegetables of every kind which they have cultivated during the preceding year. The other dog is consumed in the fire. The ashes of the pile are then gathered up, carried through the village, and sprinkled at the door of every house. When this ceremony is ended, which is always near the close of the seventh day, all the inhabitants feast together upon the contents of the kettle; and thus the festival is terminated.

This mode of exhibiting their gratitude is certainly far from satisfying the feelings of a Christian; yet I think several of the American states might learn from these savages the important lesson that it becomes a people possessing the light of revelation to render annually a public tribute of thanksgiving to the Great Benefactor of mankind for the blessings which they have received during the year from his bountiful hand. This, however, is not the only religious service which has existed among the Six Nations. Mr. Kirkland informed me that while he was crossing the Oneida Lake with a fleet of canoes, a violent storm arose, from which the fleet was in the utmost danger of perishing. The chief sachem, in whose canoe Mr. Kirkland was, took from a box in the stern a small quantity of fine powder made of a fragrant herb unknown to Mr. Kirkland, and scattered it on the water. This he found was intended as an oblation to the deity acknowledged by the sachem.

There is a stone too large to be carried by a man of ordinary strength, at some distance eastward from the Oneida village, which some of these people regard with religious reverence, and speak of it as their god. They say that it has slowly followed their nation in their various removals, and allege as decisive evidence of the declaration that a few years since it was much farther to the east than it now is. The truth is, a stout young man of the Oneidas, being a wag, resolved to amuse himself with the credulity of his tribe; and therefore, whenever he passed that way, took up the stone and carried it some distance westward. In this manner the stone, advancing by little and little, made in a few years a considerable progress, and was verily believed by some of the Oneidas to have moved this distance spontaneously. The young fellow told the story to an American gentleman, and laughed heartily at the credulity of his countrymen.

I am, Sir, yours, etc.

# REMARKS ON EUROPEAN TRAVELERS IN AMERICA

## LETTER I

*Volney*

*Dear Sir,*

In a former letter I mentioned to you that it was my original determination to avoid reading the accounts given by European travelers concerning the countries which were the immediate object of my own investigation. My reason was, I wished to come to everything which I saw without any bias from the opinions of others, and to examine everything in the very light in which it should appear to *me*. At the same time I proposed to read, after I had examined for myself, what had been written by others, for the purpose both of renouncing my own errors and correcting theirs. To this design I have rigidly adhered. Having finished my journey of investigation, I shall now commence an examination of several travelers from Great Britain and France who have thought proper to visit this country, and to give their observations concerning it to the world. I begin with *Volney*.

This celebrated Frenchman was well known in America before he visited it in person by his writings, particularly his Travels in Syria, Egypt, and Palestine, and his Ruins of Palmyra. The latter of these publications, indeed, gained him very little reputation with men of sobriety and good sense; but the former was at first in some degree, and continues still to be, a popular work in this country; although Mr. *Antes,* with every appearance of truth, has informed the public that Volney, notwithstanding his professions, never ascended the Nile a step beyond Cairo.[1] In the United States he certainly traveled extensively, to what purpose I shall now proceed summarily to inquire. My remarks will be confined chiefly to detached passages, and those such as assert the facts. The book from which I quote is a translation of Volney's View of the United States by Mr. Charles Brown, published in Philadelphia, 1804.[2]

In the second chapter of this work, page 6, the writer says: "In the year 1796, from Boston to Richmond in Virginia, I scarcely marched through a tract of three miles together of cleared, or unwooded, land." If M. Volney took the upper road from Boston to Springfield, he did not pass through three miles of wooded land till after he had passed Brookfield a distance of about seventy miles. Between Brookfield and Springfield, about thirty miles, adding all the forests, groves, and coppices on the Lyme Range and the lean plains lying west of it, perhaps we might make five miles more. From Springfield to New York, as the road then went, summing up the scattered collections of wood on the road, there may be twelve miles more. The distance is 140 miles. The whole distance from Boston to New York in this course is 240 miles. Twenty miles of wood, made up of fifty or sixty parcels, is the amount of all the wooded land which M. Volney saw in this part of his journey. Two of these parcels make up eight miles of the twenty; and two others, four. The remaining eight miles are composed of groves and coppices, scarcely sufficient in number or extent to complete the variety and beauty of landscape. This M. Volney must have seen, if he kept his eyes open; if he did not, he should have left the subject to those who did.

If M. Volney proceeded from Springfield to Hartford on the western side of Connecticut River and went on to Middletown, he rode twenty miles without passing a single grove which extended an eighth of a mile along the road. If he went on the eastern side of the river, he proceeded forty miles without passing more than two such groves.

Page 9. The writer says: "The third district, or northern forest, is likewise composed of the fir, pine, larch, cedar, and cypress. It spreads itself over the western parts of New York, and the inland countries of New England."

I have already given a sufficient account of the forests of these countries, and shall only observe here that the fir is a solitary tree, thinly scattered upon the mountains south of New Hampshire and Vermont, and that it is rarely found in these states, except on the mountains, below latitude forty-four; that the pine, south of the District of Maine, if it were all collected into one spot, would scarcely cover the county of Hampshire; that the larch, though actually existing in New England, is so rare that I have never yet seen one; that the cedar, were it all collected, would scarcely fill three townships; and that the cypress is not, within my knowledge, found either in New England or New York.

In the state of New York, there is a considerable tract of pine land, extending from Lake George and South Bay on both sides of the Hudson down to the city of Hudson. There are also a few smaller tracts, particularly on the Susquehanna and some of its branches; and on Long Island there is a large forest of pines. Cedars are scattered, to no great extent, along the lower parts of the Hudson. Firs, larches, and cypresses, I have never met with in this state. Nine tenths of all the forests in this country south of the District of Maine are composed either of oak, hickory, etc., or of beech, maple, etc.

Page 10. The writer proceeds: "On one side, in a course of nine hundred miles, are scattered ten or twelve towns, built entirely of brick, or of painted wood, and containing from ten to sixty thousand souls. Without the city are scattered farmhouses built of unhewn logs, surrounded with a few small fields of wheat, tobacco, or maize, that are still encumbered with the half-burnt stocks of trees, and are divided by branches laid across each other by way of fence."

The account which I have already given of this country furnishes the best proof of the inaccuracy of this representation. If it should be admitted to be just (and that it will be by every observing traveler who follows my footsteps, I feel thoroughly assured), it will be seen that the representation of M. Volney is merely a flight of the imagination. It will appear also that a great part of the ancient settlements in New England, instead of being scattered farmhouses, are composed chiefly of villages: most of them flourishing, many of them handsome, and not one of them in one hundred disfigured even by a log house.

In May 1810, I took a journey from New Haven to Windsor in Vermont, and thence across the Green Mountains to Middlebury, whence I returned in a direct course to New Haven. The distance which I traveled is a little more than four hundred and sixty miles. A considerable part of it is occupied also by recent settlements. Two or my companions having read, or heard of, this observation of Volney, determined before we commenced our journey to count the log houses which they should find on the road. The whole number to Middlebury was fifteen; and thence to New Haven, thirty-two.

As to the assertion that the houses are surrounded with small fields still encumbered with the half-burnt stocks of trees, and divided by branches laid across each other by way of fence, I shall only observe that M. Volney is sporting with the credulity of his reader. A great part of the enclosures in the ancient settlements are formed of stone; the remainder, of rails and of boards. Hedges we have none: all attempts to raise them having hitherto failed of success. In forests and recent settlements, fences are often made of logs raised upon each other; and sometimes trees are felled on the spot, so as distantly to resemble the enclosure mentioned by this writer.

Page 11. Speaking of the great chain of mountains which forms the principal feature of the United States, he says: "It begins in Lower Canada on the southern shore of St. Lawrence near its mouth, where its points are called by sailors the hills de Notre Dame, and de la Magdeleine. Tending southwest, it recedes by degrees from this river, and forms the frontier of the United States till it enters New Hampshire. It then stretches southward through Vermont and assumes the appellation of the Green Mountains, etc."

As M. Volney never traveled over the region which he has here described, he is certainly to be acquitted of willful misrepresentation. He ought not, however, to have asserted so roundly what he did not, and could not, know to be true. The hills which commence at the Gulf of St. Lawrence and run southwestward between Lower Canada and Maine turn directly to the south about twenty-five miles east of Connecticut River. Their western branch terminates on the Sound at New Haven. The Green Mountains, commencing their eastern ridge at West Rock, also in New Haven, run directly north to Lower Canada. At some distance before they reach that province, they subside into hills of a moderate elevation. In the account in which he pursues this subject further, there are other errors; but it is unncessary for me to mention them. I shall only add that between Lower Canada and Maine, the range of the White Mountains is only what is denominated a rising ground: there being nothing which can be called a mountain in the whole range until after it enters New Hampshire.

Page 132. "For near three years together, from October 1795 to June 1798, I never saw the wind at the same point for thirty hours at a time."

In what part of the United States M. Volney was during this period, I am ignorant. No such state of weather has occurred where I have been, either at that or at any other time. For the best comment which I am able to make on this assertion, I must refer you to the observations which I formerly made concerning the climate of New England and that of New York.

Page 133. "In summer a calm may be expected at two o'clock in the afternoon: the thermometer at 86° or 88°. Rain succeeds, with a southwest wind, at four or five."

M. Volney does not inform us where these circumstances are to be expected. That they may be expected I certainly cannot deny. But during five sixths of the summer they will ordinarily be expected in vain. Rarely is the thermometer as high as eighty-six, and not often so high as eighty. In a wet season we have usually two rains in a week; in a temperate season, one; in a dry season, perhaps one in one, two, or three months. A calm sometimes takes place from nine o'clock to eleven, or from ten to twelve; and is commonly followed by a breeze from the southwest, or some other southern point. A thundershower is usually preceded by a southwest wind, and is almost always brought on by a wind blowing between the western and northwestern points. This wind commonly lasts from one to four days.

Page 140. "At these periods, that is about the equinoxes, and in April and October, occur those tornadoes which in the United States most commonly owe their birth to the northeast wind."

I have known one tornado in the month of October; but I never knew, nor did I ever hear of one about the equinoxes, nor in the month of April. They have existed solitarily in June, oftener in July, and still more frequently in August. They never owe their birth to a northeast wind. In all instances, so far as my knowledge extends, they blow from between the west and northwest points, and are no other than violent thunderstorms. They are neither preceded, nor followed by a wind from the northeast.

Page 142. "The southeast wind in the United States bears some resemblance to the sirocco of the Levant, which also blows from that quarter, being hot, moist, light, and rapid, and producing, though in a much less degree, the same torpor of the brain and the same uneasy sensations." Again. "The southeast wind is more supportable than the same wind in Sicily, because it loses some of the qualities which the sands of Africa imparted to it in its passage over the Atlantic."

There are several unfortunate mistakes in this account of M. Volney. His facts are falsely assumed. The southeast wind is never hot. In the winter it is warm compared with the northwest and northeast, but rarely so warm as to induce a person moderately careful of his health to make any change in his dress. In the spring, summer, and autumn, it is so universally cool that I do not remember a single complaint, in the course of my life, that it was uncomfortably warm during these seasons. On the contrary, it is regularly complained of as chilly and piercing in the spring and autumn, and sometimes in the summer, particularly in June. In the summer, however, it is not frequent. When it blows it is never hot, but often of a refreshing temperature.

Equally unfortunate is M. Volney in his points of compass. A southeast course from the northern states would scarcely strike the southern point of Africa; and, from the southern states, would not touch that continent. In either case it must pass over more than six thousand miles of ocean. One would think that in this passage it must lose some of the qualities of the sirocco, if there were any imparted to it by the sands of Africa.

There is another misfortune in asigning this cause for the alleged heat of our southeast winds. They rarely last longer than two or three days,* and rarely blow with a velocity exceeding ten or twelve miles an hour. I will suppose that they blow at the rate of twenty, and that they last three days. The blast would then come from a point, fourteen hundred and forty miles distant. In six days it would reach us from the distance of twenty-eight hundred and eighty. If then these winds were to come, in a deflected course, from the nearest part of that continent, they would not, even at this rate, arrive at our shore within the longest period during which I have known them continue. But the truth is, they rarely or never blow through such a period, and never move with such a velocity for more than two or three days.

With regard to the torpor of the brain, supposed by M. Volney to be an effect of these winds, this is the first time I ever heard of the fact. These

* According to M. Volney not longer than thirty hours. [Volney, *View of the United States,* p. 132.]

winds are customarily complained of as being chilly, as other winds are which blow from the ocean; and by that class of people who are affected by what are called nervous disorders are dreaded not a little, although less than those from the northeast.

Page 145. "We should naturally suppose that a wind from the south would be hotter than one from the southeast, yet in this country it is cooler."

This observation is of no other importance than as it is unfounded. The south wind, like the north, is less frequent than those which blow from the northwest and southwest, the northeast and southeast, and rarely continues longer than forty-eight hours. It is somewhat, though very little, warmer than the southeast. As it comes from the ocean in very nearly the same latitudes, its temperature cannot be supposed to be very different.

Page 149. "At the autumnal equinox the northeast takes its turn to reign, with some intermissions, for forty or fifty days." †

On this assertion I shall only observe that I have never seen such an autumn. In this season we have usually one or more heavy storms from the northeast, continuing from one to three days. Westerly winds prevail during almost the whole of this season, which commonly is in an eminent degree serene and beautiful.

Ibid. "The west wind is the most serene and bland of any in America."

The west wind is in the summer the hottest, and in the winter the coldest, of any which blows in America.

Page 189. "From New York to Cape Cod the gale is due south."

The observations already made concerning the south wind sufficiently expose the error of this assertion. I have lived at New Haven more than thirty years, and most of that time have been an attentive observer of the weather. During this period, including the time which M. Volney spent in the United States, the south wind has never been prevalent.

Page 11. "The atmosphere is so capricious that the same day will freeze with the colds of Norway, scorch with the ardors of Africa, and present to you in quick succession all the four seasons of the year."

It has never happened to me to see one of these extraordinary days. Our weather is variable, but this is a caricature, not a description.

The errors of this writer, and of Weld, as quoted by him concerning the breadth and depth of the river Niagara, the height of the plain from which it descends, the rapidity of the current above the falls, their perpendicular height, and the thundering sound of the billows dashing against the rocky sides of the caverns below, will be easily understood from the account which I have given of these objects.[3]

† How is this reconcilable with M. Volney's assertion that no wind blows here longer than thirty hours?

If you wish to form a just opinion of Dr. Belknap's exhibition of the first colonists of New Hampshire, mentioned by M. Volney, page 317, the work will speak for itself.[4]

I have selected these assertions of M. Volney as specimens by which you may be enabled to form a judgment of the credit due to the writer. The character of the man who made them cannot be mistaken. It ought not to be alleged as an apology that the writer was a stranger who resided here but a short time and must, therefore, be necessarily ignorant of many of those things which he has handled in this work; nor that he was misinformed by others, and that the blame is chargeable to them, but not to him. M. Volney may be fairly excused in believing his informants, and in reporting their information, *as such*. The assertions of M. Volney are made in terms which are peremptory and absolute, and are plainly meant to impress upon the reader's mind a conviction that the writer knew what he thus asserted to be true. The fault, therefore, is justly chargeable to him. But what must be thought of the veracity, as well as accuracy, of a writer who asserts in such a manner such things as I have specified. It will be saying little to observe that reliance cannot safely be placed upon his information.

It is however but just to add that the book, to a person able to separate the wheat from the chaff, is not without its value. It contains some useful information, and some rational mixed with much whimsical philosophy. The great misfortune running through the whole of it, is that the reader, unless informed from some other source, knows not when to believe and when to disbelieve the writer. M. Volney appears to have been governed by that practical maxim of Voltaire: *"M. Abbé, I must be read whether I am believed or not."* [5] One declaration which he makes is undoubtedly correct: viz., that many of the Americans dislike atheists and Jacobins. In this dislike, M. Volney himself undoubtedly felt a personal interest, as will appear from the following anecdote, communicated to me by the late Mr. Ellsworth, chief justice of the United States.

When this gentleman was at Paris, as envoy extraordinary of the United States, he was visited occasionally by M. Volney. During one of his visits, M. Volney declared in the most direct manner his entire disbelief of the existence of God, a Providence, and a future state. Not long after, M. Volney passed Mr. Ellsworth at an early hour, in the Champs Élysées on horseback. "I see, friend Volney," said Mr. Ellsworth, "that although you disbelieve the existence of a God, you are willing to take some pains to preserve your life and health." "Yes," answered Volney, "this horse is my providence." We do, indeed, very generally dislike atheists. We think we have many reasons for the dislike. Among them, one is that we find it impossible to place any confidence in them.

Atheists are perhaps always Jacobins in their dispositions, and so far as a regard to their safety will permit are usually Jacobins in their conduct.

When these two characteristics are united, man becomes an absolute profligate, abandoned with respect to every moral principle, a spot on the human name, a nuisance to the creation. Whether M. Volney was a Jacobin in his political views, I am ignorant. The best thing in his book is his comparison of the character, conduct, and success of French colonists with those of English, or Dutch extraction.‡

I am, Sir, yours, etc.

‡ The settler of British or German descent, says M. Volney, is of a cold and phlegmatic temper, and deliberately forms a plan of husbandry which he steadily pursues. He attends sedulously to everything that can influence the success of his projects. He never becomes idle till his end is accomplished, and he has put his affairs on a good footing.

The impetuosity of the Frenchman leads him to embrace precipitately any plausible or flattering project, and he proceeds in his career without laboriously computing expenses and contingencies. With more genius for his portion, he laughs at the dullness and cautions of his Dutch and English neighbor, whom he stigmatizes as an ox; but his neighbor will sedately and wisely reply that the patient ox will plow much better than the mettlesome racer. And in truth the Frenchman's fire easily slackens; his patience is worn out; and after changing, correcting, and altering his plans, he finally abandons his project in despair.

His neighbor is in no haste to rise in the morning; but, when fairly up, he applies steadily to work. At breakfast he gives cold and laconic orders to his wife, who obeys them without contradiction or demur. Weather permitting, he goes to plow or chop; if the weather be bad, he prosecutes his indoor tasks, looks over the contents of his house and granary, repairs his doors or windows, drives pegs or nails, makes chairs or tables, and is always busy in making his habitation more comfortable and secure. With these habits he is no wise averse to sell his farm for a good price, and move, even in old age, still farther into the forest, cheerfully recommencing all the labors of a new settlement. There will he spend years in felling trees, building a hut and a barn, and in fencing and sowing his fields. His wife, as placid and patient as himself, will second all his labors; and they will sometimes pass away six months without seeing the face of a stranger. In four or five years, comfort, convenience, and ease will grow up around them; and a competence will recompense their solitary toils.

The Frenchman, on the contrary, will be up betimes for the pleasure of viewing and talking over matters with his wife, whose counsel he demands. Their constant agreement would be quite a miracle; the wife dissents, argues, wrangles; and the husband has his own way, or gives up to her, and is irritated or disheartened. Home perhaps grows irksome, so he takes his gun, goes a shooting or a journey, or to chat with a neighbor. If he stays at home, he either whiles away the hour in good-humored talk, or he scolds and quarrels. Neighbors interchange visits, for to visit and talk are so necessary to a Frenchmen that along the frontier of Canada and Louisiana, there is nowhere a settler of that nation to be found, but within sight or reach of some other. On asking how far off the remotest settler was, I have been told, He is in the woods with the bears, a league from any house, and with nobody to talk to.

This temper is the most characteristic difference between the two nations; and, the more I reflect upon this subject, the firmer is my persuasion that the Americans, and the northern Europeans from whom they are descended, chiefly owe their success in arts and commerce to habitual taciturnity. In silence they collect, arrange, and digest their thoughts, and have leisure to calculate the future; they acquire habits of clear thinking and accurate expression; and hence there is more decision in their conduct, both in public and domestic exigences; and they at once see the way to their point more clearly, and pursue it more directly.

On the contrary, the Frenchman's ideas evaporate in ceaseless chat; he exposes himself to bickering and contradiction, excites the garrulity of his wife and sisters, involves himself in quarrels with his neighbors, and finds in the end that his life has been squandered away without use or benefit. [Volney, *View of the United States,* pp. 345–347.]

# LETTER II

### *Weld*

*Dear Sir,*

Among the English travelers in America whose books I have seen, Weld is clearly one of the most respectable. The greater part of these men appear to be destitute both of understanding and principle. From this imputation, however, I except Harriot and Wansey: the former a military officer; the latter a plain, honest clothier, not destitute of good common sense.[1] The errors of Weld, which are numerous, are derived either from misapprehension, misinformation, or prejudice. The last of these characteristics was a predominant trait in the mind of Mr. Weld. From some unfortunate circumstances which, as I am informed, attended him not long after his arrival, he conceived a strong dislike both to the country and its inhabitants, and never resumed his candor until after his book was completed.

His work contains a multitude of misrepresentations. Yet they seem never to have sprung from the want either of understanding or of sincerity. He is, however, censurable, both for the obliquity of his views and for the absolute and downright tenor of his assertions in cases where he knew not that his assertions were true, and where, certainly, they were either wholly or partially erroneous.

As this writer, so far as he has informed us, traveled over a part only of the region which is the subject of these letters, and as I shall rarely trouble either you or myself with remarks on other parts of the United States, I shall not detain you long by my observations on his book.

In the second letter, p. 31, of the fourth edition, he observes: "In a few instances only it would be possible to find a woman at the age of forty who has had a large family."

This declaration was not improbably intended to respect only the city of Philadelphia. Even thus limited, it is a gross mistake: as I know by the evidence of my own eyes. In the countries through which the journeys mentioned in these letters lay, there are, it is believed, as many women of this description in proportion to the whole number of inhabitants as probably in any other.[2]

Page 189. "Between the town and the Posaick (Passaic) River there is one marsh, which alone extends upwards of twenty miles, and is about two miles wide where you pass over it."

Mr. Weld should have said that its breadth (as I should judge from passing over it eight or ten times) is not less than eight miles.

Page 190. "It" (that is the Passaic) "suddenly precipitates itself in one entire sheet over a ledge of rocks of nearly eight feet in perpendicular height."

For nearly *eight* feet read *seventy* feet. Mr. Weld certainly never saw the falls of the Passaic. I visited this spot in May 1811. The rocks over which this river descends rise immediately on the western border of a little settlement called Patterson. They are of green stone, or whin. The river, immediately before its descent, winds for some distance to the northeast, and, precipitating itself down a steep of seventy feet perpendicular, directs its course nearly south, forming a large and deep basin at the foot of the precipice.

To future travelers who visit this scene, the solemnity will be deeply enhanced by the remembrance of the following melancholy incident. The Rev. Mr. Cumming, minister of the North Presbyterian Church in Newark, having lately married a lady of an excellent character and fine accomplishments, and having occasion to preach at Patterson, took Mrs. Cumming with him.[3] On the Monday following, they visited this cataract. While they were standing on the brow of the precipice on the north side of the river, Mr. Cumming, having turned to look at some object behind him, found, when he again cast his eye forward, that his wife was missing. While she was looking with intense pleasure on the magnificent sheet of foam before her, she probably became giddy, and fell into the basin below. She was taken up as soon as it was possible, but she was dead. This is said, whether correctly or not I am ignorant, to be the third instance in which life has been lost in a similar manner at this fascinating spot.

Ibid. "From the Passaic to the North River, the country is hilly, barren, and uninteresting."

As Mr. Weld took the stage road, he must, after leaving the Passaic, have crossed a wide extent of marsh, perfectly flat (as will be supposed), before he reached the Hackensack, a much larger river than the Passaic. After leaving the Hackensack, the flat country continues through a moderate extent. Then the traveler ascends the elevated ground on which stands the village of Bergen: a narrow, and not a barren, neck of land, perhaps from a mile and a half to two miles in breadth.

Page 205. "General Washington told me that he was never so much annoyed by mosquitoes as at Skenesborough: for that they used to bite through the thickest boot."

A gentleman of great respectability, who was present when General Washington made the observation referred to, told me that he said, when describing these mosquitoes to Mr. Weld, that they "bit through his stockings, above his boots." Our mosquitoes have certainly a sharp tooth, and are very adroit at their business; but they have not been sufficiently disciplined, hitherto, to bite through the thickest boot.

There are in this writer several other observations concerning some of the interior parts of the state of New York which are incorrect, but are of little moment. There are also some invidious remarks concerning the character of the Americans which merit animadversion; * but as they are found in those

* Mr. Weld, after having mentioned that himself and his company stopped on his passage down Lake Champlain at one house to breakfast, and at another to dine, at the first of which he says, "We got a little milk and about two pounds of bread, absolutely the whole of what was in the house; and at the second a few eggs and some cold, salted fat pork, but not a morsel of bread," proceeds to describe the latter of these mansions. "The wretched appearance also of this last habitation was very striking; it consisted of a wooden frame, merely with a few boards nailed against it; the crevices between which were the only apertures for the admission of light, except the door; and the roof was so leaky that we were sprinkled with the rain even as we sat at the fireside." He then goes on to observe. "That people can live in such a manner, who have the necessaries and conveniences of life within their reach, as much as any others in the world, is really most astonishing! It is however to be accounted for by that desire of making money which is the predominant feature in the character of the Americans in general, and leads the petty farmer in particular to suffer numberless inconveniences when he can gain by so doing. If he can sell the produce of his land to advantage, he keeps as small a part of it as possible for himself, and lives the whole year round upon salt provisions, bad bread, and the fish he can catch in the rivers and lakes in the neighborhood; if he has built a comfortable house for himself, he readily quits it as soon as finished for money, and goes to live in a mere hovel in the woods till he gets time to build another. Money is his idol; and to procure it he gladly foregoes every self-gratification." [Weld, *Travels,* I, 291–292.]

A man of common sobriety and good nature would naturally have attributed the wretchedness of this hovel, and the miserable circumstances of those by whom it was inhabited, to their poverty, or to the recency of their settlement in the wilderness; at least he would have asked the question whether one or both of these might not probably have been the causes of what he saw. Gross prejudice and rank ill nature only could have resolutely determined that avarice must be the sole assignable source of the sufferings undergone by these unfortunate beings. It is not however my design to dwell upon this subject. I have made the transcript for the purpose of introducing another from the fair-minded and gentlemanly Lambert; who, on his passage up the same lake, was forced to land upon the same shore, and has told us the following story of his reception by an American farmer.

> We were nearly two hours before we could get the vessel off the rocks. At length having succeeded, we coasted along the shore till four o'clock in the morning, when we arrived in a small bay in the township of Shelburne, about sixty miles from St. Johns, situated in the widest part of the lake. Here we went ashore at the first farmhouse, at a little distance from the bay. The door was only on the latch and we entered, but the people were not yet up. Having awaked the master of the house and told him our situation, he said we were welcome, and that he would get up immediately. In the meantime we collected some wood, and, putting it upon the live embers in the fireplace, soon made a large fire. This was a most comfortable relief after the cold night we had passed on board our miserable sloop. We found that a considerable quantity of snow had fallen in this part of the lake, though we had not met with any during the passage.
>
> The master of the house with two of his sons were soon up; and, having put the kettle on the fire, made preparations for breakfast. About six o'clock, his wife and daughters, two pretty little girls, came into the kitchen where we were assembled, and in the course of half an hour we had the pleasure of sitting down to a *substantial American*

parts of the work which describe the states south of my own limits, I will leave them, with a single exception, to be examined by others. The remarks frequently thrown out concerning the avarice of the Americans are specimens either of very imperfect observation or illiberal prejudice. If your own books fairly exhibit the character of the people of Great Britain, the difference between you and us in this respect is very small; and those of your countrymen and of other European nations who settle here certainly acquire no advantage by being compared with our citizens. Mr. Weld observes repeatedly that the farmers of this country will sell anything for which they can find a good market, and be contented to live miserably for the sake of a little additional gain. Such remarks are unwarranted respecting the farmers of this country. The manner in which the people of New England live, I have already described, and will leave it to you to judge whether they do not live as well where the settlements are not recent as those of any other country who are not possessed of more property.

One of the most extensive kinds of misrepresentation adopted by European travelers in the United States is found in the use of the word *American*. This word, when applied to the character, manners, or morals of the people who inhabit the United States, is scarcely capable of having any meaning. Like *European,* it is an almost merely geographical or political term. Suppose I were to describe the manners, morals, or character of the British or the Spaniards with the use of this word, and should actually describe the manners of the Turks, Hungarians, or Poles. What Briton, what Spaniard would be satisfied with the description?

A few observations on the account given by Mr. Weld of Long Island will conclude what I wish to say concerning his work.

---

*breakfast,* consisting of *eggs, fried pork, beefsteaks, apple tarts, pickles, cheese, cider, tea,* and *toast dipped in melted butter and milk.* We were surprised at seeing such a variety of eatables, as it was not a tavern; but the farmer was a man of property, and carried on the farming business to a considerable extent. He showed us a great number of cheeses of his own making; and, for churning butter, he had made a kind of half-barrel, with a place for one of his young boys to sit astride as on horseback. This machine moving up and down answered the double purpose of a churn for making butter, and a rocking horse for his children.

Having made an excellent breakfast we inquired of our worthy host what we had to pay. He said he should be satisfied with a York shilling (about 7d. sterling); this, however, we considered too small a sum for the trouble we had given him and his family, and the handsome manner in which he had entertained us; we, therefore, gave him a quarter of a dollar each, that being the tavern price for breakfast. We then took our leave and went on board our vessel, equally pleased with the disinterested hospitality of the American farmer, as with the comfortable refreshment we had received at his house. [John Lambert, *Travels through Lower Canada and the United States* (London, 1810), II, 107–109. Dwight omits Lambert's last sentence which was less favorable to Dwight's argument. "His conduct formed a striking contrast to that of the tavern-keeper at Cumberland Head, who refused Mr. Lyman and the Captain admittance after their accident."]

Page 548. "The dreadful maladies which of late years have never failed to rage in these places (the large towns on the coast of America) during certain months."

The only malady which at the period specified raged in these places was the yellow fever, which began in Philadelphia in the year 1793, two years before the arrival of Mr. Weld in the United States. No other disease had, during the period which intervened between 1793 and the date of this letter, 1797, in any considerable degree prevailed. The yellow fever had spread twice in Philadelphia, once in New York, once to a small extent in Boston, never in Salem, once in Newburyport, once in Providence, never in Newport. Mr. Weld ought certainly to have been better informed before he ventured to say that any dreadful maladies had never failed to rage of late years in these places during certain months.

Page 549. "The permanent residents on Long Island are chiefly of Dutch extraction."

The number of inhabitants in Kings County in the year 1790 was 4,495. Of these, 1,432 were blacks. Subtract this number, and there will remain 3,063. There are more English residents in Kings County, by a considerable number, than there are Dutch in the other two counties. The whole number of inhabitants on the island in 1790 was 36,949, of which 3,063 is less than a twelfth part. So near is Mr. Weld's assertion to truth. Mr. Weld made a short excursion into Kings County, and finding that the greater number of inhabitants there were of Dutch extraction, he concluded that it was so everywhere. *Ex hoc uno disce omnia.*[4] European travelers in this country usually make their general conclusions from single, or at the best from a very few, insulated facts.

Page 549. "It is a common saying in New York that a Long Island man will conceal himself in the house on the approach of a stranger."

I have spent about two years in the city of New York, and never heard this saying mentioned. Had I heard it, I should have known that it was ridiculously false. It was probably told to Mr. Weld by a mere citizen, who had perhaps crossed Brooklyn ferry twice. Mere citizens in this, and I presume in all other countries, are not uncommonly profoundly ignorant of the regions by which they are surrounded, and of the inhabitants which they contain. Very generally, indeed, they are acquainted with their own business; and this but too often is the boundary of their knowledge. Few worse informants concerning this country can be found than mere citizens, and yet from these men is unhappily derived most of the information acquired concerning it by foreign travelers.

I have visited Long Island several times, and made the circuit of it. Mr. Weld himself will easily believe that I have had more intercourse with the inhabitants than he could possibly have. I shall, therefore, beg leave to inform him that, however awed they might be at his approach, they discover no peculiar marks of terror or diffidence in their intercourse with ordinary strangers; but receive them, so far as my knowledge extends, with a cheerful good will and a cordial hospitality.

Ibid. "Widely different from the Anglo-Americans, whose inquisitiveness in similar circumstances would lead them to a thousand troublesome and impertinent inquiries in order to discover what your business was in that place, and how they could possibly take any advantage of it."

This contemptible observation has been so often repeated that one would think even prejudice itself would be weary of uttering it, and that a little truth would give more pleasure to the tongue, merely as a variety. Mr. Weld has too much understanding, and ought to have too much good nature, to have stained his pages with it. For my own opinions, I refer you to observations made in preceding parts of this work.

Page 550. "Immense quantities of grouse and deer are found amidst the brushwood with which it (the Brushy Plain) is covered, and which is so well calculated to afford shelter to these animals."

Great numbers of deer inhabit and are annually killed in the forests by which the interior parts of Long Island are so extensively covered. But that they are found amidst the brushwood with which the Brushy Plain is covered, and found in immense quantities, I have first learned from Mr. Weld. Even now I must beg him to explain what he means by *quantities* of deer.

Nor can I conceive how brush, which rarely rises to the height of three feet, though it may furnish a convenient shelter for grouse, can be very well calculated to afford shelter to deer.

Ibid. Mr. Weld observes that several of the Dutch inhabitants have very extensive *tracks* of land under cultivation.

This must, I think, be a mistake, although Mr. Weld has mentioned the same thing in several places. We have *tracts,* but I believe no *tracks* of land in this country. The thing, whatever it be, which the writer means, must certainly be peculiar to Europe, if not to Great Britain; and ought, as well as *quantities* of deer, to have been explained in a small glossary at the end of the work.

Page 552. "I shall leave it," (that is, America), "without a sigh, and without entertaining the slightest wish to revisit it."

Unless Mr. Weld should revisit this country with a better temper than he displayed in his work, I presume every American who reads this concluding sentence will cordially say, Amen.

I am, Sir, yours, etc.

# LETTER III

*Duke de La Rochefoucauld*

*Dear Sir,*

I will now proceed to an examination of the Travels of the *Duke de La Rochefoucauld-Liancourt.* It is remarkable that these three travelers all visited the United States at the same time; and must, one would suppose, since in many instances they visited the same scenes, have met with the same objects. This, however, can hardly have been the fact, if we are to form our conjectures from what they have written.

The Duke de La Rochefoucauld is plainly of a superior character in several respects to either of his compeers. He is pleasant, candid, grateful, and honorable; equally remote from the scientific vanity of Volney and the ill-natured petulence of Weld. He visited the United States for the purpose of learning the nature of the country and the character of its inhabitants. Whatever object within his reach he supposed likely to be worth his investigation, he examined, and often with a patient and vigorous inquisition. To such persons as he believed capable of giving him useful information, he applied for it, and frequently found those who furnished it with a good degree of correctness. When he was treated with civility, he was pleased; when with kindness, he was grateful. Generally, he is distinguished from both Volney and Weld in not deriving general conclusions from a single fact or a very small number of facts; and from the former particularly, in showing no disposition to originate theories. In fairness of character he leaves Weld out of sight, and in honorable intentions to do justice to the country which he was exploring.

With religion, the Duke had evidently never busied himself, and cannot, therefore, be supposed to have known much of this subject. In his politics he was altogether a Frenchman. Concerning these two subjects, it was to be expected that he would exercise pretty strong prejudices; and whoever had formed such an expectation, must, in reading his Travels, have found it realized. Concerning other subjects, his prejudices are fewer than those of most travelers; I think I may say, than of almost any. To me it seems that America is not a little indebted to this nobleman for being willing to enter so thoroughly into her condition and character, and for having represented it in so long a series of details with so much truth. Whether his work has been extensively read in France, I am ignorant. In this country it has certainly been read less than it deserves.

Still the Duke has fallen into many errors. Most of them are, however, of no great importance; and few of them, the result of negligence. Almost always they appear to be chargeable to erroneous informants; to ill intentions I should not attribute any which I have discovered.

My design in the following strictures is to show you how far the Duke's information may be safely made an object of reliance. You will understand that there are many mistakes in these Travels which I have purposely omitted, because I thought the number which I have selected sufficient for my design, and because I take little pleasure in finding fault with such a man.[1]

Vol. I. Page 352. "General Schuyler, who intends to purchase all the land on his own account (i.e., of the Iroquois tribes), experiences strong opposition from Timothy Pickering, who is said to be displeased that he cannot come in for a share in the proposed indemnification. These particulars, which I have from persons who think themselves well informed, may yet be mere scandalous reports, although they carry no improbability with them."

The Duke de La Rochefoucauld is in several instances adventurous in giving characters and attributing designs. I presume that nothing of this nature could be imputed to General Schuyler. Had the Duke known Colonel Pickering at that time as well as I have known him since, he would have thought that these reports, so far from carrying no improbability with them, were mere libels on the character of this gentleman. Aristides himself would not have entered with more reluctance or indignation upon the design which is here suggested.

Page 355. Colonel St. Leger "succeeded in penetrating to the fort, which he besieged, but the intelligence of the capture of General Burgoyne's army put a speedy end to the siege." [2]

Colonel St. Leger terminated the siege of Fort Stanwix on the 22nd of August. General Burgoyne's army surrendered on the 17th of the October following.

Page 365. "The Episcopal is the principal religion (i.e., in Schenectady), although the town contains also a church for German Lutherans, and one for Presbyterians. The Germans were also the most liberal benefactors to the institution of a college, the property of which amounts already to forty-two thousand, two hundred and twenty-two dollars, and one thousand, six hundred acres of lands given by the states."

There is no German Lutheran church in Schenectady. The Episcopal is not the prevalent religion. The largest congregation by far was at that time, and still is, that of Dutch Calvinists. The Dutch, not the Germans, were the most liberal benefactors to the institution of this college. The land possessed by this seminary was given by the state of New York, not by the states.

Page 367. "Albany is one of the most ancient settlements in North America, and was formed in the year 1660."

Albany began to be settled about the year 1612. According to Smith, the first fort was built in 1614.

Ibid. "Vermont and a part of New Hampshire furnish also many articles of trade."

Vermont trades with Albany; New Hampshire does not.

Page 400. "The road from Marlboro to Boston * is a continued village. Twenty miles from this city continues an uninterrupted line of handsome houses, cleanly and pleasant villages, neat gardens, and fine orchards, which form altogether a rich and delightful prospect."

Now let us hear M. Volney's account of the same subject.

"In the year 1796, from Boston to Richmond in Virginia, I scarcely marched through a tract of three miles together of cleared land." [3]

The Duke and M. Volney certainly saw with different optics.

Ibid. "You see everywhere numerous churches, of a simple construction, but neatly painted and furnished with fine spires."

This account, which is perfectly just, is not altogether accordant with the account given of this subject by the Christian Observer's correspondent, on which I formerly made some strictures.

Page 401. "A wooden bridge including the causeway leading to it is a mile in length."

The length of this bridge and its causeway is seven thousand, nine hundred and seventy-two and a half feet.

Page 406. "His (i.e. Mr. Thomas Russell's) assessment under the sole head of capitation or poll tax amounted to fifteen hundred dollars."

Mr. Russell's poll tax was the same with that of every other man who pays this tax and, I presume, never amounted to fifteen dollars. Mr. Russell possessed a fortune of about fourteen hundred thousand dollars, and must have paid a large tax; but his poll tax was no more than that of a day laborer.

Ibid. "Many colleges have been instituted in this state, which are scattered through its whole extent."

These numerous colleges, about which somebody must have abused the Duke's confidence, are Harvard, Williams, and Bowdoin Colleges, the latter in the District of Maine.

Page 443. "The common drink throughout all America is grog."

The common drink throughout all New England, New York, and a considerable part of New Jersey, except the recent settlements, is cider.

Page 447. "Penobscot is the only town in these parts, and it consists of a thousand houses."

The township of Penobscot contained in 1790, 1,048 inhabitants. In 1796,

* About thirty miles.

it was divided into two townships: Penobscot, containing 935; and Castine, containing 665: total 1600. The number of houses in both may possibly have been from 260 to 270.

Page 448. "The young people of both sexes, however, especially the young women, are desirous of a church in which they might have an opportunity to assemble every week and to display their persons. In New England they refrain on Sunday, with weak superstition, even from the most harmless sports; but it is, in truth, because it affords them an opportunity of going from home that these people are so fond of visiting the church."

The Duke would have done wisely (as would M. Volney also) had he wholly declined meddling with religion. On this subject both these writers are of course erroneous. The Duke allows that the New England people are actually fond of *visiting* the church. As they refrain on Sunday, even with weak superstition, from the most harmless sports, they can hardly be supposed to visit the church, through life, for the sake of going from home and meeting with their neighbors: since they cannot sport with them even in the most harmless manner; and since they actually can, and do, go from home and meet their neighbors at their pleasure, and indulge themselves in whatever sports they wish. That my fair country women, especially "the young women," are willing to display their persons and their dress on proper occasions, I am not disposed to deny. But I altogether doubt whether there is in the world an equal collection of human beings, possessing in greater numbers, or in higher degrees, the piety of the Gospel, or an equal number to which the remark of M. de La Rochefoucauld is with less propriety applicable.

Again page 447. "Throughout all America the building of a new church for each parochial district is considered as a very burdensome expense."

Out of New England there are in the proper sense no parochial districts. This observation then is capable of no application, but to New England. Whether the people of this country are reluctant to build churches, and to encounter the expense of their erection, may be easily determined from the vast number which they have built from the beginning, and from the numerous instances in which they are pulling down the old ones and building others which are larger and handsomer.

Page 474. "Salem is separated from Beverly only by a bridge fifteen feet in length."

I presume this must be an error of the press. The bridge is fifteen hundred feet in length.

Page 477. "Salem contains, upon an average, sixty-nine thousand inhabitants."

Salem contained according to the Census of 1790, 7,921 inhabitants.

Ibid. "Lynn which is dependent on the former place." (i.e. Salem.)

Lynn is in no respect dependent upon Salem.

Page 478. "General Warren who commanded in the celebrated battle of Bunker Hill."

In this battle General Warren was a volunteer, and had no command.

Ibid. "The fort stood—the taking of which cost the English 90 officers and 1400 men."

The loss of the British on this occasion was in a very small degree owing in any manner to the imperfect work here styled a fort, formed in less than twenty-four hours, and capable of containing but a small part of the Americans who were engaged. The action was a regular battle, in which the line extended across the peninsula.

Page 483. "These fugitives from persecution had not been here more than two years when they declared war against the Indians."

Similar assertions are found, Vol. II, p. 152.

The Plymouth colonists landed at the close of the year 1619. The first war declared by any of the New England colonists against the Indians was that against the Pequots in the year 1637. The second was that against Philip, 1675. The former of these was seventeen and the latter fifty-five years after the landing at Plymouth. Never was there a more absolute slander than that which is contained in these assertions of the Duke. The colonists acted only on the defensive, and labored with all their might to avoid war in both cases.

Ibid. "New emigrants arrived here from time to time from Europe. Other settlements were formed. Force or artifice extorted from the Indians new cessions of territory."

Again "Without any prejudices against the colonists, or in favor of the natives, it may be reasonably believed that the greater part of the enormities and crimes attributed to the Indians originated primarily from the conduct of the European settlers on their possessions."

When the colonists of New England purchased land of the Indians, they gave a fair, full price for what they bought. Purchases of this nature extended over almost all the colonies of Massachusetts, Plymouth, Connecticut, and Rhode Island. After the wars with the Pequots, Philip, and the Narragansets, they claimed, as all other nations have done, the rights of conquest; and never were these rights claimed with more absolute justice. The war, in each case, was merely defensive; and the injustice of the aggressors was of the grossest and most provoking nature. The colonists, without an unkind act on their part, were murdered in the most brutal manner by the Indians. They made patient and earnest efforts to obtain justice, but it was obstinately refused. In this situation, if in any which has ever existed, war was demanded. After the offending tribes were vanquished, lands were given to the surviving Indians who remained in the country more than sufficient for the maintenance of them all, even in their own mode of life; and, what was at least of as much importance, were secured to them against both frauds and purchases, so that most of them are holden to the present day. Where shall we find the historic page equally clean in this respect? No transactions of men are more pure than those concerning the purchase of lands from the Indians which are left upon record: as most, if not all of them are in the town records throughout New England. There is, therefore, no foundation for this senseless calumny; unless, indeed, the falsehood has been so often told that every slanderer has acquired a right to tell it again.

Whether the enormities and crimes attributed to the Indians derived their primary origin from the conduct of the New England encroachers may be conjectured from this consideration, that they existed antecedently to the arrival of the colonists, and were found by them already existing as established customs. Accordingly they were practised on each other.

From a period not long after the termination of Philip's War, the chief source of these enormities and crimes was the French government in Canada. "We have found," says Governor Shute, "by more than three score years' experience, that we had always lived in perfect peace with our neighboring Indians had it not been for the instigation, protection, supply, and even personal assistance of the French." See letter to Rallé, February 21, 1718. Hist. Coll., vol. V.[4]

Page 485. "Pit coal and iron stone are plentiful."

Pit coal has hitherto not been found either in Plymouth or in any other part of New England, except very lately in Rhode Island.

"His family" (i.e. the family of William Rotch) "has been for some generations engaged here in trade." [5]

The truth is, the town of New Bedford was settled in 1764. Mr. Rotch himself purchased it, as has been already mentioned in these letters.

Ibid. "The bread is commonly made of maize and barley; and this is, indeed, their usual bread throughout their whole state." [6]

Barley has never within my knowledge been employed as a material for making bread in New England.

Page 496. "It is usual for young people at the age of thirteen to leave the family of their parents and go into the service of others. The parents find it vain to endeavor to detain them; for if not permitted to work as others do, they will not work at home."

The Duke must have been in a reverie when he wrote these sentences. Children in New England are usually under a very efficacious parental government, and would regard a desertion of their home as the last misfortune. Were they disposed to this conduct, the law would punish both them and those by whom they were received.

Page 511. "Ships which exceed one hundred and twenty tons burden take their lading in Connecticut River at New Haven."

New Haven is thirty-four miles west of Connecticut River, and it is presumed that no ship from that river ever took in its lading at New Haven.

In vol. I, p. 514, he observes that "the notes of the New London bank are for a dollar." On the same page, he observes that "the notes of Norwich bank are for half a dollar"; and p. 519, that "the notes of Hartford bank are for a dollar each."

The notes of these and of all other American banks are, and ever have been of just such an amount, from a dollar upwards, as the directors please; and there never was a bank which issued notes of only a single given amount.

Page 515 and 516. The Duke makes several observations on the imperfection of the husbandry in Connecticut. The whole passage is too long to be quoted, and is generally erroneous.

Our husbandry is sufficiently imperfect; but, taken together, it is inferior to that of no state in the Union. In saying this I speak the common language of the country.

Page 521. "Some silver firs are thinly scattered over this tract." (i.e. between Northford and New Haven.)

The Duke mistook a kind of juniper for silver firs, and was perfectly right in saying that they make a poor appearance. His accounts of our forests are commonly erroneous; and he often finds other trees, besides firs, where no future traveler will ever find them.

Ibid. "Two great stone buildings belonging to the college, with the church and assembly house, standing round the church yard, compose the principal part of the town."

I think the Duke must have written this sentence when he was asleep, or else must have given us one of his dreams, or else the New Haven spoken of must be that which he has placed upon Connecticut River.

There were at that time three brick buildings belonging to the college and fronting the green in a row. There were also four churches and a statehouse. It is difficult to conceive how the four buildings mentioned by the Duke could compose the principal part of a town consisting of 550 houses, the least number attributable to New Haven at that period.

Page 522. "Only one of these ships sails to Europe; another makes its voyages to the West Indies. The remaining vessels (i.e. forty-eight) are engaged in the coasting trade."

There are fourteen or fifteen coasting vessels belonging to New Haven; and the number may possibly at some time or other have amounted to twenty. The remainder have always been employed in foreign trade.

Page 523. "Most of the inhabitants" (of New Haven) "have small farms in the neighborhood."

This would be a very pleasant story, if it were correct; but very few of them were then, or are now, able to boast of such a possession.

Page 525. "The most excessive intolerance, the most violent persecution, ensued against the Quakers in particular, who were treated as the worst of heretics, were tortured, banished, beaten with stripes, even put to death."

In the year 1656, the legislatures of Connecticut and New Haven colonies, in consequence of a recommendation from the commissioners of the four United Colonies, made a law against Quakers, Ranters, Adamites, and such like notorious heretics, forbidding all persons within the colony to entertain such heretics unnecessarily, on penalty of five pounds, and all towns to suffer such entertainment on the same penalty, per week. The governor, deputy governor, and assistants were empowered to commit them to prison, or send them out of the colony. Persons unnecessarily discoursing with them were fined twenty shillings; those who kept their books, ten shillings. County courts were required to suppress their books, and masters of vessels were required not to bring them into the colony. If they did, they were ordered to carry them out again at their first setting sail from the port where they landed them, on penalty of twenty pounds. This is the only law ever made in the colony of Connecticut against heretics. It was intolerant, but did not display the most excessive intolerance. It exhibits a spirit of persecution, but not of the most violent kind. When the Duke wrote this sentence, he certainly had forgotten the scenes which were acted throughout several centuries in his own country. But he informs us that the Quakers were tortured, banished, beaten with stripes, and even put to death.

This law was made, as I have observed, on a recommendation of the commissioners. Dr. Trumbull says that it was of short continuance, and that nothing of importance appears to have been transacted upon it, either in the colony of New Haven or that of Connecticut.[7] It does not appear that an individual Quaker ever suffered in Connecticut in his person or property on the score of religion. Quakers were, therefore, not banished, tortured, abused with stripes, nor put to death.

No person was ever tortured in Connecticut, for any reason, by any judicial court; nor in New England, nor, so far as my knowledge extends, in any of the United States.

Ibid. "Before which (i.e. the legislature) all suits at law may be brought by a last appeal."

No civil suit could be brought by appeal before the legislature where the sum depending was less than five thousand dollars.

Ibid. "The governor presides in the Council, and is also speaker in the House of Representatives."

He certainly must be a strange sort of a governor to hold both these offices; and stranger still, if he executed them: since the Council sat in one chamber and the Representatives in another at the same time.

Ibid. "Besides which, he can influence the voices of several other members of the legislature."

The governor of Connecticut has no *official* means of influence, and, if he were to use any other means, besides such as are involved in the character of a wise and good man, it would cost him his place.

Ibid. "The members of the Supreme Judicial Court, those of the county courts, and the justices of the peace are nominated from among the legislature."

The judges of the Supreme Judicial Court cannot be members of the legislature. The judges of the county courts may be, and some or other of them probably always are. There is however no legislature of which many of them are members. Whether justices of the peace are thus nominated may be determined from this fact. There are fifty-seven representatives in the counties of Hartford and New Haven, and 185 justices. The proportion is probably the same, substantially, elsewhere. The truth is, this assertion of the Duke is entirely groundless.

Page 527. "Without these conditions," (i.e. the possession of a hundred dollars, or a residence of six years) "he will not obtain relief from distress in poverty."

Every person who is in distress from poverty obtains immediate and certain relief, and that equally whether he be an inhabitant or a stranger. The only difference is that the expenses incurred for an inhabitant are charged to the town, while those incurred for a stranger are charged to the state.

Page 528. "The General Assembly has likewise the power of settling ministers."

The power of settling ministers is vested solely in the several congregations.

Page 529. "Although the letter of the law has established freedom of religious sentiments in Connecticut; such freedom is, however, far from being known here. Presbyterianism reigns in all its rigor, despotism, and intolerance."

The Duke is always unhappy when he speaks of religious subjects. If freedom of religious sentiments is not established in Connecticut, if it is not known in its fullest extent, it will be difficult to say where it is known. Not a legal disadvantage is laid upon any man for his religious sentiments. Every man may here think and worship as he pleases. Even those who unhappily do not worship at all meet with no molestation. The several religious sects live together in absolute harmony. It is true we do not think very favorably of persons who are irreligious and immoral, and this perhaps may be what the Duke intends; but both the laws and the inhabitants suffer them quietly to pursue their own courses so far as their religious sentiments are concerned. Presbyterians have no peculiar privileges, and claim none. It is difficult, therefore, to conceive how Presbyterianism can here be intolerant, still more how it can reign, and most of all how it can be despotic. All these imply some superiority over others, but Presbyterianism here has none.

It ought to be remembered that Presbyterianism (that is in the New England sense) was once the established religion of Connecticut; and that, although those who profess it have always been a vast majority of the inhabitants, they by a law which themselves made voluntarily placed other denominations upon the same footing with themselves.

Ibid. "Every town forming a regular incorporation must keep a grammar school."

This is in error. Every town is incorporated, but every town is not obliged to keep a grammar school.

Page 531. "The considerations which moved the legislature to determine as they did in this business were respect to property and the fear of dangerous consequences as likely to arise from a sudden and general emancipation."

This is an error. The determination referred to was that every black born in the state after the year 1784 should be free at adult age. The considerations which prevented the legislature of Connecticut from emancipating all the slaves within the state at once were the following. A considerable number of the inhabitants believed slavery, as it existed here, to be justifiable. Many of these who were slave holders insisted that they had bought their slaves under the protection and countenance of the government; and that, therefore, if their slaves were taken from them, they should have an equitable claim upon the government for remuneration. By others it was considered as a violent act to take them away, although they cordially wished them emancipation. The legislative act which has been alluded to was really a compromise between the parties on this subject, and was the more readily acceded to because it was generally thought that those who had kept slaves, and had received the benefit of their labor throughout their working years, ought now to support them, and not to throw them as a burden upon the community. From the slaves themselves there was not, and could not possibly be, any apprehension. There was never any law authorizing slavery. The practice was adopted merely because it had been pursued in other parts of the British dominions.

The whole number of slaves in the state according to the last census was 310.

Page 536. "The ministers, who in consequence of their mutual wranglings and their fierce intolerance have lost much of the high influence which they once possessed."

The ministers of Connecticut do not wrangle, and they are not intolerant. Our brethren who inhabit the states south of us complain even to this day that the influence of ministers here is still too high.

Ibid. "Such as possess extraordinary wealth are very anxious to conceal their fortunes from the vigilant and invidious jealousy of their fellow citizens."

This is a groundless misapprehension of the Duke. There is no such jealousy on the one hand, and no such anxiety on the other.

Ibid. "No culture, but that of meadows, no tillage appears." [8] (i.e. between Fairfield and Stamford.)

There is no part of New England equally extensive in which there is a greater proportion of tillage, and a less, of meadow. Indeed the proportion of tillage is as great as can consist with good husbandry.

Ibid. "It is said that the soil in general is sufficiently good for bearing corn, but that the nature of the climate subjects the crop to a blasting that never fails to spoil it in its growth. These disadvantages affect the whole territory lying along this coast."

I will not examine the philosophy of the Duke's informants. They were erroneous in the facts. The real blast is the Hessian fly.

Ibid. "From this place (Stamford) the coast of Long Island is forty, from New Haven it is not more than twenty miles distance."

The coast of Long Island is twelve miles from Stamford and twenty-nine from New Haven.

Page 530. "Ships of small burden make their way through the Sound to New York." [9]

Ships of all sizes pass easily through the Sound to Hell Gate. American frigates of forty-four guns, and sixteen hundred tons burden, go safely through that passage.

Ibid. "The passage to the island of New York is by King's ferry, at the distance of fourteen miles from that city."

It should have been written, "The passage to New York is by King's bridge etc." King's ferry is a ferry over the Hudson about forty-four miles from New York.

Page 541. The description given of the lands on Connecticut River is in many respects imperfect and erroneous.

Vol. II, page 141. "That which above all the others most violently clashed with the maxims and interests of the synod was his declaration, 'that punishment inflicted for matters of conscience was persecution."

The whole of this story is erroneously told. But the particulars are too numerous for insertion in this place. Mr. Williams had certainly some considerable excellencies in his character, and as certainly some serious defects. *Quod sensit valde sensit.* Whatever opinion he took up as a part of his own system, he seized with a rank hold. His opinions on several religious subjects were rigid and straitened to a degree rarely paralleled; and some of them were certainly dangerous to the peace of society, and to religion. Among other doctrines, he held it to be unlawful to commune with his brethren in Boston, unless they would acknowledge themselves to have sinned in communing with the Church of England before their emigration, and declare their repentance. He denied that the magistrate could lawfully punish blasphemy, profaneness, or Sabbathbreaking; or tender an oath to a man whom he believed to be unregenerate. He declared it to be unlawful for a Christian to pray with a man whom he believed to be of this character, even a member of his family; and that it was unlawful to give thanks after the sacramental supper, or after common meals. He pronounced the churches of New England polluted and anti-Christian, and refused to commune with the members of his own church unless they would separate from the other churches. He was baptized a second time in March 1639 by one of the brethren of his church, but after a short time he determined that baptism ought not to be administered at all without an immediate revelation. For the second, third, and fourth of these tenets, he was banished. But it must be remembered that Mr. Williams was not banished for *holding* these opinions. He conversed, preached, wrote, and acted. He refused to take the oath of fidelity himself, and taught others to refuse. Morton said, "He spake dangerous words"; Mather said, "He preached furiously against the patent, which was the foundation of the government." In a similar manner he struck at the character and existence of the New England churches, and boldly pronounced them anti-Christian. Finally he refused to pray with his own wife and family, or to ask a blessing at meals with them, because they attended public worship with the church at Salem, which refused to withdraw from communion with the neighboring churches.[10]

In the infant state of the New England government and churches, such a man threatened not only their peace, but their existence. He was plainly a man of talents, bold, restless, regardless of consequences; and in his judgment and feelings, and in his ecclesiastical conduct also, at least as intolerant toward those who differed from him as they in their civil conduct towards him. They took not a little pains to reclaim him, and plainly were very much at a loss how to live with him in peace. Any alteration in his opinions and practices, except what was originated by his own mind, was hopeless. He was sure of being right. He was right when he held the doctrine of infant baptism. He was right when he was baptized anew by one of the members of his own church in Providence. He was right when, after this, he rebaptized several of them. He was right when he told them that in all this he had been deluded and had misled them, that their last baptism, as well as the first, was a nullity, and that they must renounce all that had been hitherto done and wait the coming of new apostles.

Page 142. "The accusation brought against him was only a pretext to cloak the jealousy entertained of his influence by Governor Winthrop and others. But that pretext was an effectual mean of accomplishing their views; and, Coddington being banished," etc.

This is an error. Mr. Coddington was not banished. He removed quietly from Boston to Rhode Island. All the history which I can find concerning this subject says otherwise. Mr. Coddington was an assistant; and, having become an Antinomian, probably by the influence of Mrs. Hutchinson, was left out of the list of magistrates by his countrymen. He then in company with some others purchased Aquidneck, which he named Rhode Island. In his latter days he became a Quaker.

Page 148. "Taunton and Durham, each the capital of a county of similar name."

Taunton is the capital of a county named *Bristol. Dedham,* not Durham, is the capital of a county named *Norfolk.*

Page 152. "But soon these newcomers became persecutors in turn."

On this subject see the remarks already made on the persecutions of the Indians by the people of Connecticut. The answer there given will refute this calumny, as well as that.

Page 153. "The Presbyterians, finding themselves more numerous than the other sects . . ."

There were no other sects until a considerable time after the country began to be colonized. Permit me here to observe what, so far as my knowledge extends, seems to have been passed over in the writings of others, that the first colonists of New England left their own country and came to this inhospitable wilderness with a full expectation and settled design to live by themselves. It was their darling wish, the great object of all their aims, to live by themselves, safe from the intrusions of others. They had gone through every labor, expense, and suffering to accomplish this desirable object. In their own country they had undergone everything but death on account of their religion. In this distant, solitary wild, they naturally thought that they might be undisturbed. They had purchased the country at home. They had again purchased it here. They had settled it; they had defended it. The expense and self-denial, the patience and perseverance which they had encountered were extreme, wonderful, and such as, in their own view at least, entitled them fairly to an exemption from all the trouble afterwards given them by the Baptists and Quakers. When they had gone through all these difficulties to a great extent, and changed the country into a desirable habitation, these people came in among them. Why did they come? They were not invited. They were not welcomed. They were not desired. The New England colonists intruded upon no settlements of Baptists or Quakers; nor did they meddle with the business, or break into the precincts of any other people. It was one of the privileges of *Israel* that *they should dwell alone.*[11] The people of New England wished ardently for the same privilege; and for the very same reason, viz., that they might transmit what they believed to be the religion of the Gospel, pure in its doctrine, discipline, and manners, to their posterity. Why should this privilege be grudged to them? The Baptists and Quakers, they regarded as errorists. *They* had done nothing toward purchasing, clearing, or defending the country; and, in the view of the inhabitants, came only to corrupt their principles and disturb their peace. They cordially hated the people of New England. Why did they not stay among those whom they liked better? The only answer is, they came to make proselytes: the most uncomfortable of all intruders.

Internal dissensions have been universally esteemed more serious calamities than external wars; and internal dissensions about religion are certainly as serious calamities as those about liberty. He who excites civil discord in a community is universally accounted an enemy of its peace. Why is he less deserving of this character who excites religious dissensions?

The world was sufficiently wide to furnish the same opportunities to Baptists and Quakers to plant themselves which had been found by the people of New England. Sufficient tracts might have been obtained from the Crown and purchased of the Indians. Why did they not obtain and purchase these tracts? Had they done this, the New England people would not have disturbed them. In England no man is permitted to preach *without a license from the government.* These people preached in New England in defiance of the express injunctions of the government. A number of them insulted both the government and the religious worship of the country with gross indecency and outrage.

The Duke asserts that "the Quakers, and Baptists were persecuted, imprisoned, banished, and put to death."

It is not true than any Anabaptist was put to death. Several of them, after having openly disobeyed an express injunction of the government, were imprisoned and banished; and one of them, who insulted the court, and was declared by his neighbors to be an idle, lying fellow, was whipped. So late as the year 1748, the Rev. Dr. Rodgers, of New York, was sent out of Virginia by the General Court of that province for preaching to some Presbyterians who had invited him into the country for that purpose. This gentleman did what all others ought to do in the like circumstances. Upon receiving the order of the Court he desisted from preaching and left the province.

I am no friend to persecution for religion, or for anything else; and regard it, as I believe, in all cases with at least as much abhorrence as the Duke de La Rochefoucauld or any other declaimer against the New England colonists. Still I can find no justification either for the Anabaptists, or for the Quakers, those, I mean, who are the subjects of these remarks.

Ibid. "The worst of all governments is that in which a system of religion is the main spring, and which is either conducted or influenced by the ministers of that religion."

A part of this sentence is just, and the rest may be fairly yielded to a man who had lived in a Popish country. A government conducted by the ministers of religion must certainly be a bad one, I think the worst of all governments, for the following reasons. When civil and ecclesiastical power are united in the same hands, such ecclesiastical power as has been actually possessed by men in most countries, and such as in this case would be possessed by them in all, would furnish temptations which they would never resist, and generate a system of oppression which their subjects could never sustain. The ministers would become villains, and the people would be undone. The experiment has been fairly tried in the Romish hierarchy, and happily for mankind can never be tried again. Should it be said that the ministers of religion would be persons of too good a character to be guilty of such enormities? Probably this would be true of the first set which came into these dangerous circumstances, because they would be merely ministers of the Gospel, men who came into that office for the sake of discharging its duties. But those who followed them would enter the ministry solely for the purpose of obtaining the power attached to the office. These would commence their ministry with fraud, and would soon become abandoned. The government, therefore, would be in the very worst hands; and, because the power possessed by them would be greater than in any other case, would be the worst government. But a system of religion, or in better words, the true religion or Christianity, ought to be the basis of all government. In this case human government would proceed on the same principles as that of the Infinite Ruler. All governments also ought to be regulated absolutely by these principles. Were they in fact thus regulated, an end would be put to all those sufferings which subjects feel except from the incapacity of rulers.

The question, *Whether ministers ought to have influence with respect to the affairs of government* will, if answered with truth, be answered differently according to the character of ministers, and according to the degree and perhaps the manner in which the influence is employed. By influence I intend the efficacy which the character and circumstances of one man have toward inducing others voluntarily to coincide with him in opinions and measures. Where clergymen are wise and virtuous men, it is hardly possible that their influence upon government should fail of being beneficial.

The case of Massachusetts and Connecticut alluded to at the commencement of the paragraph from which the last quotation is taken is unfortunately selected by the Duke for the purpose of proving his assertion. In these states from their first settlement, ministers, although absolutely destitute of power, have had as much influence as in any country in the world. It is no exaggeration to say that in these two communities, industry, good neighborhood, good order, useful knowledge, sound morals, and genuine piety have flourished as uniformly and as extensively as in any country on the globe.

Page 154. "The governor and judges of Salem. . . ."

There never were any such persons.

Page 206. "Indian corn bears no higher price here (i.e. in Brookfield, Massachusetts) than nine pence a bushel."

The Duke must have been egregiously misinformed concerning this subject. The Brookfield farmers would hardly be satisfied with the market which he has provided for them. The lowest price at which I ever knew Indian corn sold was two shillings † a bushel. In the years 1795 and 1796, it could not be less than four, and was not improbably five or six shillings.

I will now close the remarks which I have thought proper to make on the Duke de La Rochefoucauld. I should do justice neither to the traveler, nor to myself, if I did not observe that I have found his work much more valuable than I expected. There are, indeed, many errors in it. Some I have mentioned, and not a small number of others might have been added to them. But it contains also very many valuable truths. The writer was often misinformed, sometimes negligent, and sometimes misled by prejudice; but he discovers everywhere a wish to gain information, and a willingness to recite it. What he saw he is willing to report as it appeared to him. In the times in which he wrote, it was scarcely possible not to be prejudiced about politics; or, with the education which he had received, about religion. Generally he discovers a commendable spirit of inquiry and industry, respectable understanding, and an honorable degree of integrity and candor.‡

I am, Sir, yours, etc.

# LETTER IV

*Lambert*

*Dear Sir,*

I have lately seen Travels in Lower Canada and North America, in the years 1806, 1807, and 1808, by John Lambert, a native of Great Britain, printed in London for Richard Phillips, 1810.[1] On this book I will now make a number of observations.

Permit me to say generally that the writer is superior to most of his fellow

† One and sixpence sterling.

‡ The following may serve as specimens of the errors into which foreigners easily fall with respect to the names of persons and places, and into which they betray their readers. The Duke says:

| | | | | | |
|---|---|---|---|---|---|
| *Belly town* | for | Belchertown | *Gresworth* | for | Griswold |
| *Volwich* | for | Woolwich | *Stone river* | for | Stoney River |
| *Pepperborough* | for | Pepperelborough | *Watworth* | for | Wadsworth |
| *Saga* | for | Saco | *Golf* | for | Goff |
| *Goldhue* | for | Goodhue | *Whadley* | for | Whalley |
| *William Rush* | for | William Rotch | *Durham* | for | Dedham, etc. |

travelers in candor and justice. He came to America, as he informs us, upon business. Unexpected disappointments having frustrated his design, he found himself at leisure to travel over several parts of this continent. The result of his observations and inquiries he has given us in three octavo volumes and has in my view made a valuable present to the public. The information which he has furnished concerning Canada, unless I am deceived, is to a considerable extent new and satisfactory. In the United States his opportunities of seeing the country and acquiring information were much fewer than I should have wished, and evidently much more limited than he himself wished. Yet he has the merit of having made the most of them. What he saw, he generally observed with accuracy and good sense, and told with truth; and it deserves to be recorded to his honor that, with a victory over prejudice not often achieved by Englishmen traveling in this country, he appears plainly to have been desirous of seeing everything in its native light, and not with jaundiced eyes. For his information he was dependent as every traveler must be upon others; often he is well informed; at times he was undoubtedly led into error. He passed over several hundred miles in which I have traveled; and his accounts of what fell under his eye are just, beyond what I should expect from a foreigner to whom every object was new, and who had so little opportunity of examining with attention. Upon the whole, Mr. Lambert has claims to respect and to confidence which cannot be challenged by any other native of Great Britain who has appeared here as a traveler.

The following paragraph in the introduction to his work well deserves the attentive perusal of every Briton who considers this country as meriting his regard.

After residing a twelve month in Canada, I visited the United States, a country whose real state is almost as little known in England as that of Canada; and the manners and dispositions of whose inhabitants are seldom viewed, but through the false medium of popular prejudice.

Whatever truth there may have been in the accounts given of the United States by former writers, they present at this day but imperfect or distorted pictures of the country and its inhabitants. Those who have not seen the United States for the last twenty years would be astonished at the alteration that has taken place. No country perhaps ever increased in population and wealth, or rose into importance among other nations more rapidly than the United States. Within the space of thirty years, they have emerged from the obscurity of colonies into the rank of independent states, governed by a constitution altogether novel in the present times, but which, whatever defects it may contain, has proved the source of all their prosperity. The people of England are too apt to hold the character of the Americans in trifling estimation; but, when it is known that their country is fast approaching to importance, that their imports and exports already amount to one half of those of Great Britain, while their annual expenditure is not a twentieth and their national debt not a fortieth part of ours, we cannot avoid giving them our meed of admiration, whatever jealousy might suggest to the contrary. It is to be hoped that the two nations will no longer give way to blind and acrimonious prejudices against each other, but endeavor to cultivate the blessings of peace instead of the horrors of war.

It would be well if some of your journalists were to learn a little truth from these observations of Mr. Lambert, and to believe with him that the travelers whose malignant accounts they take a pleasure apparently not less malignant in quoting have given only imperfect or distorted pictures of the country and its inhabitants. The blind and acrimonious prejudices mentioned by this writer have been indulged by no persons with greater spleen or grosser falsehood than by the authors of some of your reviews. Great Britain has no market of so much value to her as the United States; and no body of men in the world, equally numerous, so willing to be her steadfast friends upon reasonable principles as a large part of their inhabitants. Why this body should be provoked and alienated by the torrents of abuse so liberally poured out on your side of the Atlantic, the writers to whom I have referred are yet to explain.[2]

Page 176. "From what cause the custom (of driving on the right side of the road) originated in America, I cannot say."

The cause is this: The drivers of loaded carts and wagons usually walk on the left side. If you take the right, the driver is of course between you and his own team. He is therefore able to see that he gives you sufficient room, which he could not do if you took the left side. Hence the law requires every carriage to go on the right.

Page 278. "The inhabitants of the shores of Nova Scotia and the New England states, who are enveloped in fogs more than one half the year, enjoy the same ruddy complexion as the English, while those who live in the interior under a clear sky are universally distinguished by sallow and swarthy complexions."

There are two errors in this sentence so far as it respects New England. Its shores generally enjoy a remarkably fine, clear sky; and the inhabitants of the interior are rather more ruddy, so far as there is any difference, than those on the shore.

Page 354. On this and the following pages there are several unfortunate observations concerning religion, a subject which the writer has very imperfectly examined. I mention the fact not as coming within the scope of these remarks; but merely that, after what I have said concerning the respectable character of Mr. Lambert, it might not be supposed from my silence that I approved of these opinions. In the subsequent parts of the book there are other observations of a nature generally similar. At the same time, I acknowledge with pleasure that Mr. Lambert appears to be respectful to religion and morality.[3]

Page 435. "The rabbit was never found wild in any part of America."

Wild rabbits are considerably numerous in New England.

Vol. II, page 128. "The Americans are so extremely captious on political subjects that they can never speak of them without entering into a dispute, and disputes generally terminate in quarrels."

The Americans are without a doubt sufficiently inclined to dispute about political subjects, and are in my opinion at least sufficiently captious. New England is believed to be as much interested in this controversy as any part of the American Union. Yet there are every day conversations on political subjects without disputes, and disputes without quarrels. These indeed must be very rare, for I do not remember that I have heard of half a dozen in New England during the twenty-five years which have elapsed since the establishment of the American Constitution.

Page 129. "It (the American stage coach) is always drawn by four horses, which, in well-settled parts of the United States, are as good as the generality of English stage horses."

Who could have expected this from an English traveler in America!

Page 132. "At the better sort of American taverns or hotels, very excellent dinners are provided, consisting of almost everything in season."

Ibid. "English breakfasts and teas are, generally speaking, meager repasts compared with those of America; and as far as I had an opportunity of observing, the people live, with respect to eating, in a much more luxurious manner than we do, particularly in the large towns and in their neighborhoods. But their meals I think are composed of too great a variety, and of too many things to be conducive to health; and I have little doubt but that many of their diseases are engendered by gross diet, and the use of animal food at every meal. Many private families live nearly in the same style as at these houses, and have as great a variety upon their tables."

I hope Mr. Lambert, since he is a Briton, will be considered as an exceptionable witness to the fact that the people of this country have something to eat and drink both in private houses and in inns; the testimony of your former travelers to the contrary notwithstanding. I, who have known the whole subject by experience, can testify that this has been the fact with regard to both private houses and inns from my earliest remembrance. Food in the richest variety has always abounded in this country, and has been within the reach of every man possessed even of moderate property. The principal difference between the farmers and mechanics who are in easy circumstances, or are worth from five to ten thousand dollars, and the gentlemen (that is when there is any difference) is, so far as the mode of living is concerned, found chiefly in the different modes of management, particularly in cookery. A farmer of my acquaintance, worth perhaps from twenty to twenty-five thousand dollars, kept as good a table as any man whom I ever knew.

The best old fashioned New England inns were superior to any of the modern ones which I have seen. They were at less pains to furnish a great variety of food. Yet the variety was ample. The food was always of the best quality; the beds were excellent; the house and all its appendages were in the highest degree clean and neat; the cookery was remarkably good; and the stable was not less hospitable than the house. The family in the meantime were possessed of principle, and received you with the kindness and attention of friends. Your baggage was as safe as in your own house. If you were sick, you were nursed and befriended as in your own family. No tavern-haunters, gamblers, or loungers were admitted, any more than in a well-ordered private habitation; and as little noise was allowed.

There was less bustle, less parade, less appearance of doing much to gratify your wishes than at the reputable modern inns; but much more actually done, and much more comfort and enjoyment. In a word, you found in these inns the pleasures of an excellent private house. To finish the story, your bills were always equitable, calculated on what you ought to pay, and not upon the scheme of getting the most which extortion might think proper to demand.

The Duke de La Rochefoucauld was sick at the house of Captain Williams in Marlboro. A stranger, a foreigner, appearing as he says in a very plain dress, and universally in circumstances which indicated no superiority of rank or character; after he had recovered his health, chiefly as it would seem by the kindness of the family, he exclaimed, "Surely these are the best people in the world." [4]

I am entirely of Mr. Lambert's opinion that our meals are very often composed of too great a variety to be conducive to health. A simpler mode of living would naturally prevent excess in eating and drinking. Our dinners are furnished with a great variety of vegetables as well as of meats.

Page 136. "The morning was remarkably fine."

The account which is given in the following paragraphs of the Hudson and the country bordering upon it, particularly of the beauty and magnificence of the scenery, is just, and far from being exaggerated. I hope it will contribute to persuade some of your countrymen that nature did not lavish all her charms on the eastern continent, but reserved some of her choice gifts for America. One of your countrymen a short time since questioned one of mine to the following effect: "How comes it to pass that America has no such fine scenery as we find in European countries?"

Page 146. "The first is of very considerable extent, being one hundred and twenty miles in length, and about eight miles in breadth. It is a fertile and well-cultivated piece of land, inhabited chiefly by the descendants of the old Dutch settlers."

For the truth with regard to these subjects, I refer you to my observations concerning Long Island, and to my notes on the travels of Weld.

Page 202. "A taste for reading has of late diffused itself through the country, particularly in the great towns."

A taste for reading has always been diffused throughout New England,

and social libraries were frequent at the beginning of the last century; and the libraries of ministers and other men of learning were to a considerable extent better than they are now.

Ibid. "It seems indeed that the fair sex of America have, within these few years, been desirous of imitating the example of the English and French ladies. They have cast away the gossiping and frivolous tittle-tattle which before has occupied so much of their attention."

Mr. Lambert was misinformed concerning this subject. The ladies in New England who received a good education fifty, sixty, and in various instances even one hundred years ago, were as well educated as most of those who have followed them; were possessed of as much sound knowledge, of as refined a taste, of as elegant accomplishments, and of as much dignity and excellence. The modern education is attended with more expense and parade, but is not productive of greater moral or intellectual improvement.

Page 208. "I was told of one (sailor) who carried with him a small grappling, and, while the horse was at full speed down one of the streets, threw out the anchor; which, catching hold of the stones, suddenly brought him up, broke his horse's neck, and hurled him a distance of several yards upon the pavement."

This story I heard when I was a boy; and it may serve to show you that your travelers pick up many a tale of other times, and present it to the public as an account of something that has lately happened.

Page 357. "Toward evening we lost sight of Neversink Hills, and could not help thinking upon the absurdity of their name while I beheld their summits sink into the ocean as the vessel receded from the coast."

I have been accustomed to see the name printed *Navesink,* and have supposed it an Indian word, corrupted by careless pronunciation into Neversink.

Page 399. "At the period when the Americans were so much exasperated against Great Britain in consequence of the attack upon the Chesapeake frigate," etc.

The story told in this paragraph is erroneous, and Mr. Lambert was ill-informed. I never before heard that the British subjects throughout the states were under the necessity of keeping within doors until the popular fury was abated. No Americans, so far as I remember, wore a piece of crape round their arm in those parts of the country with which I am well acquainted, nor was any man within those limits ducked under the pumps for refusing to comply with that mark of respect for his deceased countrymen.

The chief reason for which I have quoted this sentence is the improper attribution which it contains of actions and characters to all the Americans, which are due to a part only, and that probably very small. This is a very common and very unfortunate practice of your travelers in the United States. They see or hear of something which is done in this country, some local custom, some solitary incident, some good or bad treatment of a foreigner. They find two or three bad inns, make with some sharper a disadvantageous bargain, purchase lands unadvisedly of some jobber and are bitten in the contract, and are otherwise injured, teased, or abused. Immediately the character becomes in their mouths universal; the custom spreads over the whole country; the incidents become a general history; the people have all turned sharpers and land jobbers; the inns are all dirty, and the innkeepers rude, vulgar, and insolent.

The case in which this conversion of individuals into a class, and of particular into generals, is most frequent, and which an inhabitant of New England regards with very little complacency, is that in which the customs, manners, morals, and other characteristics of other states of the union are applied to his own. A traveler in one of the United States is told that the inhabitants treat their slaves with cruelty; in another he is informed that they are engaged frequently in duels, fighting cocks, gouging and horse racing; that they are rude and insolent to strangers; that their inns are wretched; their churches few, poor, and decayed; their ministers few, and many of them uneducated; the manners expensive; the income of the inhabitants anticipated, and their character extensively that of semicivilization. Now, whether these things are truly said or not, I am not at present interested to inquire. My objection lies to the manner in which they are described and attributed. They are described as general customs of the whole country, and are attributed to its inhabitants universally. Thus we are told that the *Americans* gouge, race horses, and fight cocks; and that the inns, the churches, the ministers, the manners, and the customs of the United States are such and such.

Suppose I were to travel through Spain; and, finding the Inquisition in that country, should say in the journal of my tour that this horrid tribunal is established in Europe, and that the inhabitants at the end of certain periods celebrate the auto-da-fé.[5] Suppose I were to travel through Turkey, and accommodating my journal to the manners of the Turks, should say that the people of Europe are Mohammedans, wear mustachios, keep their turbans on, and pull off their shoes in their mosques, have each four wives, and as many concubines as they can maintain, are served by eunuchs and mutes, and are obliged to go once in their lives on a pilgrimage to Mecca. Or suppose I should make an excursion into Russia, and should attribute all that Dr. Clarke has said to disgrace the people of that country to the Europeans generally; [6] or, proceeding onward to Lapland, should attribute to the inhabitants of Europe the size, structure, features and complexion of the Laplanders; what would a candid and intelligent man think of my assertions and my character? What would the inhabitants of Great Britain, France, and Germany think of a traveler who applied to them declarations which were true of Spaniards, Turks, or Laplanders only?

Yet these assertions, when made concerning the people of Europe at large, would be no less just and true than those assertions which your travelers often make concerning the inhabitants of this country under the general names of Americans, or the people of the United States: assertions adopted with even less discrimination by several writers in your literary journals. The customs, manners, and morals of the states at the southern and western borders of the Union are to a great extent absolutely unknown in New England; and the story concerning the inns, the churches, the ministers, the gouging, the horse racing, the cockfighting, the gambling, and the great variety of imputations thrown by your tourists on the character of the Americans are as little applicable to New England as to old England, and in most instances much less. Your people make horse racing an amusement of high importance; and your gentlemen, clergy, nobles, and princes frequent this diversion at Newmarket in the same manner as your jockeys. Your people fight cocks; to us the thing is unknown except by report. Gambling is carried on to an extent immeasurably greater with you than with us. Gouging, familiarly attributed to us by some of your writers, is as absolutely unknown in New England as in St. James' Palace. Our inns perhaps are not as good as yours, but I am confident that they are better than those of any other country. Our plain people have more civility than such of yours as visit this country, and are abundantly better-informed. The gentlemen are less haughty, distant, and reserved. Of our churches and ministers, I have already given you a sufficient account.

But this is not all. Your travelers seize on a single person, or a solitary fact, and make them the representatives of a whole community and a general custom. Have you no awkward persons? No sharpers? No debauchees? No profligates? No blunderers in language, both in pronunciation and meaning? If not, what are we to think concerning the representations made of morals, manners, and language of your inhabitants in plays, novels, newspapers, literary journals, travels, and moral treatises? Is an American to form his ideas of the language of Great Britain from that of the driver of a stagecoach, a porter, a Yorkshireman, or an inhabitant of Wales? Are the morals of Wapping to characterize the English nation? Is the phraseology of Billingsgate to become a specimen of their breeding? Are the coal heavers and coal miners who supply London with fuel to become the index of your manners? And are we to learn the state of your morals from Colquhoun's Police of London, or from that of the Thames? [7]

Mr. Lambert is less afflicted with this disease of turning particulars into generals, and individual facts and persons into a host than most of your travelers. Yet even he is not without some trespasses. They are however so few, and of so little moment, as scarcely to demand animadversion.

Page 431. "The militia of the United States is, for the most part, badly disciplined. In the towns, some show of military force is kept up by the volunteers; but throughout the country places the militia meet only to eat, drink, and be merry."

That this may be true of the militia of some other states in the Union, I am not warranted to deny, but it has no application to Massachusetts and Connecticut. With the character of the militia in other states I am very imperfectly acquainted. In these the militia are an excellent body of men; and, though inferior in most instances to some of the volunteer corps in the large towns, are well dressed, and to a great extent well disciplined. An American officer of distinction, who at New London saw daily the appearance and discipline of the Connecticut state troops taken by voluntary enlistment, and stationed in the neighborhood of that city, declared that he had never seen a finer body of men although he had often seen the guards of His Britannic Majesty and the invincibles of Napoleon. The militia of these states, whenever they are assembled for the purpose of discipline, instead of spending their time in eating and drinking, are very industriously employed in the proper business of the day.

Vol. III, page 80. "It (New Haven) has a harbor for small coasting vessels."

The harbor of New Haven admits easily ships of three and four hundred tons, and a number of the vessels owned in this town have *coasted* round the globe. Mr. Lambert arrived at New Haven about midnight, and left it the next morning. It is not strange that his account of it should be both defective and erroneous.

Page 86. "Hartford contains about 10,000 inhabitants." [8]

The city of Hartford contained 3,955 inhabitants; the remainder of the township, 2,048.

Vol. II, page 131. Mr. Lambert says, "Albany contains about 6,000 inhabitants."

The inhabitants of Albany by the same census amounted to 9,356, and including the little town of Colonie separated from it only by an imaginary line, 10,962.

Vol. III, page 86. "Elders go about and forbid innkeepers to suffer any person at their peril to travel," i.e. upon the Sabbath.

Somebody abused the confidence of Mr. Lambert. Such a fact I presume never took place in Connecticut. The ministers of this state have no authority over innkeepers, or any other persons except as ministers or parents, and are not accustomed to meddle with business which is not their own. The sportive observations at the conclusion of this paragraph are therefore out of place.

Page 88. "It was only within these few years that the spring was discovered."

Fifty years since it was at least as much celebrated as at the present time.

Page 89. "Throughout the states of Connecticut, Massachusetts, and New York, a remarkably neat, and indeed elegant style of architecture and decoration seems to pervade all the buildings in the towns and villages; and I understand is more or less prevalent in the northern and middle states. The houses in the small towns and villages are mostly built of wood, generally one or two stories above the ground floor; the sides are neatly clapboarded and painted white; the sloping roofs are covered with shingles and painted of a slate color; and with sash windows, green venetian shades outside, neat white railings, and steps have a pretty effect. Sometimes the entrance is ornamented with a portico. The churches, or as they are oftener termed meetings, are constructed of similar materials, painted white, and frequently decorated like the houses with sash windows and green venetian shades. The building is also surmounted by a handsome spire or steeple with one or two bells. A small town composed of these neat and ornamental edifices, and situated in the neighborhood of well-cultivated farms, large fields, orchards, and gardens, produces a most agreeable effect, and gives the traveler a high opinion of the prosperity of the country, and of the wealth and happiness of its inhabitants. Indeed those parts of the northern and middle states through which I traveled have the appearance of old well-settled countries. The towns and villages are populous; provisions are cheap and abundant; the farms appear in excellent order; and the inhabitants, sober, industrious, religious, and happy."

I wish this passage to be compared with the declarations of Volney and other travelers on this subject.

Page 94. "The inhabitants of Marlboro are nearly all Congregationalists. This denomination of Christians practice a form of worship that easily reconciles the Presbyterian and Episcopalian to meet in one church. It is in some sort a relaxed Presbyterian service. They have no written form of prayer, the service consisting of chapters of Scripture, extemporary prayers, and a sermon, with psalms or hymns at intervals. The minister frequently reads his discourse as in the Episcopal churches, and organs are often put up in the meetinghouse. The prayers of those Congregational ministers have been of that general and tolerant nature which embraces all sects and denominations of Christians, supplicating for the safety and welfare of all men without respect of persons. Their discourses were generally of an evangelical cast, but devoid of all absolute tenets, dogmas, and denunciations. Faith was earnestly recommended, but the necessity of good works was strenuously enforced."

I hope these remarks will be admitted by Englishmen, and among others by your journalists, as proofs that the inhabitants, particularly the Congregationalists, who constitute the great body of the inhabitants of New England, are extensively destitute of that bigotry so liberally fastened upon them by former English travelers, and by a multitude of their countrymen. I hope also that it will be allowed to refute the imputations of intolerance on these very people by the Duke de La Rochefoucauld, good-natured and candid on every other subject, but always erroneous and some times perverse on that of religion. I hope also that the declaration (page 86 of the same volume), "The people of Connecticut are distinguished by their industry and economy, strict piety, and devotion," will contribute to diminish the number and the spirit of those aspersions which have been so long multiplied on the moral character of the New England people in Great Britain. Page 98. "Through the whole of this journey of 240 miles from New York to Boston, I had passed over a most beautiful tract of country, which from the manners of its inhabitants, the excellent order and condition of its towns, villages, and buildings, its farms, orchards, gardens, pasture, and meadow lands, together with the face of the country, undulated with mountains, hills, plains, and valleys, watered by a number of rivers, small lakes, and streams, afforded a variety of the most beautiful landscapes and strongly reminded me of English scenery."

Compare this account with that of Volney concerning the same tract of country.

Ibid. "Much has been said by former travelers of the familiarity and rudeness of the American people. I will not attempt to contradict their assertions, but for myself I must declare in justice to the American character that I experienced the utmost civility and even politeness from the inhabitants in every part of the country through which I traveled. The coachmen were civil, and, the tavern keepers attentive; wherever I had occasion to mix with the country people, I never met with the least rudeness or shadow of impertinence on any occasion; on the contrary, they were civil and obliging."

Compare this passage with the various reports of your travelers, particularly of Weld and Ashe, concerning this subject.[9] Let them compare it with their own caricatures, and blush for the gross injustice which, through prejudice and ignorance, or from a cause still more censurable, they have done to the inhabitants of this country.

How much happier, because more just, is the spirit of Mr. Lambert than that of his predecessors.

Page 100. "Those travelers who visited the United States soon after the Americans had obtained their independence were swayed by their prejudices, for or against that country." And again, page 101. "If they (the English travelers) had been the dupes of a few knaves, the American people were branded as rogues; and the rudeness, imperfections, and chicanery of individuals were set down to the account of the whole nation. Sometimes they published their complaints to the world, and these becoming current, have tended to increase that animosity and disgust which the American Revolution had engendered, and which were already too prevalent in England."

It is sufficient to have transcribed these declarations of Mr. Lambert. They are too just to admit of a doubt; and to him who feels any regard to the subject, too important to be read without interest.

Page 105. "The females of the New England states are conspicuous for their domestic virtues. Everything in their houses has an air of cleanliness, order, and economy that display the female character to the greatest advantage. The young women are really handsome. They have almost all fair complexions, often tinged with the rosy bloom of health. They have generally good and sometimes excellent teeth. Nor did I see more instances to the contrary among the young women of America than are to be met with in England. Their light hair is tastefully turned up behind in the modern style and fastened with a comb. Their dress is neat, simple, and genteel; usually consisting of a printed cotton jacket with long sleeves, a petticoat of the same, with a colored cotton apron, or pin cloth, without sleeves, tied tight, and covering the lower part of the bosom. This seemed to be the prevailing dress in the country places. Their manners are easy, affable, and polite, and free from all uncouth rusticity. Indeed they appear to be as polished and well bred as the ladies in the cities, although they may not possess their highly finished education. Yet, in the well-settled parts of New England, the children do not want for plain and useful instruction; and the girls especially are early initiated in the principles of domestic order and economy. At the taverns and farmhouses where we rested on the road, we found the people extremely civil and attentive. We were treated with as much respect as if we had been at our own houses; and the landlord, his wife, and daughters waited on us in the most obliging manner. I do not mention this as a solitary instance, it was general at every house where we stopped; neither have I drawn my conclusions merely from the reception I met with at taverns and other places of public resort, but from my observations upon the people in general, with whom I had frequent opportunities of mixing, whether they belonged to the highest or the lowest orders of the community. I believe it is generally allowed that for a traveler who wishes to make himself master of the real character and disposition of a people, it is not sufficient that he associate only with the grandees of a nation; he must mix with the plebeians, otherwise he acquires but false ideas of the country and its inhabitants. 'The great mass of nations,' says Dr. Johnson, 'are neither rich nor gay. They whose aggregate constitutes the people are found in the streets and villages, in the shops and farms; and from them collectively considered must the measure of general prosperity be taken.' From these I have judged of the real character of the Americans; and I found it as difficult to discover a single particle of rudeness in the behavior of the men, as it was to discover an ugly face or bad teeth among the young women."

This paragraph is so just, and at the same time so honorable to my fair countrywomen, that I was willing to transcribe it all. The women of New England are very generally such as are here described, differing, however, as you will suppose they must differ, according to their circumstances in life. As I have before given their character, I will not weary you by enlarging upon it here. In one particular Mr. Lambert has contravened my own belief. I had supposed that the teeth of the New Englanders, particularly of the females, were less generally good than those of the English. Mr. Lambert has pronounced the fact to be otherwise, and is unquestionably much abler to make the comparison than I can pretend to be.

Page 112. "At the upper end of the park (in Boston) there is a stand of hackney coaches, superior in every respect to vehicles of that description in London. The horses and carriages of some of them are equal to the best glass coaches."

Thus an Englishman has found one thing in the United States which is superior to the same thing in London. I hope this will be remembered.

Page 167. "An American writer, in reviewing Mr. Moore's Epistles, Odes, and Other Poems, descants with much truth and justice upon the false estimates which the English people in particular form of the American character." [10]

" 'All ranks of people in Britain,' says that writer, 'from the prince to the peasant, appear to be most profoundly ignorant of our situation, both individually and collectively. Not even the British statesmen form aught bearing the least resemblance to a correct notion of our actual condition; and the ambassadors sent out to America from Britain, instead of searching into the character of the people, are more employed in tattling and gossiping at tea parties and routs.' "

Observe that Mr. Lambert, an Englishman, pronounces these observations of the American writer to be true and just; and therefore the English nation in particular, that is, more than other people, form false estimates of the American character. What is the sentence which Mr. Lambert thus pronounces to be just? It is no other than that all ranks of people in Britain, from the prince to the peasant, appear to be profoundly ignorant of our situation, both individually and collectively. And that not even the British statesmen, nor the British ambassadors understand this subject. And what is the reason of this ignorance? Evidently they do not think the subject worth their investigation. I am satisfied that your ambassadors should, if they please, employ themselves more in tattling and gossiping at tea parties and routs than in learning the character, interests, and relations of the people among whom they reside; and to learn whose character and circumstances is an immediate and important part of their duty. Your statesmen also may, with my consent, be satisfied with the conduct of these functionaries; and, as they have already done in many instances, may hereafter send to the Americans statesmen who, instead of promoting the interests of their own country or ours, will while away the period of their embassy in parade and pleasure. But I protest against the representations of any man who is profoundly ignorant of our character and situation when he undertakes to describe either. Let him learn what we are, and what our circumstances; or let him be silent concerning us. He who desperately ventures on falsehood in cases where he is ignorant is very little removed from him who utters it in direct contradiction to his own knowledge.

The observations which I have last quoted from Mr. Lambert's book, you will remark, are taken from an American writer who reviewed Thomas Moore's Epistles, Odes, and Other Poems; and are followed by several strictures upon some allegations of this man against the American character.

You will easily believe that every American who has reputation or worth must feel a mixture of indignation and contempt when he hears this peddler of filthy rhymes say that the American character is made up of iniquity and baseness. Let him look at his own works, and observe how small a part of them is not employed for the sole purpose of corrupting mankind. How little of his time has he spent in any other business than that of a pander to licentiousness. He has talents which might have rendered him respectable, but he has only prostituted them. Nor will any felicity of numbers, style, or imagery which his admirers may challenge for him at all lessen the infamy which has already attached to his name, and which will adhere to it so long as it is remembered. If this profligate writer possessed any optics which would enable him to look inward, the world would hear no more of his aspersions on others. His own baseness and pollution would occupy all his future thoughts, and the remainder of his life would be spent in confessions and tears.

Page 477. "They (the Vermontese) have often displayed their dexterity as horse jockeys in Canada, and exchanged their weak and rickety pacers for the hardy Canadian horses."

Mr. Lambert mentioned this fact before in nearly the same language. The reader would suppose from it that the inhabitants are generally employed as horse jockeys. The people of Vermont are employed in farming, and it is believed that few of them are horse jockeys. It would also be supposed from these declarations that pacers abound in Vermont. In my various journeys through this state I do not remember that I have seen even one. It is a great misfortune to New England at least that this breed of horses is so nearly extinct. The Narragansett horse was undoubtedly the best for the saddle which we have ever known. The few which remain of that breed are purchased with extreme avidity, and usually at a very great price. Nothing better deserves the attention of the farmer than the restoration of these fine, sprightly, vigorous animals to the possession of his countrymen.

Page 479. "I found in several instances that the people of Vermont and some other of the New England states make use of many curious phrases and quaint expressions."

Again. "Everything which creates surprise is *awful* with them. 'What an awful wind, etc.' "

Again. "A variety of other quaint expressions are equally common, and have become favorite phrases not only among the country people, but also among some of the American writers."

A number of these quaint expressions are recited by Mr. Lambert in the sentences immediately following. They are those, with little variation, which have been repeated by every English traveler who has thought it proper to mention this subject. One would think that even Englishmen must be wearied by the repetition.

The truth concerning this subject is, there are people in this country, as there are in all other countries, who use language imperfectly and improperly. Terms of exaggeration are common in the mouths of all men; and different terms are used at different periods by the same individual and the same community, and at the same period by different individuals and different parts at least of the same community. Thus the words, *grand, capital, monstrous, awful, dreadful, terrible, wonderful, surprising, astonishing, amazing, devilish, damned,* and many others have had their place and their day; and some or other of them are in use in this country at the present time. A moderate number of ignorant people employ the term *awful* for this purpose, as a number, not very moderate, of your countrymen use the terms damned and devilish with at least as much quaintness and more turpitude. But Mr. Lambert may be assured that, although he must from his birth be supposed to be infected with the English disease of finding fault with the language of Americans, yet, had he resided in New England twelve months instead of twelve days, he would have found that our language is less quaint and less corrupted than that of his own country. The reason is obvious. The people at large are much better educated: a fact which he himself recognizes in the 474th page of this volume.[11]

Page 480. "I could collect hundreds of others (colloquial barbarisms) equally absurd, which have been invented by Americans who are desirous of introducing what they call an American language."

There are probably two errors in this observation. One is that there are no such inventions. Certainly there are very few. I know but one man, a very respectable one indeed, who has made any attempts of this nature. The other is that he could collect hundreds of these colloquial barbarisms, whether invented or uninvented.

There are several other errors of serious importance in this work. But not being possessed of the means of establishing the truth with respect to the several subjects, I shall omit them. Others still, of a subordinate nature, I have thought it unnecessary to mention. Upon the whole, Mr. Lambert's work is creditable to his understanding, accuracy, and diligence in obtaining information. And what is much more honorable to himself, exhibits in a very advantageous manner his candor, justice, and integrity.

I am, Sir, yours, etc.

# LANGUAGE OF NEW ENGLAND

## LETTER I

*The English language in this country pronounced more correctly than in England —Blunders in language customary in London—Reasons why the people of New England pronounce the English language with propriety*

*Dear Sir,*

Among the things for which the people of the United States, particularly of New England, have been censured and ridiculed by your countrymen, our language, in a variety of respects, has come in for its share. We have been accused of an erroneous pronunciation, of retaining ancient words which you have discarded, of annexing to others an unwarranted meaning, of coining new ones, and of thus contributing to render the language perplexed, unsettled, and imperfect. As I have never seen this subject examined except on one side, I shall take the liberty to give you a few thoughts concerning it, and flatter myself that you will willingly accompany me through the investigat.[1]

I shall not, I believe, offend against either truth or propriety, if I say that the English language is in this country pronounced more correctly than in England. I am not indeed sanguine enough to expect that you will credit the assertion, nor that you will believe me to be a competent judge of the subject. Still, I am satisfied that the assertion is true. That you may not mistake my meaning, I observe that by a correct pronunciation I intend that of London; and, if you please, that of well-bred people in London. You may perhaps be inclined to ask how I can even know what this pronunciation is. I know it in two ways: from hearing a considerable number of Englishmen of this description converse extensively, and from information which enlightened Americans have given me concerning the subject, who have resided in London. In both ways my information has been so extensive as to forbid every reasonable doubt in my own mind concerning its sufficiency.

When I say that the language is pronounced here more correctly than in England, I do not intend that it is pronounced more correctly, or even as much so, as by some Englishmen; although in this respect I have good reason to believe the difference to be scarcely perceptible.* This I was taught before the Revolutionary War by an English gentleman, an inhabi-

* Several American gentlemen have informed me that respectable Englishmen to whom they have been introduced have taken it for granted, and even insisted, that they must

tant of London, who resided in New Haven a considerable time, and who was several years in the service of the British government. Since that period I have been often told the same thing by respectable Englishmen traveling or residing on this side of the Atlantic. I have also found the observation verified by the pronunciation of these very Englishmen, and of others.

My meaning is that the inhabitants at large speak English with a nearer accordance to your standard of pronunciation than the inhabitants of England. Of this the proof is complete. I have seen a dramatic performance written in the West Country dialect: the words being spelt according to the local pronunciation, of which I was scarcely able to understand a sentence. I have also seen a volume of poems, professedly written in the dialect of Yorkshire, in which, independently of some local phraseology, the distorted pronunciation required a glossary to explain the meaning of many sentences even to an English reader. Now, Sir, it is no exaggeration to say that from Machias to St. Marys, and from the Atlantic to the Mississippi, every American descended from English ancestors understands every other as readily as if he had been bred in the same neighborhood. I have continually and long had under my own instruction youths from almost all the American states, and am ordinarily unable to conjecture from their pronunciation the part of the country which gave them birth. There is nothing here which can be called without an abuse of language, *dialect*. This, it is believed, cannot be said of an equal number of people in any country of Europe. The differences of pronunciation here are of no moment, unless that of the vowel U deserves to be excepted.

Permit me to turn your attention to the pronunciation of London itself; and to the mistakes and abuses adopted, or rather inherited, by those who were born within the sound of Bow Bells. You would scarcely be able, if you were to search every house in New England and glean the whole number of individual blunders, to make up such a list as Pegge in his Anecdotes of the English Language has given us of the errors which for ages have found a residence in your metropolis.[2] To refresh your memory, as well as for some other reasons, I will set down a short catalogue of these elegant peculiarities.

| | | | | | |
|---|---|---|---|---|---|
| Necessuated | for | Necessitated | Obstropolous | for | Obstreperous |
| Unpossible | " | Impossible | Argufy | " | Signify |
| Least-wise | " | At least | Common-garden | " | Covent-garden |
| Aggravate | " | Irritate | Pee-aches | " | Piazzas |
| Conquest [of people] | " | Concourse | Kiver | " | Cover |
| Shay | " | Chaise | Daater | " | Daughter |
| Po-shay | " | Postchaise | Saace | " | Sauce |
| Gownd | " | Gown | Saacer | " | Saucer |
| Partender | " | Partner | Saacy | " | Saucy |
| Bacheldor | " | Bachelor | | | |

have been either born or educated in England because they spoke the language exactly like themselves.

| | | |
|---|---|---|
| Chimbly | for | Chimney |
| Perdigious | " | Prodigious |
| Progidy | " | Prodigy |
| Contagious | " | Contiguous |
| For fraid of | " | For fear of |
| Duberous | " | Dubious |
| Musicianer | " | Musician |
| Squits | " | Quit |
| Pillord | " | Pilloried |
| Scrowdge | " | Crowd |
| Squeedge | " | Squeeze |
| Vemon | " | Venom |
| Sermont | " | Sermon |
| Verment | " | Vermin |
| Palaretick | " | Paralytick |
| Postes<br>Posteses | " | Posts |
| Sittiation | " | Situation |
| Somewheres<br>Nowheres<br>etc. | " | Somewhere<br>Nowhere<br>etc. |
| Oftens | " | Often |
| Mislest | " | Molest |
| Scolard | " | Scholar |
| Regiment | " | Regimen |
| Howsomdever | " | However |
| Whatsomdever | " | Whatever |
| Commonality | " | Commonalty |
| Properietor | " | Proprietor |
| Non-plush'd | " | Non-plused |
| Unbethought | " | Recollected |
| Discommode | " | Incommode |
| Paragraft | " | Paragraph |
| Stagnated | " | Staggered |
| Disgruntled | " | Offended |
| Ruinated | " | Ruined |
| Solentary | " | Solitary |

| | | |
|---|---|---|
| Ingenously | for | Ingenuously |
| Intosticated | " | Intoxicated |
| Perwent | " | Prevent |
| Skrimidge | " | Skirmish |
| Confisticated | " | Confiscated |
| Refuge | " | Refuse |
| Radidges | " | Radishes |
| Rubbidge | " | Rubbish |
| Nisi prisi | " | Nisi prius |
| Taters | " | Potatoes |
| Loveyer | " | Lover |
| Pottecary | " | Apothecary |
| Nyst | " | Nice |
| Nyster | " | Nicer |
| Clost | " | Close |
| Closter | " | Closer |
| Sinst | " | Since |
| Wonst | " | Once |
| Industerous | " | Industrious |
| Sot | " | Sat |
| Frags | " | Fragments |
| Moral | " | Model |
| Jocotious<br>Jecotious | " | Jocose |
| Hisn | " | His |
| Hern | " | Hers |
| Ourn | " | Ours |
| Yourn | " | Yours |
| The t'other | " | The other |
| Any-hows | | |
| Some-hows | | |
| No-hows | | |
| Nolus bolus | " | Nolens volens |
| Weal | " | Veal |
| Winegar | " | Vinegar |
| Vicked | " | Wicked |
| Vig | " | Wig |

and the beautiful examples in the following dialogue between a citizen and his servant:

*Citizen.* Villiam, I vants my vig.

*Servant.* Vich vig, Sir?

*Citizen.* Vy, the vite vig, in the vooden vig box, vich I vore last Vednesday at the westery.

| | | |
|---|---|---|
| Neighbourwood, | for | Neighbor-hood, etc. |
| I don't know nothing about it | | |
| Worser | for | Worse |
| Lesser | " | Less |
| More worser | | |
| Most agreablest | | |

| | | |
|---|---|---|
| Know'd | for | Knew<br>Known |
| See'd | for | Saw<br>Seen |
| Mought | " | Might |
| Axs | " | Ask |
| Fetch a walk | " | Take a walk |

| | | | | | |
|---|---|---|---|---|---|
| Faught a walk | for | Took a walk | This here | for | This |
| Fotch | " | Fetch | That there | " | That, etc. |
| Cotch cold | " | Caught cold | A few while | " | A little while |
| Fit | " | Fought | Com'd | " | Came |
| Shall us | " | Shall we | Went | " | Gone |
| Summons'd | " | Summoned | Gone with | " | Become of |
| A-dry, a-hungry, a-cold | | | Went with | " | Became of |
| His-self | " | Himself | He is gone dead | " | He is dead |
| Their-selves | " | Themselves | He went dead | " | He died † |

Of these ornaments of the English tongue, some are found among the ignorant people in this country. A great part must, I believe, be acknowledged to be exclusively the property of your metropolis. The former class will at least serve to keep our blunderers in countenance. The latter constitute a collection of improprieties which far exceeds everything known in New England. I ought to add that here mistakes of this nature belong only to individuals, and do not extend even over a single village: much less are they spread through a considerable tract of country. It will not be supposed that uneducated men will be free from errors, either in the pronunciation or the use of language. But we have none, even among such men, so outrageous as these.

Among the reasons which here contribute to a general propriety both in the use and the pronunciation of language, the following are not without their influence.

A great multitude of the parochial schools are taught to a considerable extent by young men educated in colleges, and in this manner derive their pronunciation immediately from the common standard in a good degree.

The great body of our people are regularly at church, and thus imbibe their pronunciation in a considerable degree from the clergy.

All those who are liberally educated and polished converse, as I have heretofore observed, more freely and universally with their plain neighbors than probably was ever done in any other country; and some persons of the former character are found in almost every village.

As there are here no distinct orders in society, all men endeavor to copy the manners of those who have acquired superior importance and reputation; and that in their pronunciation, as well as in their dress and manners.

† In the next paragraph Mr. Pegge adds, "These, Sir, and a few other such wulgarities," (to use the London word) "such *vitia sermonis,* are to be heard daily throughout the bills of mortality I readily admit; but then everybody understands their meaning; and their language is not like the unintelligible gabble of nine tenths of the provincial inhabitants of the remote parts of England, which none but the natives can understand; though I doubt not but on close investigation such language (as I hinted before) might be radically justified. Bring together two clowns from Kent and Yorkshire, and I will wager a ducat that they will not be able to converse for want of a dialect common to them both." [See Samuel Pegge, *Anecdotes of the English Language: . . .* (London, 1803), p. 74.]

To acquire this resemblance is an object of direct design and active ambition.

Our countrymen, as has been observed, read; and that in such numbers that it may be justly said to be the general character. Hence they obtain the intelligence necessary to comprehend the importance of this object, and that attentive observation which secures the attainment.

Many of them also are to a considerable extent present at courts, and there acquire an additional conformity to the standard pronunciation. From these, and doubtless from other causes, some of which may have escaped my attention, we have derived a pronunciation probably more uniform than has ever prevailed in any other country in the world.

From an observation in the Eclectic Review, I am ready to believe that the writer supposed the peculiarities of Mr. Webster's pronunciation to be generally adopted in this country.[3] The opinion, if it exist, is erroneous. These peculiarities have spread very little. The friends of Mr. Webster, of whom I am one, regret that his learning and labors should be rendered less useful by his departure in several instances from the common standard.

I am, Sir, yours, etc.

# LETTER II

*The inhabitants of this country charged with retaining obsolete words, with introducing new words, with annexing new significations to words—Alterations in language less in this country than in England for the last two hundred years—Vindication of this conduct*

*Dear Sir,*

We are accused also of *retaining ancient words* brought by our ancestors from their native country, and since that period left by the English out of their vocabulary. The charge undoubtedly is to some extent well founded. That bodies of men speaking originally the same language should, when separated from each other to the distance of three thousand miles, retain at the end of two centuries precisely the same words may, I think, be justly regarded as an absolute impossibility. Certainly no instance of this nature has been hitherto known; of course, it ought not to have been expected here. Men always have such words as will express the ideas which they have occasion to communicate to each other. Nothing is more natural than that we should retain some ideas, and have occasion to communicate them, which you have not retained. Both you and we unquestionably retain some part of the manners of our ancestors, but it is scarcely credible that we should both retain exactly the same parts. About those which we severally retain, we shall severally have occasion to converse; and each must have words expressing the ideas out of which the conversation is made. These, so far as they were in the possession of our ancestors, we naturally retain. This you have done as well as we, and to as great an extent. Nay, I believe you have many more words which are not considered as classical by yourselves than we have. The peculiarity in each case is natural and necessary, and he who finds fault with it must be either very thoughtless or very silly. An American who reads such of your books as display the language and sentiments of humble life, such as plays, novels, and that excellent work, the Religious Repository, finds in them a great multitude of expressions which certainly can plead nothing to justify them except that they are idiomatic phraseology of ancient times. Many of them, at least, are absolutely without the classic pale, and are accordant with no existing grammatical rules. It is, however, sufficient for him that they were the language of those who have gone before you. On what principles are you justified in retaining these words which will not justify us in retaining ours.

But we are censured also for *making new words.* The charge is undoubtedly just. Wherever we find occasion for the use of words and have them not, we like you and all other nations make them. In the state of Connecticut a number of men are chosen annually by each town to receive from each inhabitant a list of the taxable property in his possession. This list is required by law, and is made up by the proprietor. The men who receive it are from their employment styled *listers.* If the proprietor gives in a false list, he is punished by having the falsified article increased on the list fourfold. Englishmen on both sides of the Atlantic have no fondness for circumlocution. We therefore style this punishment *fourfolding.* These are terms confined to this state: and, although sufficiently remote from elegance, yet serve to convey ideas of some importance in our state of society, which otherwise could not be conveyed without a periphrasis. A few others, local also, may be found in other parts of our country; and a small number have had a more extensive currency. Among these, *immigrate, immigration,* and *immigrant* hold a conspicuous place. The stream of population flows *out* of Great Britain, but a part of it flows *into* the United States. You, therefore, have no use for these words, but we have at least as much as you have for *emigrate* and its derivatives. Why then should we not use them, rather than be driven to a tedious periphrasis every time we have occasion to communicate the ideas denoted by these terms? In Great Britain there are few or no alluvial lands, so few at least that the most respectable of geographers, Major Rennell, has thought it proper in the Memoir accompanying his Map of Hindoostan to describe those which are formed by the Ganges, and the manner in which they are formed. I know not that you have any single word to denote them. Here, as you will easily perceive by these letters, they are objects of considerable importance, and hence have naturally received a name. In New England they are called *intervals,* denoting the land lying between the original bank and the stream to whose waters they owe their existence. This word, derived from our ancestors, we retain, and find it useful. *Freshet* is found in Johnson, who defines it to be a pool of fresh water, and quotes Milton as his authority. It is also found in Ainsworth, who says, "It is the water of the ocean, destitute of salt, near the mouth of a river." I presume he meant the water of the river immediately above the limit where it begins to mix with the water of the ocean. This definition coincides with the ancient use of the term *freshes.* Freshet, as used here, denotes a considerable addition made to the waters of a river by melted snow or rain. In this sense it was used by Sir Ferdinando Gorges in the middle of the seventeenth century. Here these accumulations of water are interesting objects, particularly in the spring. At that season, as has been before observed in these letters, the rivers of this country, particularly the Connecticut, overflow the intervals on their borders to a great extent, and rise sometimes to the height of twenty-five feet above their common level. A fact occurring so often and so regularly becomes, of course, a frequent theme of communication among the inhabitants, and needs a single word to express it. The word *grade* was probably adopted from feelings and circumstances purely republican. If I mistake not, it sprang up during the Revolution. At that period there was a strong disrelish to everything which savored of nobility. *Rank,* though originally a harmless term, was, you know, long before employed extensively to designate this object of republican dislike, and therefore became naturally offensive to an American ear. Still, as some men will ever be superior to others; as officers in an army particularly, even in one which is republican, must be distinguished in this manner; it became necessary to adopt a term by which this distinction might be expressed, and we enabled to converse about it without a circumlocution. No word more naturally offered itself in this dilemma than the word grade. Accordingly it met with a welcome reception, and has ever since occupied a place of no contemptible importance in our vocabulary.* [1]

The verb *progress* can plead nothing more in its own favor, so far as my knowledge extends, than that it is more concise than the phrase for which it is substituted.[2]

Universally, we make words just as you do, whenever we think they are

* "The prospects of the soldiery were to revel again in the plunder of other countries and to gain military promotion through war; they thought only of rising above their respective *grades.*"

Speech of Lord Castlereagh in the House of Commons, Friday, April 28, in the debate on the war with France.

wanted; and in the same manner mankind have always acted since they began to speak. The whole number of those which have been coined here falls much short of a single column in an octavo dictionary.

Among the words to which we are considered *as annexing unwarranted significations, improve* undoubtedly claims the first place. For this the people of New England have been laughed at by Dr. Franklin, kindly admonished by Dr. Witherspoon, and severely censured by many others. The unwarranted meaning which we annex to it is that of *use, employ.* Thus we say, *improve our time; improve our privileges; improve an estate, a house, a field,* etc. Those who censure us contend that the only proper meaning of the word is either to *meliorate* when a transitive verb; or, when an intransitive, to become better. Unfortunately, however, for all these critics, the original word *improve,* which has been transferred to our own language, is to *use,* to *employ.*[3] Unfortunately also, Englishmen have always used the word in the very same sense in which it has been used by us. Says Dr. Watts,

> Our souls would learn the heavenly art,
> *To improve* the hours we have.[4]

"Which is a hint," says Addison, "which I do not remember to have seen opened and *improved* by others who have written on this subject."

"I shall now conclude," says Dr. Witherspoon, "by *improving* this subject for the purpose of self-examination."

The *practical remarks* or *inferences* with which sermons are usually concluded are to a great extent by your divines called *the improvement of a sermon.*

The practical use made by Doddridge in his Family Expositor of each of those sections into which he divides the New Testament is regularly called by him the *improvement.*[5]

I need not tell you that in the instances here quoted the idea of melioration, or amendment, is incapable of being annexed either to the verb or the noun; and that *to use,* or *employ,* would be perfectly tautologous with the verb; and the corresponding substantives, with the noun.

There are other words of a similar nature involved in the same accusation, and for the use of them the same reasons may be given. There are very few of them, however, which may not be found, and found used in the same sense, in English writers. On hardly any subject has more silly pedantry been displayed than on this, or coarser and more ludicrous mistakes been made. We have retained very few words which you have not. Fewer still have been coined, and to still fewer have we annexed any new meanings.

Let us now examine the other side of this subject. How many new words, do you believe, have been introduced into the language by your own countrymen since the colonization of New England? Look at the writings of your travelers, and mark their numerous gleanings from the French and Italian, and those too given out in books intended to be universally read. I allude not here to technical words, though even among these there are many unnecessary terms inserted in their productions. I refer to words customarily used even in familiar conversation, and to those which have words exactly correspondent in our own tongue. I refer to words which are apparently introduced by these writers, and many others, merely to let the world know that they understand French and Italian. How many of these words have become already established in our own language, and how many more are advancing toward the same naturalization? Surely this right of innovation is not secured to you by an exclusive patent. I know you will claim the authority and the privileges of a parent. But permit me to ask, is our nonage to exist forever? You have ten millions of people; we have eight. How soon will our numbers exceed yours, and that in a very formidable proportion? You have more learning and more science than we, and you write better. Admit it. How long think you will this be said with truth? The period is not distant, at least as we believe, when we shall be your rivals; and when, in spite of our lakes and marshes, of the recent settlement of this continent, and of the general inundation which it experienced since the Deluge of Noah, and which kept it covered for so long a time, in spite of the malignancy of the climate, the want of matter, the want of tails on several species of animals, the sterility of the soil, the multitude of the insects, the defectiveness of the quadrupeds, the contempt of the Quarterly, and the sneers of the Edinburgh reviewers, we are fast advancing toward wealth and power, toward intellectual, and I hope toward moral and religious distinction. If God will continue to give us his blessing, as it has been heretofore given, I have no fear concerning our success in all these interesting particulars. We shall then, at least, have a language which will be understood here, and will probably answer all the necessary purposes of communication. I hope it will have sufficient force and elegance to satisfy all the reasonable demands of those by whom it will be spoken.

Think not that I am willing to see the language of this country vary from that of Great Britain. There are many reasons for which I should regret so untoward an event. It is "the tongue wherein" I and my countrymen, no less than you and yours, "were born," and to which our attachment is probably little, if at all, inferior to yours. The books already written in this language contain more learning, science, and wisdom than those in any other; and the probability is strong that such as will hereafter be written will add materially to this accumulation of treasure. It is the language of our Bible. It is the language of our laws. It is already established to a considerable extent in the four quarters of the globe, in New Holland, and in a great multitude of islands of inferior size. The two nations which speak it appear hitherto to be more interested in spreading the religion of the Gospel through the world than any other, and their common language furnishes them many facilities toward the execution of this glorious purpose. With this mighty advantage in their hands, it is difficult to conceive how far the energy of these nations, directed to the most benevolent of all objects, may proceed; or what is the boundary at which it may be truly said to them, "Hitherto shall ye come, but no further." [6]

But there is no reason to expect such a disaster. In the ordinary course of things, centuries must pass away before any very material change of this nature can take place. That we ought to make words, to express such ideas as we have occasion to communicate, and as cannot be conveniently communicated by any terms at present in the language, there cannot be a doubt in the mind of any person who is a competent judge of this subject. All mankind have invariably supplied themselves with words in every such case. It would be idle to expect in us, or in any other people, a departure from this course. It is a law of our nature, and absolutely necessary to the intercourse of intelligent and to some extent even of savage society. Climate, soil, and other local circumstances present many objects to one nation which are not known by another. Minerals, vegetables, and animals; the revolution of the seasons, nay, even the state of the weather, furnish almost every nation more or less with ideas which are peculiar. Arts, commerce, manners, government, religion, and all other objects about which the mind is voluntary, and with respect to which it is continually forming new ideas by its power to compound, abstract, and compare, furnish very many more. To communicate many of these will be felt to be indispensable; and, wherever terms are wanting to express them, new ones will regularly be made. Circumlocutory phraseology will rarely be felt satisfactorily to answer the purpose.

A variety of things in our climate, soil, and other local circumstances, in our minerals, vegetables, and animals, differ materially from the same things in Great Britain. These things generally must have names. Wherever existing words without too violent a deflection can be employed as names for them, they will be adopted. But there are cases where no such words can be found, and in these new ones will be made. Much more extensively applicable are these observations to ideas framed by the mind and derived from the state and business of society. These, being in every advanced state of civilization very numerous, require many new names to express them; and, wherever the ideas are to be communicated to others, such names will be found. Nothing but ignorance or inadvertency can permit any man to believe that the people of the United States will not act in this case, just as all other people have acted, particularly as the British nation has always acted. Within a century and a half you have introduced into the English language one third perhaps of its vocabulary. Why, when our necessity or convenience, or, to use a single term, when our exigencies require it, should we not be expected to do just what you and all other nations have done? Why should it be an object of surprise that we have thus done? The copiousness of the English language, however, is such that a long time will probably elapse before new coined words will be very numerous on either side of the Atlantic. I have never discouraged any inclination to multiply them here, and I observe a general jealousy among your philologists which cannot but check any propensities of this nature in Great Britain. A large proportion of the books which are either studied or read here are printed on your side of the Atlantic; and every writer in the United States must, in order to acquire the reputation of writing well, conform in a good degree to the standard established by the English classics. Our state of society also, though in many respects differing from yours, as every thinking man must preconceive, is yet in many more substantially the same. Our laws, religion, and very many of our customs are more like yours than those of any two nations ever were. Hence, from this copious source of change in languages comparatively few alterations will for a long time be derived. I have often wondered that so many British writers, and among them several who would hear their claim to talents questioned with very little patience, should censure the people of this country for innovations of this nature. The considerations here suggested furnish not our excuse, nor our justification, for the case requires neither; but unanswerable proof that the conduct is a thing of course, and inwoven with the very nature and circumstances of man; that we have acted as all other nations have acted in the like circumstances, and as every man acquainted with the subject would expect us to act.

On the same grounds we have retained some words in the language which are lost out of your current vocabulary. We found use for these words; you did not.

The surprise expressed by your writers at these facts, their censures, their ridicule are all groundless. To expect the contrary conduct on our part would have been an absurdity. To demand it would be to demand what never existed, and what in the very nature of things is impossible.

I am, Sir, yours, etc.

# LEARNING, MORALS, ETC. OF NEW ENGLAND

## LETTER I

*Schools—System of Connecticut—Schools of New England—Effects of this education on the people at large—The Honorable Roger Sherman*

*Dear Sir,*

The state of learning and science, or generally of information, in every country where these objects are pursued at all, cannot fail to engage the attention of an enlightened and inquisitive mind. To know this, its causes and its consequences, is to know something in the history of man which, while it awakens our sympathies, expands our views, and enables us in some respects to form juster opinions concerning our own state of society and concerning the general character of our race. Since the American Revolution, it has extensively become a custom among writers in Great Britain, who either find or make a reason for speaking of the subject at all, to treat the character of the Americans with severity and contempt. The story told there has been echoed here; and there have not been wanting natives of this country who, having learned by rote the observations, and especially the sneers uttered on the eastern side of the Atlantic concerning their countrymen, have repeated them with not a little self-complacency. These men have probably felt, as critics concerning the writer whom they are censuring, that to censure involves of course a superiority to those who are the objects of their censure; and that, therefore, while they are condemning others in the gross, they are elevating their own character to distinction and consequence. I give these men very little credit for their labors, or for the spirit by which they are dictated. Nor am I satisfied with the kindred efforts which are made in Great Britain. Generally they have exhibited very little of truth or justice, and still less of candor or moderation. For sneers or sarcasms, I have no great respect; and these are the principal weapons which have hitherto been used in this warfare.

A stranger traveling through New England marks with not a little surprise the multitude of schoolhouses appearing everywhere at little distances. Familiarized as I am to the sight, they have excited no small interest in my mind, particularly as I was traveling through the settlements recently begun. Here, while the inhabitants were still living in log huts, they had not only erected schoolhouses for their children, but had built them in a neat style, so as to throw an additional appearance of deformity over their own clumsy habitations. This attachment to education in New England is universal; and the situation of that hamlet must be bad indeed which, if it contain a sufficient number of children for a school, does not provide the necessary accommodations. In 1803, I found neat schoolhouses in Colebrook and Stewart, bordering on the Canadian line.

The general spirit and scheme by which the education given in parochial schools, for such I shall call them, is regulated throughout the New England states are substantially the same. It will be sufficient, therefore, to give a particular account of the system pursued in Connecticut.

The state of Connecticut is by law divided into school societies. These societies are empowered to divide themselves into as many school districts as their convenience may require. They are also empowered, in each case, to form school districts by uniting parts of two neighboring school societies as they shall mutually judge convenient. In this manner the whole state is divided.

The districts have severally power to build schoolhouses, and to purchase grounds on which to erect them; to repair them, and to tax themselves for the expense; to appoint a clerk to record their proceedings, a collector of taxes, and a treasurer.

For the support of the schools, the state pays out of the treasury, annually, the sum of two dollars upon every thousand dollars in the list of each school society to its committee for the benefit of the schools within its limits. It also pays to these societies half yearly the interest arising from the school fund. To form this fund, the state sold part of a tract called *"the Connecticut Reserve,"* lying on the southern border of Lake Erie within the present state of Ohio. The principal sum arising from this source was in the treasury books in May 1812, $1,341,939.* At the same time, the first of these payments amounted to $12,924. But, in order to entitle a school society to these sums, their committee must certify that the schools in said society have been kept for the year preceding in all respects according to the directions of the statute regulating schools, and that all the monies drawn from the public treasury for this purpose have been faithfully applied and expended in paying and boarding instructors.

If these monies are misapplied, they are forfeited to the state. If the committee make a false certificate, they forfeit sixty dollars. These committees are also empowered to take care of all property belonging to their respective school societies, and to dispose of it for the benefit of such schools, according to the true intent of the grant, or *sequestration,* from which the money is derived; unless where either the grantor or the legislature has determined that such grant, or sequestration, shall be under the management of persons acting in continual succession.

* The amount of the school fund in May 1821 was $1,700,000. PUB.

All the public monies intended for the benefit of any school society are to be paid into the hands of its treasurer.

Each school society is to appoint suitable persons, not exceeding nine, to be overseers or visitors of all the schools within their limits. It is the duty of the overseers to examine the instructors; to displace such as may be found deficient, or will not conform to their regulations; to superintend and direct the instruction of the children in religion, morals, and manners; to appoint public exercises for them; to visit the schools twice at least during each season; particularly to direct the daily reading of the Bible by such children as are capable of it, and their weekly instruction in some approved catechism; and to recommend that the master conclude the exercises of each day with prayer.

Any school society is also empowered by a vote of two thirds of the inhabitants present in any legal meeting warned for that purpose to institute a school of a higher order for the common benefit of the society, in which all the children whose parents wish it are to be advanced in branches or degrees of learning not attainable in the parochial schools.

If any school district within a school society expend less than its proportion of these public monies in supporting its school or schools, the surplus shall be paid over to such district or districts as have in their school expenses exceeded the sums distributed to them.

Such is a summary account of the system by which the public schools in Connecticut are regulated. By the public schools, I intend those which receive benefactions immediately from the state, whether parochial, or of a higher class. I think you will agree with me that provision very honorable to the state is here made for their existence everywhere; for the buildings in which they are to be kept; for the mode of education to be pursued in them; for the establishment of good instructors; for the faithful discharge of their duty in promoting the learning, religion, morals, and manners of the children, and universally for whatever is necessary in institutions of this nature. Committees are by law appointed and made accountable for carrying into execution the benevolent designs of the legislature, and visitors are constituted with ample power to compel the performance. A motive also is presented, of more efficacy than almost any other, to induce the inhabitants of every school society and district to see that every part of these designs shall be faithfully accomplished, viz., the sum which they are to receive, if the committee certify to the treasurer or comptroller that all these duties have been performed according to law, or to lose whenever such certificate cannot be given. Should a false certificate be given, the penalty incurred is sufficiently heavy to prevent the crime from being repeated, especially as the committee can have no personal interest of sufficient magnitude to balance the inconvenience.

Accordingly, the schools are everywhere in existence, and are everywhere managed with a good degree of propriety.

Two things only seem to be wanting to render the system complete. One is the establishment of the same scheme of education throughout the state; the other is the institution of a board of commissioners, one in each county, whose business it shall be to examine into the actual state of the schools in their respective circuits, and who should meet semiannually at Hartford and New Haven to receive the reports of the respective committees, compare them with the results of their own inspection, and make a general report to the legislature. The former of these, by making the scheme of instruction an object of public attention, would secure to us the best system; and the latter would assure us of its complete execution.

I have now given you a summary view of the schools in Connecticut. With little variation of figure, light, or shade, it will serve as a portrait, sufficiently exact in this respect, of New England at large, the state of Rhode Island excepted. In Massachusetts, New Hampshire, and Vermont, schools are everywhere established. They are often styled parochial schools. You will not suppose that each parish has a school distinguished by this title, but that each parish has a sufficient number of schools to admit all the children which it contains. To these little seminaries the children of New England are universally sent, from two, three, four, and five years of age to the period in which they have learned to read, write, and keep accounts. In many of them, other instructions are added, according to the skill and disposition of the instructors, and the wishes of the parents. At the earliest periods, children of both sexes are placed under the direction of female teachers; and, at more advanced stages of their education, under that of men. I speak of the common schools only. It ought to be observed that throughout a considerable part of the country the female pupils, whether placed under the instruction of men or women, are sent to separate schools.

It has not often happened to mankind that their children have in mass been taught to read and write. In Switzerland and in Scotland, this privilege has been extensively enjoyed; and in a subordinate degree, in several other countries. In New England, with the exception made above, it may be said to be absolutely enjoyed; although a solitary individual may here and there be found who has not availed himself of the privilege, and who is regularly viewed by those around him with a mixture of wonder and pity.

Goldsmith says, "Of all professions in society, I do not know a more useful, or more honorable one, than a schoolmaster; at the same time that I do not see any more generally despised, or men whose talents are so ill rewarded." [1] Goldsmith was a native of Ireland, and when he wrote this had long been an inhabitant of England. So far, therefore, as he is to be credited in a case with respect to which he could hardly mistake, schoolmasters must have been little esteemed and ill rewarded in these countries. Happily, as well as justly, this observation is not true in New England. A schoolmaster here adds to his reputation, instead of lessening it, by keeping a school, if he performs his duty well, and acquires more weight in society than he possessed before. The reward also for this useful service to mankind is certainly decent to say the least. Twenty dollars a month and board, including washing and lodging, amounting in the whole to three hundred and forty dollars a year, is frequently the stipend which a young man receives for keeping a parochial school.

The effects of this part of the New England manners are of the happiest nature. By this instruction, all persons here find free access to the Bible, and to many other sources of knowledge. Intellectual improvement is in some degree extended to all. Nor is the number of persons small who, availing themselves of this education in early life, have, without any other advantages than such as their own industry and habits of inquiry furnished them, acquired a considerable share of information, particularly of that practical knowledge which, more than any other, makes men useful members of society. Many such men, besides filling useful public offices of inferior distinction, and performing a great variety of that important business which under many forms and many names exists in every society of civilized men, and is indispensable to general as well as personal happiness, have become magistrates, legislators, physicians, lawyers, and sometimes divines; and through life have sustained useful, as well as honorable characters. Nay, such men have been found in several instances on the highest bench of justice and in the most dignified seats of legislation. You are not, however, to suppose that they have arrived at these offices by a mere fortunate concurrence of circumstances, by the public courtesy, or by the arts of a demagogue. Here, the public courtesy has usually been a mere tribute of respect to acknowledged worth. The men in question have generally been well qualified for their employments, and have passed through them with reputation.

The late Hon. Roger Sherman was in early life unpossessed of any other education than that which is furnished by a parochial school.[2] By his personal industry he supported, while a young man, the family left by his father, and provided the means of a liberal education for two of his brothers. By his original strength of mind and his attachment to books of real use, he qualified himself to hold, and with an uncommon degree of public esteem actually held, the successive offices of county surveyor, justice of the peace, judge of the court of common pleas, judge of the superior court, representative in the state legislature, councilor, member of the old Congress, and representative and senator in the new Congress. In these offices he acquired, and deservedly, the highest respect, not only of the people of Connecticut, but also of the first citizens in other states throughout the

Union. This gentleman, who went to the grave with unabated honor, and to whose memory I pay this tribute with peculiar satisfaction, was, what very few men unacquainted with the learned languages are, accurately skilled in the grammar of his own language. At the same time he was an able mathematician and natural philosopher, extensively versed in the history of mankind, and a profound logician, statesman, lawyer, and theologian. His character was completed by exemplary integrity, uprightness, and piety. Of how few men can all this be said with truth?

The general remarks which I have made on this subject will not be sufficiently explained by a recurrence to mere native strength of mind. There are unquestionably in every country men whose intellectual capacity and vigor raise them from the common level to eminence and honor; and those who are very great must undoubtedly have possessed great endowments. But these are too rare to satisfy our inquiries in the present case. A considerable part of the distinction found here is derived from a combination of advantages and efforts. The advantages to which I refer are such as these. Public offices are open to every man. At the same time, an unusual spirit of inquiry pervades all classes of men in this country. In consequence of these facts the most powerful motives to exertion are continually held out to those whose dispositions prompt them to exertion. In such a state of things a greater number of persons will be affected, and more powerfully affected, by these motives than in any other.

The influence of this general diffusion of knowledge is unquestionably happy. There is no department and no concern of life to which it does not extend. Even the private, neighborly visit among the common people is materially affected and sensibly colored by it, and is accordingly more rational, enlightened, and pleasant than it is believed to be in most other countries. Conversation is here carried on with a respectable degree of good sense, a variety of information, and often with wit, humor, and brilliancy. Minds may without exaggeration be said to mingle in it, and with each other. Nor will men of superior knowledge, unless possessed of a fastidious taste and character, fail either of entertainment or instruction in their intercourse with the substantial farmers and mechanics of New England.

In a republic, particularly in those of this country, a great proportion of the business which is termed public is managed by the people at large. The complicated affairs of school districts, parishes, townships, and counties demand a considerable share of intelligence, and the agency of a great number of persons. The debates of a town meeting, not unfrequently affect the interests of the inhabitants in a degree at least as intimate, and often as important, as most of those which are carried on in the legislature; and the office of the selectman is in many respects more closely interwoven with their happiness than that of the magistrate. The extensive powers entrusted to these men, and the subjects suspended on the decisions of town meetings, I have mentioned in former letters. I have also observed heretofore that probably three fourths of all the male inhabitants in the state of Connecticut sustain in the course of life some public office or other. To such a state of society, extensively found in New England at large, this general diffusion of knowledge seems indispensable. All these departments require some, and many of them much, thought, good sense, and information. Unless, therefore, knowledge were generally extended, they could not be usefully filled.

Nor is the importance of this fact less real, though perhaps less thought of in the church. A clergyman here addresses an assembly almost all the adult members of which understand with a good degree of precision the language which he uses, the doctrines which he teaches, and the illustrations which he employs, that is, if he preaches as he ought to preach. Sound and sensible discourses may here be delivered with a rational assurance that they will be well understood; and what may be called the elementary part of a preacher's instructions may be safely considered as having been already acquired from other sources. In consequence of this state of things, the churches in most of the ancient settlements of New England are more firmly established and less liable to be *blown about by every wind of doctrine* than those of many other countries. Among people possessing a good share of information, religious novelties operate with less fascination and are more reluctantly received than among those who are ignorant. In a word, knowledge here gives, and in a more desirable manner, a good degree of that stability which is elsewhere produced by energy in the government.

I am, sir, yours, etc.

## LETTER II

*Academies in New England—Colleges—State of these institutions in 1812—Law and theological seminaries—Medical, historical, and philosophical societies—Social libraries*

*Dear Sir,*

You may perhaps remember that in the account which I gave you concerning the establishment of schools in Connecticut provision is made in the law which creates the system for the institution of schools of a higher class than those which are parochial, or of such as in this country are generally styled academies. The knowledge taught in these schools is undefined by any general system, and comprehends as much and as little of languages, arts, and sciences as the trustees of each think it proper from time to time to prescribe. In this respect many of them are undoubtedly imperfect, and do not, so well as they easily might, direct the education which they profess to communicate. A wise and well-constructed scheme of education is certainly a desideratum in these seminaries, and might contribute not a little to spread knowledge in a more perfect form and to a greater extent. There is not indeed a very great difference in the objects aimed at or in the modes pursued. The law commits the inspection of these schools in Connecticut to a number of visitors, annually chosen by those for whom they act, but attempts not to control any other schools besides those which are constituted by itself. The provision of the law is insufficient, but whether a substitute will be provided within any moderate period which will remedy its defects is uncertain.

You are not, however, to suppose that these schools are not very useful seminaries. They are generally filled with students, and are directed by instructors respectably qualified for their business. Under this direction a great number of youths are continually employed in obtaining an education in branches of knowledge not communicated in the parochial schools. Here they are qualified for their entrance into colleges. At the same time they are furnished with the necessary means of qualifying themselves for other business which demands an education considerably enlarged. Thus the country possesses itself of talents which would otherwise sleep in obscurity, and is enabled to see its affairs prosperously managed in several departments which, if not of the highest consequence, are yet perhaps more interesting to its welfare than most of those which are. Here they become intelligent surveyors, navigators, happily prepared for commercial apprenticeships, and fitted for the whole routine of human business which demands a middle education between that of the parochial school and that of the college.

Of these schools there are more than twenty in the state of Connecticut. The exact number I do not know. About ten or twelve of them may be incorporated. Seven or eight are sustained by funds. Some have sprung from the combined exertions of numbers; and some, from the efforts of individuals. Of those which have funds, the principal are Bacon Academy at Colchester, amply endowed by a Mr. Bacon, one of its inhabitants; the Episcopal Academy at Cheshire, the Hopkins Grammar School at Hartford, and the Staples Academy at Weston.

In Massachusetts there are forty-eight of these schools, all incorporated, and most, if not all of them, endowed to some extent by the state. The principal of these is Phillips Academy at Andover. Two of those in Connecticut and three in Massachusetts are exclusively female seminaries. Some others admit children of both sexes.

Of the academies in Massachusetts, the District of Maine has its full proportional share.

In New Hampshire, the number of schools which may with propriety be placed on this list is thirteen. The principal of these is Phillips Academy at Exeter, formerly described in these letters.

The number of these schools in Vermont is twelve, all of which are incorporated.

I have heretofore observed that there are eight colleges in New England: Harvard College, now styled the University in Cambridge; Yale College, at New Haven in Connecticut; Dartmouth College, at Hanover in New Hampshire; Brown University, at Providence, Rhode Island; Williams College, at Williamstown, Massachusetts; the University of Vermont, at Burlington in that state; Middlebury College, at Middlebury in the same state; and Bowdoin College, at Brunswick in the District of Maine.

You observe that some of these seminaries are styled universities, and some of them colleges. You will not from this suppose that the name university indicates any superior importance, or any more extensive scheme of education. The University at Cambridge is in some respects the most considerable, and in every respect the University of Vermont is the least of all these literary establishments.

The state of these institutions in the year 1812 was the following:

*The University of Cambridge*

A president, seven professors academical, seven professors medical, three tutors, a librarian, a regent, a proctor, an instructor in the French language.

*The Academical Professors are:*

Of theology; of logic, metaphysics, and ethics; of rhetoric and oratory; of the Hebrew, other Oriental, and English languages; of Latin; of mathematics and natural philosophy; of Greek; and of natural history.

*The three Tutors teach:*

The senior tutor, geography, geometry, natural philosophy, and astronomy; the second, Greek; and the third, Latin.

*Of the Medical Professorships:*

The first is of anatomy and surgery; the second, of the theory and practice of medicine; the third, of chemistry and the materia medica; and the fourth, of clinical medicine.

The two remaining ones are assistants, or adjuncts, to that of anatomy and surgery, and that of chemistry and the materia medica.

The number of students the same year was 281.

*Yale College*

A president, five professorships academical, and three medical.

*The Academical Professorships are:*

Of theology; of law, natural and political; of mathematics and natural philosophy; of chemistry and mineralogy; and of languages and ecclesiastical history.

*The Medical are:*

Of anatomy and surgery, of the theory and practice of physic, and of the materia medica and botany.

Here also is one professorship adjunct.

*Six Tutors*

The particular provinces of these instructors have been sufficiently explained in the account given of this seminary.

The number of students was 313.

*Dartmouth College*

A president, five professorships academical, one medical, and two tutors.

*The Academical Professorships are:*

Of theology, of civil and ecclesiastical history, of mathematics and natural philosophy, of languages, and of chemistry.

*The Medical Professorship is:*

Of medicine.

The number of students was about 150.

The number of medical students exceeded 50.*

*Brown University in 1811*

A chancellor, a president, three professorships academical, and two medical.

*The Academical Professorships are:*

Of law, of moral philosophy and metaphysics, and of chemistry.

*The Medical Professorships are:*

Of anatomy and surgery, and of the materia medica and botany.

Two tutors, and a preceptor of a grammar school connected with the university.

The number of students was 128.

*Williams College*

A president, a vice president, a professor of mathematics and a natural philosophy, two tutors.

The number of students was 95.

*Middlebury College, 1812*

A president, three academical professors.

One of law, one of mathematics and natural philosophy, one of languages, two tutors.

The number of students was 113.

*University of Vermont*

A president, a professor of mathematics and natural philosophy, a professor of the learned languages, a medical professor.

* By the Catalogue of 1821, the number of students in Dartmouth College was:
157 undergraduates, 8 resident graduates,
65 medical students; total, 230. PUB.

There are also four other professorships on paper.

The number of students supposed to be from thirty to forty.

The means of medical instruction in New England will be seen sufficiently in this account of its seminaries.

The law school, heretofore mentioned in the description of Litchfield as being under the instruction of Judge Reeve and James Gould, Esq., would not, it is believed, do discredit to any country. Law is here taught as a science, and not merely, nor principally, as a mechanical business; not as a collection of loose, independent fragments, but as a regular, well-compacted system. At the same time the students are taught the practice by being actually employed in it. A court is constituted, actions are brought and conducted through a regular process, questions are raised, and the students become advocates in form.

Students resort to this school from every part of the American Union. The number of them is usually about forty.

Every theological professor in these seminaries is destined to instruct such students as apply to him in the science of theology. But the Theological Seminary at Andover has already engrossed most of the young men in New England designed for the desk. Three professors, one of theology, one of sacred literature, and one of sacred rhetoric, are already established here; and two or three more will probably be added to their number within a short time.† Fifty students may be considered as the average number for three years past.‡ As this seminary is richly endowed, and as the gentlemen employed in its instruction are pursuing their business with spirit and vigor, there are the best reasons to believe that it will hold a high rank among institutions of the same nature.

There are also in New England the following medical societies: the Massachusetts Medical Society, the Connecticut Medical Society, and the New Hampshire Medical Society.

The objects of these institutions are to unite the gentlemen of the faculty in friendship and in one common pursuit of medical science, to discourage by their united influence empiricism in every form, to furnish a center of correspondence for the reception and publication of medical discoveries, and universally to elevate and improve the art of healing.

A historical society was formed at Boston in the year 1791, and incorporated in the year 1794, by the name of the Massachusetts Historical Society. The object of this institution is to collect and publish whatever authentic documents may illustrate the past and present state of this country. Twelve volumes of its Collections for this purpose have been already published, which in a very honorable manner prove the utility of the design.

An agricultural society has been formed in Connecticut, and another in

† A professorship of ecclesiastical history was added in 1819. PUB.

‡ 1812. Now (1820) they exceed one hundred. PUB.

Massachusetts. A small collection of papers published by each has been favorably received.§

There are also two philosophical societies in New England: the American Academy of Arts and Sciences in Massachusetts, which holds its sittings at Boston; and the Connecticut Academy of Arts and Sciences, which meets in New Haven. The latter was incorporated in the year 1800. The American Academy has published three volumes. The Connecticut Academy has completed one volume of Memoirs, and also has begun the publication of a statistical account of the state. Both of these institutions are, it is believed, advancing.

I have here given you a summary, and, as I believe, an exact account of the means provided and employed for the purpose of diffusing literature, science, and general information among the inhabitants of New England.

It ought, however, to be added that in a great part of the towns and parishes there are social libraries established. In some places they are considerable; and in all, are of material use to the little circles in which they exist. The information which they spread is of importance. They also excite a disposition to read, and this employment naturally becomes a substitute for trifling, vicious, and gross amusements. It also contributes to render society and its intercourse in a good degree intelligent and refined: while thought takes place of sense and passion; civility, of coarseness; and information, of scandal. It also enables parents to give their children better instructions, and to govern them more rationally; and at the same time it renders the children more dutiful and more amiable.

I am, Sir, yours, etc.

# LETTER III

*Observations of Buffon, De Pauw, etc. relative to the deterioration of animals; of the bodies and of the minds of men in America—Genius, what and whence derived—Genius of Americans—Literature and science of the Americans—Men of learning—Causes why they are not numerous*

*Dear Sir,*

The contempt mentioned in a preceding letter as cast by some of the inhabitants of Great Britain upon this country has at times extended to a

§ Many agricultural societies have been established in New England during the last three years (1820). PUB.

great part of all which it contains: to its soil, its climate, its vegetable productions, its animals; the bodies of its inhabitants, both aboriginal and derived; the minds, particularly of the latter class; their manners, arts, literature, science, government, morals, and religion. On the continent of Europe it has proceeded still further. The Count de Buffon and M. de Pauw extend it even to the continent itself, and suppose that there is something defective in its very structure and constitution. Both of these writers imagine that America has suffered a general inundation many years since the Deluge of Noah, which kept it covered for a long time. To the recency of this inundation the Count attributes the malignancy of the climate in America, the barrenness of its soil, and the imperfect nature of its animals and people. M. de Pauw supposes that the lakes and marshes left by that inundation are the cause of its insalubrity, the great number of its insects, the defectiveness of its quadrupeds, the barrenness, both of the soil and the women, the stupidity of the men, etc., etc.

That the Americans extensively possessed traditions, and those not incorrect, concerning the general Deluge is unquestionable, traditions which it is impossible to apply to any other event. But this subsequent inundation was formed by the Count himself, whose imagination found little difficulty in deluging worlds, or making them; while M. de Pauw found as little in swallowing either the deluges, or the worlds.

The animals of America, the Count has found to be few in the number of their species, small in their size, defective in their structure, degenerate in their natures, and a great part of them unfortunately without tails. All this train of misfortunes these gentlemen ascribe to the wretchedness of our climate, the infancy of nature on this continent, the sterility of our soil, the deficiency of matter, and the great number of lakes and marshes left by this mischievous deluge. A prudent philosopher will generally choose to be sure of his effects before he looks out for their causes; while those who make causes, as generally find little trouble in creating also their effects. The man who could discover the origin of this globe in the impact of a comet against the surface of the sun, which struck off a quantity of melted glass sufficient to form the world, can discover anything and make anything which he pleases.

Unfortunately for these gentlemen, there are fewer species of animals without tails in America than on the eastern continent, the Count himself being the umpire.

I have already considered the size and weight of our animals. It is unnecessary to observe again that the elk, the moose, the brown bear, and the bison are larger than the caribou, or the tapir, boldly asserted to be the largest native animals of this continent; or than a calf a year old. I have also considered the assertion that European animals introduced into this country degenerate, and shall only add on this subject that there is now in this town a horse, twenty hands, or six feet and eight inches in height, every way well proportioned, and but four years old: a native of this land of deterioration.

An eagle was not long since killed at Brookfield in Connecticut, which had just destroyed a calf. The American *condor* is the largest known bird of prey in the world.

With regard to the bodies of the native Americans, M. de Pauw and Dr. Robertson acknowledge that there are no deformed persons among the savages of America, because they put all children of this description to death.[1] But they assert that, wherever this species of cruelty is prevented, the proportion of deformed persons is greater than in any country in Europe. It would have been well if these gentlemen had furnished us some evidence of the truth of these assertions, or at least of their probability. As they have left the story, it can only afford diversion to such as read it on this side of the Atlantic, mingled with pity for its authors.

Deformed people are certainly uncommon in this country; and the inhabitants are as tall, as well made, as strong, as agile, and as handsome upon an average to say the least as those who visit us from the eastern side of the Atlantic.

With regard to the insalubrity of the climate, I shall have occasion to consider the subject in another place.

The great object at which all this ingenuity is aimed is, I suspect, *the minds of the Americans.* Most of the followers of these gentlemen have left to them the task of carrying on a war against the subjects already specified in these remarks, and have directed their own attacks to the genius, learning, and science which are found on this side of the Atlantic. As these attacks are peculiarly pointed against the people of the American states, you will cheerfully permit me to pay some attention to them.

There are few questions on which more pedantry and more prejudice have been displayed, in which vanity has assumed sillier airs, or reason been oftener put to the blush, than on that which is so customarily started respecting the comparative genius of different nations. Were it not that pride is so pleasantly regaled by the incense regularly offered to it, whenever the question is brought up to view by those who present it, good sense must long ago have been wearied and surfeited, and decency have sickened with the service.

Genius may be generally and accurately defined to be *the power of making mental efforts.* This definition involves alike what may with propriety be termed logical genius, or the power by which intellectual efforts are made; and rhetorical genius, or that which is seen in the efforts of the imagination and the feelings. The attribute in both its forms is unquestionably communicated to some minds more than to others. The great body of mankind may, I think, be said, with some qualifications, to possess the average share, or genius at the middle point. A few are raised above it, and a few depressed below. The differences among those who are numbered in either of these classes (differences which are often very great) are derived chiefly from energy in the individual, from the motives set before him to exert it, and from the incidental advantages which are furnished to him by the mode and circumstances of his life. This truth is evidenced in a great variety of ways. In many instances, for example, individuals who have removed from the older settlements in the United States (where they had few motives to exertion because everything which prompts to effort was already in the possession of others) to the new settlements (where all things of this nature lay equally open to them as to others) have suddenly exhibited talents which before they were not suspected to possess. So common is this fact that it is here generally admitted to be a part of the regular course of things.

For similar reasons operating on other modes of life, the Greeks and Romans, during those periods of their political existence which called for great efforts and annexed to them splendid rewards, never wanted great men to lead their armies. For the same reasons the French Revolution has regularly produced a constant succession of very able generals; and if a considerable number have at any time lost their lives, their places have been immediately filled up by successors equally able. For the same reasons also, the American and British navies have regularly been supplied with commanders whose talents have been equal to every achievement within the reach of man.

From these very causes, he who wishes to satisfy himself will find derived the whole of that distinction which attended the four ages, as they are emphatically termed, of genius.

As genius is the power of making efforts, it is obvious that it will never be exerted, or in other words the efforts will never be made, without energy, that is, without the resolution, activity, and perseverance which are necessary to their existence. This energy can never be summoned into action, but by motives of a suitable nature and sufficient magnitude to move the mind. Nor can it act to any considerable purpose, unless attended with proper advantages. Wherever these causes do not meet, the fire will be smothered. Gray wrote sound philosophy, as well as beautiful poetry, in the following fine stanzas: [2]

Full many a gem, of purest ray serene,
The dark, unfathom'd caves of ocean bear;
Full many a flower is born to blush unseen,
And waste its sweetness on the desert air.

Some village Hampden, that with dauntless breast,
The little tyrant of his fields withstood;
Some mute inglorious Milton here may rest,
Some Cromwell, guiltless of his country's blood.

Th'applause of listening senates to command,
The threats of pain and ruin to despise,
To scatter plenty o'er a smiling land,
And read their history in a nation's eyes,

Their lot forbade . . .

How obviously must the real Milton have been inglorious, if he had been mute; and how obviously would he have been mute, notwithstanding all his powers, if his energy had not prompted him, or if commanding motives had not summoned that energy into action.

Various writers have attributed the existence of genius to natural causes, particularly to climate; and many others, who have not made this ascription in express terms, have yet plainly implied their adoption of it in the manner in which they have generally spoken of this subject. In the contemptuous observations concerning America, and particularly concerning the United States, to which I have referred above, this doctrine seems to have been taken for granted. Of these gentlemen I ask whether the Greeks and Romans owed their genius to this cause. If they did, why does not the same climate now produce the same genius? Greeks inhabit Greece still. But where are Homer and Sophocles, Plato and Aristotle, Pericles and Demosthenes? Where are Themistocles, Cimon, Lycurgus, and Epaminondas? The climate of Italy is unaltered. But who would think of looking for Cicero and Livy, Vergil and Horace; or for Tasso, Ariosto, and Father Paul among the inhabitants of that country? In a word, whence is it universally the fact that no climate and no country has for any great length of time been productive of this coveted endowment.

I ask again, what is the nature, what the quality of the climate? Must it be *temperate?* If so, whence were derived the talents of the two Gustavuses, Charles the XII, Peter the Great, Suvorov, and a long train of others born and educated under a frozen sky? Or on the other hand, whence were those of Moses, David, Solomon, Job, Isaiah, and Paul? Whence those of Cyrus, Kublai Khan, Mohammed, Sesostris, and a splendid train of Arabian and Persian poets? Must it be *moist?* Whence were derived those illustrious inhabitants of dry and parched regions, just now mentioned? Must it be *dry?* Why were Shakespeare and Milton, Alfred and the Black Prince, Bacon and Newton born under the dripping canopy of Great Britain? Must it be *clear?* To what cause then does the world owe Pindar, Pelopidas, and Epaminondas, Erasmus, Grotius, and De Witt? Must it be *foggy?* How shall we explain the character of Pascal and Montesquieu, Corneille and Racine, Henry the IV, and Condé?

Perhaps it will be said, however, that salubrity of climate is the immediate cause of this mental superiority. If it were true that strong health regularly accompanied vigor of mind, if the bodies which last the longest regularly sustained the highest powers of the soul, there would be some reason for resorting to this attribute of climate for an explanation of the difficulty under consideration. But how many of those minds which have attracted the admiration of mankind have inhabited frail tenements, and quitted them at a comparatively early period; while the grosser spirits which occupied the strong barracks of Pratt, and Parr, and Jenkins, and a host of Russian peasants, found them unassailed by disease and defying death many years beyond a century? At the same time, Greece, and Judaea, and Arabia, and even Italy are countries not remarkable for health.

Upon the whole, I believe, with all due respect to the Count and his position, that this scheme must be given up.

But were we to allow this curious theory all which it solicits, the result would be in the highest degree favorable in some respects to the United States at large; and, in all, to the countries which are the immediate subjects of these letters. The United States comprehend as great a variety of climates as all Europe south of the Baltic, and most of the countries which they cover are healthy. New England and New York are among the healthiest countries in the world: New England universally; New York, with the exception of a very few spots of no great extent. The miserable, malignant, niggard sky attributed to America by the gentlemen whom I have so often mentioned furnishes in these two countries more clear and bright days annually than are seen by the inhabitants of any country in Europe, except perhaps by those in the middle of Russia. The products of the soil are more various, and a great proportion of them are more exquisite. If M. de Pauw had visited this country, he would have hunted in vain for the marshes which gave him so much trouble. You will perceive that I have passed through a great part of New England in the journeys which have been mentioned. I had traveled through it extensively before. Yet I never found in it a marsh, so far as I remember, which contained more than a small number of acres. That larger marshes exist, I have not a doubt. But that they are numerous, or extensive, or of any importance is a dream of M. de Pauw.

As to the lakes whose exhalations constitute, I suppose, a serious part of the malignancy of our climate, we must plead guilty. There are three great lakes on the borders of the state of New York, and one of them washes the western shore of New England, not far from two hundred miles. It must also be conceded that some of the flat grounds along Lake Champlain and Lake Ontario are in a degree unhealthy. The small lakes in the state of New York, I have elsewhere chiefly enumerated, and have observed that little spots near the outlets are subjected to the fever and ague, and to bilious remittents. The whole of these insalubrious tracts would, I suppose, make up a country of the middle size.

In New England, as I have heretofore mentioned, there are, besides Winnipesaukee, Umbagog, and Moose Lakes, the largest of which is somewhat more than sixty miles in diameter, more than a thousand which extend from one fourth of a mile in length to perhaps nine miles. If the description which I have given of them be credited, it must be admitted that their only effect is to add to the beauty of the landscape and to the pleasure of the inhabitants. Whatever may be their efficacy on the body or the mind, it must undoubtedly be experienced in the greatest degree by those who inhabit their borders. But it has not been discovered hitherto that these have been less healthy, or less ingenious, than the rest of their countrymen.

If we suppose genius to be a gift of God, immediately communicated and independent of natural causes, it must be admitted that it is given according to his own pleasure, for his own reasons, and when, where, and to whom he chooses. Both the philosophers and the critics with whom I am now concerned would probably adopt this method of accounting for the facts in question with reluctance, and only in the last extremity. In this case, however, no reason can be assigned, a priori, why this gift should be supposed to descend on a single country in one age rather than in another, or on one country rather than another. Still, if the fact be otherwise, every such argument must, I confess, stand for nothing. Should these causes be given up, and this endowment be considered as descending like beauty, strength, and other natural attributes in the ordinary course of human propagation, it will, I suppose, be admitted to be subject to much the same laws, to proceed in much the same course, and to be liable to much the same variations as these attributes. We often see both men and women of fine talents, the parents of children of the same character, as we often see handsome persons the parents of handsome children. Sometimes also, superior talents descend through a series of generations. According to this mode of accounting for the existence of genius, the inhabitants of Great Britain will, I presume, readily admit the people of the United States to possess their full share, as the great body of them are descended from British ancestors, and the rest have derived their origin from Europe. The people of New England particularly have sprung almost universally from England itself. Vigor of mind has appeared more frequently in Great Britain than even in Greece, although, for obvious reasons, not so often employed on precisely the same objects. We therefore claim our descent from that country which, if any one in modern times can claim the title, must be allowed to be the nursery of genius.

From these observations it will, I think, appear that the preconceptions of Buffon, De Pauw, Robertson, and other philosophers concerning the American continent and its influence upon the bodies and minds of men are unsolid, and without any foundation in facts. I am, therefore, at liberty to believe my countrymen are not insuperably precluded by any law of nature, or any known decree of heaven, from the possession, in some instances at least, of those talents which may do honor to the land which gave them birth, and be the source of important benefits to mankind.

After all that has been said on the subject discussed in this letter, I am aware that many of the writers with whom I am contending, deserting the causes on which some of their predecessors have so confidently relied, make their appeal to the more decisive evidence of facts, which they say are subversive of all our claims to ingenuity, learning, and science. Unhappily, this subject is rarely treated with sobriety, and not very often with decency. Our cause, instead of being examined, is often prejudged; and, instead of being left to stand or fall by argument and evidence, is proved to be bad by a sarcasm, and condemned by a sneer.

To add to our misfortunes, a train of European travelers have passed through this country, whose books an American reads with astonishment, pity, and diversion: astonishment at the ignorance and falsehood of the writers; pity for that falsehood and that gross depravity from which it has proceeded; and diversion excited by the silly prejudices, the ludicrous mistakes, and the distorted narratives of which these books are very extensively composed. He does not commonly find even the likeness which may ordinarily be found in a caricature. In my own mind these books have lowered materially the confidence with which I have heretofore regarded travelers of reputation, and forced me to feel a continual succession of doubts concerning what they had written. If men passing through a country whose language is their own, and whose laws, customs, and religion not a little resemble their own; a country to every part of which they have free and safe access, and to every person in which they may, if men of fair reputation, be easily introduced; can be so grossly ignorant of its real state, fall into errors so numerous and so palpable, and so frequently utter falsehoods equally palpable; what judgment ought to be formed of the books written by men who while traveling are destitute of all these advantages? To what a host of mistakes must the travelers be exposed to whom the language of the countries through which they pass, the manners, government, and religion are all unknown; who often find the access to persons and places either impossible or difficult; and who at times are obliged to fly, rather than permitted to travel. Of several of these gentlemen I shall find occasion to take some notice hereafter.

Permit me to add that there is more spirit than candor or good sense in the treatment which we have received from some persons, even of reputation, on your side of the Atlantic. The process has not been a course of investigation, but a train of hostilities. The issue has been such as a mind, in the slightest degree acquainted with human affairs, could not fail to foresee.

In order to form a just opinion concerning this subject, it will be necessary for you to become acquainted with the actual state of the country, particularly with the state of society from which everything pertaining to it is derived.

Of the mode of education pursued in New England, from the parochial school to the professional seminary, I have given you a summary account. You have seen the extent, the mode, and the degree in which instruction is here communicated to every rising generation; in a higher degree to many, and in the highest degree in which it here exists to a number which, compared with that found in any other country, is great. It will not, I think, be believed that a society in which all these things are taught, and thus taught, can be very ignorant, or entitled to the character given them in the following words. "There is, however, both in the physical and intellectual features of the Americans, a trace of savage character, not produced by crossing the breed, but by the circumstances of society and of external nature." [3] Of our manners I shall speak hereafter. That our common people as a body are superior in intelligence to those of the same class in the most enlightened countries of Europe, we know with absolute certainty, not only from the information of the numerous Americans who have traveled through those countries, and the acknowledgment even of many Englishmen, but from the fact that Europeans of this class have come in shoals to America through a long period, and have exhibited to us the degree of intelligence which they possess.

The literature of this country is certainly inferior, as is also its science, to that of Great Britain. Solitary instances of proficiency in learning have existed here which would have been thought honorable there. Dr. Cotton Mather was an example.[4] The late Dr. Stiles of this town was another. There have been, there are now a few others who have accumulated as much knowledge as the length of human life would permit. The number of these is, however, small. I will explain to you the causes of this fact, and attempt to show you that it involves no disgrace to the literary men of my country.

All the people of New England without an exception, besides what is created by disease or misfortune, are men of business. The observation is applicable alike to those who are appropriately styled men of business, and to all others. The clergyman, to take an example which may serve universally, preaches two sermons every Sabbath, of forty or forty-five minutes each at an average, always composed by himself, and necessarily, if he would not sink into contempt, catechizes the young persons in his congregation; visits all the sick in his parish, and that in many instances often; attends every funeral; makes many parochial visits; receives many visits from his parishioners in turn; entertains not a little passing company; attends every associational and consociational meeting within his district; is present at ordinations, and at other ecclesiastical business; and delivers a considerable number of public and private lectures. To these are to be added all his domestic concerns, together with those of an extraneous nature, which are perpetually occurring, and constitute a considerable source of employment. Permit me now to ask you whether such a life can furnish any considerable opportunity for pursuits merely speculative. Yet from no part of this complicated business can any prudent, not to say pious, clergyman here withdraw himself. Permit me further to ask, whether the giving and receiving of some parts of these visits perhaps excepted, the performance of these things is not more useful to mankind than extensive researches into learning and science would ordinarily be. Such researches demand the whole of human life, a great part of it at least. Where in the life of a clergyman thus occupied can the time which is indispensable for them be found? The business of a clergyman, it is here believed, is to effectuate the salvation of his flock, rather than to replenish his own mind with that superior information which, however ornamental or useful in other respects, is certainly connected with this end in a very imperfect degree.

In addition to these things, it ought to be observed that clergymen here are rarely possessed of libraries sufficiently extensive to make such attainments practicable. The reason of this fact is no dishonor to them. It is that they are not able to purchase such libraries.

I have chosen to illustrate the subject by taking a clergyman for an example, because men of that class are often considered as having more leisure than those of any other. But were such pursuits easy, and the time and means for them ample, the persons engaged in them could rarely obtain a tolerable reward for their labors. No American has within my knowledge been willing to inhabit a garret for the sake of becoming an author. Books of almost every kind, on almost every subject, are already written to our hands. Our situation in this respect is singular. As we speak the same language with the people of Great Britain, and have usually been at peace with that country, our commerce with it brings to us regularly not a small part of the books with which it is deluged. In every art, science, and path of literature, we obtain those which to a great extent supply our wants. Hence bookmaking is a business less necessary to us than to any nation in the world; and this is a reason, powerfully operative, why comparatively few books are written.

A market for original literary productions is for this and several other reasons, with which I will not trouble you, so limited as to hold out little encouragement for the profession of an author. I never knew half a dozen persons who here made writing books their business for life. To write books is not merely a work of genius, or learning, or science; it is also in the proper sense an art. Accordingly, it has been not a little improved by a long progress of time in Great Britain and on the European continent. Here it has been comparatively little cultivated, because the motives for cultivating it have been comparatively few. In consequence of this fact, most men of the first distinction for genius and intelligence are not authors. Their proper business has engrossed their attention to so late a period in life as to prevent them from assuming the character. Active life has here, proportionally more than in most countries in Europe, furnished the commanding objects of ambition.

In the Universities of Oxford and Cambridge, fellowships in great numbers have supplied the means of deep research in the fields of literature and science. In these, ingenious men have found subsistence, leisure, books, enlightened companions, and every other advantage for mental excursion gratuitously supplied. The intense student obviously cannot be employed in acquiring property, and must therefore be supported by others, or starve. But on this side of the Atlantic no such support is provided for the votaries either of learning or science. Not a fellowship, as I heretofore observed, exists in any of the literary institutions in the United States. Nor do I know a single foundation on which an individual is supported for the mere purpose of enabling him to advance far in speculative pursuits.

In Great Britain also, particularly in England, the livings of the clergy, especially of the superior clergy, and the mode of life to which they are destined enable them to spend their whole time in study. In America the case is reversed. Here men are only paid for doing the business of their respective professions.

From all these facts, you will readily perceive that peculiar discouragements and obstructions of those speculative efforts which have added so much distinction to the European character exist in the United States.

I am, Sir, yours, etc.

## LETTER IV

*Opinion of the Edinburgh Review relative to the literature of America—President Edwards—Rev. Dr. Edwards—Dr. Franklin—Dr. Rittenhouse and other natural philosophers—Ingenious and useful inventions—McFingal—Progress of learning in Great Britain from the eighth century*

*Dear Sir,*

From the observations in my last letter you may possibly be induced to believe that whatever may be the deficiency of our genius and learning, it is not attributable to the causes alleged by Buffon and Pauw. In this I hope to convince you that amid all these disadvantages our character is not altogether such as it frequently appears in the the observations of your countrymen.

In the Edinburgh Review, on Ashe's Travels in America,* is the following passage: "In short, federal America has done nothing either to extend, diversify, or embellish the sphere of human knowledge. Though all she has written were obliterated from the records of learning, there would (if we except the works of Franklin) be no positive diminution, either of the useful, or the agreeable. The destruction of her whole literature would not occasion so much regret as we feel for the loss of a few leaves from an ancient classic."

These declarations are certainly uttered in a sprightly manner. But they are untrue. The late President Edwards has more enlarged the science of theology than any divine of whom either England or Scotland can boast; and the loss of his works would occasion more regret than these reviewers, and I may add without any fear of sober contradiction, than the whole literary world, would feel for the loss, not of a few leaves only, but of the whole works of half the ancient authors now extant. I do not intend that the reviewers themselves would feel this regret, but that it would be felt by a vast multitude of mankind, to whom several writers in that review have been both openly and insidiously hostile: I mean Christians. There is not a treatise written by Mr. Edwards, except those which were merely occasional, which has not enlarged science. I particularly specify his treatises on religious affections, on the qualifications for communion in the Christian church, on moral agency, on original sin, on God's last end in the creation of the world, and on the nature of true virtue.[1] The subjects of these discussions have long been acknowledged by the whole civilized world to be of the highest importance to man. They are also of the most abstruse nature, and require the profoundest thought and the most enlarged comprehension. Two of them are professedly replies to the ablest philosophers who have written on the Arminian side of the question, that on moral agency, and that on original sin; and both appear to have terminated the dispute.[2] They have now been published more than fifty years. On one side they have been steadily appealed to as immovable standards of faith, so far as these subjects are concerned. On the other, they have been bitterly complained of, denounced as heretical, pursued with sarcasms and sneers, and hunted down with contempt; but they have never been answered. Nothing can explain this fact but the acknowledgment that they have hitherto been believed to be unanswerable.

I am aware that it may, and will, be replied to a part of these observations that I have here taken for granted a main point: viz. that the scheme of Mr.

* Vol. XV, p. 398. Amer. Edit. [In the Edinburgh edition, see 15 (Jan., 1810), 445–446.]

Edwards is true. Of its truth I have not a question, but I will not assume it here. I am not ignorant how many persons disbelieve it, nor how respectable the character is of some who are in this number. Nor am I ignorant on the other hand that it is the scheme substantially adopted by all those distinguished men who, under God, produced the Reformation; nor that it is substantially found in the creeds, confessions, and catechisms of all the Protestant churches, particularly in the articles and homilies of your own church; and, let me add, in the prayers also. It was the glory of this great man that he had no love for innovation. He did not believe that theology was, like philosophy, left in such a situation that ages might pass on during which the honest inquirers in the church would be necessarily and invincibly ignorant of its fundamental truths. Nor did he think it proper to sacrifice common sense to metaphysics. Though probably the ablest metaphysician who has appeared, he never warped from the path of common sense. To the Scriptures he yielded the most profound reverence, and the most implicit confidence. At the same time he treated his antagonists with a civility, candor, and moderation which very few of them or their followers have exhibited in return.

The first of my positions is not at all affected by the supposition that Mr. Edwards' opinions are erroneous: viz. that the loss of his writings would awaken more regret than the loss of a few pages of an ancient author, or even of half the works of all the ancient authors now extant. The question here is merely concerning a matter of fact. You may say perhaps that I assert merely my own opinion. I confess it. The reviewer also asserts nothing but his opinion; and I am fairly warranted to believe that my own regret for the loss of Mr. Edwards' works would be greater than his for the loss of a few pages of an ancient author, or the whole of many ancient authors. Such a loss would be the loss perhaps of a few facts, some of them in a degree interesting to mankind; as the case might be, of a few opinions and doctrines of considerable value, or possibly of a fine narrative or interesting description.

His subjects are the most important in the universe; and his discussions are the clearest, the ablest, and the most decisive elucidations of them which the world has ever seen. He has elicited from the Scriptures truths which have escaped other men, has illustrated them by arguments which were never before discovered, and has shown their dependence, connection, and importance, with a comprehensiveness of view which elsewhere will be sought for in vain.

With regard to the principal subject under examination, principal I mean with respect to the present debate, the admission that Mr. Edwards' doctrines are erroneous will only exhibit it with still higher advantage. What must have been the talents which could have placed error in such a light that all the distinguished men who have appeared on the side of truth during the last fifty years, not only in Great Britain, but in the whole Christian world, have been unable to detect his errors? Does truth in its own nature labor under such disadvantages? Or did Mr. Edwards possess such singular and transcendent powers?

Indifference to the subject cannot here be pleaded, nor contempt for Mr. Edwards. The numerous complaints made of his writings in Great Britain, and the numerous specimens of ill nature with which he has been assailed, prove beyond debate that they have been regarded with far other feelings than indifference. That they would have been answered had those who disrelished them so strongly been able to answer them, there can be no doubt. Look into Boswell's Life of Johnson, and mark the gloom with which the biographer was distressed from fear that the system of Mr. Edwards should be the truth; and, what I principally intend, observe the dread with which Johnson himself regarded the subject of his appeal to him, and the caution with which he avoided reading the book so pathetically complained of, although Boswell ardently wished him to read it, and although he regarded the Americans with even more contempt than he felt toward the Scots.[3]

Suffer me to add that in his History of Redemption, and in his treatise on God's last end in the creation of the world, there is a sublimity of thought to which since the days of the apostles there has been no rival. I do not intend here sublimity of imagination. I intend intellectual sublimity, vast and elevated conceptions of truth. Both of these works too were only collections of his sermons, delivered as a part of his ordinary course of preaching, and the former of which was published after his decease.[4]

At the same time Mr. Edwards was a most powerful preacher. It is believed that no preacher who has appeared in this country ever engrossed the attention of his audience so often, so long, and to so great a degree, except Mr. Whitefield.[5] Yet his voice was low, and he was destitute of gesture. During the first third of his ministry he read his sermons. The remainder of his life he often preached either with short notes, or extemporaneously. The propriety of his pronunciation, his earnestness, his gravity, and his singular solemnity controlled in the most absolute manner the minds of those who heard him. The Rev. Mr. Hooker, who succeeded him, a gentleman distinguished for his learning, good sense, and elegance of mind and manners, as well as for his moral worth, said to me in a circle conversing on the nature of eloquence, "This subject is so variously understood and defined that it is difficult to determine what is intended by it; but, if it consists in making strong impressions of the subject of a discourse on the minds of an audience, Mr. Edwards was the most eloquent man whom I ever knew." The late Nehemiah Strong, Esq., a native of Northampton, and formerly professor of mathematics and natural philosophy in Yale College, observed to me that in early youth he heard Mr. Edwards deliver the sermons which now constitute the History of Redemption.[6] His mind, he remarked, was from the beginning deeply interested in the subject. As it advanced, his feelings became more and more engaged. When Mr. Edwards came to a consideration of the final judgment, Mr. Strong said, his own mind was wrought up to such a pitch that he expected without one thought to the contrary the awful scene to be unfolded on that day and in that place. Accordingly, he waited with the deepest and the most solemn solicitude to hear the trumpet sound and the archangel call; to see the graves open, the dead arise, and the Judge descend in the glory of his Father, with all his holy angels; and was deeply disappointed when the day terminated and left the world in its usual state of tranquillity.

You will not suppose that I mean in any of these observations to commend the style of Mr. Edwards. In perspicuity and precision, it was, however, excellent; in other respects it was slovenly. His thoughts were such as none of his opposers were able to form. In this respect he stands alone among moral and metaphysical philosophers. One excellence his compositions had which criticism cannot fail to approve. His sermons almost universally rise in their importance and impressiveness from the beginning to the end. This is ordinarily the only happy mode of conducting a discourse.

The late Rev. Dr. Edwards, president of Union College in Schenectady, New York, second son of this gentleman, was possessed of the same superiority of mind. His answers to Dr. Chauncy's work on universal salvation, and to Dr. West's on the subject of moral agency, particularly the latter, are efforts of reasoning to which Europe can show nothing superior in theological and metaphysical philosophy.[7]

The talents of my countrymen have been exhibited, as I think, respectably in various other modes. Dr. Franklin is excepted in this very declaration of the reviewer from the general disgrace, and has been so often pronounced a distinguished natural philosopher in the most enlightened countries of Europe, and by persons of high eminence, that it is too late to attempt a reversal of this sentence. Professor Winthrop would have done credit to any country in the character of a natural philosopher; as would also Dr. Williams, who afterwards filled the same chair in the University at Cambridge. Dr. Rittenhouse merited this character in a still greater degree. Bred to the business of a farmer, and educated only in an English school, he was obliged by ill health to quit that business, and devoted himself to the employment of a clock smith, and then to that of a mathematical instrument maker. In both he was his own instructor. He formed the science of fluxions without any knowledge of its existence in Europe, and for a number of years supposed himself to be its author. The best orrery, it is believed, in the world was invented, as well as made, by Dr. Rittenhouse. At the same time he was a man of a very enlarged and vigorous mind, and thought with peculiar felicity concerning every subject to which he directed his researches. What unhappily is not so often the fact as could be wished, he was also distinguished for moral excellence. Godfrey, of Philadelphia, was the inventor of the quadrant falsely called Hadley's, it having been villainously stolen from him by a man of that name.[8] The machinery of Whitney for the manufacturing of arms has not, it is believed, been excelled by any single mechanical effort of a mind accustomed to no mechanical pursuit. The orrery of Pope is a noble specimen of ingenuity; and, had it been constructed on a scale sufficiently large to secure its arrangement and durability, it would probably be esteemed inferior to none now in the world.† [9]

† The following account of Pope's orrery, copied from the Massachusetts Centinel, March 10, 1788, was drawn up by the very respectable gentlemen whose names are at the bottom, in conformity to a commission which they had received from the American Academy of Arts and Sciences to examine this curious piece of mechanism, and report concerning it to that body.

The subscribers, members of the committee for examining machines, in conformity to a vote of the Academy, have inspected Mr. Joseph Pope's orrery.

Upon a careful examination, the view afforded them much satisfaction.

The sun, placed in the center, revolves on his own axis, which is inclined. The several planets, at their relative distances from the sun, revolve around him in eccentric orbits, performing their diurnal motions; and the several satellites revolve around their respective primaries, all in their proper periodic times, determined by the motion of an index.

The inclination of the axes of those planets, whose axes are inclined to the ecliptic, is exhibited keeping parallel to themselves, and always tending to their respective places; and the inclination of their several orbits to the plane of the ecliptic is also shown, as is the heliocentric latitude of each planet in every part of its orbit. The motion of Saturn's ring is also exhibited.

The moon and the earth are each half covered with a black cap to represent the apparently dark parts. Around the earth are several circles, showing the siderial time, the moon's age, latitude and longitude, and her motion on her axis, which is inclined and keeps parallel to itself around the earth. This motion, being contrary to the common method of performing it, another moon is placed on the same circle with her axis perpendicular.

In the center of the machine is placed an index, which readily shows at any time the latitudes and longitudes of the several planets. The diameter of the ecliptic circle is five feet and two inches.

The machine is in the form of a dodecagon. In each square is a glass fixed to show the movements of the wheel work, which appears as accurate as it is curious. Each corner is ornamented with a statue of brass. On the top of the case are fixed twelve pillars, which support the great ecliptic circle, across which is fixed a segment of one of the celestial meridians. Between those pillars are plates with calculations. Within the ecliptic is fixed a broad circle representing the zodiac, on which are delineated the twelve signs and the fixed stars in their proper places.

The face is a plane, above which all the bodies revolve, and are put in motion by a single winch, which may be performed with the strength of a common thread. The whole is placed on an elegant stand.

While the ingenuity of the artist displayed in the workmanship pleases, the plan itself so perfectly executed excites admiration.

In justice to Mr. Pope we readily say that it is our opinion the improvements he has made are great; and that the description he gave to the Academy of his orrery is fully verified.

RICHARD CRANCH<br>SAMUEL WILLIAMS<br>JOSEPH WILLARD<br>CALEB GANNETT<br>LOAMMI BALDWIN } *Committee*

Many other specimens of ingenuity might be here mentioned, which have reflected not a little credit on the inventors and their native country. Such is the machine invented by Mr. Whitney for cleansing the upland cotton of its seeds. Such also was the submarine vessel invented by Mr. Bushnell, of Saybrook.[10] Such is the application of steam to the purposes of navigation.

The poetry of the Americans is treated by these reviewers with not a little contempt. On this subject I shall say little. It may, however, be observed, that several reviewers have spoken of it in more favorable terms. It may also be observed without any partiality that McFingal is not inferior in wit and humor to Hudibras, and in every other respect is superior.[11] It has a regular plan, in which all the parts are well proportioned and connected. The subject is fairly proposed, and the story conducted correctly through a series of advancements and retardations to a catastrophe which is natural and complete. The versification is far better; the poetry is in several instances in a good degree elegant, and in some even sublime. It is also free from those endless digressions which, notwithstanding the wit discovered in them, are so tedious in Hudibras, the protuberances of which are a much larger mass than the body on which they grow.

The painters of this country have been holden in honorable estimation in Great Britain. A high reputation has been attained by West and Copley, by Trumbull and Stuart.[12] As a portrait painter, it is believed, Stuart has rarely if ever been excelled. Several others, younger than these, are also advancing rapidly toward distinction.

Sculpture has not within my knowledge ever been attempted here. But engraving has already proceeded far, and is very fast advancing.

From the whole of this account, I cannot but persuade myself that you as a man of candor will think that the inhabitants of this country have a claim to be considered with some other emotions than those of contempt, and to receive other treatment than sneers and sarcasms. Perhaps you will think that as much has been done as in the circumstances could be reasonably expected. From what I have said in a former part of these letters, you will not consider it a small thing to convert an American forest, not merely into a habitable country, but into a pleasant residence. In New England, according to an estimate heretofore made, there are probably at the present time (1812) more than 220,000 dwelling houses. A great part of these are convenient; almost all are comfortable; a great multitude are neat; and not a small number handsome. The inhabitants probably enjoy more of the comforts and suffer fewer of the evils of life than the same number of people in any other part of the world. To accomplish this amid all the difficulties and dangers which attended the colonization of the country has involved a mass of labor, resolution, and fortitude, which in any other case would have claimed respect. To these things was added necessarily, the establishment of a government, a religion, a system of education, and universally a state of society by means of which the descendants of those on whom the burden rested might, so far as their circumstances would permit, be free, enlightened, virtuous, and happy. Occupied in this spacious and various field, the inhabitants have in few instances had either leisure or inclination to write books; and most of those which have been written were prompted by some particular occasion.

Let me request you to remember how long your own nation existed before it could boast of a single well-written book. In the eighth century you had only the venerable Bede; in the ninth, only Alfred; in the tenth and eleventh, none; in the twelfth, William of Malmesbury is entitled to respect. Roger Bacon adorned the thirteenth. From that time till the sixteenth you had no writer of any distinction, except Fortescue, Chaucer, and Gower.[13] In the sixteenth century, you number only five or six writers of respectability. The seventeenth and eighteenth have filled your hemisphere with constellations. Before Hume and Robertson, you had no historian superior to several of ours. The reviewer is disposed to speak contemptuously of Marshall's Life of Washington.[14] Yet there is no piece of biography written in Great Britain, if we except those of Johnson, which would not suffer by a comparison with it. The last volume is almost singularly excellent. It ought here to be added that the ministers sent out to Europe by Washington have holden at least as high a rank in European estimation as those who were their companions from any of the European courts. Of Mr. Jay, Lord Grenville has given a character in the British Parliament, which should have made the reviewers hesitate before they published the following declaration: "We have dwelt longer upon this article than its merits justify, not so much for the sake of the work, as for stating and exemplifying a most curious and unaccountable fact: the scarcity of all but agricultural and mercantile talents in the New World." There are the best reasons for believing that no foreign minister was holden in higher estimation by the British government than Mr. King.[15]

I will dismiss the subject with one more remark concerning my countrymen. The speeches of [Fisher] Ames and several other members of the American Congress have been rarely excelled in eloquence by British orators.

I am, Sir, yours, etc.

# LETTER V

*Manners and morals of the people of New England—Executions during the Revolutionary War—Capital punishments in the county of New Haven in 175 years—Duels in New England since its settlement—Inhabitants all required to be in the possession of arms—The poor supported and educated—Public and private charities*

*Dear Sir,*

The manners of the people of New England claim next a place in these observations. In the Quarterly Review of November 1809 article on Dr. Holmes' Annals, the writer says, "There is, however, both in the physical and intellectual features of the Americans, a trace of savage character, not produced by crossing the breed, but by the circumstances of society and of external nature." [1] The following facts will show how far this remark is applicable to the people of New England. During the eight years of the Revolutionary War, there was one man put to death by the hand of violence and one by the hand of civil justice within the limits of this country. It contained at that time eight hundred thousand inhabitants. These were then contending *pro aris et focis*,[2] and the spirit of party ran as high as it can easily be supposed to rise in such a state of society. One party seriously considered the other as engaged in a rebellion against their lawful sovereign, and was considered by the other as endeavoring to accomplish the ruin of their country. The man who fell by violence was put to death by three others on the border of Byram River between the lines of the American and British armies. His murderers were part of a banditti, living without any control upon the plunder of the poor inhabitants who inhabited this exposed ground. Yet it is fairly questionable whether they designed to take away his life. The man who fell a victim to law was executed at Hartford after a regular conviction of treason.

This fact has been mentioned in a former part of these observations. Let me recall to your recollection two or three others. From half to two thirds of the inhabitants sleep round the year without bolting or locking their doors. This, you will observe, is not done by the tenants of cottages merely, for of these we have very few; but much more numerously by the owners of good houses, well stored with the property which naturally invites plunderers.

I have lived in New Haven during the last sixteen years.*

This town contains 750 houses and about six thousand people. It employs also a trading capital amounting to $2,500,000. No house, within my knowledge, has been broken open here during this period.

New Haven is the shire town of the county of New Haven, in a state distinguished for the rigid execution of its laws. Of course all the capital punishments in the county have been inflicted here. The whole number of these in one hundred and seventy-five years has been thirteen. Of these, five were whites; five were Indians; and three were blacks. Of the whites, one was a stranger taken up as a spy as he was passing through this town, and executed pursuant to a sentence of a court-martial. Three of the remaining four were natives of England. It does not appear that any inhabitant of this town or county ever suffered death by the hand of law. There is no reason to conclude that the people of this county are more distinguished for their morals than most of the other settlements which have been established for any length of time. In this respect (the paucity of capital punishments), New England may be compared with Scotland and Switzerland, and will suffer no disadvantage by the comparison. I have observed that, since the settlement of New England, five duels have been fought within its boundaries. The first was between two servants belonging to the Plymouth colonists, within a year after their arrival; the second, by two officers of the Revolutionary army, in the state of Rhode Island; the third, by two West Indian youths, who were at school in Stratford; the fourth, by two young gentlemen, inhabitants of Boston; the fifth, by two gentlemen from New York, who crossed Byram River that they might fight without exposing themselves to a prosecution in that state. Two only, therefore, of the five were fought by inhabitants of New England.

Perhaps a still stronger example, at least one which appears to me stronger, is presented by a combined view of the government and state of society in Connecticut. There is not a spot on the globe where so little is done to govern the inhabitants, nor a spot where the inhabitants are so well governed, or perhaps, in more appropriate terms, where the state of society is so peaceable, orderly, and happy. A recurrence to the manner in which elections are carried on here, as described in a former part of these letters, will enable you to compare them with your own. Those in your country have been described to me on various occasions by authority which cannot be questioned. They are scenes of riot, tumult, and violence. Ours are scarcely less decent than religious assemblies.

I have also observed heretofore that, within a time specified, I have traveled not far from twelve thousand miles, principally in New England and New York. I may now add two thousand more (1811), and in this extensive progress have never seen two men employed in fighting. I also added at that

* 1811.

time, what is still true, that I remember no more than one instance of this nature which has fallen under my eye during my life. As I have been extensively occupied in the busy haunts of men, this fact must be considered as proof that such controversies are here extremely rare. Now permit me to call your eye to your own newspapers, and observe how often their columns are ornamented with the feats of Humphries and Mendoza, Cribb and Molineaux.[3] What a grave aspect is given to the accounts which describe the brutal contests of these bullies! Observe also that not the mob only, not the middle ranks of life only, but gentlemen, noblemen, and even princes of the blood † have been present at these rencounters. I do not believe that a gentleman of New England could be persuaded to be present at such a scene by any inducement whatever, unless to perform his duty as a magistrate in committing and punishing such disturbers of society.

Dr. Paley observes, "When the state relies for its defense on a militia, it is necessary that arms be put into the hands of the people at large"; and mentions that upon this plan a great proportion of the inhabitants must ultimately be instructed in the use of them. He then subjoins, "Now what effects upon the civil conditions of the country may be looked for from this general diffusion of the military character becomes an inquiry of great importance and delicacy. Nothing perhaps can govern a nation of armed citizens, but that which governs an army—despotism. The country would be liable to what is even worse than a settled or constitutional despotism, to perpetual rebellions and perpetual revolutions, to short and violent usurpations," etc.[4]

The people of New England have always had, and have by law always been required to have, arms in their hands. Every man is, or ought to be, in the possession of a musket. The great body of our citizens also are trained with a good degree of skill and success to military discipline. Yet I know not a single instance in which arms have been the instruments of carrying on a private quarrel. Nor do I believe that such a subject is even thought of by one person in fifty thousand so often as once in twelve months; I believe I might say with truth, so much as once during life. On a country more peaceful and quiet, it is presumed, the sun never shone. I must, however, acknowledge that there have been, since the settlement of this country, several mobs, and two or three more serious commotions. In Connecticut, the government, whether of the colony or the state, has never met with a single serious attempt at resistance to the execution of its laws. That of Massachusetts was for some time opposed during the latter part of the Revolutionary War and the three years which followed the peace. Several mobs assembled at different times, composed of people from various parts of the county of Hampshire. The first of them were employed in resisting the

† "A horse race, a fox chase, or a boxing match is never without its train of reverend attendants." *Letters to the Rt. Hon. Mr. Perceval.* [*Christian Observer*, Nov. 1811, p. 714.]

British government; the rest rose in opposition to that of the state. Their last effort was in the proper sense an insurrection, and that which immediately preceded it deserved substantially the same name. In the last, the insurgents, amounting to several hundreds, attempted to take possession of the public arsenal at Springfield, but were dispersed by Gen. Shepard with the loss of two or three of their number. Some of the ringleaders were afterwards taken, tried, and sentenced to suffer death; but were pardoned. The cause of these disturbances was the hard pressure of poverty, produced by the ruin of the Continental currency, the want of a circulating medium, and a general train of difficulties following from these, and enhanced by a taxation severe in the amount and distressing in the mode. The period was also that in which the former government was annihilated, and the new one imperfectly established.[5] In all these inroads upon good order, detestable as mobs are, not a person lost his life except those just mentioned.

In New England, horse racing is almost and cockfighting absolutely unknown. I need not remind you to what a degree these barbarous and profligate sports prevail in Great Britain. In New England there never was such a thing as a bullbaiting. Suffer me to recall to your remembrance the debates not long since held in the British Parliament on this subject, the decision of that august body, and the speech delivered at that time by the Hon. Mr. Windham.[6]

Our laws provide effectually for the comfortable maintenance of all the poor who are inhabitants; and, so long as they are with us, of poor strangers, in what country soever they are born; and, when they are sick, supply them with physicians, nurses, and medicines.

The children of the poor are furnished with education and apprenticeships at the public expense. There is not a country on earth where the provision for the wants and sufferings of the poor is so effectual as in New England. The number of these people is, I acknowledge, very small; and our contributions to their relief are of course small compared with those in England. At the same time they are abundantly sufficient for their comfortable support. The facts that the object itself is so limited, that it is distributed into so many hands, that these have no interest in stinting the public charity except what is involved in the nature of things, that they are responsible for all their conduct, and that their accounts are regularly laid before the respective town meetings, or in the instances where this is not done, may at any time be called before the public eye, secure a just application of the public bounty in a degree which I think it must be impossible to reach in England.

The private charities of New England are certainly liberal, inferior, I acknowledge, to those in Great Britain, but superior to those of every other country. Our ancestors brought with them not a small portion of the liberal British spirit. The missionary societies established here are a strong proof of the position. In this excellence of character the inhabitants of the eastern coast of Massachusetts stand at the head of their countrymen. But the same spirit spreads honorably through our country.

A poor debtor confined in prison may upon surrendering his property above the value of five pounds always be discharged, unless the creditor will be at the expense of the maintenance allowed him by law; and this is so considerable that scarcely an instance of such a nature occurs. Indeed public opinion is so hostile to this inhumanity that few men have sufficient hardihood to look it in the face. There is perhaps no country in the world where public opinion has equal influence. When one man injures another in such a manner as that the injury elsewhere would create a duel, the injurious person is ordinarily sufficiently punished by the general discountenance. The knowledge of this more effectually prevents injuries here than dueling has ever done elsewhere.

I am, Sir, yours, etc.

# LETTER VI

*Various traits of character of the people of New England, compared with similar traits of the inhabitants of Great Britain—Difficulties found by Englishmen in judging of the character and circumstances of the people of this country*

*Dear Sir,*

In the early part of this work I observed that every man in New England, almost without an exception, lives on his own ground, and that the lands are universally holden in fee simple, and by law descend to the children in equal shares. Elsewhere, I have observed also that every freeman is eligible to any office, and that a great proportion of them actually hold public offices at some time or other of their lives. The spirit of independence naturally resulting from these facts, and from the ample means of subsistence generally furnished by the former of them, you will easily believe, constitutes a distinguishing trait in the character of its inhabitants. This spirit is cherished by the frequency with which the opportunities of exercising the privilege of election occur. All officers of the parish, town, or state are elected annually, with the single exception that in Connecticut the representatives to the legislature are elected semiannually.* Nations possessed of civil lib-

* Under the new constitution, representatives are elected but once a year. PUB.

erty have ever thought it wise to cultivate this spirit. In Great Britain particularly, it has been the perpetual boast of her citizens. In the opinion of other nations, your countrymen have carried it beyond the bounds which reason can justify, and have rendered themselves less amiable and less acceptable than from their solid, sturdy virtues might be wished. That you may not think me as destitute of candor and liberality, as I think the men whose opinions I have combatted, I will subjoin the following testimony from one of the most admired of your modern poets.

Pride in their port, defiance in their eye;
I see the lords of human kind pass by,
Intent on high designs; a thoughtful band,
By forms unfashion'd, fresh from nature's hand;
Fierce in their native hardiness of soul;
True to imagin'd right; above control;
While e'en the peasant boasts these rights to scan,
And learns to venerate himself as man.
Thine, freedom, thine the blessings, pictur'd here;
Thine are those charms, that dazzle, and endear:
Too blest indeed were such without alloy;
But, foster'd e'en by freedom ills annoy.
That independence, Britons prize too high,
Keeps man from man, and breaks the social tie;
The self-dependent lordlings stand alone;
All claims that bind, and sweeten, life, unknown.
Here by the bonds of nature feebly held,
Minds combat minds, repelling and repell'd;
Ferments arise, imprison'd factions roar;
Repress'd ambition struggles round her shore;
Till over-wrought, the general system feels
Its motion stop, or phrensy fires the wheels.
Nor this the worst.†

It is unnecessary to comment on this picture, as well as on the lines which immediately follow. Allowing it to be just, it exhibits more of *a trace of savage character* than everything of which I have been a witness among my own countrymen. We are styled proud, haughty, insolent republicans. Among your literary people the republican days of Rome and of Greece are accounted their best days. Even they, therefore, do not consider a republican government as necessarily injurious to the human character. Yet the Romans and Greeks were both much more haughty than we are; nay, your own countrymen are much more haughty. This I know with certainty, both by the books and by the conversation of gentlemen from most parts of the continent of Europe. Indeed, you must have seen the names of *proud and haughty Islanders* applied to the British almost proverbially. Nay, Sir, the very same thing has been repeatedly declared to me by several of your own countrymen who have resided in America long enough to be acquainted

† Goldsmith's Traveller. [Lines 327 ff.]

with the manners and character of her inhabitants. These with one voice have frankly told me that they have found more civilities and more kind offices cheerfully rendered to them here than they should have expected, or probably have found, without the circle of their friends, from their countrymen in an equal period of time.

Of the numerous Englishmen who have visited these states, I have seen not a small number. The manners of these, of every rank, and some of them have been persons of considerable distinction, have, with a small number of exceptions, been less unassuming, less civil, more distant, more self-complacent, and more forbidding than those of my own countrymen in similar spheres of life. You will not understand by this that I think ill of British manners. A frank, intelligent, open-hearted, worthy man from Great Britain who has had the liberality to lay aside his national peculiarities is as agreeable a companion as I wish to converse with.

A principal reason why your countrymen complain of disobliging conduct in mine is that they provoke this treatment. An Englishman when he enters an inn treats the innkeeper as if he were his servant, perhaps I might say with truth, his slave; and it is remarkable that they are the only people who exhibit this treatment. Unused to it from others, the innkeeper bears it impatiently from them. Whether this behavior of the traveler is proper and defensible, I shall not now stop to inquire. It is not customary; and for this reason at least, unwelcome. As every New England man feels entirely independent, it is not strange that he should not brook what he considers as unmerited abuse. A little civility would have commanded every effort of the innkeeper to please him.‡ I think so much might be conceded to the manners of the country. Travelers ordinarily yield much more to the manners of other countries.

Another misfortune of the same nature is that Englishmen are very commonly dissatisfied with everything which is done for them. Some of them can find nothing fit to be eaten or drunk, and that apparently because they were predetermined not to be pleased. Numerous impositions have been sportively practised upon them in consequence of this characteristical spirit. The Philadelphian porter, which when known to be Philadelphian they have thought detestable, has afterwards, when they believed it to be of London manufacture, been pronounced to be excellent; and Connecticut cheese has in the same extraordinary manner changed its nature. I have the best reason to believe that your inns are better than ours, but I have equal reason to believe that ours are better than those of any other country.

We are complained of as inquisitive. We are so, but very rarely, I suspect, in any such manner as to justify the complaints. I have mentioned the extent to which I have traveled in New England and New York during the last sixteen years, and these letters are ample proof that the parts of these

‡ See remarks on Lambert. ["Remarks on European Travelers in America," Letter IV.]

countries which I have visited are very numerous. In this employment I have spent at different times between two and three years; but do not remember that I have been once asked by an innkeeper, during the whole of this progress, who I was, whence I came, whither I was going, or what was my business; nor do I recollect that I have met with a single incivility. I have found innkeepers in various instances poor, ill furnished, and unpolished, but cannot recall more than two or three instances in which they have been disobliging. All the instances in which innkeepers have seated themselves with me at table, or offered to sit in the room of which I had taken possession, except one, are, I believe, mentioned in these letters. I cannot think that cases of this nature occur very often to others. Permit me to suspect that your travelers create some of them, and see others through a multiplying glass.

At the same time, an inn is a very imperfect representative of the town in which it stands; and neither an innkeeper, nor his servants ought to be considered as standards of the intelligence, character, or manners of the inhabitants at large, certainly not of those who are the most enlightened and polished.

The Englishmen and most Europeans who travel through this country hasten with the rapidity of the stage from one great town to another. To men bred in such towns, this is certainly a very natural course, but it makes it impossible for them to know the state of the country through which they pass. A little they learn sometimes from their fellow travelers, and a little more they glean at inns. Most of what they are told is very imperfectly told, and more imperfectly understood. The remainder of their information is picked up in cities, many of whose inhabitants know as little of the country as themselves. The state of almost everything here is so different from that of the same things on the eastern continent, the habits of those who judge and the standards of thinking to which all that is judged of is referred are so unsuited to the objects which present themselves that it is scarcely possible for a mere traveler not to err materially when forming his opinions. The late Dr. Witherspoon, president of the college at Princeton in New Jersey, once observed that it was necessary for an inhabitant of Great Britain to live eight or ten years in America in order to form those opinions concerning the state of the country which he would ultimately consider as just. "For example," said he, "if you were to tell a North Briton that the people of this country universally live upon beef, mutton, veal, and other animal food, which they eat, once, twice, or thrice every day, he would believe that they were all possessed of fortunes, because none in that country besides those who have fortunes live in this manner. Whereas, if you should tell the same man that he would find a wooden latch on one or more of the doors of a great number of the houses, he would conclude at once that all these were cottages, because such latches are never found on any other buildings in North Britain."

The import of these observations is applicable in a greater or less degree to very many things in this country. Our government, our laws, our religion, our manners, the state of arts and manufactures, our literature, our science, our climate, nay, even the state of vegetation are either in their nature, or their dependence on their respective causes, or their connection with each other, or their mutual influence, of necessity imperfectly understood and regularly more or less misapprehended by every foreigner who passes through the country. This is evident beyond a debate to every intelligent American in his conversation with every foreigner.

You will naturally object to these observations that these things are chiefly the same with those in Great Britain, or very similar. You will say that our government is the same with yours, except some slight shades of difference, that our religion is the same in all its varieties, that our manners are the same, and that this is true of our whole state of society. What I mean is, that you will consider all these things as copies, imperfect indeed, but still copies of the same things in Great Britain. Where then, you will ask, is the difficulty which an Englishman will find in readily discerning and comprehending whatever meets his eye in New England?

As the subject has never been publicly discussed, and as the contrary opinion to that which I have here advanced appears universally to be adopted by Britons, particularly by Englishmen; as the effects of it have hitherto been only malignant, and as just opinions in your countrymen concerning mine must be of considerable importance if we are hereafter to be connected as friends, I will endeavor to convince you that the observations which I have made on the subject are just. For this purpose I ask your attention to the following remarks.

1. There are more differences in the state of things in the two countries than an Englishman can possibly preconceive. Almost the only difference which he is prepared to expect is involved in the general inferiority of all those things which I have mentioned to the same things in his own country. This opinion is extensively erroneous. The inhabitants of New England as a body are in many respects not inferior, and in some superior, to those of England. In the older settlements they are more religious and have better morals; not, I acknowledge, than very many of your countrymen, yet it is true of them *en masse*. We have fewer corruptions; we have more of the simplicity and innocence of youth. Centuries must pass over our heads before we shall be able, or willing, to practise one half of the enormities which are recited in Colquhoun's Police of London, or his Police of the Thames. At the same time we are behind you in learning, science, and a multitude of mechanical and manufacturing arts; in agriculture, in architecture, in commerce, and in wealth; in the fine arts, in liberality, and in various other advantages of improved society. Still we have fewer prejudices, both because we are a less important part of the human family and have therefore fewer temptations to them, and because we have had less time to

form and rivet them. Great, powerful, and splendid nations never do justice to those which are inferior. The great nations are the tribunals which decide in every case where a comparison is made between them and others. Great nations are the painters, and always paint themselves riding. Inferior nations are only painted by them, and regularly appear on the picture as ridden. The mere continuance of this progress rivets the opinions adopted by the former to such a degree that they ultimately obtain the force of a law, to revolt from which is considered as a kind of rebellion.

At the same time we are more affable, more easy of access, and universally more social and more ready to oblige.

We are also more orderly, quiet, and peaceful; are governed with less difficulty and by milder measures.

Our common people are far better educated than yours, both in the school and in the church, and for this very good reason, that they are all at school, and almost all at church. All of them can read, and write, and keep accounts. Almost all of them do read; and many of them, much. At the same time, our state of society prompts men to become acquainted with many things besides their own business. *That,* they understand generally less perfectly than the English. But they understand many things of which the same classes in England know little or nothing. An English artisan or farmer bends, and is obliged to bend, the whole force of his mind to the attainment of perfection in his proper employment; and this he accomplishes in a degree rarely reached by the citizens of any other country. A New Englander is under no such necessity, and finds many inducements to turn his thoughts toward many other objects. In this manner he becomes to a considerable extent actually acquainted with those objects, and acquires an expansion of mind and a rationality of character not often found in any other country.

We have in New England no such class of men as on the eastern side of the Atlantic are denominated *peasantry.* The number of those who are mere laborers is almost nothing, except in a few of the populous towns; and almost all these are collected from the shiftless, the idle, and the vicious. A great part of them are foreigners. Here every apprentice originally intends to establish and, with scarcely an exception, actually establishes himself in business. Every seaman designs to become, and a great proportion of them really become, mates and masters of vessels; and every young man hired to work upon a farm aims steadily to acquire a farm for himself, and hardly one fails of the acquisition. We have few of those amphibious beings of whom you have such a host, who pass through life under the name of *journeymen.* All men here are masters of themselves, and such is the combined effect of education and society that he who fails of success in one kind of business may almost of course betake himself with advantage to another.

To dismiss the subject, there is a vein of practical good sense, the most valuable of all intellectual possessions, running through the people of New England, which may be considered as their characteristical distinction. The old Roman question, *cui bono erit?* [1] is asked here perhaps more frequently and more universally than in any other country.

2. The very fact that these differences are very small, as in many instances they undoubtedly are, prevents them from being observed. It is an observation of several respectable grammarians that the English language is worse written, and its grammar less understood, because its analogies and consequently its rules are so few, and because it may be tolerably understood and written almost without any knowledge of grammar. The late Dr. Rodgers, an eminent clergyman in New York, once observed to me that it was hardly possible to give a Presbyterian minister from Scotland just and distinct apprehensions of American Presbyterianism.

3. Englishmen generally, at least those who converse with us or write about us, consider our country as scarcely meriting any attentive examination.

As I feel very little interested in this opinion, I shall not here inquire whether it is just or not. It is only necessary to remark that those who hold it will never examine sufficiently to find out what is true. Your travelers who visit us are generally in the full pursuit of either business or pleasure, and in both cases fail necessarily of learning the state of the country. Still they are generally desirous of being thought to be acquainted with it, and let me add, usually deliver their opinions with at least as much confidence as if their information was sound and comprehensive.

4. They enter the country with strong preconceptions of their own superior wisdom, and thence judge without thought, and determine without a suspicion that they are liable to error. To know beforehand is to be always deceived.

5. Their habits of thinking necessarily lead them into a train of misconceptions. A person who reads English books, or converses with Englishmen, will soon perceive that there are certain standards of opinion adopted by them which they rarely think of calling in question so far as to make them even subjects of examination. Nor does it appear to make much difference whether the opinions are just or erroneous. Thus a high churchman holds the doctrine of passive obedience and the divine right of bishops without considering either as admitting even of a debate. A low churchman would hardly allow either of them to be defensible. A member of the established church of either character pleads for the importance of episcopacy, that it secures effectually the necessary discipline of the Gospel, both with respect to ministers and private Christians. Yet the discipline of our churches is incomparably more regular, exact, and efficacious than that of yours. Examples of this nature might be multiplied in all the spheres and concerns of life. All old, established society is subjected of course to this mode of think-

ing, and by refusing to examine its opinions, continues in many cases in unnecessary errors. Sometimes these modes of thinking spring so entirely from mere circumstances that they may be excused, or at least pitied. At others they are so mingled with ill temper and perverseness as to merit censure. In both cases they are sources of errors which are numerous and unhappy.

Among these habits a sweeping one is a general conviction, perhaps I ought rather to say determination, that almost everything in England is right, and that everything which differs from it here is wrong. Englishmen, more, I believe, than any other people, employ themselves when abroad in comparing everything which they think worth their attention with that which is of a similar nature in their own country; and this, I am convinced, in many instances with a settled disposition to give the preference at all events to what is their own. The consequence is that whatever becomes the subject of their discussion is condemned almost of course. I well know that there are many things in England which are better than the same things in most other countries. Yet it is far from being true of all. I also know that many things are good which are not best; that things have an inherent, as well as a comparative value, and that this will not be forgotten by men of candor and good sense. To English travelers in the United States, it seems scarcely to be known at all. The result of such a mode of judging, I need not specify.

6. Many of your countrymen feel some hostility to America on the score of the Revolution. So often does this spirit discover itself that my assertion will not be disputed. Permit me to add that I think such a disposition, either in the British or the Americans, unwise and unhappy.

7. Your travelers, partly for the want of better information, and partly from a willingness to receive them, adopt without hesitation a collection of old tales concerning the inhabitants of New England which, I confess, have been so often repeated by contemptible prejudice as to be extensively believed by a credulity scarcely less contemptible. Generally, however, they are false even to a ridiculous degree; and, where they are true, have as little connection with the present state of this country as with England itself. We have our faults and our follies, and both are numerous; but it is unnecessary to increase the number from this source.

8. Englishmen are obliged to encounter here a considerable number of real evils, and lose a number of real enjoyments when they leave their own country and reside in this. In England, men who have sufficient property can find almost every enjoyment of life which their climate will permit, their soil yield, or their commerce and manufactures furnish provided in a sense to their hands. Business is there so far systematized, and all its fruits, if I may call them such, are so regularly brought into the market that every such man may command any of them at his pleasure. But this cannot be so

extensively or easily done here, even in our large cities. Our markets, in the literal sense, are indeed almost glutted with everything which can be eaten or drunk. In fine fruits, it is unnecessary to say, our country incomparably exceeds yours, both as to their richness and variety; and those of the West Indian islands are brought hither in profusion. Wines also are sold here in vast abundance and on very moderate terms. But articles which we eat and drink are far from constituting the whole list of what the case demands. If an Englishman here wants to build a house, he cannot always find a man who will contrive a house for him such as he wishes, and take the whole trouble of building it upon himself. If he wishes to hire laborers, he will obtain them with more difficulty, they will do less labor, and they will demand a price two or three times greater than in his own country. At the same time they will not do his work so well, will treat him with less respect; and, if he affronts them, will scarcely work for him again. Still greater will be his difficulty in obtaining and keeping servants. They are always in demand; and the competition is not for the place, but for the service. Hence they feel themselves to be important, are disobliging, rude, disposed often to change their place, and will not unfrequently quit it with little or no warning.

In addition to these things, an Englishman finds a variety of sufferings growing out of the general fact that his mode of life is in many respects materially changed from what it was in his own country. All his habits he brings with him; and these in reality form not only his enjoyments, but the man himself. In a variety of ways they are here disturbed; and in some, counteracted. Our climate is alternately severely cold and severely hot. The damp, the wet, and the mud of his own country he was accustomed to from his infancy; and, therefore, thought nothing of them, although the same weather, when it exists here, is more disagreeable to us than our heat and cold. But the cold and the heat are new to him and, therefore, extremely uncomfortable. His conveniences for traveling are materially lessened, unless indeed he will make use of his own vehicles. Our stages are fewer, less convenient, furnished by owners, and driven by coachmen less obliging.

He wishes to hunt, but often will be able to find neither hounds, nor hares, nor foxes, nor fellow sportsmen. In the same manner he looks in vain for a variety of enjoyments to which he has been attached, at least in the same perfection.

The first impressions of a traveler and still more of a resident in a foreign country are those which are made by a violation of his habits. From this source he is a loser in many ways, while the country in which he now is furnishes very little which he can substitute for what he has lost. The country in which he is cannot give him new habits until he has been in it long enough to form them; and, until they are formed, nothing which it contains will give him the satisfaction found by him in their indulgence.

The enjoyments which the native inhabitants esteem exquisite, and much superior to those in which he once delighted, yield him little pleasure, because they have not been endeared to him by habit. A native of the southern states when he comes to the North finds all his habits violated in the same manner, and would scarcely for any consideration be induced to take up his residence here. A northern man inverts these facts, and would with as much difficulty be persuaded to continue in the South. Nay, an inhabitant of New England who has spent one or two years in Great Britain feels exactly the same emotions, and returns with as much satisfaction as even Weld himself when quitting the United States for his native country. There is something so respectable in the *amor patriae* that I feel little disposition to contend with a foreigner on this subject, and can forget many of his prejudices while I look at the dignity scarcely separable from this affection. Another set of impressions, early and increasingly felt by these persons, is derived from the absence of their peculiar friends. The effect of this is in some degree to divest every pleasing object of its brilliancy, to diminish the pleasure which it might convey, and to make every painful one still more painful. The unhappiness which springs from this source will awaken the sympathy, and the character of the sufferer will command the esteem of every generous mind.

If these remarks are allowed to be just, they will certainly go far toward explaining a considerable part of the errors with which your travelers in America certainly abound. Some others are undoubtedly attributable to personal character. The number and nature of these are such that, if British travelers have represented other countries with as little skill and correctness as they have done ours, the world will derive little advantage from their writings.

I am, Sir, yours, etc.

# LETTER VII

*Modes of living—Amusements—People of New England fond of acquiring knowledge—Happy effects of this trait of character—The Sabbath observed with sobriety and reverence—Marriages—Funerals*

*Dear Sir,*

The means of comfortable living are in New England so abundant, and so easily obtained, as to be within the reach of every man who has health, industry, common honesty, and common sense. Labor commands such a price that every laborer of this character may earn from one hundred and twenty-five to two hundred and fifty dollars a year.* Hence every one may within a moderate period purchase himself a farm of considerable extent in the recent settlements, and a small one in those which are older. Even those who are somewhat below the common level in these attributes may, and do, acquire small houses and gardens, where they usually live comfortably.

The food of the inhabitants at large, even of the poor, is principally flesh and fish, one or other of which is eaten by a greater part of the inhabitants twice and three times a day. A breakfast in the large towns is chiefly bread and butter, the bread in the cool season generally toasted. In the country almost universally this is accompanied with smoke-dried beef, cheese, or some species of fish or flesh broiled or otherwise fitted to the taste of the family. So universal is this custom that a breakfast without such an addition is considered as scarcely worth eating. At dinner, the vegetables which I formerly mentioned continually succeed each other in their varieties. Fruits also, which you will remember are here very numerous and various, as well as very rich and luscious, are brought upon the dinner table, or are eaten in other parts of the day throughout most of the year. Supper in most parts of the country is like the breakfast, except that it is made up partially of preserved fruits, different kinds of cake, pies, tarts, etc. The meats used at breakfast and supper are generally intended to be dainties.

Puddings formed of rice, flour, maize, and sometimes of buckwheat very frequently constitute a part of the dinner.

Pork, except the hams, shoulders, and cheeks, is never converted into bacon. I do not know that I ever saw a flitch of bacon cured in New England in my life. The sides of the hog are here always pickled, and by the New England people are esteemed much superior to bacon. The pork of New England is fatted upon maize, a sweeter and richer food for cattle of all kinds than any other, is more skillfully cured, and is, therefore, better than that of any other country. It is also a favorite food with most of the inhabitants.

Tea and coffee constitute a part of the breakfast and supper of every class, and of almost every individual. The principal drink of the inhabitants is cider. Wine, which is here very cheap, is extensively used; so in the mild season is punch. Porter also is drunk by fashionable people; and in small quantities, ale. In the large towns, particularly in Boston, dinners are given without number, but much more unfrequently in the smaller ones. The favorite entertainment in them is the supper. For this there are two potent reasons. One is, everybody is here employed in business through the day. The evening, being the only season of leisure, furnishes the best opportunity for that agreeable intercourse which is the primary object of all

* 1812.

entertainments. The other is, the want of a sufficient number of servants to take the burden of superintending the preparation of dinners from the mistress of the family. I have been present at a very great multitude of entertainments of both kinds, and am compelled to say that those of the evening are much the most pleasant and rational. There is less excess and more leisure; the mind is more cheerful; and the conversation almost of course more sprightly, interesting, and useful.

The hours of breakfast vary in the country from six to eight in the summer, and from seven to nine in the winter; those of dinner from twelve to two; those of supper from five to eight. In the large towns all these hours vary still more. The most fashionable people breakfast late, and dine from three to four. The food of such people is principally taken at a single meal. In the summer many of the laboring people make their principal meal at supper.

The proportion of animal food eaten in this country is, I think, excessive.

At entertainments, the dining table is loaded with a much greater variety of dishes than good sense will justify. A fashion which it is difficult to resist prevails in this respect over every rational consideration.

The quantity of ardent spirits consumed chiefly by the middle and lower classes of people is scandalous to its character, although much less in its amount than that drunk by the same number of people in Great Britain.

The dress of the inhabitants is chiefly formed of the manufactures and made up in the fashions of Europe, particularly of Great Britain.

The principal amusements of the inhabitants are visiting, dancing, music, conversation, walking, riding, sailing, shooting at a mark, draughts, chess, and, unhappily in some of the larger towns, cards and dramatic exhibitions. A considerable amusement is also furnished in many places by the examination and exhibitions of the superior schools, and a more considerable one by the public exhibitions of colleges.

Our countrymen also fish and hunt.

Journeys taken for pleasure are very numerous, and are a very favorite object.

Boys and young men play at football, cricket, quoits, and at many other sports of an athletic cast; and in the winter are peculiarly fond of skating. Riding in a sleigh, or sledge, is also a favorite diversion in New England.

People of wealth, and many in moderate circumstances, have their children taught music, particularly on the pianoforte; and many of the young men play on the German flute, violin, clarinet, etc. Serenading is not unfrequent.

Visiting, on the plan of sociality and friendship, is here among all classes of people, especially among those who are intelligent and refined, a very agreeable and very rational source of enjoyment; and is usually free from the crowds and confusion, the ceremony and frivolity, which so often render scenes of this nature wearisome in great cities, and force the hours devoted to them to drag heavily, while

The heart, distrusting, asks if this be joy.[1]

Visits are here formed for the purposes of interchanging thought, affection, hospitality, and pleasure. With far less parade, less inconvenience to the family visited, and less trouble to the visitors, they are fraught with more cordiality, more good sense, more sprightliness, and incomparably more pleasure. The themes of conversation are of a superior class; the affections and sentiments are set upon a higher key; and the company part, not with eagerness, but with regret.

Reading also is a favorite employment with persons in almost all conditions of life. A considerable collection of books throughout a great part of this country is furnished to the inhabitants by the social libraries heretofore mentioned. Private libraries are undoubtedly much more limited than in Great Britain. Many of them are, however, sufficient collections to extend much useful information, and to supply not a small fund of pleasure to their proprietors and others. By these means a great number of persons are enabled to read as extensively as their other avocations will permit; and all who love reading will find, or make, opportunities for pursuing it, which in the aggregate will constitute a considerable, as well as valuable and delightful, part of their lives. Accordingly this employment is pursued by men and women in almost every sphere of life.†

† The reading of newspapers in this country is undoubtedly excessive, as is also the number of such papers annually published. Yet it cannot be denied that newspapers, conducted with moderation, integrity, and skill, are capable of being useful to a community; or that the reading of them to some extent is a pleasant, rational, and profitable employment. Several newspapers in this country are conducted by men of education and talents.

The following account of gazettes formerly published in the British colonies, for which I am indebted to the researches of Rev. Dr. Stiles, president of Yale College, cannot fail of gratifying the reader. [Corrections taken from Clarence S. Brigham, *History and Bibliography of American Newspapers, 1690–1820* (Worcester, Mass., 1947).]

There were printed in 1765 in the British colonies

| | |
|---|---|
| Quebec Gazette | Brown & Gilman, Aug. 22, No. 62 |
| Halifax Gazette | |
| New-Hampshire Gazette | Daniel and Robert Fowle, Sept. 23, No. 468 |
| Portsmouth Mercury | [Furber] & Russell, Sept. 27, No. 36 |
| Boston Gazette | Edes & Gill, Sept. 30, No. 548 |
| [Boston] Evening-Post | T. & J. Fleet, Sept. 30, No. 1568 |
| Massachusetts Gazette | Richard Draper, Aug. 15, No. 3208 |
| Boston Post-Boy | Green & Russell, Aug. 5, No. 406 |
| Newport Mercury | Samuel Hall |
| Providence Gazette | Goddard, dropped in Aug. [1765] |
| New-London Gazette | Timothy Green, Sept. 27, No. 98 |
| Connecticut Gazette, New Haven | B. Mecom, Sept. 27, No. 483 |
| Connecticut Courant, Hartford | T. Green, Sept. 30, No. 45 |
| New-York Gazette | J. Hall [Holt], Sept. 26, No. 1186 |
| New-York Mercury | Hugh Gaine, Sept. 30, No. 727 |
| Weyman's New-York Gazette | W. Weyman, Nov. 25, No. 343 |

We are often censured for diffusing a smattering of learning and science throughout a great part of the community, as well as for not communicating them in higher degrees to persons liberally educated. Is this censure just? Is

---

| | |
|---|---|
| Pennsylvania Gazette | B. Franklin & D. Hall, Sept. 26, No. 1918 |
| Pennsylvania Journal | William Bradford, Sept. 26, No. 1190 |
| Maryland Gazette, Annapolis | Jonas Green & Wm. Rind, Sept. 19, No. 1063 |
| Virginia Gazette, Williamsburg | Alexander Purdie, March 7, No. 772 |
| North-Carolina Gazette, Wilmington | Andrew Stuart, April 9, No. 78 |
| South-Carolina Gazette | Peter Timothy, Oct. 31, No. 1607 |
| South-Carolina and American General Gazette | Robert Wells, Oct. 31, No. 364 |
| Georgia Gazette, Savannah | James Johnston, No. 149 |
| South-Carolina Gazette And Country Journal | Charles Crouch, Dec. 17, No. 1 |
| Virginia Gazette | Aug. 1, No. 12 |

For the first eighty years after the British colonies began to be settled, there were no newspapers printed in any of them. The first was the Massachusetts Gazette, originally the Boston Weekly News-Letter, which was published in 1704. There were only seven published before 1750. In 1765 there were twenty-six on the continent, and five in the West India Islands. These were the Jamaica, Barbados, St. Christopher, Antigua, and Grenada Gazettes.

| | |
|---|---|
| The Massachusetts Gazette begun | 1704 |
| New-England Courant | 1721 |
| Pennsylvania Gazette | 1728 |
| South-Carolina Gazette | 1734 [1732] |
| Boston Evening-Post | 1735 |
| New-York Gazette | 1742 [1743] |
| Pennsylvania Journal | 1742 |
| Maryland Gazette | 1745 |
| New-York Mercury | 1751 [1752] |
| Boston Gazette | 1755 [1719] |
| Connecticut Gazette | 1755 |
| Portsmouth Mercury | 1765 |
| Boston Post-Boy | 1757 [1734] |

About seventeen or eighteen years since, I collected with some painstaking a list of the several newspapers published in this country. There were at that time in

| | |
|---|---|
| Vermont | 6 |
| New Hamsphire | 11 |
| Maine | 3 |
| Massachusetts | 19 |
| Rhode Island | 3 |
| Connecticut | 13 |
| In New England | 55 |
| New York | 21 |
| New Jersey | 5 |
| Pennsylvania | 14 |
| Delaware | 1 |
| Maryland | 7 |
| Virginia | 6 |
| North Carolina | 5 |
| South Carolina | 3 |
| Georgia | 1 |
| Kentucky | 1 |
| Tennessee | 1 |
| Total | 120 |

it a misfortune to any man to have his capacity enlarged beyond that of a mere peasant? Is it undesirable that men in plain life should be enabled to think rationally and soundly concerning religion, morals, the general concerns of their country, the affairs of the town and parish in which they reside, the personal and social duties, and the business which they are to pursue? Is it undesirable even to spread their views beyond the limits of their country and the age in which they live? Can the impropriety be pointed out of instructing such persons to some extent in geography or history? Can there be any disadvantage in teaching persons to generalize their thoughts, to combine facts and principles, and to reason from those which they already know to those which from time to time become objects of their investigation and are governed by the same or kindred analogies? Can it be undesirable that any classes of mankind who are destined to pass through old age, a season at the best sufficiently destitute of comforts, should acquire the means which reading and the rational conversation furnished by it supply to man of cheering the hours of declining life, and gilding the otherwise melancholy evening of their days with serenity and sunshine? Can it be proper that those who are to be parents should be precluded from the power of giving rational instruction to their children?

Were this censure uttered by a vain, pert stripling, who, having acquired a little knowledge, felt impatient at the thought of seeing others become his rivals, it certainly ought to excite no surprise, nor resentment. From men sufficiently informed to understand the value of knowledge, and to discern both the usefulness and the pleasure of which it is the natural source, it comes with a very ill grace; and the contempt with which it is expressed recoils deservedly and irresistibly upon its authors.

I know it will be said that when persons in humble life become possessed of the information here referred to they are apt to rise above their proper station and business. The peasant will no longer be contented to be a peasant; and the laborer will leave his daily task, not from indolence, but from pride. Whatever truth or force this observation may derive from the state of society in Europe, it is here destitute of force, and almost of meaning. We have no peasants, unless that name is to be applied to a number of laborers, very small, and those chiefly resident in our cities. No man here begins life with the expectation of being a mere laborer. All intend to possess, and almost all actually possess, a comfortable degree of property and independence. The ascent to better circumstances and higher stations is always open, and there are very few who do not attempt to rise. He who is discontented with his present condition is at perfect liberty to quit it for another more agreeable to his wishes, and a great multitude actually quit their original poverty and insignificance for wealth and reputation. No disadvantages result to the community from this source; the benefits derived from it are very numerous and everywhere visible.

It is further said that such a diffusion of knowledge over the community creates discontentment, an inclination to meddle with politics, the fretfulness and turmoil awakened by petty ambition, and ultimately a disturbance of the peace of society. It has always been the ardent wish of the great to keep the small quiet by such means as were in their power, and nothing is more obvious than that ignorance is one of the most effectual preventives of that uneasiness in the subordinate classes of men which at times have threatened the existence of social order. It is not, therefore, to be wondered at that the superior ranks should have looked on the mental improvement of their inferiors with an eye of jealousy; and, although ashamed to commend ignorance in the abstract, or in Protestant countries to pronounce it the mother of devotion, that they should still contemplate it with not a little degree of complacency.

That jealousy is blind is an adage. In New England no part of the fears which give birth to this objection has been realized. That diffusion of knowledge can be fraught with no inherent danger, which for near two hundred years has produced none. There is not, there never was, a more quiet or more orderly state of society than that which has existed in Connecticut from the beginning, and in all the old settlements of New England, with too few exceptions to deserve notice. Against this proof from experience, the conjectures of the most learned men on the other side of the Atlantic will to a New Englander be urged in vain. The magistrate in the meantime will here see his official duty stripped of half its encumbrances, and peace established around him by the good sense and good principles of those whom he governs. The minister will behold his church and congregation ordinarily settled upon firmer foundations and yielding less to every wind of doctrine than in most other countries. The neighborhood also will be rendered social and pleasant, and life pass on with more peace and comfort than were ever yielded by ignorance in any of its gradations.

To the individuals who are thus enlightened, enlightened, I mean, when compared with those of other countries in the same circumstances, the advantages are often incalculable. A New Englander imbibes from this education an universal habit of combining the objects of thought and comparing them in such a manner as to generalize his views with no small degree of that readiness and skill which in many countries are considered as peculiar to a scientifical education. Hence he often discerns means of business and profit which elsewhere are chiefly concealed from men of the same class. Hence, when prevented from pursuing one kind of business, or unfortunate in it, he easily, and in very many instances successfully, commences another. Hence he avails himself of occurrences which are unregarded by most other men.

From this source have been derived many original machines for abridging human labor and improving its results, not a small number of which have been invented by persons who had received no education except that which has excited these observations. A house joiner in Massachusetts, if I have been correctly informed, has invented a stocking loom, elsewhere mentioned, which weaves six stockings a day. Universally, our people are by this degree of education fitted to make the best of their circumstances, both at home and abroad, to find subsistence where others would fail of it, to advance in their property and their influence where others would stand still, and to extricate themselves from difficulties where others would despond. Universally also, they teach their children more and better things than persons of less information teach theirs, and are regularly induced to give them, if possible, a better education than themselves have received.

In a war on the land and on the water, the New Englanders, with the same discipline and experience, will be found more expert, both as soldiers and seamen, than the inhabitants of most other countries.

I will conclude this letter with a few observations concerning two or three other subjects intimately connected with the manners of this country.

The Sabbath is observed in New England with a greater degree of sobriety and strictness than in any other part of the world. As we have been very often severely censured on this very account, the truth of the observation may of course be admitted. Public worship is regularly attended twice every Sabbath by a very great part of our people, and is everywhere attended with decorum and reverence. Our laws in Massachusetts and Connecticut forbid traveling upon the Sabbath: the whole day being here considered as sequestered by God to himself, and consecrated to the duties of religion. Some of your countrymen, and not a small number of ours, regard this prohibition as an unwarrantable encroachment on personal rights, and complain of the laws with not a little bitterness. We without hesitation pronounce them to be right, founded on the law of God, and necessary to the preservation, as well to the peaceful enjoyment, of that all important institution. Some of your divines teach us that the New Testament has relaxed the severity of the law which prescribed the manner of observing the Sabbath to the Jewish nation. That the municipal law which punished a Jewish Sabbathbreaker is not obligatory upon the gentiles any more than the rest of that code in which it is found is without a question sufficiently taught in the New Testament; but, in what place in this volume the fourth command is at all relaxed, or the prescription which discloses the duties of the Sabbath in the 58th chapter of Isaiah, I am yet to learn. If these gentlemen would distinctly point us to the passages of the New Testament in which we are released from the duty *of turning away our foot from doing our own pleasure on this holy day,* and are permitted *to do our own ways, to find our own pleasure, and to speak our own words,* instead of *esteeming the Sabbath a delight and the holy of the Lord honorable,* they certainly would throw new light on the subject, and rescue many individuals from the reproaches of a wounded conscience.[2] By the Christians of this country the strict observation of the Sabbath is esteemed a privilege, and not a burden; and to be released from it, a diminution, not an increase of the blessings given to the Jewish church. Until this is done, we shall continue to believe that the Sabbath is to be kept holy unto the end.

You will not question that every government is bound to secure the religious privileges of its subjects, and that every Christian government is, of course, under obligations to secure to its subjects the undisturbed enjoyment of the Sabbath. Wherever traveling is permitted, this becomes impossible. Our churches stand almost universally, as do most of our private dwellings, upon the public roads. Every traveler, therefore, disturbs both the public and private duties of the Sabbath.

As to the plea that the prohibition of traveling or amusements is an intrusion upon the rights of strangers, I regard it as contemptible. All strangers of common sense and common decency feel themselves bound quietly to submit to the laws of any country in which they are, so long as it gives them protection; and shall it be said that a traveler is under obligations to obey the laws of Turkey, Arabia, Cochin China, and even of Kaffraria, while he resides in those countries, and not be under the same obligation quietly to submit to those of Massachusetts or Connecticut? Strangers have no right to prescribe; it is their business quietly to obey.

Marriages were formerly festivals of considerable significance in this country. It was customary to invite even the remote relations of the parties, all their particular friends, and a great number of their neighbors. A dinner was made, in form, by the parents of the bride for the bridegroom and a numerous suite. The marriage was celebrated in the evening. Cake and wine were plentifully distributed among the guests, and the festivity was concluded with dancing. At the present time the guests are usually very few.

Justices of the peace are throughout New England authorized to marry, but are rarely, if ever, employed to perform this service when a clergyman can be obtained. As it is everywhere believed to be a divine institution, it is considered as involved, of course, within the duties of the sacred office. An absolute decency is observed during the celebration.

At the funerals in New England, the friends and neighbors attend of course. When the assembly is gathered by the ringing of the parish bell, a prayer is made at the house in which the deceased lived by the clergyman, and is always adapted to the occasion. The corpse is then conveyed to the grave either upon a hearse, or upon men's shoulders. In the latter case, the young men of the town always voluntarily offer their services in sufficient numbers. A solemn procession accompanies it, and to a great extent it is attended by pallbearers. After the corpse is committed to the grave, in many places a solemn address is made by the clergyman to the assembly, and the thanks of the surviving family are returned to those who are present for their attendance; and, in cases where the disease has been of long continuance, to such as have exhibited kindnesses to the sick, and mourning family. Sometimes the procession is formed anew and accompanies the mourners to their habitation, but more frequently the company disperses. In either case an entire decorum is preserved.

I am, Sir, yours, etc.

# RELIGION OF NEW ENGLAND

## LETTER I

*History of religion in New England from the year 1755—Effects of the French and Revolutionary Wars—Evils arising from the introduction of foreigners into the country*

*Dear Sir,*

The actual state of religion in any country must, of course, be an interesting object of investigation to every sober and intelligent man. To give you a correct view of this subject so far as New England is concerned, it will be necessary for me to go back to the war which commenced in 1755 and terminated in 1763. Antecedently to the first of these periods, all the changes in the religious state of this country were such as left the principles of its inhabitants essentially the same. They were not changes of the commanding character, but shades of that character, through which it varied toward greater or less degrees of purity. From the first settlement of the country to the commencement of that war, the same reverence for God, the same justice, truth, and benevolence, the same opposition to inordinate indulgencies of passion and appetite prevailed without any material exceptions. An universal veneration for the Sabbath, a sacred respect for government, an undoubting belief in divine revelation, and an unconditional acknowledgment and performance of the common social duties constituted everywhere a prominent character. I have said that the exceptions were not material. It is not intended that the whole number was inconsiderable, nor that vice was not found in various and sometimes very painful degrees. Still, vicious men constituted a very small part of the society, were insignificant in their character, and independently of the power of example had little or no influence on the community at large. They were objects of odium and contempt, of censure and punishment; not the elements of a party, nor the firebrands of turmoil and confusion.

During this war, foreigners for the first time mingled extensively with the inhabitants of New England. The colonial officers and soldiers, whose principles had in many instances been imperfectly formed, and whose ardent dispositions qualified them to decide rather than to reason, to act rather than to think, easily imbibed in an army composed of those whom they were taught to regard as their superiors loose doctrines and licentious practices. In that army there were many infidels. In spite of their professions to the contrary, all infidels earnestly wish to make proselytes. To these men a fair field was now opened for the accomplishment of this purpose. Most of their American companions had never heard the divine origin of the Scriptures questioned, and their minds were, of course, unprovided with answers even to the most common objections. To such objections as were actually made was added the force of authority. The British officers came from *the mother country:* a phrase of high import until after the commencement of the Revolution. They came also from a country renowned for arts and arms, and regarded by the people of New England as the birthplace of science and wisdom. These gentlemen were at the same time possessed of engaging manners, and practiced all those genteel vices which, when recommended by such manners, generally fascinate young men of gay, ambitious minds, and are naturally considered as conferring an enviable distinction on those who adopt them. Many of the Americans were far from being dull proficients in this school. The vices, they loved; and soon found the principles necessary to quiet their consciences.

When they returned home, they had drunk too deeply of the cup to exchange their new principles and practices for the sober doctrines and lives of their countrymen. The means which had been pursued to corrupt *them,* they now employed to corrupt others. From this *prima mali labes,*[1] the contagion spread, not indeed through very great multitudes, but in little circles surrounding the individuals originally infected. As these amounted to a considerable number, and lived in a general dispersion through the country, most parts of it shared in the malady.

About the year 1737, a very extensive and happy revival of religion prevailed in almost all parts of New England. At this time, a vast multitude of persons united themselves to the Christian church; and, with few exceptions, testified through life by their evangelical conduct the genuineness of their profession. The influence of this body of men, many of whom survived for a long time the peace of 1763, retarded essentially the progress of the evil. All vicious men felt that religion must be regarded with reverence, and life conducted with a good degree of moral decency. Still, a relaxation of morals and a looser adhesion to principles was unhappily discernible.

During the six years which preceded the Revolutionary War in America, religion experienced no very material change; and it may be doubted whether it gained or lost ground. But in the progress of this war it suffered far more than in that of 1755. All the evils which flowed from the former were multiplied in the latter. The foreigners with whom they had intercourse were not so numerous perhaps as in the war of 1755, but many of them were of far more dissolute characters. They were Frenchmen, disciples of Voltaire, Rousseau, d'Alembert, and Diderot; men holding that loose and undefined atheism which neither believes nor disbelieves the existence of a God, and is perfectly indifferent whether he exists or not.[2] Between French and English infidelity, there has generally been a plain, marked distinction. The English infidel has commonly exhibited, in appearance at least, some degree of reverence for the Creator. The French infidel has only despised him. The Englishman has usually admitted that there may be an existence hereafter, and that men may be rewarded beyond the grave. The Frenchman knows *a priori* that there is nothing beyond the grave. The Englishman usually admits the distinction between right and wrong, and acknowledges that men are under some obligation to do that which is right, and to abstain from that which is wrong. The Frenchman, when you express your belief of these doctrines, looks at you with a stare made up of pity, surprise, and contempt, as an ignorant rustic entering for the first time, or not having entered at all, the world's great metropolis of science and improvement; and, having himself been born and educated a citizen, pities you for your weakness, is astonished at your ignorance, and is irresistibly compelled to despise the clownishness of your moral sentiments. The Englishman will rarely deny that he may be an accountable being. The Frenchman knows intuitively, if not instinctively, that God exercises no moral government over man, that moral obligation is a chimera, that animal pleasure is the only good, and that man is merely a brute upon two legs. The Englishman usually acknowledges the question to be still in debate, and feels that you have a right to demand proof of the soundness of his doctrines. The Frenchman, a very Trophonius, never mistrusts that any character belongs to him, but that of "Sir Oracle"; and takes it for granted that, if you have either sense or civility, you will receive his opinions with a confidence more implicit than he would yield to his Maker.[3] In a word, right in his view is the same with convenience, and wrong, the same with inconvenience to himself or to France; and to this opinion he expects you to subscribe.*

You will wonder that New England men could imbibe these, or any other opinions, from men of such a character.[4] These opinions they did not indeed imbibe; but they received others, less gross, but of the same general nature; and, although not corrupted with a hopeless putridity, exhibited unequivocal proofs of disease and decay.

Many of these foreigners, you will remember, were men of polished man-

* The reader will please remember that the Frenchmen here spoken of were disciples of Voltaire and his coadjutors. Many of a very different character came to the United States after the American Revolution commenced, and many more in consequence of the French Revolution. These were Catholics, men of fair minds and respectable characters. Those who were followers of Voltaire were, extensively at least, just such as are here described: possessed of the same self-sufficiency, the same hatred to Christianity, the same contempt of the Bible, the same hostility against their Maker. To speak of such men truly is to speak of them severely, that is, in the manner which will often be styled severe.

The Frenchmen whom I have found deserving of esteem and respect have been Catholics and royalists.

ners, improved minds, and superior address. They had been long accustomed to the business of making proselytes, were skilled in the various weaknesses of man, knew every avenue to the heart, and understood perfectly all the subtle and unsuspicious means of persuasion. They perfectly knew how to insinuate the grossest sentiments in a delicate and inoffensive manner, to put arguments to flight with a sneer, to stifle conscience with a smile, and to overbear investigation by confronting it with the voice and authority of the great world. At the same time they were *the friends and aids of the American cause—nos très chers et très grands amis et alliés.* From persons of this character who could suspect anything but good?

The men on whom they were to operate had in many instances been educated in morals and religion with much less care and strictness than those who had acted in the former war. A considerable number of them were young, little acquainted with the doctrines of Christianity, and still less with the evidences of revelation. Whenever the Scriptures were assailed, therefore, they were utterly unprovided with means of resistance.

To these evils was added another of a similar nature. Multitudes of their countrymen from other colonies were united with them in military life. These were often ingenious, polished, sprightly, and facetious. With the arguments on either side of the question they were indeed very little acquainted. So were those on whom they were to make impressions. Uninterested to inquire and impatient of research, they were prepared to receive licentious doctrines because they loved them. The heart here sat as judge, and decided the cause without summoning the head to its assistance, even as a witness.

Those who remained at home possessed in many instances the same character; and, although not sent to the same school for moral improvement, were yet sufficiently susceptible readily to receive from the scholars whatever they had gained from their instructors.

To aid the work of ruin, the paper currency of the country operated in the most powerful and malignant manner. At the first effusion of this evil upon the community, every sordid passion of man was stimulated to the most vigorous exertion. Wealth, for such it seemed to the fancy, was acquired with an ease and rapidity which astonished the possessor. The price of labor, and of every vendible commodity, rose in a moment to a height unexampled. Avarice, ambition, and luxury saw their wishes anticipated, and began to grasp at objects of which they had not before even dreamed. Sudden wealth rarely fails of becoming sudden ruin; and most of those who acquire it are soon beggared in morals, if not in property.

At the end of two years, this currency, in consequence of enormous emissions, began sensibly to depreciate; and the depreciation became a new source of degeneracy. The want of an established standard of estimation by which the value of commodities may be ascertained, the price of labor regulated, and bargains equitably adjusted is a greater evil than any man who has not been a witness of its consequences can be induced to believe. A general perplexity at once clouded all human dealings, and it soon became impossible for upright men to determine whether their bargains were honest, or oppressive. After a short period every case of this nature was determined, not by a general rule, but by what the parties thought its own merits; and to these avarice lent its uniform bias. Within three years from the commencement of this evil, the currency sunk so low as to be refused in exchange for the necessaries of life; and, notwithstanding the abundance of provisions in this country, those who could offer nothing else were frequently reduced to very serious difficulties. Barter became extensively the established mode of dealing, and barter is the natural parent of the low cunning and the gross knavery of a jockey. A stable currency, besides furnishing incalculable facility to commerce, is of inestimable benefit to mankind *as a known standard of commutative justice, and the great means of enforcing it in all the varieties of commercial intercourse.* For the want of such a standard, the general sense of right and obligation in buying and selling was gradually lowered; and the pride of making what are called good bargains, a soft name for cheating, gradually extended. Whatever was not punishable by law, multitudes considered as rectitude. That delicacy of mind which shrinks at the approach of wrong, that tenderness of conscience which turns with apprehension from every doubtful moral action, was extensively succeeded by those gross views which are satisfied where magistrates do not meddle, and where shame does not terrify. In the meantime the existing government was peculiarly unhappy. All regular public functionaries lost during this period either the whole or a great part of their proper efficacy. In their stead, *committees of inspection and correspondence* assumed an extensive control over both the public and private affairs of their country. The powers of these bodies were undefined; and, therefore, soon became merely discretionary. Yet they were the tribunals by which almost every cause was decided. In most instances they were composed of men unlearned in law and unskilled in public business. They had no precedents and no known rules of judging. Often they were the dupes of cunning, and often of flattery. At one time they were awed by superiority of character in their suitors; at another, they were influenced solely by the base pleasure of humbling those by whom it was possessed. Extensively they were victims of the addling pride felt by little minds when unexpectedly invested with authority and the consequent love of domineering. It is hardly necessary to ask what were the decisions flowing from this combination of ignorance, perplexity, and prejudice. Very many and very great evils were actually produced by this government, and that it did not produce many more is no small encomium on the character of my countrymen, and a proof of the superintending care and good providence of God.

*The influence of a weak and fluctuating government on the morals and happiness of mankind is,* to say the least, *not less malignant than that of an established despotism.* The men who under a better system had formed just and exact views of what was right almost necessarily receded from such views by an imperceptible declension. The rising generation grew up for a season with scarcely any other ideas concerning this immensely important subject than those which were defective. Even justice and truth, virtues mathematically defined and perfectly known in a sound state of society, were now to a great extent seen only in a fluctuating light, which half discovered and half concealed their real nature. But when these two great pillars of morality tremble, the whole building totters.

I am, Sir, yours, etc.

# LETTER II

*State of religion after the peace of 1783—Effects of the French Revolution—Circulation of the writings of infidels*

*Dear Sir,*

After the peace of 1783, the country began slowly to recover from the evils mentioned above, and from the disastrous state of morals which they produced. The former sober habits of New England, the belief of a divine revelation prevailing in a vast majority of the inhabitants, and the real Christianity of a number which, though much less than in former times, was still great, had more firmly than could rationally have been expected stood the shock of this war of moral elements. The walls, though weakened by various breaches, were still strong. The fortress, though partially undermined, was still defensible, and invited both the labor and the expense necessary to repair it. By degrees, infidelity and licentiousness began to lose their confidence, and morals to regain their former control. Men who have been accustomed to the morals of Christians can scarcely be satisfied with those of infidels. Infidels are indeed possessed, as often as other men, of natural amiableness, are sometimes taught in early life to respect truth and justice, are sometimes well informed and well bred; and from these causes are induced to adopt a decent and at times a pleasing deportment. Still, the want of principle at the bottom, and of reverence for God, the only basis of principle, leaves them always exposed without any effectual security to the combined influence of passion and temptation. The consequences of this exposure are perpetually discernible in their most guarded behavior, particularly when their conduct is daily before the eye of inspection. In every case of this nature they will be seen to exhibit a varying, zigzag morality, now wandering into the field of vice, and now retreating within the boundaries of decorum. In a regular state of society, therefore, infidelity of course loses by degrees its reputation and its influence. Thus in New England the name *infidel* proverbially denotes an immoral character, even in the mouths of those who profess no peculiar attachment to the Scriptures.

From the year 1783, the minds of the people of New England became gradually more and more settled. Business assumed a more regular and equitable character. The tumultuous passions roused by the war subsided. Men of wisdom and worth acquired an habitual influence. Public worship was more punctually attended, and the whole face of things became more promising. To all these blessings, the present system of American government added a new stability, and by the energy and wisdom with which its administration was begun furnished hopes to good men of the return of permanent order and happiness.

Just as this prospect began to dawn, the horizon was again overcast by the French Revolution. That portentous event, monstrous in its cause and horrible in its consequences, deeply affected not only the countries of Europe, but even these states. We had just passed through a revolution which, as we thought, had secured our freedom and independence. Very naturally, therefore, we sympathized with those whom we supposed to be aiming at the same important objects. The minds of the Americans anticipated with a rapturous enthusiasm the emancipation of twenty-five millions of their fellow men from the thralldom of despotism and superstition. Men of unquestionable worth, and of wisdom on other occasions equally unquestionable, united with those around them in the common feelings, and in hailing the arrival of so glorious an event. The exceptions to this remark were fewer by far than a sober man could have believed before it had taken place. In this manner an importance, a solemnity, a sanction was given to this revolution, resembling the effects of enchantment. An influence was imparted to it which for a considerable time spread a veil over its enormities and softened the aspect of its horrors: an influence which no ingenuity could preclude, and for a season no efforts resist.

In these inauspicious circumstances, the infidelity of Voltaire and his coadjutors began to make its appearance, in form, throughout most parts of this country. We had been long assailed by the reasonings of Herbert and Chubb, the subtle frauds of Tindal, the pompous insinuations of Shaftesbury, the eloquent, but empty, declamations of Bolingbroke, the wiredrawn metaphysics of Hume, and at this period by the splendid impositions of Gibbon.[1] But the country which had produced these false and sophistical efforts had also triumphantly refuted the sophistry. What was perhaps of little less consequence, it was of such a nature as to allow of a refutation. Formed in the English school of philosophy, where good sense and sound logic had always supported their reputation, it retained, insidious and illusory as it was, so much of the appearance of reasoning *as to present something which could be understood, and which, therefore, could be answered.*

But the philosophy of the French school, with which it was intended to overwhelm these states, was in a great measure new. *It was a system of abstract declarations which violated common sense, delivered in an abstract style, equally violating all just taste and sober criticism.* It is not designed to instruct or convince, but to amuse, perplex, and beguile. It is addressed, not to men of learning and understanding, the persons who should be addressed in every abtruse discussion, but to the ignorant, unthinking, and vulgar. It is directed, not to the understanding even of these, but to their weaknesses, prejudices, and passions. The language in which it is uttered, like the signs of unknown quantities in algebra, is without meaning until you arrive at the result and the application; and it is never designed to come to a result, nor to admit of an application. If you answer an argument or a book according to its obvious meaning, you are gravely informed that you have mistaken the author's intention. When you inquire for that intention, you will be left without an answer, or will receive one in the very language which you are declared to have mistaken. Proceed a few steps farther and you will find yourself in a labyrinth, compared with which that of Minos was a beaten highway.[2]

The doctrines really intended to be taught by this philosophy are like the furniture stowed in "the paradise of fools,"

> Abortive, monstrous, and unkindly mix'd.[3]

The principles upon which they apparently rest are merely hypotheses, destitute of any foundation, and without any authority besides the egotism of the author. The arguments by which they are professedly supported are usually of the *a priori* kind, attended with no evidence, and conducting the mind to no conclusion. Were they delivered in language capable of being understood, their authors would be considered as the Newtons and Aristotles of folly. At their side, Bohme and Swedenborg, those laureates in "the limbo of vanity," would lose their distinction, and return far toward the character of common sense.[4]

That men of talents should be willing to write in this manner has certainly the appearance of a paradox. Its explanation is easily found in *the purposes for which all this has been done.* One of these was *to extend the reign, multiply the means, facilitate the progress, and establish the quiet of sin;* the other, to *place the world beneath the feet of philosophical pride, ambition, and avarice.* Whenever conscience, truth, and evidence are suffered to operate, wickedness will meet with continual discouragement and distress. No man ever could believe in a season of sober reflection, or while his understanding was permitted to control his faith, that God will justify sin, or divest himself of the fear that he will punish it. These terrible suggestions of reason are by revelation changed into certainties. Truth and conscience, therefore, reason and revelation, are regarded by all men who resolve on a course of wickedness for life as their most bitter and dangerous enemies. That philosophical sinners should wish to reign and riot involves no enigma.

As the dictates of truth, conscience, and Christianity are supported by argument and evidence, they can never be reasoned down without superior evidence. This cannot be found. Still there are means which may be employed against them with no small success. He who cannot convince may perplex. He who cannot inform may beguile. He who cannot guide may entice. He who cannot explain may overbear. He who can do all these may, and often will, persuade.

The effects of this combination of causes were great and unhappy. Most men in every country are but imperfectly acquainted with both the evidences and doctrines of revelation. Most also are unaccustomed to thorough research, and impatient of the labor, which it requires. Of this multitude there are, however, many who are yet pleased with thinking, when indulged only through moderate periods and unattended with much exertion. A considerable number of these, and among them such as were brilliant and ingenious, were for a season dazzled and confounded. Youths particularly, who had been liberally educated, and who with strong passions and feeble principles were votaries of sensuality and ambition, delighted with the prospect of unrestrained gratification and panting to be enrolled with men of fashion and splendor, became enamored of these new doctrines. The tenor of opinion and even of conversation was to a considerable extent changed at once. Striplings, scarcely fledged, suddenly found that the world had been involved in a general darkness through the long succession of preceding ages, and that the light of wisdom had but just begun to dawn upon the human race. All the science, all the information which had been acquired before the commencement of the last thirty or forty years stood in their view for nothing. Experience they boldly pronounced a dull, plodding instructress, who taught in manners, morals, and government nothing but abecedarian lessons, fitted for children only. Religion they discovered on the one hand to be a vision of dotards and nurses, and on the other a system of fraud and trick imposed by priestcraft for base purposes upon the ignorant multitude. Revelation they found was without authority or evidence, and moral obligation a cobweb which might indeed entangle flies, but by which creatures of a stronger wing nobly disdained to be confined. The world they resolutely concluded to have been probably eternal; and matter, the only existence. Man, they determined, sprang like a mushroom out of the earth by a chemical process; and the powers of thinking, choice, and motivity were merely the results of elective affinities. If, however, there was a God and man was a created being, he was created only to be happy. As, therefore, animal pleasure is the only happiness, so they resolved that the enjoyment of that pleasure is the only end of his creation.

On the folly and impiety of these opinions it is unnecessary to expatiate. All which Swift in the Travels of Gulliver has poured out concerning the weakness and wickedness of our race is a faint picture of the weakness and wickedness of a world governed by these opinions. Should the Almighty suffer them to be generally and practically adopted, perdition would, I think, commence on this side of the grave. Indeed, France during the Revolution exhibited, while under only the partial influence of these doctrines, the strongest resemblance to Hell which the human eye in this world has ever been permitted to behold.

Had not the effect of these opinions threatened the very existence of virtue and happiness, they would in several instances have been sufficiently ridiculous. Men who were before inclined to vice were delighted to find themselves justified, and proceeded with new courage and strength to bolder perpetrations. Men reluctantly conscious of their own inferiority of understanding rejoiced to see themselves without an effort become in a moment wiser than those who had spent life in laborious investigation. Some were not a little gratified with the boldness and independence of character displayed in sinning, others with escaping from the shackles of conscience and the terrors of revelation. Not a few were charmed with the novelty and spirit of the doctrines themselves, and most found an addition made to the ease and quiet of an immoral life.

The efficacy of all the causes which I have mentioned was enhanced by the events which attended the French Revolution. The boldness of the enterprises, the number and the splendor of the victories, the importance of the conquests, and the vastness of the convulsion united to overwhelm minds of no more than common stability. Most eyes were disabled from seeing clearly the nature of the purposes which were in view, and of the characters which were exhibited on this singular stage. In the agitation, the amazement, the horror excited in all men, few retained so steady optics as to discern without confusion the necessary consequences of this stupendous shock. Even the crimes at which this world was lost in astonishment were by the audacity and decision with which they were perpetrated surrounded with a gloomy luster which dazzled and deluded the spectator. Actions which a few years before would have mocked all utterance, now passed over the tongue with moderate censures and reluctant severity. Robespierre, Danton, and Carrier, whose existence is perhaps the strongest argument hitherto discovered against a particular providence, were mentioned not only without infamy and horror, but at times with satisfaction and applause.[5]

The idolatry of the ancient heathen nations was the worship of calves and cats, of blocks and stones. The idolatry of the present day, still more stupid and unmeaning, is the worship of abstract terms. To the astonishment of every sober man, France has exhibited the spectacle of twenty-five millions of the human race prostrating themselves with religious reverence before the word REASON. Had the weakest of these worshippers formed a definition of this term, and by applying it to anything to which it was ever applied given it a meaning, he must have been a mere zoophyte to have continued his homage for a moment. A multitude of the Americans have paid their devotions to the word liberty. This word has a real and important meaning, but in the minds and mouths of most men appears to have no meaning at all. That which it signifies is by mankind at large respected and loved, but they *worship* only the abstract term. A few years since, I should have been hardly induced to believe that multitudes of my countrymen could so idolize this bare word as to sacrifice at its shrine the very thing which it denotes.

Amid all the thunders of the French Revolution, this necromantic term was incessantly repeated, and unhappily was distinctly heard. It was ostensibly in the cause and for the sake of liberty that the Gallic church was overthrown; its property plundered; its ministers massacred by thousands; and Louis XVI, the meekest and mildest monarch ever elevated to the throne of France, was butchered with his family.[6] Such of his subjects as were distinguished for probity and worth were entombed in prisons, or made the food of the guillotine. The realm was drenched in blood, and manured with the corpses of Frenchmen murdered by Frenchmen. All the surrounding countries smoked with conflagration and slaughter. Republic after republic was blotted out of existence. Every house in France was subjected to the domiciliary visits of a horde of villains who came only to rob, to dishonor, and to destroy. Visits and parties, *à la guillotine,* were the most gay and most genteel amusements of Frenchmen, and Frenchmen of distinction. In the cause of liberty, it was roundly asserted, Nantes and Lyons were consigned to a common grave. In the cause and for the sake of liberty, the Bible and the vessels of the Eucharist were placed on an ass and paraded through the streets in mock procession to degrade religion and its God. The former was laid on a bonfire, and the latter were polluted by a company of modern Belshazzars. In the mother club of Jacobins at Paris, a comparison was formally instituted between the Redeemer of mankind and *Marat*; and this twin brother to Judas was solemnly pronounced a greater benefactor to the world than the Saviour. For the sake of liberty, the Sabbath was annihilated, and the decade substituted in its place, as a rest from business for villainy and pollution, that ample opportunity might be furnished of enjoying without reins the horrors of the club or the brutism of the brothel. Finally the souls of men, I mean of Frenchmen (for the National Convention were not, I presume, invested with dominion over the souls of other men), were for the sake of liberty doomed by the legislature of France to eternal sleep in the dreary caverns of annihilation.

But I am losing both you and myself in this forest of enormities. Future ages will hardly believe that any part of this portentous story could pass for truth with men of acknowledged wisdom and piety. Nothing, however, is more certain. The man who does not in a considerable measure give up his understanding and suffer his virtue to be impaired in a season of popular frenzy may be safely pronounced more firm, or more fortunate, than most of his race.

At this period Europe, which annually ships for our shores a vast quantity of useful merchandise, and together with it a proportional assortment of toys and mischief, consigned to these states a plentiful supply of the means of corruption. From France, Germany, and Great Britain, the dregs of infidelity were vomited upon us at once. From the Système de la nature and the Philosophical Dictionary, down to the Political Justice of Godwin and the Age of Reason, the whole mass of pollution was emptied on this country.[7] The two last publications particularly flowed in upon us as a deluge. An enormous edition of the Age of Reason was published in France and sent over to America to be sold for a few pence the copy; and, where it could not be sold, to be given away. You may perhaps be astonished that such men as these, the mere outcasts of creation, could do harm at all. In my apprehension they were exactly fitted for a sphere of mischief of vast import in the empire of destruction which perhaps no other men could have filled. Satan needs his scullions and scavengers, as well as his nobles and heroes. They were industrious, bold, and enterprising. They were impudent beyond example, were not destitute of imagination, and possessed a popular manner of writing. It is true, they were incapable of understanding the force of an argument, or the nature of evidence; but they were no less delighted with falsehood than better men are with truth, were equally triumphant in a victory and a defeat, and like the Lernaean snake had a spare head for every new combatant. At the same time, they were conveniently lost to principle and to shame; and uttered villainy, obscenity, and blasphemy, not merely with a brazen front, but with the sober, intrepid serenity of apparent conviction. Such men are incomparably better fitted to persuade ignorance and embolden vulgar iniquity than superior villains. The writings of such villains are beyond the reach of mankind at large. These men are fitted to invade the cottage and ravage the fireside. On the people of New England their influence, though sensibly felt, was not extensive; on other parts of the Union, it is declared, as I believe with truth, to have been great.

In a recital of the causes which have contributed to the moral corruption of this country, its political dissensions ought never to be forgotten. The spirit of party when roused to vigorous exertion soon becomes deaf to remonstrance and blind to moral obligation. In my own view, and in that of all the wise and good men with whom I converse, this spirit has had an efficacy on the American character not less malignant than any, perhaps than all the other causes whch have been mentioned. On this subject I may hereafter expatiate.

I am, Sir, yours, etc.

# LETTER III

*The effects of the principles avowed by the leaders of the French Revolution, counteracted and destroyed in a great measure by their cruelties and impiety, and by the miseries they brought on other nations—These effects likewise lessened by the efforts of the clergy and of many other respectable inhabitants, but principally by an extensive revival of religion—Comparison of the religious and moral character of the first settlers with that of the present inhabitants*

*Dear Sir,*

When these numerous and fruitful sources of depravation have passed in review before you, it will seem wonderful that religion and morals have not bidden this country a final adieu. That they have not absolutely forsaken us, nay, that they extensively prevail, and that there are even more religious persons in New England than at any former period is, however, undoubtedly true. The causes of this fact I will briefly explain.

Before I enter upon this part of my design, I ought, however, to apologize to you for so extended a discussion of the subject, particularly for the historical detail which I have given you concerning the causes which have heretofore contributed to the deflections of our moral character. Among my reasons are the following. The subject is unquestionably of considerable importance in the philosophy of man. No account of it has been published by others; and those who have been eyewitnesses of its progress, and who alone could exhibit it truly, are either gone or will soon go to the grave. The probability, therefore, is great that it will never be communicated to the public by any other hand. To my own countrymen at least, it must be interesting, and may be useful. Yet most of them are chiefly unacquainted with the particulars which I have recited. The resistance which the inhabitants of my native country have made to this mass of evil is honorable to their character; and from this account of their difficulties, and the example which they have furnished of opposing them successfully, succeeding generations may derive both instruction and motives for future resistance.

I have heretofore mentioned the efficacy of the New England institutions. These, operating everywhere and every moment, and, although silently and insensibly, yet powerfully operating, have with a constant accumulation of energy greatly contributed to wear away this formidable combination of mischiefs. Habits are proverbially the only important sources of permanent good. From steady, national habits only can great national good in the ordinary course of things be derived. From the New England institutions such habits have long since sprung, and from a very early period have constituted a stable, national character. Such a character can hardly be materially changed unless by the ravaging hand of conquest, or the slow progress of time. It becomes the common nature, and

Si *Naturam* expellas furca, tamen usque recurret.[1]

There is a constant renitency of the mind against all those innovations which sensibly affect this character, an elastic tendency toward the recovery of its original position. To such habits, under God, New England owes in no small measure its escape from that degeneracy which has so miserably affected many other countries.

The influence of the French Revolution, which for a time threatened us with moral ruin, was to a great extent counteracted by the evils of the revolution itself, by the character of the men who successively conducted it, and by the evils which flowed from it as consequences. I need not tell you that the calamities of this revolution outran all expectation, example, and belief. When the Americans began to read and believe the successive massacres of Paris, a considerable number of them were startled. Blood here has rarely been shed but under the solemn decision of a jury. Nay, it has been rarely shed at all, except in a period of war. The ferocity of the Parisian women, those fiends in a female dress, filled the mind of the whole sex in this country with horror. The guillotine curdled the blood even of coarse and unfeeling men, and the death of Louis XVI awakened general detestation. The ravages of La Vendée, Nantes, Toulon, and Lyons completed the picture of woe.

Nor was the impiety of France and its violation of all other moral principles much less impressive than the tales of its cruelty. There was a grossness of immorality, a brutal atheism in the speeches and measures of the national legislature; a disregard of evidence, truth, and justice in the proceedings of its judicial tribunals; a ferocity in the conduct of its judges and juries; and a savageness in the behavior of its executive officers, which, if reported by others, would have been considered as an outrage upon credulity itself.

Happily for us, they were their own historians; and the truth of their recitals could not be questioned.

Nor were the minds of my countrymen less advantageously affected by the treatment exhibited to the successive leaders in this revolution by those who followed them. The hero of yesterday was regularly murdered by the hero of today, and the possession of the supreme control was only a regular introduction to the guillotine. There was something amazingly solemn in seeing these Goths and Vandals, these Alarics, Attilas, and Genserics, successively led up by the hand of divine justice to the block, to make a feeble expiation of their crimes by their blood.[2] About one hundred of them perished in this manner. These facts taught my countrymen that the attachment professed by these men to the liberty of their country was nothing but a pretense to help themselves into place and wealth; and this hypocrisy they naturally, as well as justly, transferred in the end to all their coadjutors.

At the same time the widespread calamities brought upon other nations by France, particularly upon such as had enjoyed a free government, contributed to the same general effect. My countrymen saw with astonishment, as well as with regret, one republic after another blotted out from under heaven; and this by the hands of the very men who had solemnly announced to the world that France would make no conquests.

Finally, the termination of this convulsion established the views which had been thus formed beyond the possibility of any material alteration. Every wise and dispassionate man saw with conviction that infidelity is hostile to all public and personal happiness; that without the influence of religion, political freedom can never be long enjoyed; and that a connection with the leaders and disciples of this revolution would only be baleful to his own country. Even the French nation itself by quietly settling down under the military despotism of a single man, as an asylum from the tremendous oppression of their Directory, proved beyond debate that no government of mere force is equally terrible with that of infidel philosophy.

Another great truth of no less importance was impressed on a contemplative mind by these events. It is this: that infidelity naturally and necessarily becomes, when possessed of the control of national interests, a source of evils so numerous and so intense as to compel mankind to prefer any state to these evils. No fact of a political nature was ever more instructive to thinking men than the torpid submission of France to the rod of the Emperor Napoleon. Even the infidels of this country, particularly the intelligent ones, saw in this fact and in those which preceded it the efficacy of their own principles, and the danger which they threatened to mankind. Alarmed by the prospect, they first ceased from their endeavors to make proselytes, then began to speak favorably of the Christian religion, and finally insisted that it was absolutely necessary to good government, liberty, and safety.

For a considerable time the clergy of New England generally were plainly unaware of the extent to which this degeneracy of principle and practice prevailed. With the propagators of infidelity and vice, they naturally had very little intercourse; and the evil proceeded for a considerable time with so much silence and decency as to be unobserved by men who were either employed in their studies, or in their active business were chiefly conversant with persons of a better character. Some of them, however, from a peculiarity of circumstances, discovered the danger at an early period. These gave the alarm; and, although scarcely credited at first, because the change was too great to be easily admitted in such a country as New England, yet gradually gained the ear, not only of their brethren in the ministry, but of all the sober inhabitants. From that period, men of wisdom and piety in considerable numbers made vigorous efforts against this invasion of human happiness. A great multitude of judicious discourses were preached throughout the country, and not a small number published on the various branches of the deistical controversy. These, the enemies of religion were never able to answer. The subject became at the same time generally the theme of conversation, and was handled with an efficacy which was both extensive and powerful. Nor was personal influence less exerted, or less successful. The danger was so obvious and so great as to alarm all men of consideration. Even many infidels, terrified as they were by the events mentioned above, united heartily with others in repelling evils which they saw daily thickening and threatening everything which they held dear. Nay, in considerable numbers they openly renounced their principles, and became professed adherents to the cause of Christianity.

At the same time also, a series of efforts made by men of talents and worth in Great Britain formed a strong mound against the tide of iniquity. Several writers, to whose labors all succeeding generations will be deeply indebted, exposed the weakness of the arguments, the base designs, and the contemptible character of the principal agents in this system of corruption. Of those by whom their writings were read, most were convinced and the rest put to silence.

You will easily believe that when infidels became thus interested to oppose their own principles, all sober men who believed in the divine origin of the Scriptures, but had not hitherto made a public profession of Christianity, felt the subject still more deeply. These with a single voice united in strengthening the government and religion of their country. Accordingly they conversed in favor of both with new earnestness, exhibited a more marked reverence for the constituted authorities of their country, frequented more punctually the house of God, regarded and treated its ministers with enhanced respect, and appeared openly and everywhere as the determined supporters of religion. From these exertions made by a body of men so numerous and influential, society may be said to have assumed a new aspect.

Finally, a revival of religion commencing at this season spread gradually through a great part, not only of Connecticut, but of New England. This revival, which is still spreading over many parts of the country, has been attended with the happiest circumstances and followed by the best consequences. Among the many thousands who have been solemnly affected with religious considerations, and greatly as well as evidently reformed, very few have exhibited any appearance of enthusiasm. Almost all have at the same time presented to the observing eye proofs of vital Christianity, which could not be rationally questioned. Perhaps there has been no extensive reformation of mankind in which fewer instances have occurred either of hypocrisy or delusion. In consequence of so auspicious an event, the church of Christ has been increased by the addition of many thousands of professors; the zeal and the charity of Christians have been materially enhanced; and the labors of ministers have become more abundant and exemplary, more strenuous and successful.

Among the happy effects of this reformation, one particularly ought not here to be forgotten. A large number of those who have personally shared in it have emigrated to the new settlements, and have already begun to build churches, settle ministers, and establish the public worship of God. In this manner the state of society is there assuming in many instances a new aspect. In this manner succeeding generations will find themselves in these countries born and educated in the house of God, trained up to piety, invested with invaluable privileges here, and entitled to immortal happiness hereafter.

With all these facts before them, the people of New England can scarcely fail to say with St. Paul, "Having thus obtained help of God, we continue unto this day." [3] When I look back upon these events,

> Quæque ipse miserrima vidi,
> Et quorum pars fui: [4]

for I have lived through the whole of this period, and have been an eye and ear witness of almost all the things which I have recited so far as they have taken place in this country; when I look back upon these events; when I consider their magnitude, their portentous efficacy at times on the morals and religion of my native country; when I reflect on the dangers which threatened, and the evils which distressed us; when I remember how the wisest men were perplexed, and the firmest trembled; I cannot willingly avoid saying, and I hope my countrymen will say with me, "Had not the Lord been on our side when men rose up against us, they had swallowed us up quick, and the proud waters had gone over our soul. Blessed be the Lord, our soul is escaped as a bird out of the snare of the fowler; the snare is broken, and we are escaped. Our help is in the name of the Lord, who made heaven and earth." [5]

It is strange, but after a minute and extensive investigation, I believe it to be true that the Christian church in New England has at no time since its settlement included so great a number of members as at the present time.* The proportional number was for a long period after the colonization of Plymouth much greater; the absolute number I am satisfied was never so great. Churches which are expensive and handsome are now zealously built throughout all parts of the country and carefully repaired; ministers also are settled in the same universal manner, and with stipends which, though often less in their real value, are yet nominally much more considerable. Public worship is also numerously attended in most places, and with a good degree of solemnity and decorum.

At the same time the disposition of the inhabitants has appeared with much advantage in the liberality with which they have contributed to several charitable objects. Missions have been continually and extensively supported in the numerous infant settlements so widely spread over the interior country. Eleven societies for the promotion of this benevolent purpose have been for some time established in New England: seven in Massachusetts, one in Vermont, one in New Hampshire, one in Rhode Island, and one in Connecticut: each of the four last including the whole state in which it exists. The exertions of these societies have been in the highest degree laudable, honorably supported, and in my opinion followed by the best consequences. In the year 1810, several young gentlemen educated for the ministry in the Theological Seminary at Andover offered themselves to the General Association of Massachusetts as missionaries, to be employed under the direction of that body in foreign countries. The General Association, after deliberating on the subject, constituted a Board of Commissioners for Foreign Missions: five of the members from Massachusetts, and four from Connecticut. In 1811, the same body chose five for Massachusetts, and the General Association of Connecticut also chose four. This Board of Commissioners may now be considered as a permanent body to consist of nine members to be chosen annually by these two associations. It may, however, be augmented hereafter by members chosen from other communities.†

By these commissioners five missionaries have been already sent to Hindustan and the Burman Empire. To defray the expense, several charitable societies have been formed in New England, by whom considerable collections have been made. Mrs. Norris, relict of the Hon. John Norris, of Salem in Massachusetts, left in trust to the Board of Commissioners by will the sum of $30,000, for the purpose of supporting foreign missions.

A Bible society has also been formed at Boston, and another in Connecti-

* 1816.

† This body has been since incorporated by the legislature of Massachusetts.

cut, which holds its meetings at Hartford. By both, Bibles in considerable numbers are annually distributed.‡ The spirit of doing good in these and other charitable methods has been regularly increasing here during the last twenty-five years.

The present state of our moral and religious character cannot perhaps be more advantageously illustrated than by a comparison of it with that of our ancestors. The religion of former times was more zealous, rigid, scrupulous, and uniform. At the same time it was less catholic, gentle, indulgent in lawful cases, graceful, and amiable. The strictness, the energy, the commanding character of their religion, we have in a great measure lost. Where they stood firmly against the blast, we bend to escape its force. Where they watched, we are asleep. Where they fought manfully, we are employed in parleying. Where they triumphed, we are satisfied with a drawn battle.§ On the other hand we have in some respects advantageously relaxed from their austerity and rigor. We live more kindly and evangelically with Christians of other denominations. Our religious controversies are less violent, and we regard fewer things as fundamental grounds of difference. On the other hand, they educated their families more virtuously, regulated society with greater skill, executed laws with more exactness, and settled the affairs of men on a more solid foundation. They chiefly exhibited the magnanimous, we the gentler virtues. Ours are more amiable, but less firm. Theirs were

‡ Since the text was written, ten other Bible societies have been established in New England: six in Massachusetts, one in New Hampshire, one in Rhode Island, and two in Vermont.

There are now (1815) sixty-three in the United States.

Besides these, there are several female associations of the same nature: two in the state of New York, one at Boston, one in New Jersey, three in Pennsylvania, and one in Virginia; and probably others of which I have not been informed.

There are also numerous associations of both sexes formed to aid missions and for a variety of other charitable purposes. The rapidity with which these benevolent institutions increase may be understood from these facts. When the text was written, in the summer of 1809, there were three Bible societies in the United States; there are now sixty-three. N. B. Eight more have been added to the number since this note was written.

A great number of auxiliary societies have been formed to promote foreign missions, and their contributions have been very liberal. Domestic missions have at the same time rapidly increased. With all these exertions the increase of religion in many parts of the United States has gone hand in hand; and, although we are yet very far behind the wishes of every good man, there is much, very much, which will make the heart of a good man rejoice.

(It ought to be stated that the labors of the American Bible Society had but just commenced at the time of the decease of the author. That society as appears by their fourth Annual Report, published May 1820, has 207 auxiliaries. The number of Bibles and Testaments issued the last year exceeded 41,000. The amount of the receipts by the treasurer was $41,361.97. PUB.)

§ A Moral Society for the state of Connecticut, supported by a considerable number of auxiliary societies, has been established since the text was written. Several societies under the same title have been formed in Massachusetts, Vermont, and, I believe, New Hampshire. The object of these societies is to oppose vice, especially Sabbathbreaking, gaming, profaneness, and intemperance. Their success has already proved the wisdom of their institution.

rough and uninviting, but more to be relied on. In justice to these excellent men, it ought to be added that to them we are indebted for almost everything in our character which merits commendation. In some respects we have polished, but upon the whole, instead of improving, we have impaired their system. Formerly New England was inhabited almost exclusively by two classes of men: public professors of religion, and men of decent moral characters. The latter class universally believed without a doubt in divine revelation, and intended one day to become religious. All of them also regularly attended the public worship of God, and almost all of them observed in their conduct a respectful conformity to the precepts of his word. Every immorality was regarded as a crime, and confessed to be incapable of justification or defense. When crimes were committed at all, they were committed with a consciousness of guilt, in secrecy and solitude, without a hope that principles could be found to palliate them, and with a certainty of shame and censure in every case of detection. They were committed only under the pressure of sudden or powerful temptations, when gain bewildered, when provocation stung, and when the mind was goaded by passion or appetite. After the perpetration, as he himself perfectly foresaw, the criminal was declared by the universal voice to be an offender against law and a sinner against God. He might be pitied, but he was never excused. He went, therefore, to the perpetration with trembling, and shrunk from the universal frown whenever he was detected.

In such a state of society, you will readily believe, crimes were rare. Capital convictions were scarcely known, and a capital punishment was a prodigy. In almost all instances also, the persons convicted were foreigners. Inferior offenses, though more frequent, were few; and the stocks and the whipping post had little other use besides that which was monitory. Few infidels existed, and hardly one of them avowed his principles.

The present state of our society is in some respects the same with that which has been here described. In others the variations are marked by small shades of difference; in others still, the diversity is sufficiently evident. From the middle or neutral class of men, infidelity has received a considerable accession of recruits. You will not suppose that these men have been convinced of the truth of infidel principles, or of the falsehood of those which are contained in the Scriptures. They are merely men who love sin, and without conviction or evidence hail whatever will enable them to perpetrate it in peace. They are men who conclude without reasoning and resolve without inquiry.

It is scarcely possible that an infidel should not encourage vice in others, as well as foster it in himself. This he does without, as well as with design. To quiet his own conscience, he is obliged to justify his conduct to others, for the countenance of others is the only real support which he finds either for his principles or his practices. For the same reason also, he feels himself obliged to attack the Scriptures, and the whole system of virtues which they enjoin. The religion which they teach, he styles superstition, enthusiasm, and fanaticism. In this manner every infidel degrades religion in the eyes of the little circle around him, and emboldens them to the commission of sin. All his conduct, however decent, is at the same time vicious; and his example becomes of course the means of enhancing this corruption. Such, uniformly, has been the progress of vice here wherever infidelity has had influence. Crimes to a considerable extent are now practised, avowed, and vindicated; are made the materials of a jest, and gloried in as proofs of ingenuity and independence, which our ancestors knew only by report, and of which they spoke only with horror. Inferior deviations from rectitude are extensively become familiar and regarded as things of course. Loose men only laugh at them; and good men, discouraged by their frequency, cease in a great measure to censure them with severity. The man who fifty years since sunk under the consciousness of his own guilt, and withdrew from the detestation of others, now clears his brow and lifts up his front, while he repeats by rote the latitudinarian opinions of those who have employed their talents in seducing their fellow men to guilt and perdition. Of these opinions, it is true, he knows frequently neither the author, the evidence, nor the meaning; but he understands them sufficiently for his own purpose. In other words, he believes them to be justifications of his sins, and this is all which he wishes.

From these and other causes, we have lost that prompt energy in behalf of what is right and that vigorous hostility to what is wrong which were so honorable traits in the character of those who have gone before us. The spirit with which we resist wickedness is languid, and the measures are lax.

At the same time piety has received still larger accessions from the class of decent men. Gross crimes are also still rare, and capital executions solitary.

New Haven was settled in 1638, 174 years since. The capital punishments in the county of New Haven, as I have before remarked, have all been inflicted here. The whole number of these is thirteen. One of them, however, was inflicted by a court-martial in the time of the Revolutionary War on a soldier in the British service who was picked up in the neighborhood of this town. Of the remaining twelve, five were Indians, and three, blacks. The remaining four were whites. The whites were all executed within the first twenty-four years from the date of the settlement; three of them were born in England, and not improbably the fourth. The first settlers of New Haven brought with them a collection of peasants and servants remarkable for their profligacy, and of these classes were the criminals which have been mentioned. I have not been able to find any proof that a native of the township or county of New Haven was ever executed. With small variations this account will exhibit the state of New England at large. The number of native inhabitants who have been capitally punished has from the beginning been extremely small. In this respect New England bears a stronger resemblance to Scotland and Switzerland than to any other countries in the world.

Upon the whole it is probable that the morals and religion of this country, particularly of the ancient settlements, may without disadvantage be compared with those of any other.

I am, Sir, yours, etc.

# LETTER IV

*Establishment of the public worship of God in Connecticut*

*Dear Sir,*

The religion of the Congregationalists, the great body of the people in New England, differs little in its doctrines from that of most Protestant countries. In its forms and discipline, it strongly resembles those of Scotland, Holland, and Protestant Switzerland, and still more that of those English dissenters who are denominated Independents and Congregationalists. In several particulars, it differs from them all. These I will attempt to explain in an account of the religious system which prevails in Connecticut.

The state of Connecticut is universally divided into parishes, each containing one or more congregations, or, in the language of the laws, *ecclesiastical societies.* These societies are corporate bodies for various purposes.

In those parishes which contain but one, the society is constituted of all legal voters who hold generally the scheme of religion adopted by the society.

Each society is to meet once a year to transact its legal business. To render such meeting legal, notice must be given to the inhabitants at least five days before the meeting by the society's standing committee; or, for the want of such committee, by the clerk. This meeting is empowered to choose a moderator, clerk, treasurer, and standing committee, possessing the same authority in society affairs as the corresponding town officers possess in town affairs.

When thus met, the society is also empowered to levy taxes and choose collectors by a major vote of the numbers present.

Persons unpossessed of real estate rated at nine dollars annual income, or personal estate rated at one hundred and thirty-four dollars, or exempted (on account of dissenting) from the payment of taxes for the support of the usual worship and of the minister, and for the building and repairing of the churches in which such worship is celebrated, cannot vote or act in society meetings. The latter class, however, are disqualified only so far as these particular subjects are concerned.

Persons refusing to serve in the business of the society are subjected to fines in the same manner as those who refuse to serve in the business of the town, and the fines are to be paid to the treasurer of the society. Unqualified persons are also fined for voting, acting, or intermeddling in society meetings.

All persons at any time within twelve months after arriving at the age of twenty-one years, or within the same period after becoming widows, or after settling anew in any parish, have liberty to enroll themselves in any society by lodging their names for this purpose with the clerk. In the case of non-enrollment, a son belongs to the same society to which his father was attached, a widow to that of her husband, and new settlers to that which is lowest in the list.

All persons joined to a society continue members unless they remove or obtain leave of the General Assembly or of the society to separate themselves. Persons, however, who soberly dissent from the worship celebrated by the ecclesiastical societies in this state shall upon lodging a certificate of their dissent with the clerk of the society be exempted from all society taxes, so long as they shall ordinarily attend on the worship of the church or congregation to which they shall join themselves.*

Any society by a major vote may call and settle a minister and provide for his support. A minister so settled is styled in law the minister of the society, and is entitled to all the privileges of this office. The persons qualified to

* Since the death of the author, a new constitution has been adopted by the people of Connecticut. As some important alterations have been made, particularly in the provision for the support of the public worship of God, the article relative to religion is subjoined.

PUB.

It being the duty of all men to worship the Supreme Being, the Great Creator and Preserver of the Universe, and their right to render that worship in the mode most consistent with the dictates of their consciences; no person shall by law be compelled to join or support, nor be classed with, or associated to, any congregation, church, or religious association. But every person now belonging to such congregation, church, or religious association shall remain a member thereof until he shall have separated himself therefrom in the manner hereinafter provided. And each and every society, or denomination of Christians in this state, shall have and enjoy the same and equal power, rights, and privileges; and shall have power and authority to support and maintain the ministers or teachers of their respective denominations, and to build and repair houses for public worship, by tax on the members of any such society only, to be laid by a major vote of the legal voters assembled at any society meeting, warned and held according to law, or in any other manner.

If any person shall choose to separate himself from the society or denomination of Christians to which he may belong, and shall leave a written notice thereof with the clerk of such society, he shall thereupon be no longer liable for any future expenses which may be incurred by such society.

vote for these purposes are those who have a freehold estate in the same society rated at nine dollars annually, or are rated at one hundred and thirty-four dollars in the common list, or are of full age and in full communion with the church in said society. All the members of the society and their successors are, as in other corporations, bound by the votes of the majority.

The salaries of the ministers are to be paid according to the real value of the salary voted. For this purpose a tax is annually granted by the vote of the majority, and proportioned on the list in the same manner as public taxes. Negligent collectors are to have distress taken out against them by the society's committee, and the deficiency which is occasioned by their negligence levied and collected out of their estates. If the committee neglect their duty, they are to be fined, and to pay the deficiency out of their own estates. If the society omit to choose a collector, a selectman or justice of the peace is to appoint one.

If the society do not agree with the minister for his salary, nor support him, the General Assembly will order him a sufficient maintenance to be paid by the society. If a society be without a minister for a year, or years, the General Assembly will appoint a sum to be paid by such society, and to be disposed of for the use of the ministry in such society.

It is incumbent upon the society's committee to see that these duties are performed, and that the tax is speedily collected and paid, viz., within two months after the salary shall have become due.

All funds, estates, and donations given for the support of the ministry are under the care and management of the committee, who are accountable, and are empowered to make all proper contracts, and to use all proper and necessary measures to accomplish the purpose of the trust.

Nonresident proprietors of lands lying in parishes containing more than one society are to pay the tax on such lands to the society which is lowest in the list, if that society supports its minister by tax according to law.

Such societies as are unable to maintain a minister may yet, having obtained leave of the General Assembly, perform similar duties and enjoy similar privileges so far as to obtain the preaching of the Gospel and accomplish other necessary purposes.

In parishes containing more than one society, each is constituted by the enrollment of the names of its members with its clerk.

A considerable number of the towns in the state contain each but one society. Such towns are invested with all the preceding powers and privileges. In all such cases the functions of the officers of the society are performed by those who hold the corresponding town offices. Thus the selectmen perform the duties of a society's committee.

All churches and congregations which form themselves into bodies for the maintenance and support of the public worship of God have the same powers and privileges for building and repairing churches, and for every other ecclesiastical purpose, as the societies constituted by law.

Whenever a society shall by a lawful vote declare it necessary to build a church, the place on which it shall stand is to be fixed by the court of common pleas; and, if a society, or any part of it, proceed to build before they make application to said court, they are to be fined one hundred and thirty-four dollars.

If, after the place is fixed, the society neglect to build the church, this court is to notify the negligence to the General Assembly, who will order a sufficient tax to be laid on the society, and direct the money to be laid out for this purpose.

After societies are formed, churches erected, and ministers settled, the law for the further support of public worship, and for securing the quiet enjoyment of the Sabbath, requires all persons to attend the private duties of religion; and on public worship, if there be any such worship on which they can conveniently and conscientiously attend. As there are churches everywhere in the state, not more than five or six miles asunder, inconvenience can rarely be pleaded in ordinary circumstances. The law also forbids all secular business and diversion; traveling, except for necessary or charitable purposes; assembling in companies; going to taverns and receiving those who go; setting up warnings or notifications; and serving civil processes on the Sabbath. It also forbids all interruptions or disturbances of public worship, and all rude behavior during its celebration. The penalties on which these offenses are forbidden are included between half a dollar and thirty-four dollars.

Grand jurors, constables, and tithing men are to inspect the public behavior of all persons on the Sabbath, and due presentment make of all profanations and breaches of the Sabbath.

Parents and guardians are to correct their children for such offenses, on penalty of half a dollar.

Assistants or justices of the peace are to apprehend offenders upon sight or knowledge; to examine, and, if need be, to command any person to seize, arrest, and secure any travelers on the Sabbath; and to hold them till judgment be had in the case.

Constables, sheriffs, and grand jurors are to apprehend without warrant and to carry before a justice of the peace all offenders against this law.

Persons refusing to obey the commands of these officers, or neglecting to afford them their utmost assistance to apprehend and secure any offenders against this law, are subjected to the same penalties as when refusing to assist sheriffs and constables in the ordinary execution of their offices.

Sheriffs, constables, and indifferent persons are empowered on warrant to pursue and apprehend offenders against this law anywhere within the limits of the authority of the magistrate granting the warrant. No appeal lies from the sentence for breaches of this act.

I am, dear Sir, yours, etc.

# LETTER V

*Vindication of the establishment of the public worship of God by law*

*Dear Sir,*

In the preceding letter I have given you, if I mistake not, a complete account of what has been often, though improperly, called *the ecclesiastical establishment of Connecticut.* This phrase, as applied to other countries, has usually, if not always, denoted *the establishment of a national or state church, or the establishment of exclusive privileges in the possession of one class of Christians.* To Connecticut, therefore, it can have no proper application, because in this state all classes of Christians are placed on the same level. Formerly the case was different. A religious establishment existed in the colony of Connecticut antecedently to the Revolution, and gave exclusive privileges to the Congregationalists, the class of people by whom it was originally settled. This has been changed for the system detailed above. Whatever advantages or disadvantages, therefore, may be supposed to attach to religious establishments in the appropriate sense, they can have only a partial relation to the ecclesiastical system of Connecticut. The principal arguments in favor of such establishments, and the principal objections against them, can be applied to it only in the same imperfect manner. In my own view the system might, in better language, be styled, "*the legal establishment of the public worship of God in this state.*"

I have brought all the parts of this system into one view because they are all parts of a single design, naturally expressed by the phrase adopted in the preceding sentence, and because I wished you to see them in their connection with each other. In this scheme you will see the whole country formed into religious congregations styled ecclesiastical societies. These societies are vested with ample powers to tax themselves, to collect taxes, to hold property, to receive donations, and to manage their property for the purpose of building and repairing churches, and maintaining the public worship of God. This worship they are required to attend; churches they are required to build; and ministers they are required to settle and support. In doing these several things they are secured, so far as may be, against intrusion, opposition, interruption, and even indecency from others. The great object in view, the public worship of God, is required, provided for, enforced, and defended. Some of the means by which it is to be accomplished are pointed out, and all which can consist with the certain attainment of the object are left to the societies themselves.

You cannot but have perceived that *all classes of Christians are here vested by law with the same privileges.* You must also have perceived that ample provision is made for all those changes of opinion and those scruples of conscience which, where they honestly exist, are entitled to tenderness and respect, for which men very jealously claim regard, and which, therefore, demand regard from every wise legislature.

If it be admitted, as by the sentence of both reason and revelation it ought to be, that a legislature has a right to establish the worship of God, it will also be admitted that the legislature of Connecticut has adopted a wise and liberal system for this important purpose. They have done most of that which is necessary, and nothing which is not necessary to this end. So far as is consistent with the design, they have also placed everything in the hands of those who are chiefly concerned, and left them to the guidance of their own choice. At the same time they have made them responsible to the proper tribunal, the supreme authority of the state.

There are two classes of men who contend against the interference of the legislature for the support of public worship: those *who consider it as inexpedient,* and those *who regard it as unlawful.*

On this subject it would be easy to fill a volume. It cannot be supposed that I can here discuss it at length, nor that, if this were in my power, you would with patience read the discussion. But it has been so often a theme of contention and complaint, on this as well as on the other side of the Atlantic, and particularly in the states south of New England, as to render it proper to examine the subject with some degree of minuteness even here. To the former of these classes then, I address the following observations.

The legislature of every state is the proper superintendent of all its prudential concerns. It has not only a right, but is obliged by an authority which it can neither oppose, nor question, to pursue every lawful and expedient measure for the promotion of the public welfare. To this great purpose religion in every country is not only useful, but indispensable. But religion cannot exist, and has never existed, for any length of time without public worship. As every man ought, therefore, willingly to contribute to the support of whatever increases his own prosperity, he is by immovable consequence obliged to support the religion which by increasing the common prosperity increases of course his own.

Should an advocate for the doctrine which I oppose demand proof that religion is indispensable to the welfare of a free country, this is my answer. Morality, as every sober man who knows anything of the subject discerns with a glance, is merely a branch of religion; and, where there is no religion, there is no morality. Moral obligation has its sole ground in the character and government of God. But, where God is not worshipped, his character will soon be disregarded, and the obligation founded on it unfelt and forgotten. No duty, therefore, to individuals or to the public will be realized or performed. Justice, kindness, and truth, the great hinges on which free society hangs, will be unpractised, because there will be no motives to the practice of sufficient force to resist the passions of man. Oaths of office and of testimony alike, without the sanctions of religion, are merely solemn farces. Without the sense of accountableness to God, without the realizing belief of the future retribution, they are employed only to insult the Creator, deprave the juror, and cheat his fellow men. This sense nothing but religion can inspire or preserve. With the loss of religion, therefore, the ultimate foundation of confidence is blown up; and the security of life, liberty, and property buried in the ruins.

In aid of these observations I allege that no free government has ever existed for any time without the support of religion. Athens, Sparta, and Rome stood and fell with their religion, false and gross as it was, because it contained some of those great truths and solemn sanctions without which man can possess no conscience, exercise no virtue, and find no safety. To their religion, Britain, Switzerland, and the United Netherlands have owed most of their happiness and their permanency; and might say to this celestial denizen in every period of their prosperity, as the devout and humble Christian to his God, "Having obtained help of Thee, we have continued to this time." [1]

In the history of the globe there is recorded but one attempt seriously made to establish a free government without religion. From this attempt has sprung new proof that such a government stripped of this aid cannot exist. The government thus projected was itself never established, but was a mere abortion, exhibiting doubtful signs of life at its birth, and possessing this dubious existence only as an ephemeron. During its diurnal life it was the greatest scourge, particularly to those for whom it was formed, and generally to the rest of mankind, which the world has ever seen. Instead of being a free, just, and beneficent system of administration, it was more despotic than a Persian caliphate, more wasteful of life and all its blessings than an inundation of Goths and Vandals. Those who lived under it, and either originated or executed its measures, were the authors of more crimes than any collection of men since the termination of that gigantic wickedness from which nothing but an universal deluge could cleanse this polluted world.

These evils, my antagonist is further to be informed, were the result of the only experiment ever made of erecting a government without religion. They are the only specimen of the genuine efficacy of infidelity and atheism on the mind and on the happiness of man, during the only opportunity which they have enjoyed of possessing an unlimited control over human affairs. Until the remembrance of this experiment shall have been lost, it can never be made again.

Finally, he is to be informed that it is wiser, more humane, and more effectual to prevent crimes than to punish them. He is to be told, what he cannot deny, that religion is the only great preventive of crimes, and contributes more, in a far more desirable manner, to the peace and good order of society than the judge and the sheriff, the jail and the gibbet united. He is to be reminded that mankind, with all the influence of religion added to that of the civil government, are still imperfectly governed; are less orderly, peaceful, and friendly to each other than humanity must wish; and that, therefore, he who would willingly lessen this influence is a fool; he who would destroy it, a madman.

I am well aware that in spite of this and any other reasoning, in spite of demonstration itself, there are men who may, and in all probability will, say that, however good and useful the public worship of God may be, they do not wish to avail themselves of its benefits, and owe, therefore, no contributions to its support. To these men I reply that he who has no children, or who does not wish to send his children to school, and he who does not use the roads and bridges of his country because he is either necessitated or inclined to stay at home, may on exactly the same ground claim an exemption from supporting schools, roads, and bridges. To such an objector it is a sufficient answer that these things enter into all the happiness which he enjoys, and that without them he and his countrymen would be hermits and savages. Without religion, man becomes in a short time a beast of prey, and wastes the happiness of his fellow men with as little remorse as the wolf or the tiger, and to a degree which leaves their ravages out of remembrance. Even if this were not the melancholy fact, the list of individual enjoyments is as much more valuable in a community where religion prevails than where it does not as the safety, peace, and pleasure of civilized society are more desirable than the exposure, discord, and misery produced by the furious and malignant passions of uncultivated man.

Those who consider the legislature in supporting the public worship of God as doing that which is unlawful found this doctrine upon what they conceive to be revelation. In support of it they allege such things as the following: that Christ has declared his kingdom not to be of this world; that the gates of Hell shall never prevail against it; and that he said to the apostles, "Freely ye have received; freely give"; [2] together with various other things of the like nature.

Every man who soberly alleges scruples of conscience in any case has a claim to be answered with seriousness and delicacy. To this class of objectors, therefore, I answer, When Christ declared his kingdom not to be of this world, he had not even the remotest reference to the subject in hand. He merely replied to the accusation which the Jews brought against him to Pilate, viz., that he claimed to be a king and was therefore a rebel against the government of Caesar.

It is, however, admitted in the fullest sense that the kingdom of Christ is not of this world; that as Christ declared, it is within man; and that, as St. Paul declares, it consists in "righteousness, peace, and joy, in the Holy Ghost." [3] But I ask, what reference had this to the point in debate? For myself I confess, I am unable to see the application of it so far as to find anything to be answered. In the interference of the magistrate to support the public worship of God, there is not even a reference to this doctrine, either friendly or hostile. Nor can I conceive how man can intermeddle with the subject at all, unless by declaring himself to be the author of regeneration, or to be able and disposed to resist the real author, the Holy Ghost. When the public support of the worship of God shall be shown to be unfavorable to the existence of regeneration, or to the disposition produced by it, and thus to oppose the spiritual kingdom of Christ, it will then be a proper time to cite this text as an argument against such an interference of the legislature. But should their interference be favorable to this great purpose, as, if we argue from all human experience, it must be; he who, understanding the subject, would hinder it, must renounce every pretension to the character of a Christian.

"But Christ," it is said, "has promised that the gates of Hell shall never prevail against his church"; [4] and, as he himself has engaged to support it, the aid of the civil magistrate can neither be necessary, nor proper. This promise I believe without a doubt, but the inference I shall take the liberty to question. The promise is this, and nothing but this: that there shall be throughout the ages of time a church of Christ in the world. It contains not, therefore, the least encouragement that for any length of time the kingdom of Christ will exist in any given country. In perfect accordance with this promise, Great Britain may be the seat of Christianity; and New England, a forest of savages, or a reveling house of infidels. But the first and great concern of the people of New England is to secure the blessings of this kingdom to themselves and to their posterity. To this object, I assert in contradiction to the above-mentioned inference that the aid of the magistrate is both proper and necessary. Miracles have ceased. The extraordinary and immediately perceptible agency of Christ in this business cannot, therefore, be expected, and will not be employed. Whatever is to be done, except the work of sanctification, which man cannot do, is to be done by man as the instrument of his Maker. Man is to *plant and water;* and then, and then only, is warranted either to hope or to pray that *God will give the increase.*[5]

Men are to build churches, to qualify themselves to become ministers of the Gospel, to preach the Gospel, to settle ministers, to support them when they are settled, to secure to them that support that they may be enabled to fulfill the duty of *providing for their own households,* and thus be safe from the charge of having *denied the faith and being worse than infidels.*[6] Of this safety there is no other possible foundation but a contract. Every contract which is not immoral, or of which the fulfillment is not impossible, the legislature of every country, especially of every Christian country, is not only authorized, but, so far as it is able, bound to enforce. In this manner, and in this only, will they and their children be furnished with ministers qualified to teach them divine knowledge and to impress on their hearts the duties of the Gospel. In this manner only will they secure themselves and their children from being left to the guidance of ignorant men, who, instead of being qualified to teach, are neither able, nor willing to learn.

In this manner will they shut out of the desk men to whom common sense instinctively cries, *Physician heal thyself.*[7] These men, who in all countries have been the disturbers of ecclesiastical peace and good order, will in this manner, and in this only, be silenced. For no body of decent men will vote a decent, fixed salary to a person of this character.

But it is said that *the apostles received freely,* and were commanded *freely to give.* The apostles on a miraculous mission and endued with miraculous powers were commanded *to heal the sick, to cleanse the lepers, to raise the dead, to cast out devils, and to preach,* as they went, *saying, "The kingdom of heaven is at hand."* [8] The supernatural powers by which these miracles were to be wrought, and which they had received freely from the bounty of Christ, they were commanded to exercise freely for the benefit of those by whom they should be welcomed into their cities and houses. Is this the commission under which ministers now act? If it is, let them obey its call as did the apostles. Particularly, *let them provide neither gold, nor silver, nor brass, in their purses; nor scrip; nor two coats, nor shoes, nor yet staves.* According to this very commission, *they are forbidden to preach the Gospel to any who will not furnish them with these things. A*gainst those who do not perform this duty, they *are directed to shake off the dust of their feet;* and it is declared *that it shall be more tolerable for Sodom and Gomorrah in the day of judgment than for them.*[9]

The ninth chapter of 1 Corinthians has settled this point forever. Here *Christ has ordained that they who preach the Gospel shall live of the Gospel.*[10] To cut off all debate, so far as debate can be cut off, St. Paul has sanctioned the ordinance that *they who preach the Gospel shall live of the Gospel* by an appeal to the law of Moses,[11] the express injunction of Christ, and the authority of his own inspiration.

But *why,* it will be asked, *may not this living be furnished by a voluntary contribution?* There are undoubtedly cases in which it may. In large towns congregations may be ordinarily gathered, sufficiently numerous and sufficiently liberal to build one or more churches and to support one or more ministers. In smaller towns this would ordinarily be impossible; and I suppose the objector himself will admit that it is at least as necessary for the inhabitants of smaller towns to have ministers as for those of cities, especially as they constitute the mass of people in all countries. In such towns the whole burden of supporting ministers by contribution would fall upon a few individuals. But these could not sustain this burden, and ministers, of course, could not live. In such towns, therefore, there will upon this plan be no ministers, I mean, none such as the Gospel requires: *Workmen who need not to be ashamed, who rightly divide the word of truth; who give attendance to reading, to exhortation, and to doctrine; who meditate upon these things, and give themselves wholly to them, so that their profiting may appear unto all.*[12]

Besides, St. Paul, 1 Cor. xvi, *has determined that a tax is the right and proper manner of doing all this.* In the second verse, he *commands the Corinthians to lay by them somewhat,* as a contribution to the relief of their fellow Christians, *every man as God had prospered them.*[13] Between contributions for their fellow Christians and contributions for ministers, there is no moral difference. *The contribution of a sum in proportion to the prosperity God has given men is a tax*: for a tax is nothing but a regular and proportional contribution. This proportion cannot be established but by authority, for, except by authority, men cannot be required to render an account of their circumstances. Nor can any proportion approach so near to equity as that which is formed under the direction of the legislature. Here, then, the rule of St. Paul, the rule established by God, is as exactly pursued as it can be by human wisdom: and, if it was a right rule in one ecclesiastical case, it is a rule equally right in every other.

If we look to facts, we shall find the same doctrine supported with illustrious evidence. In the year 1793, I was a member of the General Assembly of the Presbyterian Church. There were then, if I do not misremember, 412 congregations belonging to this church within the United States south of New England, and 209 congregations in the state of Connecticut alone. To supply these Presbyterian congregations, there were 204 ministers. In Connecticut there were in the year 1790, 237,946 inhabitants, and in the states south of New England, 2,920,478. In the year 1798, there were, belonging to the Presbyterian Church, 242 ministers, of whom thirty-three were without any charge; or, in the language of New England, were not *settled ministers.* Two hundred and nine ministers, therefore, supplied so far as they were supplied at all the whole number of Presbyterian congregations south of New England. The number of congregations at that time cannot be ascertained, as the returns were in this respect imperfect. These ministers supplied 290 congregations, eighty-one being what are called pluralities; and there were 142 vacancies returned. Five presbyteries made no returns of the vacancies within their bounds. If we suppose the vacancies in these presbyteries to be eighteen, the number will be 160. This number will make the whole 430. With this numerous train of vacancies, there were thirty ministers still who were unsettled. It follows irresistibly, either that the congregations were so small as to be unable to support ministers, or so indifferent to religion as to be unwilling.

The number of vacancies in Connecticut at that time, I am unable precisely to ascertain. Twenty may perhaps be assumed as the probable number. There were then at that time within the state 189 ministers.

In the year 1800, there were in Connecticut 251,002 inhabitants; and in the states south of New England, 4,033,775. The whole account according to this estimate will stand thus.

There were in 1798

| | Congregations | Ministers | Vacancies | Pluralities | Ministers not settled | Inhabitants |
|---|---|---|---|---|---|---|
| In Connecticut | 209 | 189 | 20 | 0 | 5 | 251,002 |
| In the states south of New England | 430 | 242 | 160 | 81 | 33 | 4,033,776 |

In Connecticut, then, a sixteenth of the number of inhabitants form 209 congregations, and support 189 ministers. Of these congregations, twenty were vacant; and five of the ministers were unsettled. In the states south of New England, sixteen times the number of inhabitants formed 430 congregations, of which eighty-one were pluralities, and 160 were vacant or without ministers. The ministers supported and settled were 209. If these states contained congregations, and were supplied with ministers, in the same proportion as Connecticut, the whole number of congregations would be 3,344; and the whole number of ministers, settled and supported would be 3,024. In this estimate we have a fair specimen of the natural consequence of establishing, or neglecting to establish, the public worship of God by the law of the land. In Connecticut every inhabitant who is not precluded by disease or inclination may hear the Gospel and celebrate the public worship of God every Sabbath. In the states specified it is not improbable that a number of people, several times as great as the census of Connecticut, have scarcely heard a sermon or a prayer in their lives.

The only objection which I can foresee against this estimate is that although the number of Presbyterian congregations in Connecticut is much greater in proportion than that in the states specified, yet this difference is, to a great extent, lessened by the superior proportion of congregations formed by other classes of Christians in those states. The number of Episcopal congregations in Connecticut, including twenty-six pluralities, is sixty-one; the number of Baptist congregations, sixty-seven; making in the aggregate 128. It is doubted whether a correct estimate of the congregations, formed by these and other classes of Christians, in the two fields of inquiry, would be materially different from that which has been already given. This estimate, however, cannot be made, their being no data from which it may be derived. I have chosen the Presbyterian congregations as the subject of inquiry because the numbers were attainable from returns in my possession.

An examination of the religious state of Massachusetts would have given a result not essentially different.

In a happy conformity to this estimate and the scheme here supported has been the prevalence of religion in these two states. It is doubted whether there is a collection of ministers in the world whose labors have been more prosperous, or under whose preaching a greater proportion of those who heard them have become the subjects of real piety. I know of no country in which revivals of religion have been so frequent, or in proportion to the number of inhabitants so extensive, as in these two states. God, therefore, may be considered as having thus far manifested his own approbation of the system. If at the same time we advert to the peace, the good order, the regular distribution of justice, the universal existence of schools, the universal enjoyment of the education which they communicate, and the extension of superior education, it will be difficult for a sober man not to perceive that the smiles of heaven have regularly accompanied this system from its commencement to the present time. I need not, however, have gone any farther for the illustration of this subject than to a comparison of the states of Rhode Island and Connecticut. The former of these, independently of Providence, Newport, and two or three other small towns, is in all these important particulars a mere contrast to the latter. Yet these states were planted by colonies from the same nation, lie in the same climate, and are separated merely by a meridional line. A sober man who knows them both can hardly hesitate, whatever may have been his original opinion concerning this subject, to believe that a legislature is bound to establish the public worship of God.

I am, Sir, yours, etc.

# LETTER VI

*Education of candidates for the ministry, and settlement of clergymen*

*Dear Sir,*

Few subjects, within a moderate number of years, have been more frequently canvassed by many Americans than *the character and privileges of the New England clergy:* I mean the Presbyterians. Perhaps no subject has been environed with more error, misrepresentation, or abuse. My observations will be confined to a mere explanation of the character and situation of the clergy. It is my wish to remove misapprehensions from the minds of candid men. Others I shall leave to themselves. It will be unnecessary to go beyond the limits of Connecticut for this purpose, as the differences between this state and most other parts of New England are not in this respect very material.

The progress of every clergyman in the state of Connecticut until he arrives at the desk is the following.

From infancy to manhood his whole character is subjected to the inspection of his parents, of his schoolmaster, of the parish in which he is born and bred, of the government of the college in which he is educated, of the church to which he is united, and of the clergyman by whom he is instructed in theology.* The inspection of the parish is here a serious object, for in no country is personal character so minutely scrutinized or so well known as in Connecticut. After his preparatory studies in theology are ended, he is licensed to preach; and, whenever he finds a congregation sufficiently pleasing to him and sufficiently pleased with him to render his settlement in it desirable, he is ordained, and has the congregation committed to his care. During every part of this progress he is subjected to a series of strict examinations concerning his character, conduct, and improvements. Besides earlier investigations of this nature, he is examined with regard to his learning and character in order to his admission into a college. Here he passes through eight public examinations before he can be admitted to the degree of bachelor of arts. Before he can be received into a church, his Christian character is scrupulously investigated. Before he can receive a license, he is again particularly questioned on this subject, and passes through a minute and comprehensive examination concerning his acquaintance with theology, the doctrines which he believes, and the talents which he possesses. If he is approved, he receives a license, limited to six months, a year, or sometimes to two years. When this license expires, he cannot without being disorderly continue to preach unless it is renewed; and it will not be renewed unless his character continues to be incensurable. While he is a licentiate, he is under a kind of daily examination. His sermons, his elocution, his doctrines, his moral and religious character, his manners, and the prudence of his conduct, all undergo a species of ordeal, both from the friends and the enemies of religion.

When he offers himself for ordination he passes through a new, more

* Until within a few years, there were no seminaries for the instruction of students in theology in New England. Previously to their establishment, young gentlemen, after completing their collegiate education, placed themselves under the direction of clergymen of respectability for the purpose of preparing themselves for the ministry. PUB.

solemn, and still more critical trial, conducted according to the pleasure of a consociation, a tribunal hereafter to be explained, every member of which has a right to protract his inquiries till he is satisfied. At this time, it is absolutely necessary that the candidate should appear unexceptionable in his knowledge, prudence, and piety.

Before he can become a settled minister, he is invited to preach, merely for the purpose of conducting for a moderate number of Sabbaths divine service in a destitute congregation. If both his preaching and manner of life are sufficiently agreeable, he is invited to preach, as it is termed, upon probation: that is, to give a fair and full exhibition of his talents and character, and to disclose his views of the principal doctrines contained in the Christian system.

Soon after this a further trial commences. A standing committee of the association within whose district the society is included assembles upon notice from the society's committee to hear him preach a lecture, and to converse with him freely on the topics mentioned above. When their inquiries are ended, these ministers advise the society to proceed in the design of giving him a call or to desist, as they find there are or are not any serious objections. After the period of his probation has been sufficiently extended, a legal meeting of the society is warned for the announced purpose of determining whether they will invite him to settle with them in the ministry. At this meeting every member makes every objection to the candidate and to the proceedings which he thinks proper. When the deliberation is ended, the question is put by the moderator. If it is carried in the affirmative, the quantum of his salary is next decided. In this particular the society vote just what they please, having nothing to influence them but their own judgment and inclinations.

Immediately before this meeting of the society, the church assembles to determine whether they will receive him as their minister. As the prime relation between a minister and his fellow men is his relation to the church, it is indispensable that the question concerning this relation be determined before the subjects mentioned in the last paragraph can be properly brought forward for discussion.

If both the church and the congregation unite in inviting him to be their minister, certified copies of their records containing all these proceedings are transmitted to him. When he has sufficiently considered the proposals, he gives written answers, which are also recorded in the public books of the church and the society. If he accepts the call, a day is appointed for his ordination. The consociation of the district, or a council mutually chosen, assembles on the morning of the preceding day. He is then examined in the manner already mentioned. If the members of the council are satisfied with his answers, they proceed the following day to his ordination. The parts of this religious service are a psalm; an introductory prayer; a second psalm; a sermon appropriated to the occasion; a consecrating prayer, conjoined with the imposition of hands upon the candidate; a charge in which his duties as a minister are explained and enjoined, and the church and congregation solemnly committed to his care; sometimes another charge to *them,* explaining and enjoining their corresponding duties; the giving of the right hand of fellowship in the name of the ordaining council as a token of their cheerful admission of him into their Christian fraternity and to the office and privileges of a minister; a concluding prayer; a third psalm, or an anthem; and the evangelical blessing.

In all the votes above mentioned a large majority must coincide. Three fourths constitute the smallest proportion which in any ordinary case can be supposed. Often, the opposition of a small number of respectable individuals will be a sufficient reason to the council for postponing, and in the end declining, the ordination.

After a minister is settled, his conduct is watched with more attention than that of any other man. He must not only be substantially free from censure, but, like the wife of Caesar, unsuspected: [1] uniting and exemplifying the wisdom of the serpent and the harmlessness of the dove.

Notwithstanding the rigidness of the laws heretofore recited, and the apparent security which they furnish to him, he holds his place in the congregation which settled him and the living attached to it by a more precarious tenure than that of almost any other man. Should a very moderate number of his parishioners, should even an individual of peculiar consequence, become opposed to him, it may in the end be the cause of his removal. His living in the meantime furnishes barely a comfortable subsistence. The average salary of ministers in Connecticut, including all the perquisites annexed to it, does not, I believe, exceed four hundred dollars. There are, perhaps, from six to ten within two hundred and fifty dollars. I know of but one which amounts to eleven hundred dollars. When it is remembered that the public sentiment demands that a minister in his dress and manner of living should appear as a gentleman, and that the price of all the means of subsistence has during the last twenty-two years † been doubled, it must be seen that such a salary is sufficiently stinted.

I am, Sir, yours, etc.

† 1816.

# LETTER VII

*Influence of the clergy in Connecticut: its nature and derivation*

*Dear Sir,*

The *powers of a clergyman,* about which so much has been lately said, are a power to marry within the county in which he lives; and a power, when he is chosen, to preside as moderator, or when he does not preside, to vote in ecclesiastical meetings where none but ecclesiastical subjects are considered. In the meetings of his own church, he is the moderator *ex officio.* I doubt not but a multitude of those who read this declaration will read it with astonishment. Hardly will they believe that the formidable stories, the alarming suggestions which have been so often reiterated concerning *the New England hierarchy* can have grown out of these puny things. Yet these are the only powers of a New England clergyman. Let the men who have uttered these suggestions blush over this account, if a remaining, solitary drop of crimson yet wanders through their cheeks.

Whence then, it will be asked, is all that clerical consequence about which such a multitude of tongues have been so long busied? That it exists in some degree cannot be doubted, or it could not have been made the subject of so much obloquy, or even of discussion. I will answer the question frankly. *The real weight of clergymen in New England,* particularly in Massachusetts and Connecticut, *consists wholly in their influence:* an influence derived from their office and their conduct.

Their office is, and is acknowledged to be, sacred, instituted by God himself, eminently useful to the present and immensely important to the future well-being of mankind. There is something so reasonable in the consciousness of an intimate and permanent connection between rational creatures and their Creator, and a conviction of the duties owed by them to him and to each other; something so self-recommendatory in virtue and so intuitively odious in sin; something so rational in accountableness, so irresistible in the decisions of conscience, and so probable, and awful, in the idea of a future retribution, that the mind, left to its own views, unbiased by adventitious prejudice, unperplexed with sophistry, and unhardened by habitual wickedness, will admit all these things of course, and will scarcely think of opposing either their evidence or their influence. He who, with a character known and approved, approaches the mind with fair, frequent, and solemn injunctions on these amazing subjects will, therefore, be respected instinctively. When in addition to this he comes as a messenger of God, authorized by him to explain them to the understanding and to impress them on the heart, from a book written by the divine finger, on a day, in a place, and on an occasion made sacred by the same Lawgiver, and accompanied by ordinances supremely affecting, it is impossible that he should not be an object of veneration.

To this reverence, high endearment will be added of course by his presence in the hour of sorrow, in the chamber of sickness, and at the bed of death. The man who is always employed in mitigating distress, administering comfort, and aiding the return of serenity cannot but be hailed as a friend of no common character. Other men are from necessity more or less employed in originating, or enhancing, trouble to some or other of their fellow men; and, although occupied perhaps in their duty and praiseworthy for performing it, are yet by the ordinary association of ideas regarded as sources of pain. A minister is active only in the production of enjoyment or the alleviation of suffering.

At the same time he is every man's minister. Between him and each of his parishioners a relation subsists found in no other case. From this relation arises an interchange of affections and offices, wholly peculiar, strongly endearing, soon rendered habitual, and easily regarded as indispensable. He is the common friend; the common peacemaker; the common father; the general solicitor of charity for the poor, of assistance to the sick, and of relief to the suffering; the general instructor of the children in wisdom and piety; and, in the beautiful phraseology of the Scriptures, the shepherd who guides the flock and walks before them in the way to heaven.

To these means of influence his learning, prudence, and personal character make an important addition. By these he is placed in a superior and, what is not true of any other man, an uninvidious light. He is no man's rival in the chase for honor or wealth. The miser may make his bargains and the candidate compass his election without fearing any competition from him. In his place, office, and pecuniary circumstances, he is fixed; and they will neither be coveted, nor envied by others.

Finally, he must possess an unspotted character. The character of a clergyman in this country, like that of the delicate sex, is enclosed by mounds which he cannot safely pass, although he sees them daily passed without the least injury to themselves by other men of fair reputation. These form a security to him, of high importance as they keep him at a distance from danger. Watched by every eye and exposed to the censures of every tongue, he is compelled to be on his guard. Should he trespass, therefore, beyond the haltings of mere human infirmity, he must, to say the least, be very inattentive or very imprudent.

From these observations you will easily perceive the true state of this subject. The clergy of Connecticut have no power, but they have much influence: an influence which every sober man must feel to be altogether desirable in every community. It is the influence of wisdom and virtue. Clergymen here are respected for what they are and for what they do, and not for anything adventitious to themselves or their office. Miserable, indeed, must be the state of that society in which character and conduct, known and approved, fail of their proper influence: for plainly no means hitherto furnished by the providence of God have so happily promoted the welfare of mankind. Order and peace have hitherto been established either by force or persuasion, by power or by influence. Who would not rather have his own children influenced to behave well, than punished for behaving ill? Who that can claim the name of a man, who that cherishes a particle of the humanity which derives its appellation from that name, will not rejoice to see crimes prevented by the desk rather than rewarded by the gibbet? Who would not rather see churches crowded, than jails? Happily for themselves and their children, the people of this state have chosen rather to prevent the commission of crimes by the efficacy of religious instruction, than to expect either reformation or good order from the terrors of the dungeon or the halter.

Let me solicit you to take a cursory view of the care and caution used from the beginning in introducing a candidate into the ministry. Let me then ask you whether in any business of human life you have known more prudent or more effectual expedients employed. Is not the utmost security here attained of receiving only the proper candidates? If these measures will not insure a learned, pious, and faithful ministry, what will?

The ministry here is safe also from the temptations presented in several other countries by rank and opulence. I am far from believing that rank and opulence necessarily conduct those by whom they are possessed to criminal conduct. I well know that many such persons have been distinguished for their wisdom and piety. But you will agree with me that these splendid objects involve serious temptations. You will also admit that, where they are annexed to places of any kind, the votaries of wealth and splendor will covet, and not unfrequently obtain, these places. It is here believed, and I think with no small appearance of reason, that great secular enjoyments would open the desk in spite of every precaution to the intrusion of loose and worldly men. But no devotee to wealth or honor will be allured into this office by the salary connected with it, or the tenure on which it is holden. I neither deny, nor doubt, that the former is too small, and the latter too precarious. As both are, however, there is probably no class of men more unblamable than the clergy of Connecticut.

You are not to conclude from anything which I have here said that ministers do not in the great body of instances continue firmly fixed in the places where they are originally settled. Almost all of them continue in their stations during life, unless when they are voluntarily exchanged for others. This fact, however, has its foundation *chiefly in the manners and habits of the people.* Ministers and schoolmasters to a great extent form the manners, and the manners support the ministers and schoolmasters. Hence the situation of ministers is justly asserted to be stable and permanent: as great a proportion of their whole number probably terminating life where they were originally settled as in most parts and perhaps in any part of the Christian world. The greatest source of separation between ministers and their people is the smallness of their salaries: and this, I confess, threatens, at the present expensive period, a more numerous train of evils than have hitherto been known of a similar nature in New England.*

I am, Sir, yours, etc.

* There is an evil relative to this subject, and that of no small magnitude, which has arisen from the peculiar state of the country since the commencement of the American Revolution. During the progress of that event, the salaries of ministers, which had before furnished them, generally at least, a decent subsistence, dwindled to nothing by the depreciation of the Continental currency. The poverty of the country produced by a war of eight years prevented the mischief from being remedied, except in part, for a considerable period. As the wealth of the inhabitants increased, the salaries of ministers were enlarged, particularly of such as were then settled, with a design to make them adequate to their maintenance. The war in Europe introduced a total change into the economic affairs of this country. The prices of labor and of all the necessaries and many of the conveniences of life were suddenly doubled and trebled. Salaries of course sunk again in their real value to one half and one third of their original value. Farmers, who in most places constitute the body of parishioners, and whose farms still supply them with the same means of supporting their families, are almost necessarily ignorant of the difference in the expense of living created by this state of things. Men of this class rarely make any calculations concerning the subject; and, from mere ignorance, are with great reluctance induced to believe the real state of the fact. Accordingly, some of them within my knowledge, having had such calculations presented to them, have confessed their mistakes concerning the subject, and totally changed their views and measures. It is reasonably believed that such would be the conduct of very many others were they to possess the same advantages for forming a just estimate.

From this state of things it has arisen that, although salaries have been materially increased in their nominal value, their real value, as means of living, has been materially lessened. From the colonization of the country to the year 1763, the stipends of ministers, including all the means which they possessed of supporting and educating their families, were better, throughout the country at large, than they have been at any subsequent period.†

† At the present time (1820) the expense of living is much lessened, and the value of salaries is proportionally increased. PUB.

# LETTER VIII

*Confession of faith and articles of church discipline agreed to at Saybrook in 1708 by the delegates of the churches—History of the proceedings relative to this subject —Observations*

*Dear Sir,*

On the 9th of September, 1708, the elders and messengers of the churches of Connecticut in New England, by virtue of the appointment and encouragement of the General Assembly, convened by delegation at Saybrook; and unanimously agreed, "that the confession of faith, owned and consented unto by the elders and messengers assembled at Boston in New England, May 12, 1680, being the second session of that synod, be recommended to the honorable General Assembly of this colony at their next session for their public testimony thereto, as the faith of the church of this colony: which confession, together with the heads of union and articles of the administration of church government herewith emitted, were presented unto, and approved, and established by the said General Assembly, at New Haven, on the 14th of October, 1708."

The confession here alluded to and adopted is in substance the same with the Westminster and Savoy confessions.

At the same time this synod agreed unanimously upon articles for the administration of church discipline in the churches of the colony. Such of these articles as are of importance to my design, and as will be sufficient to give you a just and comprehensive view of the scheme agreed upon by these good men, I will summarily exhibit, and, as far as may be, in their own words. They acknowledge that there is a catholic church, comprehending all who are united to Christ, whether in heaven or on earth; but disclaim the notion of a Catholic, visible church, collected under a visible common head in this world.

They agree that particular societies of visible saints, statedly joined together for communion in the ordinances of Christ, are particular churches, and are to be owned by each other as instituted churches of Christ, though differing in apprehensions and practice in some lesser things.

That none shall be admitted as members, but such as are knowing and sound in the fundamental doctrines of the Christian religion, without scandal in their lives, and to a judgment regulated by the word of God are persons of visible holiness and honesty, credibly professing cordial subjection to Jesus Christ.

A competent number of such persons declaring their consent and agreement to walk together in the ordinances of Christ become a church. The members of such a church ought, as far as may be, to live near one another.

Every such church has a right to choose its own officers; and, being furnished with them agreeably to the Gospel, has a right to exercise government and to enjoy all the ordinances of worship within itself. It belongs to the pastors and other elders of every particular church, if such there be, to rule and govern; and to the brotherhood, to consent, according to the rule of the Gospel. Professors are bound, when they have an opportunity, to join themselves as fixed members to some particular church; and to continue steadfast with the said church, its ministry, and ordinances, until regularly dismissed and recommended to another.

Ministers ought to be indued with competent learning and ministerial gifts, as also with the grace of God, to be sound in judgment, not novices, without scandal, and such as devote themselves to the work of the ministry. Ordinarily none ought to be ordained to the work of the ministry, but such as are called and chosen to it by a particular church.

In the business of calling and choosing a pastor, every such church ought to consult and advise with pastors of the neighboring congregations. After such choice and advice, the candidate is to be duly ordained and set apart to his office over the church by which he has been called. Candidates for the ministry ought in ordinary cases to give proof of their gifts and fitness for the ministry to ministers of known abilities.

Ecclesiastical censures are admonition and excommunication.

Admonition in case of private offenses is to be performed according to Matthew xviii, 15, 16, 17; and in case of public offenses, openly before the church.[1] If the offender is penitent, all further proceedings cease; if not, after all due means have been used to bring him to repentance, he is to be excommunicated.

If a member, not otherwise scandalous, fully withdraw and separate himself from the communion of the church, the church may justly declare itself discharged of any further inspection over him.

Particular churches ought to exercise care and tenderness toward each other.

Pastors ought to have frequent meetings, for the purpose of strengthening the hearts and the hands of each other.

No particular church is to be subordinate to another; and no church, nor its officers are to exercise power over another church and its officers.

Members of a particular church may have communion with another in the ordinances of the Gospel, except when lying under some imputation.

No church is to be blamed for its proceedings by another until after it shall have been heard.

The office of a deacon is of divine appointment; and it belongs to that office to receive, lay out, and distribute the alms of the church, by the direction of the pastor and brethren, if need be.

Some persons believe that there is, and some that there is not, such an office as that of ruling elders. The synod declared that this difference of opinion should make no breach among themselves.

In weighty and difficult cases, ministers ought to be consulted; and both the elders and members of particular churches ought to have a reverential regard to their judgments, and not to dissent therefrom without apparent grounds from the word of God.

We think ourselves obliged to pray continually for the blessing of God upon our rulers. We ought to yield them subjection and support. If they please at any time to call together any number of us and require an account of our affairs and the state of our congregations, we shall most readily express all dutiful regard to them herein.

As to what appertains to soundness of judgment in matters of faith, we esteem it sufficient that a church acknowledge the Scriptures to be the word of God, the perfect, and only, rule of faith and practice; and own either the doctrinal part of those commonly called the Articles of the Church of England, or the confession, or catechism, shorter or larger, compiled by the assembly at Westminster, or the confession agreed on at the Savoy, to be agreeable to the said rule.

It is the duty of Christians to bear a Christian respect to all Christians, according to their several ranks and stations, though not of our persuasion or communion.

To those who are ignorant of the principles of the Christian religion, or of vicious conversation, we will endeavor to explain the doctrine of life, and to our utmost persuade them to be reconciled to God.

Such as appear to have the essential requisites to church communion, we shall willingly receive them in the Lord, not troubling them with disputes about lesser matters.

Articles for the administration of church discipline, unanimously agreed upon by the synod at the same time and place:

The elder, or elders, of a particular church, with the consent of the brethren, are to exercise the discipline of the Gospel in relation to all scandals that fall out within the same. In cases of difficulty, advice should be asked of the elders in the neighborhood before they proceed to censure.

The churches shall consociate for mutual assistance in their ecclesiastical concerns. The pastors and churches of a county shall form one, or, if they judge meet, more than one consociation.

All cases of scandal within the consociational limits, when there shall be need of a council for the determination of them, shall be brought before the consociation.

Nothing shall be deemed an act or judgment of a consociation which hath not a major part of the elders concurring, and such a number of the messengers or delegates present as to constitute a majority of the whole.

A trial before a consociation shall be final, and the consociation shall see their judgment duly executed agreeably to the word of God.

If any pastor and church refuse conformity to such a judgment, they shall be reputed guilty of scandalous contempt, and the sentence of noncommunion shall be declared against them; and the churches are to approve of the said sentence by withdrawing from the communion of such pastor and church.

If any case of difficulty shall arise in any church, the church, or the minister, or member aggrieved shall apply to the consociation to which said church belongs; which, if they see cause, shall thereupon convene, hear, and determine the case. If the consociation shall judge it best, they may call upon another consociation in the same county, or, if there be none, in a neighboring county to sit with them; and this united body shall hear, judge, determine, and finally issue such case according to the word of God.

A particular church in which any difficulty shall arise may call the consociation to which it belongs before a sentence is pronounced. But this may not be done by an offending brother without consent of the church.

Every church may choose one or two delegates to represent them in the consociation, who are to stand until others shall be chosen.

Consociations have power to adjourn themselves as need shall be for the space of one year after their first session, and no longer. The moderator of a consociation, with the advice and consent of any two ministers belonging to it, may summon a special meeting; or in case of the moderator's death, two ministers of the consociation shall have the same power. Every consociation is empowered to form rules for its own proceedings. A person regularly complained of to a consociation, or a witness to such complaint, being regularly notified to appear, who shall refuse or neglect to appear at the time and place specified, shall, unless a satisfactory reason be given to the consociation, be adjudged guilty of scandalous contempt.

The ministers of each county shall be formed into one or more associations as they shall see cause, shall assemble twice a year at least, at such time and place as they shall appoint, to consult concerning the duties of their office and the common interest of the churches, shall consider and resolve questions and cases of importance presented by themselves or others, and shall have power to examine and recommend (i. e. to *license*) candidates for the ministry.

The said associated pastors shall take notice of any among themselves accused before them of scandal or heresy, shall examine the matter carefully; and, if they find just occasion, shall direct to the calling of the consociation, where such offenders shall be duly proceeded against.

The said associated ministers shall be consulted by destitute churches belonging to their association, and shall recommend to them such persons as may be fit to be called and settled in the ministry among them; and, if such destitute churches shall not seasonably call and settle ministers among them, the said associated pastors shall lay such cases before the General Assembly, that they may take such order concerning them as shall be found necessary for their peace and edification.

It is recommended as expedient that all the associations of this colony meet in a general association by their respective delegates, one or more out of each association, once a year: the first meeting to be at Hartford at the time of the general election, next ensuing the date hereof; and so annually, in all the counties successively, at such time and place as the said delegates in their annual meeting shall appoint.

You have here the system of faith, communion, and discipline unanimously adopted by a synod formed by delegation of all the ministers and churches in the colony of Connecticut. A short history of this subject will place it in a more conspicuous light.

The trustees of Yale College, being met at Guilford, March 17, 1703, wrote a circular letter to the ministers, proposing to have a general synod of all the churches in the colony to give their joint consent to a confession of faith, after the example of the synod in Boston in 1680.

This proposal was universally acceptable; and the ministers and churches of the several counties met in voluntary consociation, and gave their consent to the Westminster and Savoy confessions of faith, and agreed upon certain rules of union in discipline, which were designed to be preparatory to a general synod. Still there was no visible, acknowledged, and authoritative bond of union among them; and the disadvantages necessarily attendant upon a want of system were felt to a considerable extent. Where there is no general rule acknowledged, different bodies will of course make different and often clashing rules for their own regulation. Where there is no common scheme of proceeding, almost all proceedings will be irregular and imperfect. In such a state of things it is in vain to expect harmony or happiness.

Accordingly, a variety of inconveniences sprang up year by year in the colony of Connecticut from this source, and both the clergy and laity felt them deeply. The venerable Hooker, whose opinions were almost oracular, observed with great earnestness about a week before his death, July 7, 1647, "We must agree upon constant meetings of ministers and settle the consociation of churches, or else we are undone." Soon after his death, the ministers of Connecticut formed themselves generally into associations.

The Heads of Agreement, drawn up and assented to by the united ministers in England called Presbyterian and Congregational in 1692, were highly approved in this country, and contributed to increase the disposition in favor of establishing a scheme of faith and discipline here.

In May 1708, the legislature passed an act requiring the ministers and churches to meet by delegation at Saybrook at the next commencement to be held there, and form an ecclesiastical constitution. This they were directed to present to the legislature at their session at New Haven the following October, to be considered of and confirmed by them.

In the same act they directed the ministers and churches of the colony to meet (the churches by delegation) in the county towns of their respective counties, there to consider and agree upon those rules for the management of ecclesiastical discipline which they should judge conformable to the word of God, and to appoint two or more of their number to form the synod at Saybrook. They also directed the synod to compare the results of these ecclesiastical meetings of the several counties, and out of them to draw a form of ecclesiastical discipline. The expenses of all these meetings were to be defrayed out of the public treasury.

The system agreed upon by the synod was presented to the legislature at the time specified, upon which they passed the following act:[2]

At a General Court, holden at New Haven, October 1708.

The reverend ministers, delegates from the elders, and messengers of this government met at Saybrook, September 9, 1708, having presented to this assembly a confession of faith, heads of agreement, and regulations in the administration of church discipline, as unanimously agreed and consented to by the elders and messengers of all the churches in this government; this assembly doth declare their great approbation of such an happy agreement, and do ordain that all the churches within this government that are or shall be thus united in doctrine, worship, and discipline be, and for the future shall be, owned and acknowledged established by law; provided always that nothing herein shall be intended and construed to hinder or prevent any society or church that is or shall be allowed by the laws of this government, who soberly differ or dissent from the united churches hereby established, from exercising worship and discipline in their own way according to their consciences.

A true copy, Test.

Eleazar Kimberly, Secretary

I will now make a few observations on this scheme. You have here an exact account of the ecclesiastical authority and power of two ecclesiastical judicatories established in the state of Connecticut: a particular church and a consociation. A particular church, with its pastor at its head, has the power of exercising the discipline of the Gospel with respect to all scandals which take place among its members. With respect to this subject it is declared to be the province of the pastor, together with the ruling elders wherever they exist, to govern; and that of the brotherhood to consent, and of course, if they see occasion, to dissent. This constitutes two distinct powers: one of which (the elder or elders) is to originate decisions; and the other has the right of a veto with respect to every decision. This certainly is a judicatory attended with circumstances of extreme delicacy, for should the brotherhood refuse their consent, the measures originated must regularly fall. It might not unnaturally be expected that in such a division of authority most measures actually proposed would fail. The very same is, however, the constitution of every representative government so far as a veto is concerned: each branch of the legislature having, of course, a negative upon the other. Here also each branch has additionally the power of originating measures.

At the same time this appears to be a mode of ecclesiastical government founded upon the Scriptures. St. Paul in 2 Corinthians ii, 6, says: *Sufficient to such a man* (the incestuous person mentioned in a former epistle) *is this punishment* (i. e. excommunication) *which was inflicted of many;* ὑπὸ τῶν πλειόνων; *by the majority.* The majority of the members of the church at Corinth were, therefore, active as an authoritative power in inflicting this punishment. As this transaction was approved by St. Paul without any qualification, it should seem certain that it must have been agreeable to the will of God and must, therefore, be a rule for all other churches.

Whatever is scriptural is right, and will ordinarily be successful. Accordingly, no churches, it is believed, have a stricter or more efficacious discipline than those of Connecticut. None within my knowledge, amounting to an equal number, have so strict a discipline. Even ours, however, is less exact in many instances than a good man could wish. From the decision of the church an appeal lies in the cases specified to the consociation; and from that of the consociation a kind of half appeal, in cases of great difficulty, to a body formed partly of the consociation which has already heard and determined the cause, and partly of a neighboring consociation invited to act as assessors. This certainly is an absurdity in the system. There is little reason to believe that those who have once heard and adjudged a case will recede from their adjudication: perhaps the less reason, the more patiently and carefully the cause has been heard. Should the assessors judge differently from the original tribunal, there will be consociation against consociation, and sentence against sentence. Both parties will, therefore, feel themselves completely justified; and the contention, whatever it may be, will be still undecided, at least so far as the opinions and feelings of the interested persons are concerned.

The reasons why an appeal lies from a particular church to a consociation are the supposed incompetency of the church to judge in certain cases, or the apprehension of biases, particularly where the parties differ materially in weight of character, influence, and the number and power of their connections. The same reasons would in some instances make an appeal equally necessary from a consociation to a higher tribunal. These, I acknowledge, will be few; still they will exist. For the decision of such cases a general consociation seems necessary to complete the ecclesiastical polity of Connecticut. As the system is, however, the affairs of the church have generally gone on with much harmony and good order; not always, it must be confessed, with equal harmony, yet probably with as few difficulties as can be found elsewhere.

Anciently, ruling elders existed in many of the churches of New England. At the present time there is not a single officer of this description in any Congregational church in this country. This I think unhappy. Such offices plainly existed in the apostolical times. This is explicitly declared by St. Paul, 1 Timothy v, 17, Romans xii, 8; and 1 Corinthians xii, 28.[3] They are also sufficiently alluded to by several of the Fathers, particularly by Ignatius, Hilary, Cyprian, and Augustine.

The General Association of Connecticut is a body merely advisory, yet its recommendations have no small part of the efficacy derived from authority. The business transacted by it, with one exception, consists in a general superintendence of the prudential affairs of the churches, in receiving applications from the several ministers individually and associated, and from the several churches, particular or consociated, concerning their respective interests or the general ecclesiastical interests of the state; and giving their advice, recommending such measures originally as they judge to be beneficial, etc., etc.

The exception which I mentioned above is this: the General Association is the incorporated missionary society of the state. Their executive business in this character is transacted by a board of trustees, annually chosen by them, and annually reporting to them whatever they have done.*

The General Association also appoint committees of certification in all the particular associations, for the purpose of certifying authoritatively the good standing and character of ministers or licentiates within their bounds intending to travel and reside within the bounds of the Presbyterian and other Congregational churches in the United States. A certificate from either of these committees, each of which consists of an individual, gives the person certified a regular access to the desk wherever he may be and churches may have occasion for his labors. The General Association also receives annually a particular account of the state of religion, ministers, and churches in their respective districts from all its members, which consist of two delegates from each of the thirteen associations in this state; three, four, or five from the General Assembly of the Presbyterian Church, two from the General Association of Massachusetts, two from that of New Hampshire, and one from the General Convention of Vermont: all these bodies being united in a common bond of union for general purposes affecting them all. The General Association of Connecticut sends a corresponding number of

* In 1816 the General Association became also the Domestic Missionary Society of the state.

delegates to these several ecclesiastical bodies. All these delegates have, in every case, the same rights of deliberating and voting. This union may be considered as a serious improvement in the ecclesiastical affairs of the United States. It has extensively become a source of unity, cordiality, more expanded and liberal views, and more generous affections. At the same time it spreads everywhere, brings up to public view whatever of importance is done or needs to be done to promote religion, gives energy to all its friends, and presents serious discouragements to its enemies. It also prevents the depredations of unauthorized preachers by making a regular certificate from the proper authority indispensable to every preacher in order to his admission into the desk wherever he is a stranger.

I cannot here omit mentioning the catholicism of this synod. One of the Heads of Agreement mentioned above, and unanimously adopted by them, is this. "We esteem it sufficient that a church acknowledge the Scriptures to be the word of God, the perfect and only rule of faith and practice, and own either the doctrinal part of those commonly called the Articles of the Church of England, or the confession, or catechisms, compiled by the assembly at Westminster, or the confession agreed on at the Savoy, to be agreeable to the said rule." [4]

When we remember how many sufferings the immediate ancestors of these men had experienced from the hands of those who ruled in the English church, and how easily men become hostile to everything associated with those by whom they suppose themselves, or theirs, to have been injured, it is certainly a proof of a disposition much more moderate than that which has been generally attributed to the religious people of New England that this synod has unanimously said, "As to what appertains to soundness of judgment in matters of faith, we esteem it sufficient that a church acknowledge the Scriptures to be the word of God, and the only rule of faith and practice, and own the doctrinal part of those commonly called the Articles of the Church of England to be agreeable to said rule." [5]

Permit me further to observe that the divines in England who formed the Heads of Agreement, and the synod at Saybrook, and let me add the great body of Presbyterian and Congregational ministers who have lived in this country since that time, have thought your articles sufficiently Calvinistic for them, so much so that they placed them on the same level with the Westminster and Savoy confessions of faith. These, I am well aware, will not be acknowledged as a decisive tribunal in this case. An impartial one I think they must be acknowledged.

The business of ordaining ministers, and all that pertains to it, is here appropriately the province of a consociation. This body takes cognizance of the call given by the church and congregation; the answers of the candidate; the proposals for his support; and all the circumstances of the case which may contribute to render his union with the people happy, or unhappy, and himself useful, or unuseful, to them. They also, as has been heretofore observed, examine his qualifications for the ministry, literary, religious, and prudential. From all these things they make up their judgment, which is final; and their proceedings are all recorded by their standing clerk.

I am, Sir, yours, etc.

# LETTER IX

*Comparison of the state of religion in England with that in New England—English representations of the state of religion here refuted*

*Dear Sir,*

In the Christian Observer for November and December 1811, I have found a Review of Letters to Mr. Perceval on the State of the Established Church of England.[1] The observations contained both in the Letters and the Review are too intimately connected with my design of defending, so far as truth and candor will permit, my own country, and of illustrating its situation by comparing it with that of yours with respect to the same things to be neglected on the present occasion. I beg you to believe, Sir, because it is true, that although an American, a republican, and a Presbyterian, I take no pleasure in the humiliation of your church or the country in which it is established. Nor will it be any part of my design at the present time to enhance, or enjoy, the calamities of either. To see your country virtuous and happy, and your church restored to the highest religious excellence and moral distinction which it has ever enjoyed, will hardly give a more sincere pleasure to any Englishman than to me. While I remember anything, I shall not forget that it is the country *avorum meorum, atavorum, et omnium, a quibus genus ducitur meum.*[2] The subjects which I shall briefly touch, and with respect to which I shall institute an informal comparison between our circumstances and yours, are the following, forming, as you will see, only a part of those mentioned by the writer: the state of the universities, examination for orders, disposal of patronage in the church, neglect of ecclesiastical discipline, neglect or carelessness in the pastoral duties, and want of churches.

On the first of these subjects the writer says that "there are more vice and profligacy of manners countenanced at the universities than would be suffered to take place among its members afterwards when they arrive at situations in life which present no positive restraints; and that the scenes of riot and debauchery which pass unnoticed, or at least are ineffectually noticed by those who cannot be ignorant of them, would in the metropolis subject the perpetrators to the correction of the police." These evils he also attributes to "the example of too many among the preceptors." He also says, "Chapel is not attended till it is half over. Many go there intoxicated, as to a roll call; and, although the assumption of the Lord's Supper is peremptory on the students, no care is taken to teach them its importance." [3]

These, Sir, are unpleasant declarations. Such an account concerning any college in this country would be a libel. Almost all our students are decent in their deportment; most of them are irreproachable; and not a small number of them, religious. Nor can any known, scandalous conduct pass without a sufficient reprehension. At the same time, the great body of them are industrious, and many of them intensely laborious.

I know not that I have ever heard of any person in New England who appeared at church in a state of intoxication. The great body of our students are always at prayers and public worship in the proper season, and behave usually in a decent and reverential manner.

The letter writer says that "the assumption of the Lord's Supper is peremptory upon the student"; that is, as I suppose, they are required peremptorily to partake of the Lord's Supper at stated seasons. This requisition is certainly unhappy. No person ought ever to appear at that ordinance unless he is in his own view hopefully a Christian. All attendance of this nature ought to be only voluntary. No human power can meddle here; no unhallowed feet intrude. Permit me to say that this requisition of itself, by making the attendance in question an object of human law, like that upon recitations, lectures, or other academical employments, degrades religion in her most sacred exercises to a merely secular character, and prepares the students to esteem her duties of no superior importance. I cannot wonder that students under such a requisition should be ready to trifle with the whole subject, and find in it little or no restraint upon their vicious propensities.

With respect to *examination for orders,* the letter writer goes on, "So very lax has become the examination for orders that there is no man who has taken a degree at the university who cannot reckon on ordination as a certainty, whatever his attainments in learning, morals, religion, etc.—speaking generally, I believe the only qualifications are to be able to construe a chapter in the Greek Testament and answer a few questions out of Grotius." [4] At this account I am astonished. I have been always taught to believe that the clergy of the English Church were, as a body, at least decently learned; and, when Englishmen in this country speak of our clergymen with contempt in comparison with their own, and when English writers of travels declare that we have neither learning, nor eloquence, it seems almost necessarily concluded that they have been accustomed to much of both in their native land. Paley,[5] and many other respectable English writers in modern times; and Hooker, Burnet, and others, in those which were more ancient, have complained with not a little feeling concerning the ignorance of many of your clergymen; "by reason whereof," says the venerable Hooker (that is, of careless ordination) "the church groweth burdened with silly creatures more than need, whose noted baseness and insufficiency bringeth their order itself into contempt." Still I could not have imagined that such an examination as this would have been the passport to the desk. Scarcely less am I surprised at the admission of the Christian Observer, if I construe it right, that * "a large majority of regularly educated dissenting ministers are better versed in the common places of theology, and that knowledge of the Bible on which as a science it rests, than even a small minority of our rising ministry." [6]

Suffer me to call to your recollection the account which I gave you of the manner in which young men are educated for the ministry in this country. You will see in it an attention to this subject which, from the united testimony of these Letters to Mr. P[erceval] and this Review of them, you will, I fear, look for in vain in your own church. You will also see men destined to the desk, not because it is the wish of their parents, but because it is their own; not to provide a child with a living, but to furnish a congregation with a pastor. No youth is admitted into sacred orders, except within the precincts of the *liberal* Christianity mentioned in my observations on the District of Maine, who has not been twice strictly examined (after having received a liberal education) concerning his knowledge of the doctrines and duties of religion, and who is not to the eye of charity *cordially* a Christian. It is a radical and most melancholy evil in your church that men designate children for the desk from their infancy, and push them into it whether they are persons of piety or not. How tremendous in the mouths of many such candidates for holy orders must be the declaration that "they verily believe themselves moved to the assumption of the sacred office by the Holy Ghost!" With how much more truth and propriety might they say with the twelve disciples of John mentioned by St. Luke, *"We have not so much as heard whether there be any Holy Ghost!"* [7]

On the subject of *church patronage,* I shall only observe that in the manner in which it is holden in Great Britain, I cannot but think it eminently unhappy. The Christian Observer prefers it to that which has been often proposed in lieu of it, viz. *popular suffrage.* I have a high respect for the opinions of the gentlemen to whom the public are indebted for this excellent periodical work. Still I cannot but think the preference the result of education and habit merely. In this country, in the Congregational,

* Christian Observer 1811, p. 713.

Presbyterian, and Baptist churches, every congregation chooses its own minister, a practice which has been continued without intermission from its settlement. It is also divided universally into parochial districts. Yet no considerable evils have flowed from the practice throughout this long period. It is questioned whether any collection of churches, equally numerous, have been more peaceful, more virtuous, or more happy. Of the evils which have arisen also, very few have, I believe, sprung from this source. At the same time to choose, or to have a voice in choosing, for myself and my family the man who is to guide us to immortal life is a privilege which I deem inestimable, and to be yielded up only when it cannot be retained. But the prime proof of the injuriousness of your church patronage to the cause of religion is found in its effects, particularly in those recited by this letter writer, and by the Earl of Harrowby: † effects which, it should seem, could hardly spring from any other cause.[8] Were it in your power to adopt a different system, I cannot but suspect that you would scarcely continue the present.

On the *neglect, or carelessness, of your clergy in their pastoral duties,* the letter writer observes that a great proportion of them are wrapped up in secular pursuits; and betray, he fears, an indifference of conduct and a dissoluteness of manners which, while it is most shameful in them, would not be borne with in any other state of life. "A horse race," he says "a fox chase, a boxing match is never without its reverend attendants; and the man who in the house of God hurries over the offices of devotion as beneath his attention will be seen the next day the noisy toastmaster or songster of a club." Their professional indolence, he contrasts with their occasional activity at a county election, in a cathedral, county, or town. "You have the honor of finding yourself in such contests," he says "acting in concert with deans, chancellors, archdeacons, prebendaries, and minor canons without number—on such occasions grave, very grave persons indeed, are to be seen shouting the chorus of some election ribaldry." [9]

*"Single* duty," that is, I suppose, going through the service once upon the Sabbath, he says, "is performed sometimes only every other Sabbath." As to the manner of the performance he observes, "A clergyman who gallops to the church gallops through the service, and gallops away again. The Decalogue is hurried over in the desk with as little ceremony as the detail of a fox chase; and in many parishes the whole morning service does not, including the sermon, occupy three quarters of an hour." "Original composition," he observes, "is scarcely known among the clergy;" and even their selections he represents as injudicious, and so often repeated as to be quite familiar to the audience; and finally he declares that "pastoral visits are not only greatly neglected, but even their obligation is denied; and the clergy are

† See Review of a Speech of the Earl of Harrowby, Christian Observer 1811, p. 380.

convinced that the duties of hospitality, and of domestic instruction, and consolation, to the young, the depraved, the decrepit, and the dying, form no part of the demands which their parishioners have upon them." [10]

The Christian Observer, speaking with reference to this part of the subject, says, "These are times in which we must sorrowfully own that the ministry of the established church are held in a disrespect unknown in former days. There is but little or no respect to their office, as such."

I have chosen to appeal to these papers for two reasons. One is that, living in a distant country, and having never been in Great Britain, it cannot be supposed that I am personally acquainted with the state of the established church. Whatever knowledge I possess of this subject, derived from books and men, whether Englishmen or Americans, you, or others, might perhaps be disposed to question; and thus my remarks, however just, might be left in a state of uncertainty, or perhaps absolutely discredited. The other is that, as I am a Presbyterian, you might believe me less candid with respect to this subject than I intend to be.

To the present appeal no objection can, I presume, be reasonably made. Permit me then to say, with the exception heretofore made, that in the collection of churches in New England which are Presbyterian or Congregational such clergymen as are here described are unknown. We have some bad ministers, they are, however, *rarae aves*. But a minister who spent his time, or any part of it, in the dissipation specified by this letter writer would here be regarded as a prodigy. I never knew one who in this country could have these things said of him with truth. Few have I known, very few, who were not believed to be persons of piety. No minister belonging to these churches thinks of such a thing as selecting sermons. Every minister preaches two sermons every Sabbath, and always composes them both himself. Let me add, the great body of them are of course religious, fraught with the spirit of the Gospel, and very generally judicious. Many of them are excellent. It is impossible that a man who devotes himself at all to his study, or his parochial concerns, should compose so many sermons and get them by heart. They are, therefore, generally read; and the inhabitants are so far persuaded that written discourses, taken together, are more instructive and profitable than extemporaneous ones that they are well satisfied with this manner of preaching, and usually prefer it. There is, however, a considerable exception to what I have here asserted. A number of ministers, and not a very small one, when they have arrived to middle life, and have become familiarized to the doctrines and duties of theology, preach either from short notes, or extemporaneously: studying their discourses, however, more laboriously perhaps than when they are written. Instruction is here the ruling character of preaching, rather than addressing the feelings or the imagination. In behalf of this mode I allege three reasons. One is that religion has nowhere more prevailed than in the old settlements of New England. Another is that the people are nowhere less blown about by every wind of doctrine. The third is that sound instruction is more satisfactory to an audience, and generally more popular.

I have read a considerable number of the most celebrated British sermons, and think it no injustice to say that we have many which are not at all inferior to most of them in good sense, sound theology, or the power of making deep impressions on the conscience. None of them can boast the eloquence and sublimity of Robert Hall, but some of them are eloquent and sublime. At the same time they are rarely trifling; rarely are they merely attempts to display the preacher to advantage. We have no Sydney Smith sermons, gewgaws intended to be shown, like a diamond ring or snuffbox, to prove that the preacher is the owner of such trinkets. Rarely are they intended to be mere means of whiling away the time. We have no fifteen minute sermons. Rarely are they regarded by the preacher as an oppressive tax upon his industry, a hard task through which he struggles, as a lazy schoolboy through his lesson, because he cannot escape from his thralldom. We have few, very few, of those preachers whom the author of *The Task* reprobates; but many, very many, of those whom he commends.[11] Our preachers in great numbers are:

> simple, grave, sincere;
> In doctrine uncorrupt; in language plain;
> And plain in manner. Decent, solemn, chaste,
> And natural in gesture. Much impress'd
> Themselves, as conscious of their awful charge,
> And anxious mainly, that the flock they feed,
> May feel it too. Affectionate in look,
> And tender in address, as well becomes
> The messengers of peace to guilty men.

On the subject of *nonresidence,* I cannot express my astonishment. The Christian Observer excited it to a high pitch by recording the numbers of nonresident clergymen for three years. The speech of Lord Harrowby left me in absolute amazement. This is the most rotten part of your whole system. What, Sir, do your clergymen, after the solemn vows of ordination, feel themselves at liberty to desert their cures and give up the salvation of their flocks to the care of accident, to "a stranger whom they will not follow," to "a hireling whose own the sheep are not," and, who, "when he seeth the wolf coming, leaveth the sheep and fleeth; and the wolf catcheth them, and scattereth the sheep."? [12] For what purpose were the ministers ordained? For what purpose were they presented to benefices? Was it that they might obtain sufficient money to support them in a pleasant town, in an agreeable circle of acquaintance, in a round of pleasures, and those, if this letter writer is to be credited, not unfrequently gross and openly sinful? Is a minister then to forsake his people entrusted to him by the Eternal God, that by "taking heed unto himself, and unto the doctrine of the Gospel; and by continuing in them, he might both save himself and them that should hear him," [13] for a horse race, a card table, a fox chase, a drawing room, and a theater? Are those whose great duty it is to "watch for souls, as they who must give account," [14] to leave these very souls to perish, without an effort and as it would seem without a wish to save them? And are there 6,120 such ministers in the established Church of England? I cease to wonder that men of consideration among her members are alarmed for her danger. I cease to wonder that dissenters multiply in the astonishing manner mentioned by Lord Harrowby. Such clergymen certainly believe nothing of the Gospel, and care nothing about their ordination vows or the duties of their ministry.

*There is not, there never was, a nonresident clergyman in New England.* In the account which I gave of Keene in New Hampshire, I mentioned a Mr. S[prague], of Dublin in that vicinity, who in a very limited sense might be entitled to this appellation. But even in this sense he was nonresident only for three or four years, and during that period spent a considerable part of the week and the whole Sabbath regularly among his parishioners. To your *advowsons,* this evil is owing. Were your ministers chosen by their respective congregations, the nonresidence of the clergy would be terminated forever.

With regard to *ecclesiastical discipline,* I shall only observe that in circumstances like these, it must be expected in vain. In New England no clergyman can be seriously defective in his duty without incurring an ecclesiastical censure. For half the charges recited by this letter writer, he would be deposed.

With respect to the *want of churches,* a few more observations will be necessary.

A writer in the Christian Observer for August 1809, after having advanced a number of arguments in favor of an ecclesiastical establishment, and particularly that there is no single instance upon record where religion has long survived an establishment, says, "It has been usual to controvert this argument by alleging the case of America." [15] He then goes on to present his readers with a table, in which he exhibits what appears to be the amount of the provision made here for the maintenance of religion, and then to trace out, as far as his scanty materials will allow, the consequences of this inadequate provision. I used to wonder at the ignorance of intelligent Englishmen concerning America, and at the mistakes so frequently occurring in respectable publications. I finally concluded, and I presume justly, that the true cause of these facts was that you considered us as too insignificant to merit your attention. Of this I have no wish to complain. But I have a right to be dissatisfied with your *misrepresentations.* You ought to represent us truly, or not at all; and not to begin your representations until you have informed yourselves sufficiently to know what is true.

The table formed by this writer is erroneous in a variety of particulars.

For example, he states that Massachusetts has made full maintenance for the clergy, and that Connecticut has made none. You have already seen the provision made by Connecticut for this body of men. I add that it is as complete, to say the least, as that of Massachusetts. The writer, who signs himself C., says that Massachusetts has a complete establishment. Though this is an unfounded assertion, yet that of Connecticut is not less complete than that of Massachusetts, as you may perceive by recurring to the account already given of it in these letters. Substantially the same is true of New Hampshire also. Imperfectly it is true of Vermont. I am, however, very little interested to rectify the errors of this table. My principal concern is with C.'s account of the consequences of this state of things.

> The full consequences of this system of imperfect establishments are not yet felt in America. Time has not been given for the evils consequent on such an arrangement to come to maturity. But as far as the argument reaches, it is altogether in our favor. Religion, in many provinces, is altogether in ruins; and in the rest the dilapidations are great. *Throughout the whole continent a principle of decay is visible; and everything indicates the speedy downfall,* not only of the regular fabrics of religion in the land, *but of the miserable hovels in which her disciples have hitherto found a refuge.**

Permit me to say that, so far as New England is concerned, this account is essentially untrue. We have no "hovel in which the miserable disciples of religion have hitherto found a refuge"; and her regular fabrics manifest no "principle of decay", nor does anything indicate their "speedy downfall." There are 869 Presbyterian congregations and eighty-one Episcopal in the states of New Hampshire, Massachusetts, Vermont, and Connecticut. Every one of these has a church. Almost every church is decent and in good repair. Almost all are painted, except such as are of brick or stone; and nineteen out of twenty have steeples. A great number have been built in the new settlements; and many others, in the places of such as have been pulled down because the proprietors have wished for larger or handsomer buildings. A multitude of these churches may be pronounced handsome, not indeed in the same sense in which the fine specimens of architecture exhibited by various churches in the city of London are styled handsome. Still, though not answering the demands of the taste and science of a connoisseur in that art, they are beautiful objects to the eye. Nor can anything be more delightful to a traveler than the continual succession of these buildings at intervals of three, four, five, and six miles throughout all the ancient settlements of this country, where, drest in snowy white, they appear like stars amid the universal verdure, unless perhaps his agreeable surprise at finding the same objects in settlements so new as to forbid even the hope, and much more the expectation of seeing them at a period apparently premature. It ought to be added that the spirit which prompts to the settlement of ministers, and to the rebuilding and repairing of churches, is rapidly increasing;

* Christian Observer 1809, p. 502.

not, I confess, everywhere alike, but so extensively as to be fairly pronounced the general character of the country.

C. goes on to observe:

A person distinguished by his rank, virtue, and talents has transmitted the following account to this country. "In consequence of the want of a religious establishment in America, infidelity daily increases; and the very semblance of religion decays rapidly. The congregations are fewest where the population *is greatest,* and are not likely to increase. Many Presbyterian ministers have been dismissed by their congregations without any complaint either against their life or doctrine. There are only three Presbyterian congregations *in Philadelphia,* all which were erected *under the English government.* They have been endeavoring for these thirty years past to erect a fourth congregation, but have not yet been successful. As there is no professor of divinity in many of the seminaries of this country, students put themselves under the care of any minister that they choose. Every minister in the country is also a farmer, and has more dependence on his farm than on his stipend for subsistence. For, although congregations in the country subscribe at an average about ninety pounds sterling a year for their minister, yet subscribing, and paying, are two very different things in this country. No law can oblige the subscribers to pay their subscriptions, as they sometimes ask time, and when that is expired they plead the statute of limitations. A country minister, therefore, generally speaking, is obliged to work at the *plow* and *wagon* like another farmer, for servants do little work in this country; and most of them can only spare two hours on Saturday afternoon to prepare their sermons and to instruct their students in divinity." Similar testimony might be extracted from other sources. It may be added that there are now in the country letters from various persons in America, stating the general indifference to the interests of religion to be such that, unless the Christian liberality of individuals on this side of the Atlantic afford the necessary rescue, the race of orthodox ministers is likely soon to be extinct. Here then is the result of an experiment made under the most favorable circumstances. Such is the state of America that she now petitions to relight her extinguished fires at the altars of that church she once contemptuously deserted.

This is certainly an extraordinary story. Let us examine it. The first assertion is that infidelity daily increases in America. This "person distinguished by his rank, virtue, and talents" has, you will observe, included within his assertions the whole of the United States. Had he stopped at the southern and western border of New York, it would have been unnecessary for me to have made any remarks upon these declarations, however erroneous. So far as they respect the countries which are the subject of these observations, I feel myself obliged to say that his "virtue and talents" were very unhappily employed. With regard to the state of infidelity and the state of religion in New England, I have already given you my own views. It will be unnecessary to repeat them. It is sufficient to say that the number of professed infidels is small; that the cause of infidelity is broken down; and that not only the semblance, but the substance of religion, instead of decaying rapidly, has rapidly increased, and is still increasing.

"The congregations," the writer asserts, "are fewest where the population is greatest." What I have already said will show that this is untrue. Massachusetts and Connecticut are far the most populous states in the American

Union. I have already shown you the number of congregations contained in these states. I have also given you an estimate of the congregations which would exist in the countries south and west of New England were they as generally established in proportion to the number of inhabitants.

"Many Presbyterian ministers," the writer says, "have been dismissed from their congregations without any complaint against either their life or doctrine." When ministers are dismissed here, which is sometimes the fact, they are almost always dismissed without any complaint against their life or doctrine: for usually neither affords any ground for complaint. But dismissions are few; and, when they take place, the parish is soon provided with another minister of course; and the minister, almost of course, with another parish. Compare this small evil (for that it is an evil I admit) with your own 6,120 nonresident ministers, who dismiss themselves from their cures and their duties.

The writer goes on, "Every minister in the country is also a farmer, and has more dependence on his farm than on his stipend for subsistence." I wish every minister in New England had a farm, and a farm which would contribute more than his stipend to his subsistence. I presume, however, that scarcely one in fifty can boast of such a possession. Land in the old settlements, and often in those which are comparatively new, is sold at such a price as absolutely to forbid this important convenience.

"Subscribing, and paying, are two very different things in this country. No law can oblige the subscribers to pay their subscriptions, as they sometimes ask time, and when that is expired they plead the statute of limitations." In the states of Massachusetts and Connecticut, and I believe in New Hampshire, "subscriptions" of this nature are unknown; and the law compels every man to pay his tax to his minister, and makes all the lands in the parish liable for the salary. In addition to this, a great number of congregations have provided either partial or complete *funds* for the support of their ministers.

It ought further to be added that it is a very unfrequent fact for any part of a clergyman's salary to be collected by law.

This "person distinguished by his rank, virtue, and talents" goes on, "A country minister, therefore, generally speaking, is obliged to work at the *plow* and *wagon* like another farmer, and most of them can only spare two hours on Saturday's afternoon to prepare their sermons and to instruct their students in divinity." I have lived in New England from my birth, with the exception of a single year, and am perhaps as familiarly acquainted with it as any one of its inhabitants; yet, I have never seen a minister working at the plow or the wagon. That such facts have existed I can easily believe, particularly in new settlements, the inhabitants of which are few and poor. For such parishes it is incomparably better that ministers should be settled in them whose subsistence is to be derived partly from their farms, and even from their labor, than that they should be without ministers.

That "most of the clergymen in this country can spare only two hours to prepare their sermons and to instruct their students in divinity" cannot have been said by this writer from his personal knowledge, because it is said without a shadow of truth. That we have some lazy men in the sacred office ought not to be questioned. That the incumbents are generally industrious can no more be questioned. But that there is *one* who can ordinarily "spare only two hours" for either of these purposes, "credat Judæus Apella, non ego." [16]

C., after asserting that other testimony might be obtained to the same purpose, says that "there are now in the country letters from various persons in America, stating the general indifference to religion to be such that, unless the Christian liberality of individuals on this side of the Atlantic afford the necessary rescue, the race of orthodox ministers is likely soon to be extinct." Of this assertion, what I have already said will enable you to judge. If the doctrines universally declared by the editors of the Christian Observer to be orthodox are to be admitted as such, there is no danger that the ministers who hold them in New England will soon be extinct: for their number has long been increasing, is now increasing rapidly, and is likely to increase through an indefinite period.

From this statement you will see that the situation of America is not such, in this part of it at least, "that she now petitions to relight her extinguished fires at the altars of that church which she once contemptuously deserted."

Finally, let me observe that with regard to the number of our churches, and the convenience of their distribution so as to accommodate the wants of the whole community, we have greatly the advantage over the Church of England itself. I believe I might safely add that the churches in your small towns and villages are, taken together, much less beautiful than ours.

I am, Sir, yours, etc.

# LETTER X

*Articles of faith held by the first settlers of New England—Episcopalians, Baptists, Universalists, Methodists, and Antinomians—Jemima Wilkinson—Roman Catholics —Friends—Sandemanians—Shakers*

*Dear Sir,*

There is another view in which the religion of this, and indeed of every other country, ought to be considered by him who would either describe or understand it in a comprehensive manner. To this I will now proceed.

The original planters of New England, viz. the Plymouth colonists, held:

1. That the Scriptures only contain the true religion, and that nothing which is not contained in them is obligatory upon the conscience;

2. That every man has the right of judging for himself, of trying doctrines by them, and of worshipping according to his apprehensions of their meaning;

3. That the doctrinal articles of the Reformed Churches of England, Scotland, Ireland, France, the Palatinate, Geneva, Switzerland, and the United Provinces are agreeable to the holy oracles;

4. That the pious members of all these churches were to be admitted to their communion;

5. That no particular church ought to consist of more members than can conveniently watch over one another, and usually meet and worship in one congregation;

6. That every such church is to consist of those only who appear to believe in Christ and to obey him;

7. That any competent number of such persons have a right to embody themselves in a church for their mutual edification;

8. That this ought to be done by an *express covenant;*

9. That, when embodied, they have a right to choose all their officers;

10. That these officers are pastors or teaching elders, ruling elders, and deacons;

11. That pastors are to oversee, rule, teach, and administer the sacraments, and that they are to be maintained;

12. That the ruling elders are not temporary, but permanent officers, who are to aid the pastor in overseeing and ruling;

13. That the pastors and ruling elders constitute the presbytery, which should be found in every particular church;

14. That the deacons are the treasurers and almoners of the church, and are also to minister at the sacramental table;

15. That these officers can only rule and minister with the consent of the brethren;

16. That no church or church officers have any power over any other church or church officers, but all are equal in their rights and independent in the enjoyment of them;

17. That baptism is a seal of the covenant of grace, and should only be administered to visible believers, together with their unadult children, and that without the sign of the cross, or any other invented ceremony;

18. That the Lord's Supper should be received, as it was at first, in the table posture;

19. That excommunication should be wholly spiritual, and not involve any temporal penalties;

20. That the Lord's day was to be strictly observed throughout, and that fasts and thanksgivings are to be observed as the state of providence requires.

With these tenets the first colonists of New Hampshire, Massachusetts, and Connecticut generally agreed.

The great body of the present inhabitants of New England hold them in substance at the present time. In a few particulars, the Hopkinsians have superadded to the doctrinal part of this system.[1] A considerable number of Arminians and perhaps a greater number of Unitarians inhabit the eastern parts of New England, especially of Massachusetts. A few of both are found elsewhere. In Connecticut I do not know a single Unitarian clergyman among the Congregationalists, and scarcely half a dozen Arminian.

The Episcopalians in the northern states appear generally to hold the Arminian doctrines, and rather as they were taught by Episcopius than by Arminius himself.[2] Their favorite authors among the moderns appear to be Dr. Daubeny and the Bishop of Lincoln.[3] To those who in the English church are called evangelical divines, they are apparently not very friendly. Overton's "True Churchman Ascertained" they seem to regard with a kind of abhorrence.[4]

The Christian Observer has for some time been republishing here, and among the Presbyterians and Congregationalists is one of the most popular periodical works which is at present published in this country. I was informed a short time since by one of the publishers that the number of subscribers who are Episcopalians is almost nothing. The American Episcopalians, at least in the northern states, are generally, I think, of the class who are called high churchmen. At least, this is apparently the character of their clergy.

The Baptists are here divided, as they are in England. One part of them are Calvinistic. The other are, what used to be called in Great Britain, and what are now extensively called here, *Freewillers*. These do not, however, appear to be Arminians in the proper sense. So far as my information extends, they are in considerable numbers fast approximating to deism. Very extensively they appear to consider religion as consisting chiefly in being plunged, to deny the Sabbath as a divine institution, to contemn family prayer, to have few settled ministers, and little even of the external appearance of religion. Many of their preachers are itinerants, and the solemnities of public worship are celebrated by them only occasionally. The moral extent of this evil, I need not explain.

The Calvinistic Baptists are serious, regular, and, to as great an extent as their Calvinistic brethren of other classes, religious. An evil of incalculable magnitude is that their ministers are many of them uneducated men. Another of no small magnitude, common perhaps to all sects living among more numerous bodies of Christians, is the spirit of proselyting. This spirit seems to be always more engaged to make proselytes to the party than converts to religion.

There are a few Universalists scattered through this country, some of whom admit no future punishment; and others, one which will be temporary and disciplinary.

In Vermont and New Hampshire, a sect has lately risen up, the prominent tenet of which is *that the wicked will be destroyed at the Day of Judgment.* Some of the Freewill Baptists are said also to have adopted the same doctrine.

The Methodists in New England, and generally in the United States, are almost all followers of Wesley.[5] I know of but two congregations of Whitefieldian Methodists in New England. These are both at Newburyport, and are supplied with ministers from England.

There is in this country a moderate number of Antinomians.

These are found chiefly in a class of men formerly called *Separatists,* most of whom for the purpose of avoiding the legal obligation of supporting ministers became Baptists. They were generally extremely ignorant, and possessed of strong feelings and warm imaginations, in the exercise of which they chose to find religion, rather than in the faith and obedience of the Gospel. To demand obedience to the divine law, not as the means of justification, but as the duty of men, was stigmatized by them as *legalism,* or as an exaltation of the law of God against the grace of the Gospel; and they appeared to choose to "continue in sin that grace might abound."* [6]

Between twenty and thirty years since, a young woman named Jemima Wilkinson is said while laboring under a fit of sickness to have slept a much longer time than is usual or natural. When she awaked, she announced that she had been in a trance, and had received a great variety of important revelations. She declared herself to be the elect lady to whom St. John addressed his second Epistle.[7] Having collected a small number of followers, she removed with them soon after into the western country of New York, I believe to the borders of the Crooked (Cayuga) Lake. The number of her followers has very little, if at all, increased. Of her peculiar tenets I have no knowledge.

There is in Boston a congregation of Roman Catholics, under the superintendence of two ministers; and there are two others in the District of Maine.

There are several societies of Friends in different parts of Massachusetts, and several more in the state of Rhode Island.

* It is often said, with how much truth I have no means of determining, that a considerable number of the Baptists are Antinomians. I have stated in the text the number as small because I did not feel myself warranted to say otherwise.

In Newport there is a society of Moravians, and a synagogue of Jews.

There is a Sandemanian congregation in Danbury, Connecticut, and another in Portsmouth, New Hampshire.

These with the Shakers are all the classes of religions which I recollect in New England. The five last mentioned classes, exclusive of the Shakers, hold, so far as I know, the same religious opinions which are generally held by their respective denominations.

I am, Sir, yours, etc.

# LETTER XI

*Number of congregations and of ministers in Massachusetts, Maine, New Hamsphire, Connecticut, and Vermont—Churches distributed at small distances*

*Dear Sir,*

I will now give you a particular account of the religious state of this country in another point of view: viz. *as it appears in the number of its congregations* and ministers. These also I shall distribute into their different classes.

| | Congregations |
|---|---|
| Massachusetts | 531 |
| Maine | 221 |
| New Hampshire | 160 |
| Connecticut | 355 |
| Vermont, at least | 154 |
| Rhode Island | |

*In Massachusetts there are*

| | |
|---|---|
| Presbyterian, or Congregational | 341 |
| Presbyterian proper | 6 |
| Episcopal | 10 |
| Baptist | 128 |
| Methodist | 26 |
| Friends | 12 |
| Universalist | 7 |
| Roman Catholic | 1 |
| | 531 |

*In Maine*

| | |
|---|---|
| Presbyterian, or Congregational | 84 |
| Presbyterian proper | 1 |

| | Congregations |
|---|---|
| Episcopal | 4 |
| Baptist | 104 |
| Methodist | 17 |
| Friends | 6 |
| Universalist | 3 |
| Roman Catholic | 1 |
| Lutheran | 1 |
| | 221 |

*In Connecticut*

| | |
|---|---|
| Presbyterian, or Congregational | 216 |
| Episcopal | 61 |
| Baptist | 67 |
| Independent | 9 |
| Sandemanian | 1 |
| Universalist | 1 |
| | 355 |

*In New Hampshire*

| | |
|---|---|
| Presbyterian, or Congregational | 117 |
| Presbyterian proper | 9 |
| Episcopal | 3 |
| Baptist | 22 |
| Methodist | 1 |
| Universalist | 1 |
| Friends | 6 |
| Sandemanian | 1 |
| | 160 |

| In Vermont there are | Ministers |
|---|---|
| Presbyterian, or Congregational, at least | 85 |
| Presbyterian proper | 1 |
| Episcopal | 3 |
| Baptist | 64 |
| Methodist | 1 |
| | 154 |

I have no method of exactly ascertaining the number of congregations in this state. The number of townships is 247. Many of these, however, are recent settlements, and contain but a small number of inhabitants. If we are to judge from the past, particularly from what has taken place within the last fifteen years, there is good reason to conclude that a considerable number of these townships also will establish ministers among them. The legislature, however, has by an act of violence thrown very serious difficulties into the way. The former law on which the regular support of ministers rested, in a manner somewhat similar to that in Connecticut, was not long since repealed; and a new one substituted for it, of a loose and very imperfect nature. By this act the ministers already settled were unsettled in a moment, and their congregations not only released from their engagements to support them, but precluded from the power of renewing those engagements on the former principles. They were compelled to embody themselves anew, and to act in a new manner. Each individual bound himself by a subscription to contribute a certain amount, or his proportion of a stipulated sum, for the future support of his clergyman. The whole transaction appears to have been designed and executed by a spirit of the most determined hostility against religion, and to have been originated by minds totally destitute even of common honesty. Had not the inhabitants at large possessed a better character than that of a majority in their legislature, it should seem that Christianity must have received a fatal blow at this time, and the inhabitants been condemned, in future, to hear nothing from the desk but the wretched harangues of ignorance, clownishness, and separatism. But to the immortal honor of these people, not an individual minister, so far as I have been informed, was compelled to leave his cure. The congregations zealously determined, almost with a single voice, not to be deprived of their ministers; and, availing themselves of the means still in their power, resolved to support them according to the new law. In few cases has such a collection of detached bodies of men acted without concert and in a manner perfectly spontaneous, and yet so honorably to themselves and so beneficially to their children.

Of the Presbyterian congregations in Massachusetts, 341 in number, 333 were supplied with ministers in 1810. Of course there were but eight congregations vacant.

Of the 128 Baptist congregations in the same state, thirty-seven were vacant.

Of the ten Episcopal congregations, three were vacant.

Of the six Presbyterian proper congregations, three were vacant.

Of the seven Universalist congregations, three were vacant.

Of the 216 Presbyterian congregations in Connecticut, twenty-seven were vacant the same year, and 189 were supplied with ministers.

Of the sixty-one Episcopal congregations, thirty-two are pluralities. Of the remaining twenty-nine, four were vacant. Pluralities, you will remember, are congregations too small to be able to support a minister.

Of the sixty-seven Baptist congregations, twenty were vacant.

Of the nine Independent congregations, three were vacant.

The number of congregations in New Hampshire, I am unable to determine with certainty, but have reckoned up 160. The number of townships is 207. It is probable the true number of congregations lies between 160 and 180. These are furnished with 134 ministers, of whom:

| | | |
|---|---|---|
| 104 | are | Presbyterian |
| 5 | " | Presbyterian proper |
| 3 | " | Episcopal |
| 18 | " | Baptist |

| | | |
|---|---|---|
| 2 | are | Methodist |
| 1 | " | Sandemanian |
| 1 | " | Universalist |

I have given you the number of ministers in Vermont; and, therefore, the number of such congregations only as have ministers. The number of those which may properly be called vacancies here cannot be conjectured. The congregations which I have specified amount to 154. The whole number of inhabitants is 217,913. The proportion of ministers to the number of people is, therefore, 1 to 1,415.

In the year 1810, there were in Massachusetts, 472,040; in Maine, 228,705; in New Hampshire, 214,460; in Connecticut, 261,942; in Vermont, 217,913; in Rhode Island, 76,931. There is, therefore, in Massachusetts one congregation to every 888 inhabitants; in Maine, a congregation to every 1,004 inhabitants; in New Hampshire, according to the number stated above, a congregation to every 1,340 inhabitants; in Connecticut, a congregation to every 737 inhabitants.

There were at this time in Massachusetts 438 ministers of different denominations, or one to 1,077 inhabitants; in Connecticut, 265, or one to 988 inhabitants; in Maine, 171 ministers, or one to 1,337; and in New Hampshire, 134 ministers, or one to 1,600 inhabitants.

This proportion, you will remember, is exclusive of the societies of Methodists and Friends.

In the older settlements, these congregations may be said to be evenly diffused, so as to cover the whole ground, each occupying a tract from three to six miles square: the larger towns being excepted. Accordingly, the churches rise everywhere at these distances. Ministers are of course stationed everywhere at a small distance from every inhabitant. This is but partially true of the more recent settlements, but there are the very best reasons to believe that it will soon be true to the same extent of them also.

Every one of these congregations, you will also remember, has its church. Almost all the churches of the Presbyterians are decent buildings, in good repair, comfortable, sufficiently large to contain the whole congregation, painted, and ornamented with steeples. A few are so ancient that the congregations consider them as not worth repairing, particularly as they are able and willing to build new ones; and, in a number of instances much smaller still, the congregation itself may have been lessened by sectarian inroads to such a degree, or may have been originally so small, as to be unable to maintain its minister and repair its church. The new churches built within the last twenty-five years are both numerous and handsome. These also are annually increasing in their number.

The Baptist churches, a few excepted, and those of the Methodists, are small and indifferent buildings. The congregations also of both classes are small, and their ministers are very generally uneducated.

It ought to be observed here that there are a few Methodist congregations in the state of Connecticut. They are universally small, and the number of them I am unable to ascertain.

Both the religious and political writers of England often complain that in many parts of your country churches are not sufficiently numerous to furnish the inhabitants with the means of attending conveniently on public worship. The difficulties which embarrass the raising of new ones, and even of obtaining seats in those which are already erected, are mentioned by them also, with not a little feeling. What cannot fail to surprise an American, it is said that the dissenters find fewer obstacles in increasing the number of their places of public worship than the members of the established church in adding to theirs.

From these evils the people of New England, except those of the recent settlements, are exempted. I have remarked that our churches stand everywhere at convenient distances. Their number in all the established settlements keeps full pace with the population. Every inhabitant also who enters a church finds a seat of course. In Boston, the sexton has customarily waited at the door until the service has begun for the purpose of introducing strangers who may enter it to a seat. In the country towns, where all the inhabitants are known to all, the moment a stranger enters the church door he will see the doors of the pews immediately opened to invite him in. The poorest man, whenever he will come, is of course welcomed to the house of God.

We have, it is true, no cathedrals. These vast and magnificent edifices, so much boasted of by English writers (nor will I say improperly), have not yet begun to ascend the American shore. There is not in New England, and I believe not in the United States, a single church so large as not to be conveniently filled by the voice of the preacher. But if our churches are not distinguished by the grandeur of cathedrals they are perfectly suited to the convenience of the inhabitants and the great design for which churches are erected. They are in the strict sense houses for public worship. I mean that this is their whole destination. The expense laid out upon one of your cathedrals would build many churches. I will not say that it was not well laid out; but I will say that every man in England, and every other country, ought to be able, as in the older settlements of this, to find a church within a reasonable distance of his own habitation, and to find a seat in that church which he may occupy without molestation and without impropriety.

I am, Sir, yours, etc.

# CHARACTERISTICS OF THE MEN AND WOMEN IN NEW ENGLAND

## LETTER I

*The personal appearance of the inhabitants—Their gravity, etc.—General remarks on the influence of theaters and plays on society*

*Dear Sir,*

The persons of the New Englanders, their complexion, manners, and language, so much resemble those of Englishmen that the similarity has, as you know, been the subject of not a little discussion on both sides of the Atlantic in the knotty case of impressing seamen. Differences, however, exist which are discernible without much difficulty. The English, if I may be permitted to judge from those whom I have seen, are as a body fairer than we, have oftener hair of a light color and blue eyes. They are more frequently fleshy. Our countrymen are taller, more agile, have frequently dark hair and black eyes, and the muscles are more strongly marked both in the limbs and in the face.

The climate of this country, and perhaps the mode of living, have, I think, had a perceptible influence on both the complexion and figure of the New England people. Still, a multitude of very fair complexions are found everywhere; and flaxen, auburn, golden, and still lighter colored hair is seen in very numerous instances.

The natives of New England are generally straight and well formed. I have seen great numbers of Europeans from Great Britain, Ireland, France, and Germany, and from these specimens have no reason to believe that we are inferior to either of these nations in personal appearance. Deformed persons are found here; but, I have good reason to believe, as rarely as in any country under heaven. There is however one particular in which we are said to fall behind most and probably all of these nations. It is supposed that our teeth more generally decay at an untimely period than theirs.

The philosophers and reviewers of Europe have already decided that our talents are below the European standard. From such tribunals it will be in vain to appeal. In energy and activity of mind we are behind no people. There is nothing which promises a benefit at all adequate to the expense of the effort which a New Englander will not cheerfully undertake. Nor are the inhabitants of any country possessed of more numerous or more efficacious resources in their own minds to insure success to the undertaking. Whether we are brave or cowardly, I will leave to be decided by the battles of Breed's Hill, Hoosick, Stillwater, and Saratoga, and by the attack on Stony Point. Their energy is evinced by the spirit with which they have subdued an immeasurable wilderness, and with which they visited every part of the ocean for fishing, and every town on its shore for commerce. And let me add that their ingenuity is scarcely less conspicuous in the unceasing succession of inventions with which they have improved and are still improving the methods of performing operations in agriculture, manufactures, and the mechanic arts, and increasing the various conveniences of life.

With this active spirit, they unite a general disposition to a quiet, orderly, and obliging deportment, to treat strangers and each other with civility, to submit readily to lawful authority, and to obey even the recommendations of their rulers. They are also social; attached to conversation; accustomed from early life to take an interest in the concerns of others; and habitually to feel from childhood that they have, and ought to have, a real interest in these concerns.

We are said to be grave. Gravity is merely a comparative term. It is therefore impossible to know precisely what is meant by it, unless we know also the standard of comparison referred to by him who uses it. That which is grave to the eye of a Frenchman would be levity in the view of a Spaniard. The New England people appear to discern with as much readiness, clearness, and certainty as any people perhaps in the world what is commonly or indeed justly intended by propriety, and as regularly to estimate things according to their real value. The truth unquestionably is, our social meetings are probably as cheerful, sprightly, and replenished as often with sallies of wit and good humor as those of any other people.

On grave subjects we are grave, and on such subjects we are more accustomed to dwell with pleasure than men less disposed to admit the doctrines and duties of divine revelation. It must be acknowledged that we think, converse, and write much less concerning theaters and actors than the inhabitants of London, as they do than the inhabitants of Paris. Amusements are not here the principal concern of life; nor, among amusements, do we consider plays as possessing the best character, or the happiest influence on the interests of man. The views of the New England people at large are not unhappily expressed by Riesbeck, in his Travels through Germany, Letter thirty-six:

> You may recollect the excellent note of a Tyrolese monk upon a passage in Columella, published by the author of *Voyages en différents pays de l'Europe*. It contains the strongest evidence that history can give that a country in which those arts which contribute chiefly to amusement are held in high estimation, and are the most successful way of gaining honor and fortune, is a country verging fast to ruin. You will say that the fault is not in the arts and sciences themselves. Right;

but when they get a certain superiority throughout a nation over the other employments of the mind, they must draw destructive consequences after them. Frivolity, weakness, profusion, neglect of more laborious pursuits and occupations, ostentation, wrong judgment in choosing the servants of the state, a warm and immoderate desire of ornaments, etc. are necessary consequences of all these elegancies when they are carried to that abuse which borders so near on the good use of them. And what do they contribute to the real happiness of men? Are they anything more than a splendid dream? How short too has this era been with all nations! After the generation of wits, generally there has succeeded a totally illiterate horde, who have awakened those the arts had put to sleep with blows, and laid them in chains before they had well rubbed their eyes. How long is it since the days of Corneille and Racine? And we are already exhausted! Poor nation! [1]

There are certainly much higher interests among mankind, even in this world, than amusements; and, in my own view, and as I fully believe in that of ninety-nine hundredths of my countrymen, there are many amusements in the whole number amply sufficient for such a life as this, which on the one hand are less questionable as to their moral tendency, less expensive, and less injurious to the public welfare than those of the drama; while on the other, they are more within the common reach, more satisfactory to the retrospective eye, and better fitted to invigorate the languishing powers both of body and mind.

To common sense hardly anything seems more frivolous than the unremitted attempts at criticism which load the journals of travelers and reviewers, magazines, and other periodical publications concerning plays, unless perhaps the sagacious remarks of the same writers which unhappily abound also concerning the players. Of how little consequence to the happiness of man are the former of these subjects; and how insignificant, when estimated on the scale either of morality or intelligence, are in almost every instance the latter. I have read many plays, particularly such as have been most celebrated, and many criticisms upon them, for criticism has always been one of my favorite studies; nor have I been unacquainted with the history of players, or with strictures upon their talents and merits. I am also perfectly aware that a well-acted play of superior merit is capable of affording a high degree of pleasure to a mind attempered to such a performance. Still, I believe that a great part of the importance given to these exhibitions by the writers in question owes its existence merely to fashion. Were theaters once to become unfashionable resorts, I am satisfied that the greater part of the connoisseurship now lavished upon them would vanish; and that most of the writers who now make so much bustle concerning these subjects would be ashamed of the employment, and regret that they had trifled in this manner with their own talents and with the public.

The truth, if I mistake not, is that these persons pour out very few of these effusions from the heart. The subjects of their criticism are less important in their own view than we are taught to imagine. They are seized because it is believed, on the one hand, that they will engage the attention of the public, and, on the other, that they furnish advantageous materials for displaying the ingenuity and taste of the writer. When, therefore, I see criticism drained to its last dregs upon these subjects, I cannot avoid asking: Of what real use are either the subjects or the criticism? Can mere means of amusement pretend even decently to claim such regard? Much more, can means of amusement, scarcely ever free from gross immorality, and usually little else but means of corruption, claim any regard at all? Can men and women almost invariably profligate, among whom were you to collect them together from all ages and countries, you would hardly find the decade required for the exemption of Sodom from the flaming ruin which hung over her polluted ground to save them from a similar destruction; can such men and such women as are presented to the world in the "history of the greenroom"; can men and women whom the ancient church would not baptize, and even the Romish Church will not bury, engage from generation to generation the sober thoughts, the diligent labors of learning and good sense, of taste and criticism? Nay, what is unspeakably more, shall they employ the time of men professing to be Christians, men professedly bound toward Heaven, solemnly renouncing in the house of God the vanities of this world, and engaging to abstain from all appearance of evil? Still more, shall plays and players command the pens of clergymen, men declaring themselves to be, in their own belief, *verily moved by the Holy Ghost to the assumption of their office,* and promising with the most awful vows to devote themselves wholly to the great duty of turning mankind to righteousness and conducting them to endless life?

I shall be told in answer to these questions that the drama includes within its precincts some of the first efforts of human genius. The names of Aeschylus, Sophocles, and Euripides, of Corneille and his splendid train of followers, of the immortal Shakespeare and his, and perhaps too of Schiller and Kotzebue, will be conjured upon the stage to refute these observations, and convict their authors of weakness and folly.[2] I am not to be informed at this period of the talents of these writers. The superiority of their powers I acknowledge in its full extent; but I assert, and without fear of seeing the assertion disproved, that they were employed in such a manner as to produce little good and much evil. Among all their productions there is scarcely one which an apostle would even read. How great a part of them are little else than splendid vehicles of vice. Taken together, and especially when presented on the stage by such men and women as act, and to such men and women as look on, they are only a vast and fascinating system of profligacy. Shall genius command respect while employed in poisoning mankind, or in gilding the poison?

But I shall be charged with bigotry. The force of argument contained in this accusation, I do not feel sufficiently to wish to refute it. What man of common sense can be solicitous about the disgrace attached to it, when he remembers that the Athenians accused Socrates of this crime, and the Jews, the apostles and even the Saviour.

Finally, I shall be declared to be destitute of taste. From this decision I shall make no appeal. If it is the proper prerogative of taste to be sustained in the world at the expense of morals and religion, if it is the criterion of taste to approve of the stage, if it is the dictate of taste to prefer amusement to virtue, I shall feel no interest in repelling the censure.

Permit me to add that nothing but the countenance of respectable men, respectable for their talents at least, would, as I believe, continue the existence of dramatic exhibitions, certainly not on any plan which has hitherto been executed. It is the splendor of this countenance which has so long dazzled the eyes even of sober men, and prevented the mighty moral considerations which are marshaled against this evil from driving it out of the world.

But whatever may be thought of the value of amusements, or of the nature of the stage, it is certain that the people of New England consider the former as of far less importance than the sober business of life, and the latter as having little claim to respect or even to indulgence. It is here extensively believed that the profession of a player is scandalous, and that the stage is a nuisance. The clergyman who should make a business of attending dramatic exhibitions would probably lose his parish, and not improbably his office. This jealousy for the purity of the ministerial character will, I presume, be denounced as bigotry by not a few fashionable people. For myself, I rejoice in it, and cordially hope that the time will never come when a minister in this country can be safely destitute of the character required of all who hold this office by St. Paul in his Epistles to Timothy and Titus.

In every case respecting amusements, the sound common sense of my countrymen induces them to ask the old Roman question, *cui bono erit?* [3] The answer to this question usually determines the cause at issue.

I will only add that the people of New England find no want of amusements. Time rarely hangs heavily upon their hands. In the acquisition of property for themselves and their families, in educating their children, in attending to the affairs of their school districts, parishes, and townships, in being present at elections and courts of justice, in performing the duties of piety and charity, in riding, visiting, reading, and various other employments of a nature not dissimilar, they pass through life as easily, cheerfully, and usefully as most of their fellow men.

I am, Sir, yours, etc.

# LETTER II

*Opinion of a writer in the Quarterly Review relative to the women of this country examined—The features, manners, and employments of the women of New England —Their education*

*Dear Sir,*

The female sex in every country have a high claim to the minute attention of an inquisitive traveler. As it has been decided by high authority that there is, "both in the physical and intellectual features of the Americans, a trace of savage character, not indeed produced by crossing the breed, but by the circumstances of society and of external nature," it is, I presume, believed in Great Britain that, as the men here are either partially or wholly Indians, our women must of course be squaws. We ought to feel ourselves not a little obliged to this writer in the Quarterly Review for saving a part of the little reputation allowed to us, by informing the world that our savageness is not derived *"from crossing the breed."* [1] Unquestionably it does not flow from this source. Of all the inhabitants of this world, there are none so delicate on this subject as those of New England. If their blood was pure at first, it remains pure. Still we are destined, it seems, to a savageness less remediable and more absolutely hopeless; a savageness derived not only from the state of society, but also from circumstances of an external nature. As our forests through a great part of this country have for a century been so extensively felled as scarcely to have left sufficient timber and fuel for the necessary use of the inhabitants, and as the waters of the Atlantic flow in much the same manner here as on the shores of Europe, the cause of this great national calamity must undoubtedly be sought for in our hills and valleys, our plains and mountains, our lakes and rivers. Whether all these are supposed to contribute their share towards the production of our savage character, or whether the calamity is to be ascribed to a part or to one of them, I am unable to determine. I have indeed seen some remarks of a British writer concerning the cataract of Niagara in which he plainly considered that stupendous work of nature as fitted to inspire feelings only wild and horrid.

We construe passages in the book of nature as well as in the book of revelation very differently. The sentiments awakened in my own mind and in the minds of my companions by the sight of this wonderful object were only those of amazing grandeur and singular elevation. The mighty hand which formed the universe and rolls its worlds through immensity seemed here to be peculiarly visible, and the mind traced with the eye of intuition the footsteps of its Maker. Permit me to congratulate myself that the intense pleasure which I found in surveying this scene was not disturbed by the unfortunate emotions awakened here in the mind of the writer to whom I have alluded. The view of Lake Erie also, although considered as a part of that inundation which has so recently overspread the continent of America, and although plainly regarded by the Count de Buffon and expressly assigned by M. de Pauw as one cause both of our bodily and mental imperfections, excited no ideas in my own mind but those of pre-eminent beauty, magnificence, and splendor.

The loftiest elevation in the United States is Mount Washington. Its height has not, I believe, been ascertained. It is, however, several thousand feet below the summit of Mont Blanc, and not a little inferior to other Alpine eminences. What influence these lofty points have on the minds and manners of those who live beneath and around them, I acknowledge myself to have learned but very imperfectly. I have been accustomed to believe that the Swiss have long been distinguished for mild and charming simplicity of manners, and to this opinion I had been led particularly by some of your own writers of reputation. Nor did I discover anything peculiarly savage in those inhabitants of New Hampshire who lived in the neighborhood of Mount Washington. My friend Rosebrook, whose Arcadian name may, however, have had a benign influence upon his character, was certainly, though when I last saw him he had resided fifteen years within five miles both of the notch and the summit of the White Mountains, as good-natured, mild, and soft-tempered a farmer as will easily be found. There was, it is true, one trace of savageness in his wife. She unfortunately preferred Bohea tea to Hyson, and was therefore unwilling to keep Hyson in her house, observing with some degree of decision that, "if Bohea tea was good enough for her, it was good enough for travelers." This trace of savage character certainly was not derived from crossing the breed. From the circumstances of society it could not be easily derivable, for there was no society with which the good lady could mingle except that of travelers, and most of these would undoubtedly have voted in favor of the Hyson tea. We must, therefore, however reluctant, believe that she caught it either from the summit or the notch of the White Mountains. I ought in justice to observe that, bating this untoward fact, the whole family were kind, gentle, and obliging. Even the old lady herself in other respects merited this character. For although she had a prejudice against green tea, she very cheerfully furnished her guests with coffee.

There is one circumstance relative to this subject which it seems difficult to reconcile with the learned decision quoted above. It is this. Not one of one thousand of the New England people ever visited the White Mountains, the Great Lakes, or the cataract of Niagara. It seems therefore that the *sensible* influence of these objects must be so limited as not materially to affect our national character. This, I acknowledge, does not prove the evil to be underived from the efficacy of their *insensible* influence. With respect to that efficacy I will not dispute the malignant operations of the St. Lawrence and the Mississippi, the great western lakes, the White, or even the Mexican Mountains upon the character of my countrymen. Among the last, candor obliges me to acknowledge that there is one summit, named the Great White Mountain, which was determined by a mensuration of Colonel Pike to be eighteen thousand feet in height.[2] Possibly I may all this time have been puzzling myself, therefore, to no purpose in attempting to find in neighboring objects the cause of this characteristical defect, while the malignant efficacy may have been silently floating in the westerly winds from the Mississippi, or the Mexican Mont Blanc.

Had it not been for this unfortunate decision, I should have boldly asserted that there is not in the world a more amiable collection of women than those of my own country. Permit me to describe their character as, notwithstanding the authority of this sentence, they still appear to my own eyes.

The women of New England are generally well, and often elegantly, formed. Their features have usually a good degree of regularity, are comely, and frequently handsome. Their complexion, like that of the men, is not so generally fair as that of the Irish, British, and other European women in the north, but very sensibly fairer than that of the French women; and a vast number of them have complexions inferior to none in the world. In great numbers they have fine eyes, both blue and black, and generally possess that bloom which health inimitably suffuses over a beautiful countenance. But regular features united with the most delicate complexion cannot form beauty. This charming attribute so coveted by one sex, and so fascinating to the other, is, as an eminent poet of your country has said:

> an air divine,
> Through which the mind's all gentle graces shine;
> They, like the sun, irradiate all between;
> And the face charms, because the soul is seen.[3]

In this respect the women of New England to a great extent triumph. Their minds, often possessing a fine share of intelligence, are remarkably distinguished by amiable dispositions. A gentle and affectionate temper, ornamented with sprightliness and gilded with serenity, may be fairly considered as being extensively their proper character. They are said by some of your countrymen to be too feminine, and are certainly less masculine than most of their sex who have visited these states from England or the European continent. To us, this is a delightful part of their character.

Their manners are in entire symmetry with their minds and faces. An universal sweetness and gentleness, blended with sprightly energy, is their most predominant characteristic. There is nothing languid in their deportment, and rarely anything affected. They are affable, obliging, and cheerful; while they are at the same time grave, discreet, and very rarely betrayed into any impropriety.

Very many of them are distinguished for moral excellence; are unaffectedly pious, humble, benevolent, patient, and self-denying. In this illustrious sphere of distinction, they put our own sex to shame. Were the church of Christ stripped of her female communicants, she would lose many of her brightest ornaments, and, I fear, two thirds of her whole family.

In perfect accordance with this representation, the women of New England perform in an exemplary manner the various duties of life. They are almost universally industrious, economical, attentive to their families, and diligent in the education and government of their children. They are to a great extent excellent wives, mothers, and daughters. Few countries, it is believed, present in proportion to the number of their inhabitants so many instances of domestic good order, peace, and happiness.

The employments of the women of New England are wholly domestic. The business which is abroad is all performed by men, even in the humblest spheres of life. That of the house is usually left entirely to the direction of the women, and is certainly managed by them with skill and propriety. Domestic concerns admit of improvement and even of science; and it must, I believe, be acknowledged that we might learn in this particular several useful things from you. Our economy is less systematical and less perfect than yours, and our activity sometimes less skillfully directed. I am apprehensive, however, that we approach nearer to you in the house than either in the shop or the field. The houses in this country are, with their furniture, almost all kept in good order; and a general neatness prevails, even among those who are in humble circumstances. Indeed a great part of the women in this country exert quite as much industry as is consistent with the preservation of health.*

There is another employment in which I think they merit high encomiums. This is the diffusion of beneficence among the suffering. In this they far excel the other sex, and discover more skill, more patience, more activity, and universally more excellence.

From these observations you will easily perceive that the female sex hold here an honorable station in society and have an important influence upon

* See on this subject at large, the remarks on Lambert. ["Remarks on European Travelers in America," Letter IV.]

its concerns. The first place at the table in the family, in the social circle, and in every other situation where they are found is given to them of course. On all occasions they are treated with marked attention and respect, and the man who behaves rudely or insolently to a woman is considered as hardly meriting the name.

I have already given you a summary account of the manner in which young misses are educated in this country. They are all sent early to school, where they are taught to spell, and read, and write. From parochial schools, many of them are transferred to boarding schools and academies. Here they learn to understand arithmetic, which indeed is usually taught them in parochial schools, and study English grammar, geography, history to some extent, criticism, and composition. In a few instances they are taught moral science, and in some ascend to higher branches of mathematics, the Latin and French languages. To these are added embroidery, drawing, and music.

On this subject I feel bound to observe that we are in my own opinion seriously defective. Efforts of a higher nature than any which we make are due to their daughters from all persons who are possessed of wealth. The great doctrines of physical and moral science are as intelligible by the mind of a female as by that of a male; and, were they made somewhat less technical, and stripped so far of some of their unnecessary accompaniments as to wear in a greater degree the aspect of common sense, might be introduced with advantage into every female academy where the instructor was competent to teach them. It is evidently high time that women should be considered less as pretty, and more as rational and immortal beings; and that so far as the circumstances of parents will permit, their minds should be early led to the attainment of solid sense and sound wisdom. The instructions which are, or ought to be, given by mothers are of more importance to the well-being of children than any which are, or can be, given by fathers. To give these instructions, they ought, as far as may be, to be thoroughly qualified, even if we were to act on selfish principles only. Such a design, extensively reduced to practice, would in any country change the whole state of society, and raise it to a dignity of which it is otherwise incapable.

The disposition to provide a superior education for female children is in this country widely diffused and continually increasing. No regular scheme, however, has been formed on this subject within my knowledge; and I have hitherto met with no books which treat the sciences last specified in a manner satisfactory either to my views or to my wishes. It is earnestly to be hoped that ere long both these defects may be supplied, and that the women of this country, who, so far as they possess advantages, appear in no respect to be behind the other sex either in capacity or disposition to improve, may no longer be precluded from the best education by the negligence of men.

It is said, and I suspect with truth, that the American women lose their beauty and the brilliancy of youth at an earlier period of life than in

England. A great part of them are slender. Multitudes lose their teeth at an untimely date, and many of them part with their bloom before they are thirty years of age. The causes of these disadvantages belong to the province of the learned among physicians. I may be permitted, however, to observe that among them abstemiousness, which here is very general in that sex and often excessive, probably has its share. The want of sufficient exercise abroad has a still more malignant influence. Sedentariness seems regularly to be considered as intimately connected with the gentility of the female character. Walking is very little practised; and riding on horseback, notwithstanding it exhibits the female figure to so much advantage, is almost out of the question. Until there is a material change in these respects, the women of New England must be satisfied to yield their health, and youth, and bloom, and beauty, as an untimely sacrifice to the moloch of fashion. The teeth of children, their mothers might preserve. Nothing more would be necessary than to compel them to commence life with vigorous exercise, and continue it; to avoid hot drinks, particularly, by requiring their children to eat milk, or thoroughly to dilute with it their tea and coffee; and to make their teeth cold by agitating cold water in the mouth five times a day, that is, once in the morning, once in the evening, and once after each meal. Could we learn wisdom from the Asiatics and habituate ourselves to regular bathing, and follow that of our ancestors by permitting children when at school to play during the session half an hour in the morning and half an hour in the afternoon, encouraging those of both sexes to vigorous activity, the work of preserving health would in a great measure be accomplished.

To the character which I have given of the women of New England, there are unquestionably many exceptions. We have homely women, we have ignorant women, we have silly women, we have coarse women, and we have vicious women. At the same time we have no reason in these particulars to dread a comparison with other countries. In the most fashionable life we have frivolous women, who, having nothing to do, or choosing to do nothing of a useful nature, find time hangs heavily on them. To relieve themselves from the ennui flowing of course from the want of regular and useful engagements, women of this description crowd to the theater, the assembly room, the card table, routs, and squeezes; flutter from door to door on ceremonious visits, and from shop to shop to purchase what they do not want, and to look at what they do not intend to purchase; hurry to watering places to recover health which they have not lost, and hurry back again in pursuit of pleasure which they cannot find. Happily, the number of these is not very great, even in our cities.

I am, Sir, yours, etc.

# MANUFACTURES OF NEW ENGLAND

*Extracts from the Report of the Secretary of the Treasury, April 19, 1810—General account of the manufactures of Massachusetts and of Connecticut—Account of the manufactures of Rhode Island, with a history of their origin*

*Dear Sir,*

I will now present you with a few observations on the manufactures of this country. Before I attempt to specify the agency and influence of New England, it will be proper to take some notice of the general state of manufactures in the country at large.

Returns were made to the national government at the time when the last census was taken of all the manufactures which were of any considerable importance, and Congress committed to several gentlemen the business of arranging and publishing in a volume the particulars of which they were composed. For this volume I have hitherto waited in vain. Should it see the light before these letters are finished, I shall certainly avail myself of the information which it shall communicate. At present my guide must be a Report drawn up by the secretary of the treasury and referred, April 19, 1810, to a committee of the House of Representatives.[1]

The following manufactures, Mr. Gallatin observes, are carried on in the United States to such an extent as to supply the wants of the inhabitants, those of the same kinds which are imported amounting to less than those which are exported:

Manufactures of wood
Leather
Soap
Tallow Candles
Spermaceti Oil
Spermaceti Candles
Linseed Oil
Refined Sugar
Coarse Earthenware
Snuff
Chocolate
Mustard
Hair Powder

The following manufactures, he observes, are firmly established, and supply in some instances the greater, and in all a considerable part of the whole consumption:

Bar Iron
Manufactures of Iron
Cotton, Wool, and Flax
Hats
Paper
Printing Types
Printed Books
Playing Cards
Spirituous and Malt Liquors
Several manufacturers of Hemp
Gunpowder
Window Glass
Jewelry
Clocks
Several manufactures of Straw Bonnets and Hats
Lead
Wax Candles

Progress, Mr. Gallatin observes, has also been made in the following branches:

- Paints and Colors
- Several Chemical Preparations
- Medicinal Drugs
- Salt
- Manufactures of Copper and Brass
- Japanned Ware
- Plated Ware
- Calico Printing
- Queen's and other Earthenwares

Many other articles, the secretary supposes, are undoubtedly omitted, the information actually obtained having been in many respects imperfect.

Under the head of manufactures of wood, he observes that they consist of vessels, household furniture, and carriages for pleasure and for transportation. All of them are carried to a high degree of perfection.

Of vessels above twenty tons burden, there were built during seven years from 1801 to 1807, 774,922 tons: a little more than 110,000 tons in a year, worth more than six million dollars annually. Two thirds of these were registered for the foreign trade, and the remaining third for the fisheries and the coasting trade.

The annual exportation of furniture and carriages amounted to 170,000 dollars.

The yearly value of all the manufactures of wood was 20,000,000 dollars.

Of pot and pearl ashes referred by the secretary to this head, 7,400 tons are annually exported.

Of manufactures of leather, Mr. Gallatin observes that the exportations amount to more than twice the value of the importations, and that the whole value of all the articles of this class annually manufactured is 20,000,000 dollars. The value of the soap and the tallow candles, he estimates at 8,000,000 dollars. The annual importations were candles, 158,000 lbs.; soap, 470,000 lbs.

The annual exportations of domestic manufacture were candles, 1,775,000 lbs.; soap, 2,220,000 lbs.

Of spermaceti oil and candles annually manufactured, the value was 300,000 dollars.

Of refined sugar, five million pounds were annually made, worth 1,000,000 dollars.

Concerning the manufactures of cotton, the secretary observes that he has from the returns formed the following table:

Mills, 87; spindles, 80,000.

Capital employed, $4,800,000.

Cotton used, 3,600,000 lbs.; value, $720,000.

Yarn spun, 2,880,000 lbs.; value, $3,240,000.

Persons employed, men 500; women and children 3,500.

The goods into which the yarn is spun in the cotton manufactories in Rhode Island are principally bed ticking, stripes and checks, shirting and sheeting, ginghams and counterpanes.

Elsewhere are made webbing, coach laces, tablecloths, jeans, vest patterns, cotton kerseymeres, blankets, fustians, cords, and velvet.

Wool, the secretary observes, is principally spun and woven in private families. Fourteen manufactories, however, have been reported to him, each of which, on an average, yields ten thousand yards of cloth annually, at from one to ten dollars a yard. Wool, especially fine wool, was seriously deficient in quantity, but is rapidly increasing. The merino sheep particularly since this report was published have increased to a very great number.

Manufactories for spinning and weaving flax were few. Three are mentioned at which 662,000 yards of cotton binding, sailcloth, and other coarse linen were or might be made annually.

From Martha's Vineyard, nine thousand pairs of stockings were annually exported.

The value of all the goods made of cotton, wool, and flax, the secretary estimates at more than 40,000,000 dollars, household manufactures included.

Whittemore's machine for making cards had completely excluded foreign importations of that article. The quantity manufactured annually, before the embargo lessened the supply of wire, was worth 200,000 dollars.

Of hats the number exported of American manufacture was one hundred thousand. The number imported was 350,000. The value of the number made is estimated at nearly 10,000,000 dollars.

Most of the paper consumed in the United States was of home manufacture. Books for which an adequate number of purchasers can be procured are printed and bound here.

Paper hangings and playing cards were also extensively manufactured.

A supply of printing types was furnished, sufficient for the consumption, chiefly at Philadelphia, New York, and Baltimore.

The annual importations of foreign hemp amounted to 6,200 tons; but, from the increased cultivation of this article in Massachusetts, New York, Kentucky, etc., the secretary believed that a sufficient quantity would soon be produced in the United States.

The manufacture of cordage of all descriptions was equal to the demand. That of duck was less prosperous, and far from supplying a sufficient quantity.

The aggregate value of spirituous and malt liquors annually made was 10,000,000 dollars; yet the quantity imported, of spirituous liquors only, amounted in 1806 and 1807 to 9,750,000 gallons a year: a fact immeasurably disgraceful to the country.

At a loose estimate, the bar iron annually used in the United States amounts to fifty thousand tons, of which ten thousand were supposed to be imported, and forty thousand to be manufactured at home. A great part of the American iron was, however, inferior in quality to that which was imported.

Five hundred and sixty-five tons of sheet, slit, and hoop iron were annually imported, and seven thousand annually manufactured in the United States.

The cut nails amounted yearly in value to $1,200,000. Of these 280 tons were yearly exported.

Fifteen hundred tons of wrought nails and spikes were annually imported.

The manufactures of iron consist principally of agricultural implements and other products of the blacksmith's forge, anchors, shovels, spades, edged tools, and a great variety of the coarser articles of ironmongery. But the finer species of hardware, cutlery, etc. were imported, almost wholly from Great Britain.

Balls, shells, and cannon of small caliber were cast in several places; and three founderies for casting solid, boring, and finishing those of the largest caliber were established: one at Richmond, Virginia; one in Cecil County, Maryland; and one near the city of Washington. Each of the two first could cast three hundred pieces of artillery in a year; and a great number of iron and brass cannon were made at the other.

The castings of hollow ware were sufficient for the consumption.

At the two public armories, at Springfield and Harpers Ferry, nineteen thousand muskets were annually made. About twenty thousand more are made at other manufactories, all private, except one established at Richmond by the state of Virginia. This number might be immediately enlarged. Gunsmiths were in various places employed in making rifles and other species of arms.

The iron, manufactured and unmanufactured, was estimated at an annual value of from twelve to fifteen million dollars; the imported at near four million.

Rich copper mines are found in New Jersey, in Virginia, and near Lake Superior; but none of them were wrought.

The principal manufactures of copper and brass are stills, bells, cannon, andirons, chandeliers, sconces, vessels of various kinds, etc.

Zinc was lately discovered in Pennsylvania.

Lead is found in Virginia, and in several other places. The richest mines of this metal are however in Upper Louisiana, and it is said also in the adjacent country east of the Mississippi. They were not wrought to a sufficient extent; and, after supplying the western country, furnished only two hundred tons a year to the Atlantic states.

The principal American manufactures of lead were shot and colors of lead. There were two establishments for the manufacture of shot in Philadelphia and one in Louisiana, more than sufficient to supply the demand of six hundred tons a year. Five hundred and sixty tons of red and white lead, litharge, and some other preparations of that metal were made in Philadelphia alone.

Other paints and colors are also prepared in Philadelphia and some other places.

The manufacture of tinware is very extensive, and Connecticut supplies the greater part of the United States with that article.

Plated ware, chiefly for coach makers and saddlers, employs at Philadelphia seventy-three workmen. It is also made to a considerable extent in New York, Baltimore, Boston, Charleston, New Haven, Northampton, and elsewhere.

Saltpeter is found in Virginia, Kentucky, and several other places, but is principally imported from the East Indies.

The manufacture of gunpowder was nearly, and might at any moment be made wholly adequate to the consumption. The importation of foreign powder amounted annually to two hundred thousand pounds; the exportation of American, to one hundred thousand.

A sufficient quantity of the coarser species of pottery was made everywhere. Four manufactories of a finer kind had lately been established, which made ware resembling that of Staffordshire.

Twenty-seven thousand boxes of window glass were made annually at ten glass manufactories, or two million, seven hundred thousand square feet. Exactly the same quantity was annually imported. The glass made at Boston was inferior to none brought from Europe. The rest made green or German glass.

Other glasswares, such as bottles, etc., were made also; and at two glassworks in Pittsburgh was manufactured flint glass of every description, and of a superior quality.

Copperas was extracted in large quantities from pyrites in Vermont, New Jersey, and Tennessee. About two hundred thousand pounds of sulphuric and other acids are annually manufactured at a single establishment in Philadelphia. Other preparations and drugs were also made in that city and several other places, and the annual exportations exceeded thirty thousand dollars in value.

The salt springs in the state of New York furnished about three hundred thousand bushels a year, and those in the western states and territories about the same quantity. The Wabash Saline, the property of the United States, yielded annually one hundred and thirty thousand bushels. The annual importation of foreign salt amounted however to more than three million bushels, and could not be superseded by American salt, unless by establishments on the coast.

Straw and bonnets and hats were made in a small district in Massachusetts and Rhode Island to such an extent that the exportations to other parts of the Union amounted in value to two hundred and fifty thousand dollars annually. Work of this kind in great quantities is made also in many other places.

An establishment had been formed near Baltimore for the printing of calicoes, at which twelve thousand yards might be printed in a week.

I have now given you the substance of the secretary's report, which is to be considered as the most correct and extensive account of the manufactures of the United States which to that time had been obtained. He adds that, from this imperfect sketch, it may with certainty be inferred that the products of the whole manufacturing interest annually exceeds one hundred and twenty million dollars.

Since the loose return on which the above report is founded, another, which with some abatements may be considered as complete for the year 1810, was forwarded to the secretary of the treasury by order of the government. That rendered by Massachusetts is included in the following table.

GENERAL RECAPITULATION OF THE MANUFACTURES OF MASSACHUSETTS PROPER

| | *Estimated value* | |
|---|---|---|
| Ashes, 123 tons | $20,619 | |
| Breweries, 716,805 gallons | 86,450 | |
| Buttons | 20,000 | |
| Bricks, 25,295,000 | 139,067 | |
| Straw bonnets | 551,988 | |
| Brushes, 1,666 dozen | 5,000 | |
| Corn brooms, 70,000 | 4,000 | |
| *Cloth and Clothier's work* | | |
| 54 Cotton Factories, 19,448 spindles, 838,348 pounds | | $931,906 |
| 22,564 Looms, 4,048,209 yards | | 2,060,576 |
| 1 Factory woolen cloth, 6,860 yards | | 10,290 |
| 180 Carding Machines, 797,236 pounds | | 236,193 |
| 221 Fulling Mills, 730,948 yards | | 442,401 |
| 9 Spinning Jennies, 56 Looms, 36,000 yards | | 28,600 |
| Playing Cards, yearly amount | | 97,500 |
| 4 Wool Card factories, 9,953 dozen | | 78,998 |
| do. 14,400 feet | | 33,000 |
| Cabinet work, yearly amount | | 318,622 |
| Chairs, 1,694 dozen | | 96,060 |
| Combs, 49,905 dozen | | 80,624 |
| Candles, tallow, 1,436,550 pounds | | 217,060 |
| do. spermaceti, 465,000 pounds | | 178,300 |
| Cooperage, 37,995 casks | | 69,318 |
| Clocks and Watches, amount | | 46,185 |
| Catgut | | 2,000 |
| Chocolate, 255,500 pounds | | 73,100 |
| Coaches and Chaises, 667 | | 122,674 |
| Distilleries, Molasses, 2,472,000 gallons | | 1,404,350 |
| do. Grain, 63,730 gallons | | 42,590 |
| do. Cider, 316,480 gallons | | 181,386 |

| | |
|---|---|
| *Cloth and Clothier's work (Continued)* | |
| Duck, Hemp, 3,025 pieces | $80,813 |
| do. Cotton, 200 pieces | 6,000 |
| do. Bagging, and Tow Cloth, 60,000 yards | 33,000 |
| Fishery, Mackerel, 5,400 barrels | 44,550 |
| Glass | 36,000 |
| Gloves, 4,875 dozen | 14,625 |
| Fire engines, 1 Factory | 4,000 |
| *Founderies of Brass and Copper* | |
| Brass guns, 12,976 pounds | 7,136 |
| Copper, 32,159 pounds | 22,828 |
| Bells, 21,410 pounds | 8,555 |
| Brass and Pewter, 99,288 pounds | 41,700 |
| Composition, 251,503 pounds | 109,781 |
| Hats, 142,645 | 415,167 |
| Jewelry and Silver work | 161,625 |
| Printing Ink, 6,000 pounds | 3,000 |
| 37 *Forges,* 11 *Triphammers* | |
| Bar Iron, 978 tons | 121,930 |
| Anchors, 440 tons | 92,712 |
| Hollow ware, 2,340½ tons | 132,200 |
| Edge Tools | 44,000 |
| Wrought Iron | 521,718 |
| Lace for coaches, yearly amount | 10,000 |
| Leather, Boots, 63,307 pair | 412,509 |
| do. Men's Shoes, 844,864 pair | 973,033 |
| do. Women's Shoes, 1,310,500 pair | 816,250 |
| do. Saddlery, harness, jockey caps, etc. | 188,726 |
| Lead mines | 200 |
| Muskets, 19,095 | 229,085 |
| Musical instruments | 17,880 |
| 16 Marble works, 89,000 feet | 38,000 |
| Nails wrought | 69,235 |
| do. Cut, 2,925¼ tons | 644,990 |
| do. Small | 1,360 |
| Oil, Spermaceti, 77,696 gallons | 68,832 |
| do. Whale, 249,728 gallons | 171,688 |
| Oil mills, 44,460 gallons | 46,982 |
| Paper mills, 95,129 reams writing | 257,451 |
| do. 63,000 rolls hanging | 33,500 |
| Ores, ocher and nitrous beds | 1,350 |
| 6 Powder mills, 120,000 pounds | 72,000 |
| 84 *Gristmills* | |
| Wheat and Rye, 460,476 bushels | 350,896 |
| Corn and Oats, 49,054 bushels | 35,273 |
| 150 *Sawmills* | |
| Pine, 10,725,000 feet | 80,480 |
| Oak, 490,000 feet | 6,855 |
| 1 Rake factory, 11,000 rakes | 1,870 |
| Ropewalks, Cordage, 2,808½ tons | 1,030,661 |
| do. Twine, 85,200 pounds | 37,383 |

| | |
|---|---|
| Shipbuilding, 23,410 tons | $656,095 |
| Soapstone manufactory | 13,000 |
| Spectacles, yearly amount | 10,000 |
| 1 Steel factory, 20 tons | 4,000 |
| Spinning wheels, 6,393 | 17,982 |
| Spruce essence, 1,250 pounds | 2,500 |
| Snuff, 118,400 pounds | 37,281 |
| Soap, hard, 2,043,720 pounds | 239,697 |
| do. soft, 4,190 barrels | 18,400 |
| Sewing Silk, 103 pounds | 618 |
| Loaf Sugar, 422,000 pounds | 82,400 |
| Slitting mills, 1,900 tons | 318,600 |
| Saltpeter, 23,600 | 9,303 |
| *Saltworks* 468,198 *feet* | |
| Salt, 118,757 bushels | 79,526 |
| Glauber's salt, 334,238 pounds | 13,369 |
| Sheep, Merino, 73 | 18,250 |
| do. mixed blood, 2,062 | 154,650 |
| do. common, 103,141 | 226,282 |
| Woolen Stockings, 37,951 pair | 28,453 |
| Essence of Turpentine, 6,000 gallons | 18,000 |
| Steel Thimbles | 10,000 |
| Tanneries, Morocco skins, 261,800 | 130,160 |
| do. Hides, 174,596 | 1,022,661 |
| do. Calves' skins, 65,888 | 129,078 |
| do. Sheepskins, 62,536 | 52,140 |
| do. Hogs skins, 2,800 | 9,100 |
| Tacks, 11,000,000 | 2,000 |
| Tin Plate, works, amount | 73,715 |
| Whips 7,050 dozen | 7,990 |
| Wagons 2,260 | 43,600 |
| Earthenware | 18,700 |
| Wire factories, amount | 24,912 |
| Woodenware | 31,000 |
| Sheep's wool, 35,000 pounds | 14,175 |
| Total | $18,595,323 |

I have been so fortunate also as to obtain the same return for Connecticut. A copy of it, so far as the heads of it are concerned, is subjoined under the following title.

Abstract of the Manufacturing Establishments and Annual Manufactures in the District of Connecticut, as taken from the returns of the assistants to the marshal of the said district, made in pursuance of the several acts of Congress providing for the 3rd Census etc., A. D. 1810.

*Cloths and their value*

| | *Estimated value* |
|---|---|
| Looms, 16,132 | |
| Yards of linen, 2,362,078 | $800,358.81 |
| Yards of woolen, 1,119,145 | 1,098,241.92 |

*Cloths and their value (Continued)*

| | Estimated value |
|---|---|
| Yards of Cotton, and cotton and linen, 605,675 | $241,222.99 |
| Fulling mills, 218, Carding machines, 184 | |
| Pounds of wool carded, 504,088 | |
| Woolen manufactories, 15, Cotton Manufactories, 14, Spindles, 11,883 | |
| Value of cotton yarn, stockings, and suspenders | 111,021.50 |
| Value of raw and sewing silk | 28,503 |
| Value of Hats | 522,209 |
| Distilleries, 560 | |
| Gallons of distilled spirits, 1,374,404 | 811,144 |
| Tanneries, 408 | |
| Value of Leather, tanned and dressed | 476,338.80 |
| Value of Saddlery, shoes, etc. | 231,812 |
| Ropewalks, 19 | |
| Value of Cordage | 243,950 |
| Value of duck and cotton bagging | 12,148.40 |
| Paper mills, 19 | |
| Value of paper | 82,188 |
| Oil mills, 24 | |
| Value of oil | 64,712 |
| Powder mills, 7 | |
| Value of Gunpowder, etc. | 43,640 |
| Forges, 48 | |
| Tons of Iron and Steel, 1,450 | |
| Value of do. and Anchors | 183,910 |
| Furnaces, 8 | |
| Value of Cast Iron | 46,180 |
| Guns and Pistols, 4,400 | 49,050 |
| Manufactories of cut nails, 18 | |
| Value of Nails cut | 27,092 |
| Rolling and Slitting mills, 3 | |
| Trip hammers, 32 | |
| Value of Scythes, Axes, etc. | 91,145.60 |
| Brass founderies, 4 | |
| Value of Brasswork, Jewelry, and Plated ware | 49,200 |
| Type foundery, 1 | |
| Glassworks, 2 | |
| Value of Glass | 23,360 |
| Potteries, 12 | |
| Value of Earthen and stoneware | 30,740 |
| Wooden Clocks, 14,565 | 122,955 |
| Value of Coachwork, etc. | 68,855 |
| Value of marble and stonework | 11,000 |
| Value of Bricks exported | 2,000 |
| Value of Straw bonnets | 27,100 |
| Buttons, number of gross, 155,000 | 122,125 |
| Value of tin japanned and plain | 139,370 |
| Value of Combs | 70,000 |
| Manufactures of Tallow, Sieves, Tobacco, Ink, etc. | 71,612 |
| Total value of annual manufactures as returned, | $5,887,175.08 |

Concerning this abstract it ought to be observed that several articles are omitted in it which are of considerable importance. The manufacture of wagons, for example, is carried on to a vast extent. A great number of carriages of that sort are now employed both for the transportation of burdens and for pleasure. The latter are a novelty in this country. They are drawn by one horse, and by two, are made of neat forms and with nice workmanship, and have lately been multiplied to such a degree that they appear to be taking the place of most other vehicles.

From my friend Mr. L———, of Providence, I have received the following account of the manufactures of Rhode Island. Had other gentlemen in New England and New York equally interested themselves in furnishing the information which I had requested of them it would have been in my power to have done more justice to many subjects mentioned in these letters. But, unhappily, a disposition to sit down seriously to the employment of writing is far from being a prominent trait in the character of my countrymen. Generally, I shall give this account in the words of my obliging correspondent.

The natural sources of wealth in the state of Rhode Island, observes Mr. L., are limited. She has no mines, her territory is small, and her fisheries are of little importance. Her soil also is naturally unfruitful, producing barely what is sufficient for the subsistence of her own population.* Her prosperity, therefore, depends eminently upon the industry of her citizens. This industry is now almost exclusively devoted to the advancement of her manufactures. It would be no exaggeration to say that five eighths of her inhabitants are directly or indirectly employed in the manufacture of cotton, and the several branches of business to which it gives birth. Whether this direction of the industry of Rhode Island will promote her moral prosperity, time only can determine. There can be no doubt from experience that it will increase her wealth and population.

To Samuel Slater, a native of England, is this state indebted for the introduction of Sir Richard Arkwright's method of spinning cotton.[2] He came to this country about the year 1790, and soon after established the first cotton manufactory, under the patronage of Messrs. Almy and Brown, of Providence. The machinery of this establishment was made solely under his direction. Efforts of the same nature had been before begun, but had proved unsuccessful.

For five or six years after Slater's arrival, comparatively little progress was made in extending this branch of business, except by Messrs. Almy and Brown. It was regarded as a mystery difficult of acquisition, and as an experiment hazardous to the undertakers. Those also by whom the first attempts were made cautiously concealed from the public the profits which they derived from the pursuit. The attention of the public was, however, excited

* The average quantity of maize in the southern part of this state is about twenty-five bushels an acre; in the northern, about thirteen.

by the eagerness with which these gentlemen enlarged their business, and the fearlessness with which they employed considerable additions to their capital in erecting new manufactories. At length several other persons were induced to adventure their property in the same undertaking. Artificers, skilled in all the complicated branches of machinery employed in manufacturing cotton, were allured from England by the prospect of high wages to this country. The workshops in which these foreigners employed themselves were in a short time crowded with mechanics and apprentices from our own citizens, who soon made themselves masters of all the knowledge thus imported, and with that vigorous ingenuity so often found among them added in many instances improvements of no small importance. The consequences were soon apparent. The Rhode Island workmen supplanted their foreign brethren to such a degree that scarcely fifty foreigners are now employed in the state in this business. They have transferred their skill to other states where the art is yet in its infancy. It is not known that a single article of cotton machinery was ever imported into Rhode Island.

From their first establishment to the year 1800, the increase of these manufactures was gradual. Men who possess a monied capital require a certainty of profit before they are willing to vest their property in any business. As soon as it had been ascertained by experience that the American cotton manufactures could so far come into competition with the English in our markets at prices which secured a handsome profit to the manufacturer, the citizens of Rhode Island embarked eagerly in the business. None but an eyewitness can imagine the rapidity with which this species of manufacturing increased in the state after the year 1800. At least three fourths of the existing capital have been added since that period, and a new animation has been awakened in almost every other pursuit. Common laborers, diggers of canals, lumber merchants, dealers in hardware, brass and iron founders, burners of lime, carpenters, masons, curriers, wagoners, sellers of wood, and blacksmiths are all employed in greater or less degrees by the erection of a cotton manufactory.

To these are to be added the superintendents, clerks, overseers, agents at home and abroad, dyers, and that numerous class of men, women, and children who are immediately engaged in manufacturing the yarn. What is perhaps of still more consequence to the general prosperity, the weaving is all done in private families; and, being spread throughout a circumference of sixty miles to the northeast and west of Providence, engrosses a number of hands which it would be difficult to estimate. The agricultural interest is estimated by the rise of land, the rise of produce, and a nearer and readier market. For example, a piece of land on a millstream fifteen miles from Providence was sold lately for fifteen hundred dollars an acre, which fifteen years ago could scarcely have been sold for one hundred. A manufactory of fifteen hundred spindles will soon accumulate a population sufficient to form a village.

I cannot say that the following account of the extent of our manufactures is precisely accurate, but it approaches as near to accuracy as those acquainted with the business can make it. It involves a tract of territory alluded to above, none of the manufactories being thirty miles from Providence. Several of them are in Connecticut and several in Massachusetts, but all to which I refer are owned by citizens of Rhode Island.

Within these limits there are now in motion above 120,000 spindles. The yarn spun each week is not far from 110,000 pounds, or 5,500,000 pounds a year. This, manufactured into cloth, is worth $8,140,000. If you deduct from this sum the raw material, say six million pounds, which at an average of 25 cents per pound is $1,500,000, the annual profit of the Rhode Island manufactures is $6,640,000. From this sum must be farther deducted the expenses of manufacturing, the interest of capital, etc., in order to ascertain the net profit.

The capital requisite to set a spindle in motion is $75. The whole amount of the cotton manufacturing capital of this state is $9,000,000. Of this there are three investments: one in houses, lands, machinery, etc.; another in raw cotton, and manufactured stock in the hands of the weavers; and a third in goods in the market.

The most extensive manufacture of wool in this country has just commenced its operations at the north end of Providence. It is moved by a steam engine possessing the power of thirty horses, and is intended to manufacture daily two hundred yards of broadcloth. None but merino wool is used, and the cloths are of the finest quality. Mr. Sanford, of Connecticut, is the superintendent of this business.

The use of steam as a moving power is superseding that of water. Two new engines will soon be erected in Providence.

On Rhode Island proper, there are two small woolen manufactories, and one of cotton, now erecting. The number of sheep on this island, according to an estimate made by three intelligent farmers, is 16,500, and is rapidly increasing. Permit me to add that there is also on this island a coal mine in full operation, which employs about fifty hands through the year.

In Pawtucket there is a manufacture of muskets, and in Smithfield one of swords. At the latter place also, the business of plating is carried on to a considerable extent.

Few kinds of business have been pursued with more spirit or with more success in the United States than the printing of books. Within the last twenty years, many large works have issued from our presses; and all of them have found ample support. The Bible has gone through a vast multitude of editions, several of them expensive, among which are three of Scott's Bible, and one of Dr. Clarke's.[3] The latter, and one of the former, are however not yet finished. Three encyclopedias have been printed in this country: the British, the Edinburgh, and that of Dr. Rees.[4] An edition has proceeded far of distinguished British writers in sixty volumes. Pinkerton's Collection of

Voyages and Travels is another expensive work, the engravings in which would have been admired in any country.[5] The American Ornithology, executed in a very superb style, was begun by the late Mr. Alexander Wilson; and, it seems, with ample encouragement. The subscription price was one hundred and twenty dollars a set. It has however been completed in nine instead of twelve volumes. Our best printing is little, if at all inferior to the best in Europe. For a large proportion of the very expensive books printed in the United States, we are indebted to the presses of Philadelphia.

A great multitude of machines have been invented in America, both to abridge and perfect human labor, which are honorable to the ingenuity of my countrymen. The most important of these is undoubtedly the cotton gin of Mr. Whitney; next after this may be placed his machinery for the manufacture of muskets, Evans' machinery for manufacturing flour,[6] the machine of Mr. Perkins, of Newburyport, which cuts and heads two hundred thousand nails in a day, and other machines of the same ingenious artist, that of Mr. Whittemore for cutting, bending, and setting card teeth at a single operation, and a stocking loom (the name of the inventor unknown to me) which will weave six stockings in a day. To these might be added an almost endless train of others applied to various purposes of life.

The fabrics of the loom woven here are chiefly those which are worn by the middle and lower classes of mankind. Beautiful cloths are however made in considerable quantities, and of such a quality as not to be distinguished from the superfine cloths of Europe. For these, the merino sheep furnish the material. Happily for us, this useful animal, instead of declining as was expected, has visibly improved in our pastures, having increased both in its size and the quantity of its wool. For the introduction of this invaluable breed, the United States are greatly indebted to the Hon. David Humphreys, formerly minister plenipotentiary at the courts of Lisbon and Madrid. They are now, together with the crossbreeds, filling the country.

I am, Sir, yours, etc.

# MASSACHUSETTS

## LETTER I

*The state of Massachusetts—Its boundaries, population, and government*

*Dear Sir,*

I am now quitting Massachusetts and will therefore take this opportunity to make some general observations to you concerning this state, the largest in New England; and, when considered as to the extent of its territory, population, wealth, power, commerce, and advancement in civilization, one of the largest in the American Union.

The topography of this state has been already sufficiently exhibited, except in a small number of particulars which will hereafter be occasionally mentioned.

Massachusetts proper is divided into twelve counties. Berkshire begins at the western boundary; Hampshire * and Worcester extend across the breadth of the state fifty miles, and are entirely inland. Middlesex, which lies immediately east of Worcester, touches the ocean at its southeastern corner. Essex, the northeastern county, Suffolk, Norfolk, and Plymouth are bordered by Massachusetts Bay. Barnstable is washed on one side by this bay and on the other by the ocean. Bristol is bordered on the south by the ocean. Duke's County is formed by Martha's Vineyard and the Elizabeth Isles, and the county of Nantucket consists of the island of that name. The three inland counties contain 177,092 inhabitants; the maritime counties, 294,948. The inhabitants of the county of Hampshire, amounting to 76,275, live all within less than twenty-five miles of Connecticut River, which passes through the middle of the county from north to south, and furnishes a conveyance for their produce to the ocean. Those of the county of Berkshire upon its western limit are at about the same distance from the Hudson. A considerable number of the inhabitants of Worcester County are not more remote from the harbor of Providence.

The face of the country is divided by nature in the following manner: the Taconic Range; the valley of the Housatonic; the Green Mountain Range; the valley of the Connecticut; the Lyme Range; a tract formed of hills and valleys reaching from their eastern base to the ocean; and a tract of sandy ground spreading from Bridgewater to the ocean both eastward and southward, chiefly formed into extensive plains, but rising in several

* Since divided into three counties. [Franklin, Hampden, and Hampshire.]

places into hills, some of them of considerable height, particularly in the county of Barnstable.

Massachusetts is subdivided into 290 townships, of which: Berkshire contains thirty-two townships and 35,907 inhabitants; Hampshire, sixty-four townships and 76,275 inhabitants; Worcester, fifty-one townships and 64,910 inhabitants; Middlesex, forty-four townships and 52,789 inhabitants; Essex, twenty-three townships and 71,888 inhabitants; Suffolk, two townships and 34,381 inhabitants; Norfolk, twenty-two townships and 31,245 inhabitants; Plymouth, eighteen townships and 35,169 inhabitants; Bristol, sixteen townships and 37,168 inhabitants; Barnstable, fourteen townships, and 22,211 inhabitants; Duke's three townships and 3,290 inhabitants; Nantucket, one township and 6,807 inhabitants. Total, 290 townships and 472,040 † inhabitants.

There are no peculiarities in the character of these inhabitants which are not marked with sufficient minuteness in the course of these letters. Those of Berkshire, Hampshire, and Worcester so much resemble their neighbors bordering upon them in Connecticut that a traveler is conscious of no sensible change when he passes within these limits from one state into the other. The only general characteristical difference which I have observed is that the people of Massachusetts are somewhat more ardent, impassioned, and sudden in both their feelings and actions than those of Connecticut.

The produce of Massachusetts is exactly the same with that of Connecticut. The tender fruits are, however, somewhat less prosperous, and are cultivated with more difficulty.

The government of Massachusetts is formed into three independent branches: the legislative, executive, and judicial. The legislature consists of a Senate containing forty members, and a House of Representatives. The Senate are chosen on the first Monday in April annually. The electors are the male inhabitants twenty-one years of age or upwards, having a freehold estate within the commonwealth of the annual income of ten dollars, or any estate worth two hundred. The selectmen preside in the freemen's meeting.

The governor and five of the Council examine the returns of votes taken from the town clerks' offices and made to the secretary's office, seventeen days before the last Wednesday in May; and fourteen days before the said Wednesday the governor shall issue his summons to such persons as shall appear to have been chosen by a majority of the voters in each senatorial district to attend on that day and take their seats accordingly.

The Senate is the final judge of the elections returns and qualifications of its own members.

If the whole number of senators shall not appear to have been duly elected, then such as are chosen shall take the names of such persons in the

† By the Census of 1820 Massachusetts contained 523,287 inhabitants. PUB.

vacant district as shall appear to have the highest number of votes, amounting to twice the number of senators wanting; and, with the House of Representatives, shall by a joint ballot fill up the vacancies; and so, in cases of vacancy by death, removal, or otherwise. No person can be a senator who does not possess a freehold in his own right of $1,000, or a personal estate of $2,000, or both, to the amount of the same sum; and who has not been an inhabitant of the commonwealth five years immediately preceding his election, and is not at the time an inhabitant of the district for which he is elected.

Sixteen members make a quorum.

The Senate is a court to hear and determine impeachments made by the House of Representatives against any officer or officers of the commonwealth. Their judgment extends no farther than to removal from office and disqualification to hold or enjoy any place of honor, trust, or profit under the commonwealth.

Every corporate town containing one hundred and fifty ratable polls may elect one representative, and one more for every additional two hundred and twenty-five ratable polls.

Every representative is chosen by written votes, must have been an inhabitant of the town in which he is elected one year at least immediately preceding his election, and must have possessed in his own right a freehold worth $334 within said town, or other ratable estate of the value of $667.

When these qualifications cease, his right to represent the town ceases.

Representatives are to be chosen annually in the month of May, at least ten days before the last Wednesday.

The House of Representatives is the grand inquest of the commonwealth.

Money bills are originated in the House of Representatives, but the Senate may propose amendments.

Sixty members make a quorum.

The House of Representatives is the judge of the election and qualifications for its members.

No senator or representative can be arrested, or held to bail, on mesne process while going to, returning from, or attending the General Court.

The governor is chosen annually, must have been an inhabitant of the commonwealth for seven years immediately preceding his election, and must at the same time be seized in his own right of a freehold in the commonwealth worth $3,334.

The governor is empowered to call together the councilors of the commonwealth for the time being; and, with a quorum of said councilors amounting to at least five, may from time to time hold a council for ordering and directing the affairs of the commonwealth, agreeably to the constitution and the laws of the land. The governor, during the session of the

General Court, is empowered to adjourn or prorogue the same to any time which the two houses shall desire; and to dissolve the same on the day next preceding the last Wednesday in May; and in the recess of the General Court, to prorogue them from time to time, not exceeding ninety days in any one recess; and to call them together sooner than the time to which they may be adjourned or prorogued; and, in case any infectious distemper or any other dangerous cause shall require it, may direct the session to be held at some other, the most convenient place.

The governor is commander in chief of the military force of the state by sea and land; but cannot transport any of the inhabitants by sea, or oblige them to march out of the limits of the state, without the consent of the General Court, or their own, except where this may be demanded for the defense of some part of the state.

The governor is empowered to pardon offenses, to nominate all judicial officers, the attorney general, solicitor general, sheriffs, coroners, and registers of probate; and, by and with the advice and consent of the Council, to appoint them. He also commissions all military officers; and, with the advice of Council, appoints all officers in the army of the United States who are to be appointed by this commonwealth.

No monies are to be issued out of the treasury of the commonwealth, except sums appropriated for the redemption of bills of credit or treasurer's notes, or for payment of interest arising thereon, but by warrant under the hand of the governor for the time being, with the advice and consent of the Council, agreeably to the acts and resolves of the General Court.

The governor is to have an honorable stated salary, of a permanent value, amply sufficient, and established by standing laws.

The lieutenant governor is elected in the same manner as the governor, is always a member of the Council except when the chair of the governor is vacant, and then he is vested with all the powers and performs all the duties of the governor.

Nine councilors are annually chosen among the persons returned for senators, on the last Wednesday in May, by the joint ballots of the senators and representatives assembled in one room. If the persons thus chosen, or any of them, decline, the deficiency is to be made up from among the people at large. The councilors rank next after the lieutenant governor. Their business is to advise the governor in the executive part of government.

Not more than two councilors can be chosen out of any one district.

The resolutions and advice of the councilors are recorded in a register, and signed by the members present. This record may be called for at any time by either house of the legislature, and any member of the council may insert his opinion contrary to the will of the majority.

If both the offices of governor and lieutenant governor are vacant, the Council succeed to their powers.

No man can hold the office of treasurer more than five years.

The courts in this state are substantially the same with those in Connecticut.

Justices of the Supreme Judicial Court and of the courts of common pleas, and judges of probate, hold their offices during good behavior. The judges of the Supreme Court are by the constitution to have, and actually have at the present time, honorable salaries, which cannot be diminished during their continuance in office.

The state is by the constitution obliged to uphold and encourage the University of Cambridge, and to cherish the interests of literature and the sciences, and all seminaries in which they are taught.

Such is the substance of the constitution, or rather of the most important parts of the constitution upon which the government of Massachusetts is founded. It is prefaced by a declaration of rights, containing most of those general principles which the ablest jurists have agreed upon as essential to a free government, included in thirty articles. Among them is this declaration: "The people have a right to keep and bear arms for the common defense." [1]

The provisions in this constitution are few, and in that respect are a proof of wisdom in the framers: for they are probably most or all that are necessary. Generally also, they are very good in themselves. There is, however, one of them which is singularly unhappy: that which establishes the ratio of representation.

The number of representatives is greater than that of the imperial parliament of Great Britain and Ireland, falling little short of seven hundred. Nothing can be more preposterous than to assemble such an enormous multitude of men to deliberate on the interests of seven hundred thousand inhabitants. This is exceedingly regretted by the people of the state, but cannot be altered until party spirit shall have fallen from its present height.

The laws of this state are generally similar in their substance to those of Connecticut. In the following letter I shall mention a few of its institutions, and am,

Sir, yours, etc.

# LETTER II

*Laws relative to schools and the qualifications of schoolmasters; concerning the maintenance of ministers and the establishment of public worship—Early laws for the support of Harvard College—Crimes punished by death—Militia*

*Dear Sir,*

The system of Massachusetts concerning schools is the following. Every town or district in the state containing fifty householders is required to provide a schoolmaster to teach children to read and write, and to instruct them in the English language and arithmetic, six months in each year. If a town or district contain one hundred householders, twelve months; if one hundred and fifty, one school six months for writing, arithmetic and orthography, and for the English language, one school twelve months. If two hundred householders, a grammar schoolmaster, well instructed in the Latin, Greek, and English languages, and an English schoolmaster, each twelve months.

The towns establish the school districts. The selectmen determine on the qualifications which fit the children to enter into the grammar schools.

All instructors of the university, colleges, academies, and schools, and all private instructors are required to take diligent care and exert their best endeavors to impress on the minds of children and youth committed to their care the principles of piety, justice, and a sacred regard to truth, love to their country, humanity, and universal benevolence, sobriety, industry, and frugality, chastity, moderation, and temperance, and all other virtues; and to show them the tendency of these virtues to secure the blessings of liberty, and the tendency of the opposite vices to slavery and ruin. Schoolmasters of grammar schools must have received an education at some college or university; must produce a certificate from a learned minister well skilled in the Greek and Latin languages, or from two such ministers in the vicinity, that they have reason to believe him well qualified to discharge the duties of his office; and a certificate from the minister of the place where he belongs, or from the selectmen of the town, or from the committee of the parish, that to the best of his or their knowledge he sustains a good moral character. This certificate is unnecessary to a person who is to keep school in his native place, but the selectmen or committee are in this case required specially to attend to his morals.

If a town or district of fifty householders neglect this duty, they are fined £10; if of one hundred householders, £20; if of one hundred and fifty householders, £30; if of two hundred, for neglect of grammar school £30; and for partial neglects proportional fines are inflicted. These penalties are to be appropriated by the court of sessions for the county to which the deficient town or district belongs, according to their discretion.

The ministers and selectmen, or other persons specially chosen for the purpose in the towns or districts, are required to use their best endeavors that the children regularly attend the schools, and to visit them once in every six months at least.

With respect to other schools not contemplated in these provisions, it is enacted that no person shall be a master or mistress of any school and keep the same without obtaining a certificate as above, under a penalty of twenty shillings. The duty of every such master or mistress is also made the same in substance as above.

If a person who is not a citizen shall keep a school in the commonwealth for one month, he shall be subjected to a fine of £20.

Grand jurors are diligently to inquire and presentment make of all breaches and neglects of this law.

This is in the main an excellent law. It is questionable, however, whether the number of grammar schools provided for is not greater than necessity or even convenience requires. It would also have been better if no person besides a native American had been permitted to keep a school. Such shoals of foreigners have, since the enaction of this law, been naturalized, that the present exclusion is little more than a dead letter.

Schools are as universally kept in this state as in Connecticut. The number of academies is much greater; and, as a body, they are better endowed. Indeed the efforts of this state to promote useful knowledge are not exceeded on this side of the Atlantic. The benefit of these efforts is realized in every corner of the state.

The spirit and views of those who formed the Constitution of Massachusetts are fully as well as solemnly disclosed in the second and third articles of the Declaration of Rights. These I will here recite.

II. It is the right, as well as the duty, of all men in society, publicly, and at stated seasons, to worship the Supreme Being, the great Creator and Preserver of the universe. And no subject shall be hurt, molested, or restrained in his person, liberty, or estate for worshiping GOD in the manner and season most agreeable to the dictates of his own conscience; or for his religious profession or sentiments; provided he doth not disturb the public peace, or obstruct others in their religious worship.

III. As the happiness of a people, and the good order and preservation of civil government, essentially depend upon piety, religion, and morality; and as these cannot be generally diffused through a community, but by the institution of the public worship of GOD, and of public instructions in piety, religion, and morality: therefore, to promote their happiness, and to secure the good order and preservation of their government, the people of this commonwealth have a right to invest their legislature with power to authorize and require the several towns, parishes, precincts, and other bodies politic, or religious societies, to make suitable provision at their own expense for the institution of the public worship of GOD, and for the support and maintenance of public Protestant teachers of piety, religion, and morality, in all cases where such provision shall not be made voluntarily.

And the people of this commonwealth have also a right to, and do, invest their legislature with authority to enjoin upon all the subjects an attendance upon the instructions of the public teachers aforesaid, at stated times and seasons, if there be any on whose instructions they can conscientiously and conveniently attend.

Provided notwithstanding that the several towns, parishes, precincts, and other bodies politic, or religious societies shall at all times have the exclusive right of electing their public teachers, and of contracting with them for their support and maintenance.

And all monies paid by the subject to the support of the public worship, and of the public teachers aforesaid, shall, if he require it, be uniformly applied to the support of the public teacher or teachers of his own religious sect or denomination, provided there be any whose instructions he attends; otherwise it may be paid toward the support of the teacher or teachers of the parish or precinct in which the said monies are raised.

And every denomination of Christians, demeaning themselves peaceably, and as good subjects of the commonwealth, shall be equally under the protection of the law; and no subordination of any one sect or denomination to another shall ever be established by law.[1]

The laws respecting the settlement and support of ministers and the building of churches, for the observation of the Sabbath and the preservation of good order in the public worship, are in substance the same with those in Connecticut.

The same observation is generally true concerning the great body of regulations adopted in this state for its internal government.

Generally, the inhabitants are highly respectable for their intelligence, manners, morals, and religion; and will suffer little by a comparison with most communities in the world. They are ardent also in their love of liberty, and yet prompt in obeying and supporting government.

These characteristics of Massachusetts, like those of Connecticut, commenced with its settlement. A law for the support of schools, the substance of which is found in that recited above, was enacted by the legislature of Massachusetts Bay in 1654; another, to prevent breaches on the Sabbath, in 1652; and a second, in 1653. In 1641 a law was passed which may be considered as a declaration of ecclesiastical rights; in 1646 another, prohibiting open opposition or contempt of ministers and their preaching in any congregation, disturbance of the order and peace of churches, and unnecessary absence from public worship. In 1654 another law was passed requiring the inhabitants of every town to provide houses and maintenance for their ministers.

I have already mentioned the founding of Harvard College. The first law passed with respect to it was enacted in the year 1636, the second in 1640, the third in 1642. These established the government of it substantially as it is now established, and recognize a gift of £400 from the legislature, and the appropriation of the revenue of the ferry between Charlestown and Boston for its support. In 1659 another law was passed by the General Court granting £100 a year to be paid to the college out of the public treasury. As a reason for this gift, the General Court allege their fear lest they should show themselves ungrateful to God and unfaithful to posterity if so good a seminary of knowledge and virtue should fall to the ground through any neglect of theirs.

In 1642 a law was passed requiring the selectmen of every town not to suffer so much barbarism in any family as that the parents and masters should not endeavor to teach, by themselves or others, their children and servants to read the English tongue and to know the capital laws. The penalty for every such neglect was twenty shillings.

The selectmen were also required by this law to see that all masters of families catechised their children and servants, once a week at least, in the grounds and principles of religion; or, if unable to do it themselves, that they should procure it to be done; and that they bring up their children and apprentices in some honest, lawful calling, profitable for themselves and the commonwealth, whenever they were unable to train them up in learning to fit them for higher employments. If masters of families, after suitable admonition, refused or neglected to perform these duties, then the selectmen with the help of two magistrates or the next county court were required to bind the children and apprentices to other persons who would perform these duties.

Thirteen offenses were made capital by the original laws of Massachusetts Bay:

Idolatry
Witchcraft
Blasphemy
Murder
Bestiality
Sodomy
Adultery
Rape
Man stealing
False witness
Conspiracy, or rebellion against the government
Cursing, or smiting the father or mother after passing sixteen years of age, unless with justifying provocation, or with unchristianly neglect in education, and
Filial rebellion after sixteen years of age

To these were added in 1692:

High treason
Concealing the death of a bastard child
Arson, and
Piracy

At this time also a particular law was made against witchcraft. You will remember that this was the year in which the colony was convulsed by the Danvers witchcraft.[2]

In the original laws of Connecticut, revised and published by order of the court in 1672, the former of these lists is adopted with the addition of arson; as are also in substance the ecclesiastical law, that concerning schools, and many others, not however without various alterations. No particular law against witchcraft is found in this statute book. All the original laws of Massachusetts and of Connecticut also discover everywhere a high sense of the duties of piety and morality, of the value of liberty, and of the importance of exact submission to government. In some respects they would now be thought severe, and in my opinion are so. If they are considered with candor, and with a due deference to the circumstances of the people for whom they were made and to the existing opinions of the age, they will be pronounced to be generally wise and just.

The militia of this state are on a better footing than those of any other in the Union. They are distributed into thirteen divisions, twenty-eight brigades, and 103 regiments of infantry. The cavalry contains seventy-one companies, and the artillery seventy. The whole number included in these several bodies is 70,710.* The whole number of white males between sixteen and forty-five was in 1810, 133,354, exceeding the number of militia by 62,644. The period of service is from eighteen to forty-five. The deficiency is partly made up of persons between sixteen and eighteen and partly of persons excused.

The militia are clad universally in a handsome uniform, and are well armed, accoutered, and disciplined. The laws by which this body of men are formed and regulated are, so far as I may be allowed to judge, wise and efficacious; and their is an uncommon, if not singular, ambition and energy in both the officers and privates of whom the militia is formed.

I am, Sir, yours, etc.

* 1811.

# PROSPECTS OF THE UNITED STATES

## LETTER I

*Opinions of foreigners relative to the future prospects of our country—Bishop Berkeley's views of this subject in verse—Extent, waters, soil, productions and population of the United States*

*Dear Sir,*

My countrymen, in a variety of fugitive publications, have given the world their views concerning the future progress of the American republic in respectability and greatness. Most of these efforts have been extemporaneous, the result of feeling rather than of thought, specimens of idle declamation rather than of rational discussion.

British writers have also busied themselves with the same subject, sometimes seriously, at others contemptuously. In the nature of this subject there is sufficient importance to make it a proper object of interesting examination to a philosopher, whether a politician, a moralist, or a divine. Yet it must be acknowledged that scarcely an individual on either side of the Atlantic has investigated it with the degree or with the kind of attention which is evidently demanded even by subjects of very inferior magnitude.

Among the foreigners who have published their thoughts concerning the future destinies of this country, Berkeley, bishop of Cloyne, a man to whom few have been equal and scarcely any superior in endowments or acquisitions, has published *his* in a small poem inserted in his works, and not unfrequently transferred to the pages of other writers. This extraordinary man, as has been already mentioned in these letters, and as you must have undoubtedly known from other sources, came to America in the year 1732 in order to establish a college in the island of *Bermuda*. During this excursion he visited several parts of the continent, particularly New England, New York, New Jersey, and Pennsylvania, and resided a considerable time at Newport in Rhode Island. It is hardly necessary to observe that the British colonies were then in their infancy and exhibited little to attract the attention of ordinary observers. Berkeley was not of this class. With the glance of the eye he discovered more than such observers by the examination of a life. Raised by the capacity of his mind and not less by his disposition far above the level where most other men walk through life, and standing always on a commanding eminence, he took a comprehensive and at the same time an exact survey of the scenes beneath him. From such a survey he derived the thoughts expressed in the following:

*Verses [by the Author] on the prospect of Planting Arts and Learning in America.*

The muse disgusted at an age and clime,
Barren of every glorious theme,
In distant lands now waits a better time,
Producing subjects worthy fame:

In happy climes, where from the genial sun
And virgin earth such scenes ensue,
The force of art by nature seems out-done,
And fancied beauties by the true.

In happy climes, the seat of innocence,
Where nature guides, and virtue rules;
Where men shall not impose for truth and sense
The pedantry of courts and schools;

There shall be sung another golden age,
The rise of empire and of arts,
The good and great, inspiring epic rage,
The wisest heads, and noblest hearts.

Not such as Europe breeds in her decay;—
Such as she bred, when fresh and young,
When heavenly flame did animate her clay,
By future poets shall be sung.

Westward the course of empire takes its way:
The four first acts already past,
A fifth shall close the drama with the day:
Time's noblest offspring is the last.[1]

I know not how Bishop Berkeley, if he were now alive, would be able to make his peace with your reviewers. The predictions to which he has subscribed his name and lent his reputation are, it must be confessed, of quite another cast than those which these gentlemen have thought proper to utter from the Trophonian retreats in which they reside. The bishop may, however, be partially brought off, and his character in some measure saved by the consideration that he has given his prophecy in *verse,* and may therefore be fairly believed intentionally to have given us fiction and not sober truth.

The United States of America, including Louisiana, form a territory of 1,800,000 square miles, or 1,152,000,000 acres: [2] a larger empire than any which the world has ever seen except the Russian and the Chinese. This territory lies in a single, solid mass, in a form as near to a square as in a region of so great an extent our globe can well be supposed to admit.

The climates through which it passes are undoubtedly those which are most favorable to the prosperity of mankind. The seasons are not indeed as mild as those of Europe in the same latitudes, and the temperature is both higher and lower. The difference, however, is not such as to be of any material importance either to the health or the happiness of man. Perhaps the defect is balanced by the superior brightness and serenity of the sky. This extensive region is well watered. Throughout as great a part of it as of any equal region of the globe, and incomparably more than in most, springs, brooks, millstreams, and rivers abound. Wells also, so far as there has been occasion to make experiments, are found near the surface, abounding in good water. It is indeed doubted whether these advantages exist in the same degree in any other country of the same extent.

The navigation supplied by the ocean, lakes, and rivers is hardly excelled. These waters are so situated that they spread the means of conveyance at little distances throughout almost the whole of this vast tract. The coast with its windings extends about 1,700 miles. The St. Lawrence with its lakes furnishes a navigation of between two and three thousand. The Missouri, of which the Mississippi, the Ohio, the Arkansas, and the Red River are only mighty branches, is navigable almost four thousand. When to these are added the numerous, navigable rivers which everywhere divide our coast into a succession of peninsulas, it will easily be admitted that few countries are furnished by the hand of the Creator with more numerous, more universally diffused, or more important accommodations of this kind.

The soil of this vast region is of every kind and of every degree of fertility. It is also fitted to every species of vegetation found within the same climates.

Considerable *tracts* are lean, but almost all of them are capable of being made fertile by a skillful cultivation. The great mass is fertile by nature, and the parts which are not are less in their extent than the inhabitants will hereafter find to be necessary for furnishing them with timber and fuel.

Throughout a great part of this territory, the surface exhibits all that is beautiful and magnificent in landscape.

The mineral productions which it contains are hitherto imperfectly known. Of the metals, we have iron and lead in inexhaustible quantities. On a more limited scale we have discovered gold, copper, bismuth, antimony, zinc, and cobalt.

Coal mines are already found, inferior in quality and quantity to none in the world. Limestone, marble, and gypsum appear to be inexhaustible. Salt springs are wrought in considerable numbers throughout a part of the regions which lie west of a line drawn at the distance of two hundred miles from the Atlantic.

The indigenous vegetation of this country is various, to a degree which it will require many years to ascertain. Most of the productions which have been thought valuable by man, except a part of those which are the result of agriculture, are included in their number.

The artificial vegetation extends to almost all the valuable productions of the field and the garden, and to a great multitude of such as are merely ornamental. The sugar cane is prosperously cultivated in Georgia, furnishes a large article of commerce in southern Louisiana, and will soon occupy a great part of the Mississippi territory. From two to three hundred thousand square miles on the southern limit of the United States may be considered as fitted to be a prosperous sugar country: a tract sufficient to supply all the demands of the inhabitants for ages to come. Rice, indigo, cotton, tobacco, all the kinds of corn, flax, and hemp are cultivated with ease and success. Silk is produced with similar ease and success in Connecticut, and may be in every part of the Union. Wool of every quality is already furnished in great quantities, and is increasing with astonishing rapidity. All the domestic animals abound. It is unnecessary to mention the variety or the plenty of fruits.

The whole tract which lies north of the latitude of the Roanoke, except the flat country of Virginia, may be justly considered as healthy, and all the hill country which is south of that river. The inhabitants within these extensive limits are well made, robust, and hardy, and are fitted for every enterprise which demands energy of body or strength of mind.

The population of the United States amounted in the year 1790 to 3,950,000; in 1800, to 5,350,066; in 1810, to 7,230,514.[3] In twenty-five years from 1790, that is in 1815, they will amount, according to the same ratio of increase, to 8,050,642, that is, to 150,642 more than double the original number. This, however, is short of the real number, because the ratio of increase advances regularly in an arithmetical progression, being least in the first and greatest in the last of the twenty-five years. Accordingly, during the first term of ten years, the ratio was thirty-four and a third per cent; and in the second ten years it was thirty-six and a quarter per cent. During the remaining five, it has been greater still, although, as the whole amount is unknown, the ratio cannot be accurately estimated. Probably twenty-four years may be assumed as the period within which the people of the United States have actually doubled their numbers. But, as I would rather fall short in my estimate of the real number than exceed it, I will assume twenty-five years as this period. In the year 1825, the number of the people in the United States will be 10,700,132; in 1850, 21,400,264; in 1875, 42,800,528; in 1900, 85,610,056: [4] and this, independently of any additions from abroad: the allowance made at the commencement of this calculation being much more than a balance for any such additions. With this population, our territory will allow more than thirteen acres of land for the support of an individual, or about eighty-seven acres to a family consisting of six and a half, which may be assumed as the average number. It will undoubtedly be admitted that this quantity will be more than sufficient for the sustenance of such a family.

I am, Sir, yours, etc.

# LETTER II

*Enterprise, ingenuity, intelligence, means of acquiring knowledge; laws, morals, language, and liberty of the people of the United States—Extent of country yet to be settled—Institutions of the country in a state of improvement—Increase of evangelical religion and catholicism—Future prospects of the United States*

*Dear Sir,*

In the preceding letter I have remarked that the great body of those extensive regions which form the territory of the American States enjoy a salubrious climate; and that the inhabitants, already thinly spread over it, are possessed of vigorous constitutions. In this manner they are fitted to be able defenders of their country, and to encounter with success those difficulties which in the progress of human life so frequently occur, and so imperiously demand firmness of body as well as resolution. The inhabitants of no country, it is believed, unite more strength with more agility.

At the same time no people have more enterprise. There are two important facts which demonstrate this position in the clearest manner. Antecedently to the commencement of the restrictive system by our government, we were the most commercial nation in the world except that of Great Britain. Every corner of the earth was visited by our ships, and the tonnage owned by the people of Massachusetts was probably greater than that possessed by any equal number of individuals on the globe, unless where the whole, or a great proportion of them, were inhabitants of some great commercial city.

The other fact in which our enterprise is decisively discovered is the conversion of an immense wilderness into a fruitful field. Of the magnitude of this work it is not expected that Europeans will easily form adequate conceptions. Even *they* must acknowledge it to be very great, although it cannot be supposed that they should comprehend its extent without actual experience or inspection.

It is to be remembered that these are the objects by which the enterprise of the Americans will for an indefinite and it is hoped for a very long period be principally demanded.

My countrymen are also possessed of their full share of ingenuity. This you may perhaps be disposed to question. Were you to reside in the United

States a short time and to make yourself an eyewitness of the many new and successful modes which they have invented for the purpose of facilitating useful business, and which they are every day inventing, the question would be at an end. With this ingenuity they are now adding continually to the number, kind, and degree of their enjoyments, reducing the prices of very many of the products of human labor, and giving the best proofs of still more numerous and important improvements of this nature to be made hereafter. From this cause, to a considerable extent, is derived the extraordinary fact that the manufactories of the United States have within a few years risen from small beginnings to the amount of two hundred millions of dollars. From this cause also, my countrymen have built a vast number of bridges over large rivers within a little period, and have carried the arts of building and navigating ships to a degree of perfection which, it is believed, has not been excelled.

The colonization of these states was begun by civilized men, and not by a horde of hunters, nor of shepherds. Those who directed their affairs had been educated in many instances at universities of high distinction, and brought with them the learning, science, arts, and refinements of their own country. These men laid the foundation of our state of society. The disadvantages with which they had to struggle were, I acknowledge, numerous and great. Still they conveyed their own views, spirit, and character into the institutions which they formed, both literary and civil; and sowed effectually in a soil where they could not fail of taking root, the seeds of future improvement. The fruit which they have already borne has been extensive and valuable, and they are now promising to bear much more.

Among the blessings which they conveyed to succeeding generations, the universal establishment of schools for the education of every human being within their precincts was certainly of very high importance. In this manner they laid the foundation of thought, ratiocination, active invention, and good sense in every one of their descendants who was willing to think. In this manner they fitted them to think and judge as freemen, and furnished them with the proper means of becoming Christians upon the solid basis of sober conviction. In a word, they raised in this manner the national character, that is, the character of the many of whom nations are everywhere constituted, to a degree on the scale of intellectual existence not often reached by other nations.

The benefit under consideration has been chiefly realized hitherto by the people of New England, but is fast diffusing itself, and at no great distance of time will in all probability be actually diffused throughout the Union.

In most of the mechanical and many of the manufacturing arts, our workmen have already acquired a considerable degree of skill; and the products of their labor continually enter the markets with success. In these and other useful pursuits, we are also improving with a rapidity which is honorable both to the industry and the ingenuity of my countrymen.

The circle of literature and science taught at English universities is also taught here, on a less extensive scale, I acknowledge, than in Great Britain, but on one which is perhaps sufficient to satisfy every existing demand of utility. As our state of society advances and these demands increase, the scale of instruction is regularly enlarged, and within a moderate period will probably reach the European extent.

Our laws are substantially the same as yours; in some instances worse, and in some better. Your common law is adopted, *mutatis mutandis,* in most of our states. Much of your written law is copied as to its substance into our statute books. What you make worse, from your prejudices in favor of ancient customs, we, in consequence of our freedom from those prejudices, make better. What you make better by superior skill, we, for the want of it, make worse. Indeed, most of our jurisprudence is little else than a copy of yours.

The morals of this country differ, it must be acknowledged, materially in its different parts. As a whole, they are, I suspect, at least as good as yours; and in the best states, much better. Massachusetts and Connecticut will in this respect not suffer by a comparison with any other countries. All the same observations are equally applicable to our religion. Indeed, where the principles of the Reformation are adopted, it can be hardly necessary to observe that religion and morals are exactly parallel in their progress: morality being only one branch of religion thus understood.

The language spoken in the United States, with two or three exceptions of no great importance, is the same. The French and Spanish are spoken in Louisiana; and the German in Pennsylvania, and to a small extent in a few other places. These, however, as a part of current speech will soon be lost and forgotten; and the English, within fifty years from the present time, will probably be the only language spoken throughout the American republic.

The white population of this country is universally free. This I trust, will ere long be true of the black population. In 1810, near two hundred thousand of these people had been emancipated, or been born in a state of freedom. The number is annually increasing. The disposition to emancipate slaves, and the conviction that they ought to be emancipated, are gaining ground; and there is no reason to doubt that they will spread wherever slaves are holden. In every other respect our freedom is as entire as that of any country, ancient or modern.

If you admit the justice of these summary observations, I think you will agree with me that no such scene has hitherto been presented to the eye of men as that which the American States may be justly said to exhibit. The colonization of almost every country in the world, and of every country occupying any great extent, has been begun, and usually carried on, with very few of the advantages which have been recited. The colonists very generally have been either savages, or at best but half civilized. Where they have not been mere hunters or shepherds, or, in other words, mere Indians or Tartars, they have had few arts and scarcely any learning or science. Long after Canada had been settled, it did not contain a single man who could either construct or tend a mill. The whole colonial population of Europe in its early ages did not contain a single tribe of civilized men, although they were not all in the grossest sense savages. Greece had neither arts, nor sciences, till she gained them from Phœnicia and Egypt; nor Rome, till she learned them from Greece. The first collection of men in possession of learning, laws, freedom, arts, and true religion who colonized a wilderness were derived from Great Britain. The event was novel; its consequences have hitherto been singular.

No less singular is the field of colonization. In a sense it is a world. It requires little forecast to perceive that the people of the United States will in their progress fill almost the whole continent of North America, populate in the end all the extensive regions which are north of the kingdom of Mexico, and station themselves within half a century on the shores of the Pacific Ocean. This is a tract larger than the whole Russian empire; and from its climate, soil, and commercial advantages is capable of supporting twice as many inhabitants.

This population, you will observe, will consist of freemen: of men enlightened by the liberal arts and sciences, governed by equitable laws, and professing the Protestant religion. They will of course be intelligent, refined, and, it is hoped, virtuous, and happy.

When the descendants of Noah began to fill Persia and its environs with inhabitants, "the whole earth," we are told, "was of one language and one speech." [1] Such substantially is the fact with regard to the colonists of this western world. One language will ultimately be spoken throughout the vast region and by the immense population which I have mentioned. The only parallel fact is found in the empire of China, that is, in China proper. In less than two centuries the population of the American States will in all probability exceed that of China, and the extent of territory occupied by it will be quadrupled. The language spoken in it is wonderfully superior to that of the Chinese. It is written with alphabetical letters. It already includes nearly all the learning and science, and generally all the useful information found in the world. In words which denote different ideas, it is more copious than any other. The people of this country will, therefore, enjoy advantages in their intercourse with each other, and in their access to fountains of knowledge and improvement, which were never enjoyed by so extensive a population. The Russian empire will soon contain, perhaps it would be more proper to say it already contains, a very numerous population. Besides other disadvantages under which it labors, it must, for a considerable period at least, struggle with the serious inconveniences arising from the great diversity of its languages. Here there will be but one; and, if we may argue from our experience hitherto, it will probably be spoken with hardly a dialectic variation. Let me request you to contemplate this subject for a moment. Consider how many minds will here be set in motion by a single interesting book on any and every important subject of information. How many useful thoughts will be started at once by every serious advancement in knowledge. What strong motives to intellectual exertion will be awakened by the amplitude of the field of mental labor; by the multitude of those who will read, examine, and, in cases of real merit, approve. How vast will seem the prospect of usefulness to the writer who feels that he is to labor for such a multitude, and that he is to write in a language which every one of them can understand. Must we not believe that the mind will put forth all its powers, that its views will be unusually expanded and dignified, and that its efforts will partake largely of that energy and ardor with which the navigators of Europe formerly pursued discoveries in the western world, or with which warriors have attempted the conquest of the eastern.

The prospect which here opens to the eye of contemplation is certainly extraordinary: I think it is singular. Almost all our institutions, perhaps all which deserve to be permanent, have with as much regularity as seems compatible with the present state of mankind been in a course of improvement. Manners, laws, learning, and in some respects religion may be justly considered as being *now* progressive. The mechanical, manufacturing, and liberal arts, literature, and science are at the present time advanced, upon the whole, beyond any preceding attainments. Agriculture and domestic economy are better understood and more skillfully pursued. Roads, bridges, and canals are multiplied and constructed in a better manner. The number of schools and colleges is increasing, and those which already exist are more successfully directed. Judicial proceedings are daily becoming more accurate, and more conformed to the best principles of legal science; and political measures, although for some time past in a state of deterioration, are yet teaching us several valuable lessons, out of which improvement will one day spring. In spite of the pride of self-consistency, it is now acknowledged by those who are most opposed to making the acknowledgement that a navy is the proper means of our defense and safety; that our principal harbors ought to be fortified; that our form of government is ill suited to offensive war; and that for defraying the expenses of war, taxes are indispensable. We are also learning, though it must be confessed by slower degrees, that we are not so much wiser and better than the rest of mankind as many of our people have heretofore believed, or at least professed to believe. Persons of this cast are beginning to suspect that modesty is one excellence of the human character, and a proof of other excellencies; and that boasting furnishes fewer and smaller claims to respect than they have been accustomed to imagine. This melioration of our character will undoubtedly make a slow progress, yet I believe it is really progressive. The religious part of the community also are evidently assuming a higher character. A catholicism, heretofore not generally cherished by religious men, a catholicism real and evangelical, far removed from that gross indifference to truth and falsehood, to right and wrong, so often boasted of under the sacred name of catholicism, is fostered and exercised extensively by men of real piety. The "tithing of mint, anise, and cummin" makes a less, and "judgment, mercy, and faith" [2] make a much more prominent appearance on the roll of Christian attributes. The minds of good men are becoming more expansive; their prejudices are beginning to disappear; and the benevolence of the Gospel is exhibiting itself in its own proper character with vigor and success. Seen in a light more its own, and operating in a mannner more suited to its nature, it is claiming higher respect from mankind, and daily finds its claims more and more readily acknowledged. The world, bad as it is, is willing that Christians, in some modes at least, should do good: and to do good has, to a considerable extent, become their favorite, and even their acknowledged employment.

With all these objects in view, you will suffer me to indulge the feelings of an American while I contemplate the prospect which futurity presents concerning my country. Permit me to remind you of the extent of these states: the climate, the soil, the productions, the population; the character of the inhabitants; their arts, commerce, education, learning, science, freedom, laws, manners, morals and religion. Let me bring to your recollection the rapid progress of our population, the progressive state in which most of the articles which I have recited actually exist at the present time, and the promise which they give of superior advancement. With these objects in contemplation, a traveler passing through the countries which I have described, surveying the scenes which they everywhere present to his eye, and remembering within how short a period and amid how many difficulties they have been raised up in a howling wilderness, will think it no extravagance of imagination to believe that throughout this vast empire, villages innumerable will everywhere speedily adorn its surface with the same beauty and cheerfulness which he beholds around him. To these he will add the flourishing towns and splendid cities which not only the shore of the ocean, but the numerous lakes and rivers, will in the interior see rising on their borders, the seats of various useful manufactures and of an inland commerce resembling and excelling that of the Chinese empire. Everywhere he will foresee neat schoolhouses stationed at little distances, diffusing each over its proper circle the education necessary to every human being, and contributing to create a new national character by elevating the minds of those of whom the great body of every nation is formed. To these his fancy will add, at distances somewhat greater, the vast collection of superior schools communicating more extensive information to a multitude, less indeed, but still very great. Within every twenty thousand square miles, his mind will easily station a college, where literature and science will shed their light upon a number of votaries sufficiently great to perform all the kinds of human business which demand extensive information. Nor will he hesitate, since he sees the work already begun, to fix here and there seats of professional science, in which shall be taught whatever is known by man concerning medicine, law, policy, and religion; or to superadd those national institutions designed not so much to teach as to advance the knowledge of man. From what he has already seen, he will easily anticipate the rise of temples consecrated to the worship of God, diffusing, like so many stars, light and splendor over the whole horizon of his view. In these temples a hundred thousand enlightened ministers of the Gospel may be fairly supposed to teach the way of life through the Redeemer of mankind to an equal number of congregations, containing at least as many millions of worshippers; of human beings worshipping, not the idol Fo, nor Juggernaut, nor Jupiter, nor the sun, nor Osiris, but JEHOVAH. The ministers intended will be such as are enlightened by learning and science, and by the beams of the Sun of Righteousness; and will illuminate the mass of inhabitants, in most lands and ages covered by the clouds of ignorance, but here enjoying the means of that education which is indispensable to all men, and sufficient to raise them to the proper character of intelligent beings.

The Chinese with very corrupt morals have as a nation mild and gentle manners. May not such manners grow as effectually out of freedom, intelligence, and Christianity, as out of idolatry, ignorance, and slavery? Particularly, will not such manners spring up from these sources if my countrymen should as a body come to understand the true nature of war and hate it accordingly, and should they, as would be the necessary consequence, prize peace according to its inestimable value? The manners of the people of New England, unless I mistake, are already more gentle, more softened, in the middle and inferior classes than in those of the same classes in most other countries. Perhaps also, they more generally detest war. The institutions which have given these characteristics to the people of New England will give them to any other people, and these institutions are spreading both their reputation and their efficacy through the United States; their progress is silent indeed, and is made amid many prejudices and difficulties, but, as I believe, is real. Christianity stamps an immense value on human life as the period in which the blessings of immortality are to be obtained. In this manner it exterminates duels and all other wars besides that which is purely defensive. From these two sources have arisen most of the coarse, harsh, tigerlike feelings of the human mind, and most of that gross, odious, and brutal behavior extensively seen both in countries which called themselves civilized, and in men who challenged to themselves the character of gentlemen. Religion is plainly extending its influence over these states, although much less rapidly than every good man must wish; and, wherever it prevails, softens and humanizes both the heart and behavior. That it will hereafter increase with wonderful celerity, and that at no great distance of time, is the general belief of Christians. That it will first shed its happy influence upon the nations where it already exists may be regarded as a thing of course; and here, certainly, as probably as in any other country. Should this expectation be realized, both the manners and the morals of the Americans as a people will be raised to a higher degree on the scale of intellectual existence than the world has hitherto witnessed.

As a consequence of this "consummation," so "devoutly to be wished," the inhabitants of these states may be fairly expected to unite their efforts with those of their brethren on the eastern side of the Atlantic in spreading the blessings of Christianity through the world. Already they are extensively and deeply engaged in sending the Gospel and faithful ministers to preach it into the "regions of darkness and the shadow of death." [3] The spirit with which this is done, and the exertions to which it gives birth, are as you have seen rapidly increasing. It is difficult to assign limits to their future progress or their future efficacy. When we consider the number of those who within a few years will in all probability unite to accomplish this glorious object, when we remember that the efforts made hitherto have only invigorated the disposition to make more and greater efforts, there will be nothing romantic in believing that colleges here may regularly send out their quotas of missionaries, or that ships extensively freighted with Bibles may convey these messengers of peace and good will over every ocean, and to every benighted corner of the globe.

It will be very naturally objected to these observations that the American States will soon be dissevered and will then form separate empires. These empires, it will be further observed, will then, like those on the eastern continent, have discordant interests; and, like them, will of course carry on a series of wars which will partly prevent, and partly destroy, that state of prosperity here described.

All this may, I acknowledge, be true; and, possibly, to an extent not even dreamed of by the objector. We certainly have hitherto had sins enough to merit such a punishment, and folly enough to adopt and voluntarily to contrive and execute the measures by which it will be effectuated. The causes which to my eye furnish a rational hope of brighter scenes may cease to operate, and the era of peace and prosperity to the human race may be more distant than I have imagined. As I have not intended to prophecy, I shall not insist upon the probability that these conjectures will be verified; but shall still take the liberty of indulging hopes that events substantially like those which I have exhibited will be found in the future destinies of my country.

It ought to be remarked, however, that the mere separation of the American empire into independent districts will not, of course, either prevent or destroy the happiness in question. It may retard its advent, or preclude the perfection which it might otherwise reach; but it may also hasten the former, and insure the latter. Small states, when safe from foreign invasion, have been usually happier than great ones. The limited powers of the human mind seem hitherto to have been incompetent to direct with success the internal affairs of a great empire so as to secure to its inhabitants that degree of happiness which has been realized in states of a moderate extent. The present arrangement of the American territory was intended to promote the internal prosperity of the people by the division, and their safety by the union of the states. How far it will answer this end is yet to be proved. For aught which man can foresee, other divisions and other unions may be unnecessary.

Should these hereafter take place, New England and New York will, almost of course, be united in the same political body. The inhabitants are now substantially one people. Their interests of every kind are inseparably blended, and not a natural or rational cause of division can be found in either their physical or moral circumstances. Should they be separated from their sister states, there cannot be a doubt that their citizens will hereafter find in their local situation, soil, and climate; in their religious and political systems; in their arts, literature, and science; in their manners and morals; in their health, energy, and activity, ample, perhaps peculiar sources of national greatness and prosperity.

I am, Sir, yours, etc.

# *NOTES*

# ABBREVIATIONS

### DWIGHT MANUSCRIPT NOTEBOOKS AMONG THE DWIGHT FAMILY PAPERS AT THE YALE UNIVERSITY LIBRARY

"Cape Cod No. 1": Timothy Dwight ["Cape Cod No. 1"] (Sept. 17, 1800).

"Cape Cod No. 3": Timothy Dwight, "Cape Cod No. 3" (Newport Indian Converts, Tues. Sept. 23; also at end ". . . to be added after the account of Yarmouth in No. 4").

"Hallowell No. 1": Timothy Dwight, "Hallowell No. 1" (New Haven to Hallowell and to Portsmouth, Sept. 15–Sept. 29, 1807).

"The Trip to Cape Cod Journal #1": [Benjamin W. Dwight], "The Trip to Cape Cod Journal #1."

"Vergennes No. 5": Timothy Dwight, "Vergennes No. 5" (Middlebury-Onion River, Sept. 30–Oct. 1798).

"Vergennes No. 7": Timothy Dwight, "Vergennes No. 7" (State of Vermont-Glen's Falls, n.d.).

"Vergennes No. 8": Timothy Dwight, "Vergennes No. 8" (Glen's Falls, New Haven, n.d.).

### SECONDARY SOURCES

A. A. A. S. *Memoirs:* American Academy of Arts and Sciences, *Memoirs.* Vols. I–III. Boston, 1780–1815.

*Appletons':* James G. Wilson and John Fiske, eds., *Appletons' Cyclopaedia of American Biography.* 6 vols. Revised edition, with supplement. New York, 1898–1899.

Belknap, *New Hampshire:* Jeremy Belknap, *History of New Hampshire.* 3 vols. Philadelphia and Boston, 1784–1792.

*D. A. B.:* Allen Johnson and Dumas Malone, eds., *Dictionary of American Biography.* 22 vols. New York, 1928–1958.

Dexter, *Yale Graduates:* Franklin B. Dexter, *Biographical Sketches of the Graduates of Yale College.* 6 vols. New York, 1885–1911; New Haven, 1912.

*D. N. B.:* Leslie Stephen and Sidney Lee, eds., *Dictionary of National Biography.* 22 vols. London, 1921–1922.

Dwight, *Descendants:* Benjamin W. Dwight, *The History of the Descendants of John Dwight of Dedham, Mass.* 2 vols. New York, 1874.

Hubbard, *Narrative:* William Hubbard, *A Narrative of the Troubles with the Indians in New England . . . to this Present Year 1677 . . .* Boston, 1677.

Hutchinson, *History of Massachusets-Bay:* Thomas Hutchinson, *The History of the Colony of Massachusets-Bay . . .* 3 vols. Vols. I and II, Boston, 1764–1767; vol. III, London, 1828.

Mather, *Magnalia:* Cotton Mather, *Magnalia Christi Americana: or, the Ecclesiastical History of New England . . . unto the year of Our Lord 1698 . . .* London, 1702.

M. H. S. *Collections:* Massachusetts Historical Society, *Collections.* Especially 1st series, vols. I–X, 1792–1809.

Shipton, *Sibley's Harvard Graduates:* Clifford K. Shipton, *Sibley's Harvard Gradu-*

*ates . . . Biographical Sketches of Those Who Attended Harvard College . . .* Vols. IV–XIV. Cambridge, 1933; Boston, 1937–1968.

Sibley, *Harvard Graduates:* John Langdon Sibley, *Biographical Sketches of Graduates of Harvard University in Cambridge, Massachusetts.* 3 vols. Cambridge, 1873–1885.

Sprague, *Annals:* William B. Sprague, *Annals of the American Pulpit; or, Commemorative Notices of Distinguished American Clergymen of Various Denominations . . .* 9 vols. New York, 1857–1869. Especially vols. I and II, "Trinitarian Congregational," 1857.

Trumbull, *Connecticut:* Benjamin Trumbull, *A Complete History of Connecticut, Civil and Ecclesiastical, from the Emigration of its First Planters from England in MDCXXX to MDCCXIII.* Hartford, 1797.

Williams, *Vermont:* Samuel Williams, *The Natural and Civil History of Vermont.* 2 vols. Burlington, Vt., 1809.

## JOURNEY TO NIAGARA

### LETTER I

1. Proverbs xxvi, 16.

2. Lewis Evans (c. 1700–1756), Pennsylvania-born surveyor, known particularly for his maps of the middle colonies, was the author of the pamphlet, *Geographical, Historical, Political, Philosophical and Mechanical Essays: The First, Containing an Analysis of a General Map of the Middle British Colonies in America* (Philadelphia and London, 1755); see pp. 8–9.

3. Samuel Andrew Law (1771–1845), Yale 1792, studied law at the Litchfield school of Tapping Reeve, and, after admission to the bar in 1795, ran a school in his hometown of Cheshire, Connecticut, until his move to Delaware county, New York, in 1797. There Law acquired several excellent farms in Meredith and later served as postmaster and judge of the court of common pleas.

4. Allan Ramsay (1686–1758), Scottish poet, wigmaker, and bookseller, published his poems at Edinburgh in broadside form from 1715; his *Collected Poems* appeared in 1721 and several other volumes by 1730.

5. John Lincklaen (d. 1822) came to America about 1791 to investigate lands in Pennsylvania and New York for purchase by Dutch speculators; as agent for the Holland Land Company which was formed in 1796, he concentrated on the improvement and sale of lands in the vicinity of Cazenovia, New York.

### LETTER II

1. Many of the names of these towns have changed since the time of Dwight's visits to them; for example, Galen is now Clyde; Ovid, Covert; Milton, Genoa; Oghquaga, Windsor; Chenango, Binghamton; and Tioga, Athens.

2. Three Swartwout brothers, Samuel, Robert, and John, were merchants in New York. Of the three, Samuel Swartwout (1783–1856) gained dubious fame first as an accomplice of Aaron Burr and subsequently as a witness against him. In the office of collector of the port of New York, Swartwout appropriated more than a million dollars in public funds.

3. Centering on a legendary third-century hero of the Celts, Ossianic literature was revived in the eighteenth century by James Macpherson (1736–1796), many of whose translations were in fact original drafts.

4. Charles Williamson (1757–1808), British officer and land promoter, became a naturalized citizen during the period in which he administered a tract of 1,200,000 acres bought from Robert Morris by three London speculators, Sir William Pulteney, John Hornby, and Patrick Colquhoun. In order to encourage settlers, Williamson built roads, bridges, and a hotel at Geneva, New York. He served in the New York legislature, 1796–1800, and with the aid of Aaron Burr succeeded in guiding through the New York Assembly a bill permitting aliens in the state to hold title to land for a limited period of time. Williamson's connection with the London Associates was severed (c. 1802) when his expensive improvements met with disapproval. For an account of Williamson's activities, see Orsamus Turner, *History of the Pioneer Settlement of Phelps and Gorham's Purchase . . .* (Rochester, N.Y., 1851), pp. 249–279.

5. The respectable clergyman of Geneva, New York, was Jedidiah Chapman (1741–1813), Yale 1762, formerly pastor of the Presbyterian Church of Orange, New Jersey. In 1800 Chapman was sent by the General Assembly of the Presbyterian Church to carry the dual responsibilities Dwight describes.

## LETTER III

1. William A. Williams (1763–1834), Yale 1780, originally from Connecticut, came to Canandaigua in 1793 after practising medicine for a short time in Hatfield, Massachusetts.

2. Timothy Field (1775–1844), Yale 1797, had studied theology with President Dwight and upon his recommendation was called to the church at Canandaigua, where he was ordained and installed in February 1800. Finding the work there discouraging, Field moved to Westminster, Vermont, in 1806.

3. With limited education Joseph Ellicott (1760–1826) made his way in the world as a surveyor. In the employ of the Holland Land Company from 1794, Ellicott surveyed the Holland Purchase, opened roads in the area, supported the building of the Erie Canal, and founded the city of Buffalo. Ultimately he was the political "boss" of the Democratic party in western New York. See *Reports of Joseph Ellicott* (ed. Robert W. Bingham) in Buffalo Historical Society *Publications*, 32 and 33 (1937–1941).

4. The counties of Genesee and Niagara were further subdivided subsequent to the date Dwight's table was compiled, and his figure for the population of Niagara county appears to be erroneous. From Genesee County, Monroe, Orleans, and Wyoming were taken; Erie was taken from Niagara. In terms of these subdivisions of New York, Dwight's table should read:

| | | *Townships* | *Inhabitants in 1810* |
|---|---|---|---|
| Genesee | contains | 1 | 3,660 |
| Monroe | " | 4 | 4,683 |
| Orleans | " | 1 | 1,164 |
| Wyoming | " | 2 | 2,736 |
| | | | |
| Niagara | " | 1 | 1,465 |
| Erie | " | 3 | 4,667 |

| | | Townships | Inhabitants in 1810 |
|---|---|---|---|
| Allegany | contains | 4 | 1,443 |
| Cattaraugus | " | 1 | 458 |
| Chautauqua | " | 2 | 2,381 |
| | | | 22,658 |

See New York. Secretary of State, *Census of the State of New York, for 1855; . . .* (Albany, 1857), pp. xvi–xxxii.

### LETTER IV

1. David Bacon (1771–1817), after studying theology with the Rev. Levi Hart, was in 1800 commissioned by the Connecticut Missionary Society to work with the Indians beyond Lake Erie, and was the first Protestant to preach at Fort Mackinac. Later he failed in his experiment to establish a theocratic community in the Western Reserve. Josiah Dunham published in the A.A.A.S. *Memoirs,* 3, I (1809), 116–118, his "Abstract of Meterological Observations made at Michillimakkinak . . . August 1802 to April 1803 . . ." John S. Edwards, Esq., was probably Dwight's cousin John Starke Edwards, son of Pierpont Edwards of New Haven (Dwight's mother's youngest brother), and a lawyer in Trumbull County, Ohio.

### LETTER V

1. In the *Reports of Joseph Ellicott,* I, 27–28, 31–32, Philip Stedman is described as the holder of a large tract of land granted to his uncle by the Seneca Indians in 1763. The Holland Land Company claimed about five hundred acres of the land, and Theophile Cazenove made inquiries of Ellicott concerning Stedman's legal rights and the amount of compensation he sought.

2. Dwight is probably referring to Andrew Ellicott (1754–1820), brother of Joseph Ellicott and also a surveyor and mathematician. With Joseph he made the earliest topographical study of the Niagara River, and was later active in surveying the site for the national capital. A letter dated December 10, 1789, from Andrew Ellicott to Dr. Benjamin Rush, which estimated the elevation of Lake Erie above Lake Ontario as about three hundred feet, was widely published at the time, in the *Massachusetts Magazine,* July 1790, the *Columbian Magazine,* June 1790, and others. The letter is reprinted in *Studies of the Niagara Frontier* (ed. Frank H. Severance) in Buffalo Historical Society *Publications,* 15 (1911), 384–385.

3. A Major Prescott of Connecticut, who was surveying for the Holland Land Company, is mentioned in the *Reports of Joseph Ellicott,* I, 31–32.

### LETTER VI

1. A Hamiltonian Federalist of Salem, Massachusetts, Timothy Pickering (1745–1829), Harvard 1763, became increasingly intolerant and unpopular in his varied career of public service. While secretary of state, he schemed against President Adams, and bitterly opposed Jefferson's and Madison's administrations, while encouraging disunionist sentiment among Federalists from 1804. In contrast to his political attitude, Pickering's efforts in improving agricultural conditions were progressive. On his friendship with Dwight, see Editor's Introduction, pp. xxv, xxvii–xxviii.

## LETTER VII

1. Captain Tobias Shandy is a major character in Laurence Sterne's *The Life and Opinions of Tristram Shandy, Gentleman* (9 vols., London, 1760–1767).

2. Constantin-François Chasseboeuf, Comte de Volney (1757–1820), imprisoned by the Jacobins during the Revolution, came to the United States in 1795 intending to settle permanently. On being accused of being a French spy, Volney returned to France and in 1799 accepted a senatorship under Napoleon. He never wrote the critique he had planned on American social and political institutions, but did publish *Tableau du climate et du sol des États-Unis d'Amérique* (Paris, 1803); see the English translation by Charles Brockden Brown, *A View of the Soil and Climate of the United States of America: . . .* (Philadelphia, 1804), pp. 102–131.

3. A successful lawyer and one of the shrewdest Federalist politicians, Uriah Tracy (1755–1807), Yale 1778, trained at Tapping Reeve's law school at Litchfield, Connecticut, and served in the United States House of Representatives, 1793–1796, and in the Senate, 1796–1807.

4. Cambridge-educated historian and traveler William Coxe (1747–1828) published his *Travels in Switzerland* in three volumes. See the second London edition (1791), I, 397–406, for Coxe's views about goiters.

5. Horace-Bénédict de Saussure (1740–1799), Swiss scientist and professor of philosophy at Geneva, 1762–1786, included both travel information and scientific observations in *Voyages dans les Alpes . . .*, (4 vols., Neuchatel, 1779–1796), which is cited by William Coxe, *Travels in Switzerland* (2nd ed., London, 1791) I, 402–405.

## LETTER VIII

1. Sir William Pulteney (d. 1805) was one of the three London capitalists to whom Robert Morris sold the lands in western New York which he had purchased from Phelps and Gorham in August 1790. The new owners, Pulteney, John Hornby, and Patrick Colquhoun, placed title and control of the property in the hands of Charles Williamson, who settled in Bath, New York. Oliver Phelps (1749–1809), Connecticut merchant, officeholder, and land promoter, had purchased with Nathaniel Gorham the pre-emptive rights to six million acres in western New York. They were unable to meet the financial obligations, and, after returning part of the original purchase to the state of Massachusetts, sold the tract mentioned above to Robert Morris. By 1796 further speculation in Mississippi lands had put Phelps deep in debt. In 1802 he took up residence in Canandaigua, New York, and served one term in Congress, 1803–1805.

## LETTER IX

1. For Skenandoa (1706?–1816), see Dwight's account in a later footnote, in "The Iroquois," Letter II. Skenandoa may have been born into another tribe and adopted by the Oneida at an early age.

2. Concerning the brothers Thomas and Seth Jenkins, early proprietors of Hudson, New York, see Stephen B. Miller, *Historical Sketches of Hudson* (Hudson, 1862), pp. 6–18; and Anna R. Bradbury, *History of the City of Hudson* (Hudson, 1908), pp. 16–45. For more than three decades members of this family became mayors of the city.

## FIRST JOURNEY TO LAKE WINNIPESAUKEE, OR WENTWORTH

### LETTER I

1. Nathaniel Peabody (1741–1823), as a member of the New Hampshire legislature from 1776 to 1795, was a leader in the reorganization of the colony as a state. A successful physician, Peabody helped found the New Hampshire Medical Society as well as the academy which Dwight describes.

2. A Charles Little was listed as a selectman in Center Harbor, New Hampshire, in 1801, 1805–1808.

### LETTER II

1. The Scottish Presbyterian clergyman John Witherspoon (1723–1794), educated at the University of Edinburgh, came to America to accept the presidency of the College of New Jersey in 1768, and, while in this office, promoted the unification and expansion of the Presbyterian Church. Known for his activities in support of the Revolution, Witherspoon was also one of the commissioners of the Scotch-American Company which arranged for immigrants from the vicinity of Inchinnan to settle in Ryegate and Barnet. President Witherspoon also invested extensively in lands in Vermont, especially in Ryegate and Newbury. See Edward Miller and Frederic P. Wells, *History of Ryegate, Vermont* . . . (St. Johnsbury, Vt., 1913), pp. 9–12, 39–40.

2. Dwight quotes himself, *Travels,* "Journey to the Canada Line," Letter VI.

3. Numerous members of the Hale family lived in and about Newbury, Vermont, in 1812. A respected citizen, Joshua Hale (1764–1853), lived in the village of Wells River and served in the militia, although he is not identified as ever having attained the rank of major. See Robert Safford Hale, *Genealogy of the Descendants of Thomas Hale* . . . (Albany, N.Y., 1889), especially p. 313.

4. Dwight's eulogy of Federalist Roger Griswold (1762–1812), Yale 1780, son of Gov. Matthew Griswold, does not convey Griswold's inability to accept the growing democratization of American politics. By contrast, David H. Fischer in *The Revolution of American Conservatism* (New York, 1965) states, p. 298: "His public career, which included a famous fracas with Matthew Lyon on the floor of the House of Representatives, and complicity in Timothy Pickering's . . . conspiracy of 1804, was unstable and occasionally violent."

## SECOND JOURNEY TO LAKE WINNIPESAUKEE, OR WENTWORTH

### LETTER I

1. Dwight retained profound respect for John Wentworth (1737–1820), Harvard 1755, the Loyalist Anglican governor of New Hampshire from 1765 to 1775,

who was thereafter exiled from his native land because of the Revolution. In the early 1770's Wentworth had shared the labors of the farmers in his frontier settlement at Smith's Pond (later Lake Wentworth), explored the White Mountains with Jeremy Belknap, and encouraged his historical labors. In the same spirit Wentworth had attended to the establishment and sustenance of Dartmouth College (to which he remained devoted even when he governed Nova Scotia, 1792–1808). Despite his stand in the Revolution, Wentworth held the affection of Belknap, John Eliot, and classmate John Adams, who like Dwight never forgot Wentworth's many contributions in converting the New Hampshire wilderness into a civilized community. See Shipton, *Sibley's Harvard Graduates,* XIII, 650–681.

## JOURNEY TO UTICA

1. Jesse or James Deane (1748–1829), Dartmouth 1773, who associated with Indians from childhood, began his missionary labors in 1773–1774. After the Revolution he received land from the Oneidas which he exchanged for a tract in Westmoreland; from 1786 he lived there and served as a judge for Oneida county, New York. Dwight used Deane's unpublished manuscript on Indian mythology.

## THE IROQUOIS

### LETTER I

1. Cadwallader Colden's work was first published under the title, *The History of the Five Nations Depending on the Province of New-York in America,* New York (1727). Under a slightly different title the second and enlarged edition appeared in London (1747). Dwight used the third edition (London, 1755).

2. Dwight refers to William Smith, *The History of the Province of New-York* . . . (London, 1757).

3. De Witt Clinton's *A Discourse Delivered before the New-York Historical Society, at their Anniversary Meeting, 6th December, 1811* (New York, 1812) was also published in the New York Historical Society *Collections,* 2 (1814), 37–116.

4. Pierre François Xavier de Charlevoix (1682–1761), French Jesuit explorer and scholar, compiled a series of letters about his travels from Canada to New Orleans, and the customs and manners of the Indians, entitled *Journal historique,* published as an appendix to his three-volume *Histoire et description générale de la nouvelle France* (Paris, 1744). The first English edition of the *Journal of a Voyage to North-America* appeared in London in 1761. Baron Louis-Armand de Lom d'Arce de Lahontan (1666–c.1713), soldier and traveler in New France, wrote *Nouveaux voyages de mr. le baron de Lahontan dans l'Amérique Septentrionale* . . . (The Hague, 1703; English edition, London, 1703). "Except where he wilfully misled his readers . . . in many particulars [his book of travels] is the best account of New France in the late seventeenth century," according to Louise Phelps Kellogg. *D.A.B.,* X, 548. Louis Hennepin (1640–c.1701), chaplain at Fort

Frontenac with LaSalle in 1678, accompanied the explorer on other expeditions. He wrote *Description de la Louisiane . . .* (Paris, 1683); and *Nouvelle decouverte d'un très grand pays situé dans l'Amérique* (Utrecht, 1697), which was published a year later at London in translation. His accounts are considered unreliable.

### LETTER III

1. A popular English author, Thomas Salmon (1679–1767) wrote *Modern History: or, the Present State of All Nations . . .* (4 vols., London, 1736–1738) and *The Universal Traveller, or a Compleat Description of the Several Nations of the World . . .* (2 vols., London, 1752–1753).

2. Red Jacket or Sagoyewatha (1751–1830), a Seneca chief, allied with the British during the Revolution and with the Americans in the War of 1812. Dwight was probably aware of Red Jacket's complete opposition to Christianity. See De Witt Clinton, *A Discourse,* in N.Y.H.S. *Collections,* 2 (1814), 74–75.

3. Horace, *Epistulae,* I, vi, 1: "Marvel at nothing."

4. Cornplanter or Garyan-wah-gah (1732–1836), a Seneca half-breed, shifted his loyalties from the French in the Seven Years' War to the British in the Revolution and to the Americans in the War of 1812. He has been described as "the first temperance lecturer in the United States." *Appleton's,* I, 743.

5. Dwight refers to Thaddeus Osgood (1775–1852), Dartmouth 1803, a native of Methuen, Mass., ordained in 1806, who was active in founding churches and Sunday schools in newly settled areas.

## REMARKS ON EUROPEAN TRAVELERS IN AMERICA

### LETTER I

1. John Antes, *Observations on the Manners and Customs of the Egyptians; the Overflowing of the Nile, and its Effects . . .* (London, 1800).

2. Charles Brockden Brown (1771–1810), a Philadelphia lawyer and the first professional author in the United States, wrote *Alcuin: A Dialogue* (New York, 1798), a treatise on the rights of women, and utilized the American setting in his novels, including *Arthur Mervyn* (Philadelphia, 1799–1800) and *Ormund* (New York, 1799); thereafter he turned to editing and business enterprises. Dwight's page citations in C. F. Volney, *A View of the Soil and Climate of the United States of America . . .* (C. B. Brown, tr., Philadelphia, 1804) are correct, although in some instances the quotations are only approximate or have been condensed by Dwight.

3. Volney quotes Weld in *View of the United States,* pp. 86–91.

4. See Belknap, *New Hampshire.*

5. This remark of Voltaire has not been located. Leon Howard, *The Connecticut Wits* (Chicago, 1943), p. 348, notes that Dwight's knowledge of Voltaire and other modern infidels was frequently derived from secondary references rather than from direct reading of their works.

## LETTER II

1. The Dublin traveler Isaac Weld (1774–1856), arriving in Philadelphia in 1795, went by foot, canoe, horse, and wagon throughout the country. His acquaintances ranged from friendly Indian guides to the nation's leaders, including Washington. Upon his return to England Weld published *Travels through the States of North America, and the Provinces of Upper and Lower Canada, during the Years 1795, 1796, and 1797* (London, 1799). The mathematician Thomas Harriot (1560–1621), tutor to Sir Walter Raleigh, was sent by him to Virginia as a surveyor. Thereafter he wrote *A Briefe and True Report of the New Found Land of Virginia . . .* (London, 1588). Henry Wansey (1752?–1827), a retired clothier, became an antiquarian and traveler. After visiting the United States in 1794, he published *The Journal of an Excursion to the United States of North America . . .* (Salisbury, 1796).

2. Dwight (or the original printer), by leaving out the word "fine," misrepresented Weld's meaning. Weld, in talking about the appearance of American women, said, "In a few instances only would it be possible to find a *fine* woman at age forty, who has had a large family." Dwight alleges to be referring to the fourth edition of Weld and his page references indicate that it was a one-volume edition. The only fourth edition I have been able to locate is in two volumes (London, 1807), and it is possible that the edition Dwight used had such an omission. The equivalent page references to the two-volume, fourth edition of Weld are: p. 31, I, 22; p. 189, I, 261–262; p. 190, I, 262 (Here Weld says: "eighty feet," not eight as Dwight alleges.); *Ibid.*, I, 263; p. 205, I, 285; p. 548, II, 371; p. 549, II, 372; p. 549, II, 372; *Ibid.*, II, 372; p. 550, II, 374; *Ibid.*, II, 373; p. 552, II, 376.

3. Hooper Cumming (d. 1824), College of New Jersey 1805, D.D. Allegheny 1821, was pastor of the Second Church in Newark, New Jersey.

4. Dwight repeats a favorite phrase, which he probably adapts from Vergil, *Aeneid*, II, 65–66: ". . . et crimine ab uno disce omnis": ". . . from one learn the wickedness of all."

## LETTER III

1. Some of Dwight's quotations from the Duc de La Rochefoucauld are only approximate. His page citations are correct except as separately noted.

2. La Rochefoucauld, *Travels*, I, 356.

3. Volney, *View of the United States*, p. 6.

4. Dwight refers to "A Letter from Governor Shute to Rallé the Jesuit," M.H.S. *Collections*, 5 (1798), 112–119; the quotation is from p. 118. Samuel Shute (1662–1742), governor of the Massachusetts Bay Colony, 1716–1727, in addition to his problems with the Indians had difficulties with the colonists in the Assembly over his salary and powers.

5. The Duke misidentifies the family name as Rush, *Travels*, I, 492.

6. The reference should be to La Rouchfoucauld, *Travels*, I, 493.

7. Trumbull, *Connecticut*, pp. 313–314.

8. This reference as well as the two following should be to La Rouchfoucauld, *Travels*, I, 538.

9. This reference and the one following should be to La Rouchfoucauld, *Travels*, I, 539.

10. Dwight's source for the Latin, "Quod sensit valde sensit" (What he felt, he felt strongly) has not been identified. For the judgments on Roger Williams cited

here see Nathaniel Morton, *New-Englands Memoriall* (Cambridge, 1669), p. 79; Mather, *Magnalia,* VII, 8.

11. Numbers xxiii, 9: "For from the top of the rocks I see him, and from the hills I behold him: lo, the people shall dwell alone, and shall not be reckoned among the nations."

## LETTER IV

1. Little is known of the life of John Lambert (fl. 1811), the British author who published his observations after he had visited North America, 1806–1809. Unsuccessful in his attempts to foster the cultivation of hemp in Canada, Lambert remained to study the effect of its new government and to explore the countryside. Sir Richard Phillipps (1767–1840), at one time a sheriff of London, was an author, bookseller, and publisher of miscellaneous popular literature.

2. Dwight's quotations from Lambert are sometimes approximate or condensed. The page references are correct except where separately noted.

3. Dwight is here referring to the fact that Lambert prefers Roman Catholic to Protestant Christianity.

4. La Rochefoucauld, *Travels,* I, 398.

5. The auto-da-fé was a ceremony similar to the "sermo generalis" of the medieval inquisition. Accompanying the pronouncement of judgment by the inquisition and followed by the execution at the hands of the secular authorities of those sentenced as guilty, the auto-da-fé had come to mean the execution alone, particularly the burning of a heretic.

6. Edward Daniel Clarke (1769–1822), mineralogist, antiquarian, and traveler, published *Travels in Various Countries of Europe, Asia, and Africa* (6 vols., London, 1810–1823).

7. Patrick Colquhoun (1745–1820), lord provost of Glasgow, 1782–1783, and police magistrate in London from 1792 to 1818, was the author of many publications including *A Treatise on the Police of the Metropolis . . .* (London, 1796); and *A Treatise on the Commerce and Police of the River Thames: . . .* (London, 1800). Colquhoun also speculated in lands in western New York state.

8. Lambert, *Travels,* III, 85.

9. Thomas Ashe (1770–1835), Dublin-born traveler and novelist, was the author of *Travels in America, Performed in 1806, for the Purpose of Exploring the Rivers Alleghany, Monongahela, Ohio, and Mississippi . . .* (London and Newburyport, Mass., 1808).

10. Irish poet, Thomas Moore (1779–1852), while at Trinity College, 1795–1799, prepared a metrical translation of *Anacreon* (London, 1800). After a visit to America, 1803–1805, he expressed his criticisms of the United States through his *Epistles, Odes, and Other Poems* (London, 1806).

11. In his *Travels,* III, 474, Lambert says: "This general information among the country people of the United States, tends to remove that air of honest ignorant rusticity, which distinguish the peasantry of Europe; and hence they often appear to have the knowledge and cunning of the town, with little of its polish. . . . Yet a nation whose peasantry is thus instructed and enlightened, must, I should think, feel the benefit of it, and possess advantages which others, whose people are whelmed in ignorance and superstition, can never enjoy."

# LANGUAGE OF NEW ENGLAND

## LETTER I

1. Dwight was doubtless familiar with John Pickering's "Memoir on the Present State of the English Language in the United States of America; with a Vocabulary, containing various words and phrases which have been supposed to be peculiar to this country," A.A.A.S. *Memoirs,* 3, part II (1815), 439–536. Pickering notes that a great part of the work had been submitted to friends before its publication (p. 536). Although Pickering adopts the opposite point of view from Dwight, much of Dwight's material, particularly that about the usage of individual words, bears a marked resemblance to that presented by Pickering. Many of the words cited by Dwight are also discussed by Belknap in the "Preface" to volume III of his *New Hampshire.* Pickering also frequently uses Belknap as a source.

2. The reference is to Samuel Pegge (1733–1800), poet, musical composer, and author of *Anecdotes of the English Language: Chiefly Regarding the Local Dialect of London and its Environs* (London, 1803). Dwight's abbreviated list is drawn from the catalogue of errors among the natives of London which is found on pp. 53–248 of the *Anecdotes.*

3. Dwight is referring to a review of Noah Webster's *A Compendious Dictionary of the English Language* . . . (Hartford, 1806) in the *Eclectic Review,* 3, part I (London, 1807), 82–86. The reviewer speaks of Webster's pronunciation on page 85.

## LETTER II

1. All the words here discussed by Dwight are included by Pickering in his "Memoir" (A.A.A.S. *Memoirs,* 3, part II, 439–536). Pickering cites Webster as his authority for "lister" (p. 495) and "fourfold" (p. 480). For "immigrate, immigration, immigrant" (p. 487), Pickering cites Belknap, *New Hampshire,* "Preface," III, and surmises that Webster included these words on the authority of Belknap. The full citation for Dwight's reference to James Rennell (1742–1830) is: "An Appendix, Containing an Account of the Ganges and Burrampooter Rivers," in the second edition of the British geographer Rennell's *Memoir of a Map of Hindoostan; of the Mogul Empire* . . . (London, 1792; first edition without appendix, London, 1783), pp. 333–364. Pickering (p. 491) again cites Belknap, *New Hampshire,* "Preface," III, 6, for "intervals" (this word was not in Webster) and for "freshet" (pp. 480–482). The quotation that Johnson gives from Milton's *Paradise Regained,* II, 345, is:

> all fish from Sea or Shore,
> Freshet, or purling Brook, or shell or fin,

Samuel Johnson, *A Dictionary of the English Language* (2 vols., 6th ed. rev., London, 1785), I. Johnson's quotation from Milton, as well as a reference to Ferdinando Gorges, *Description of New England* (London, 1658), p. 29, are taken from Belknap by Pickering. Dwight's reference is probably to Robert Ainsworth's (1660–1743) *Thesaurus Linguae Latinae Compendiarius, or A Compendious Dic-*

*tionary of the Latin Tongue* . . . (London, 1736), which went through many editions and revisions; this quotation is not included either by Pickering or Belknap, nor have I been able to locate an edition which includes the word "freshet." "Grade" is also discussed by Pickering (p. 483).

2. See Pickering on the word "progress," (p. 509).

3. See Pickering on "improve" (pp. 487–489), including a letter from Franklin to Noah Webster, December 26, 1789, about the use of the word "improve." Pickering also refers to John Witherspoon's comment on "improve" in *Druid,* VII. Witherspoon's *Druid,* nos. V–VII (published in *Miscellaneous Works* [Philadelphia, 1803], pp. 180–197) is a general discussion of American usage of the English language.

4. Isaac Watts, *The Psalms of David* . . . (ed. Timothy Dwight, Albany, 1804), p. 237, Psalm 90, stanza 7.

5. Philip Doddridge (1702–1751), an English nonconformist minister, wrote *The Family Expositor: or A Paraphrase and Version of the New Testament with Critical Notes, and a Practical Improvement of Each Section* (6 vols., London, 1739–1756). Dwight had a copy of this work in his personal library.

6. Job xxxviii, 11.

## LEARNING, MORALS, ETC. OF NEW ENGLAND

### LETTER I

1. Oliver Goldsmith, "On Education," *The Bee,* No. VI (November 10, 1759), reprinted in Goldsmith's *Collected Works* (ed. Arthur Friedman, Oxford, 1966), I, 457.

2. Roger Sherman (1721–1793), whose biography is well covered by Dwight, had the distinction of being the only man to sign the Articles of Association of 1774, the Declaration of Independence, the Articles of Confederation, and the Constitution.

### LETTER III

1. The works of William Robertson (1721–1793), Scottish Presbyterian minister and historian, include *The History of America* (London, 1777).

2. Thomas Gray, "Elegy in a Country Churchyard," lines 53–65.

3. The quotation is from the *Quarterly Review,* 2 (1909), 331.

4. Dwight acknowledges briefly the contribution to New England's culture of Cotton Mather (1662–1728), Harvard 1678, pastor with his father, Increase Mather, of the North Church in Boston, member of the Royal Society, and author of more than 450 books. Reputedly the most learned man of his time, Cotton Mather made the *Magnalia* a repository of sermons, biographies, and historical narratives, which amounted to an ecclesiastical history of New England in the seventeenth century. In several instances the author of the *Travels* reveals his reliance on the *Magnalia.* A sanctimonious person and constant meddler in Massachusetts' politics, Mather was frustrated in his ambition to follow his father as president of Harvard and looked with favor on the new college at New Haven.

## LETTER IV

1. Dwight refers to the works of his grandfather, Jonathan Edwards: *A Treatise concerning Religious Affections* (Boston, 1746); *An Humble Inquiry into the Rules of the Word of God, concerning the Qualifications Requisite to a compleat Standing and full Communion in the Visible Christian Church* (Boston, 1749); *A Careful and Strict Enquiry into the Modern prevailing Notions of that freedom of Will, which is supposed to be essential to Moral Agency, Vertue and Vice, Reward and Punishment, Praise and Blame* (Boston, 1754); *The Great Christian Doctrine of Original Sin defended; Evidences of it's Truth Produced, and Arguments to the Contrary Answered* (Boston, 1758); *Two Dissertations, i. Concerning the End for which God created the World. ii. The Nature of true Virtue* (Boston, 1765).

2. Edwards' work on moral agency was a reply to Daniel Whitby's *A Discourse Concerning I. The True Import of the Words, Election and Reprobation, and the Things Signified by them in the Holy Scripture, etc.* (London, 1710). Edwards' work on original sin was in response to John Taylor's *The Scripture-Doctrine of Original Sin Proposed to Free and Candid Examination* (London, 1740).

3. James Boswell (1740–1795), Scottish man of letters, immortalized his friendship with Samuel Johnson in *The Life of Samuel Johnson . . .*, published in two volumes (London, 1791).

4. Dwight is referring to Jonathan Edwards, *A History of the Work of Redemption. Containing the Outlines of a Body of Divinity, in a Method Entirely New* (Edinburgh, 1774). This work was edited by John Erskine from sermons Edwards had preached in Northampton in 1739. *Two Dissertations, i. Concerning the End for which God created the World. ii. The Nature of true Virtue* (Boston, 1765).

5. In seven trips to America George Whitefield (1714–1770), Oxford 1736, the eloquent evangelical English Methodist, preached out of doors as well as in churches to large and responsive audiences from Massachusetts to Georgia. Originally inspired by the Wesleys, by 1741 Whitefield differed from them in adhering, like Jonathan Edwards, to the Calvinist tenet of predestination. On his last visit Whitefield died in Newburyport, Massachusetts.

6. Nehemiah Strong (1729–1807), Yale 1755, tutor 1757–1760, and pastor at East Granby, Connecticut, 1761–1767, was elected Yale's first professor of mathematics and natural philosophy in 1770. Strong engaged in a variety of employments after his resignation in 1781. He was the author of *Astronomy Improved . . .* (New Haven, 1784).

7. Charles Chauncy (1705–1787), Harvard 1721, great-grandson of President Chauncy of Harvard, as minister of the First Church gave leadership to the liberal opposition to Edwards among Boston's Congregational clergy. Chauncy's *Seasonable Thoughts on the State of Religion in New England* (1743) stated his objections to revivalism, upheld by Edwards. Dwight refers specifically to Chauncy's *The Mystery Hid from Ages . . . or The Salvation of All Men,* published anonymously in London in 1784. Jonathan Edwards Jr.'s answer to this work, following his father's thought, was *Salvation of All Men Strictly Examined* (1790). On the intellectual development of Chauncy see Conrad Wright, *The Beginnings of Unitarianism in America* (Boston, 1955). Samuel West (1730–1807), Harvard 1754, S.T.D. 1793, learned minister in Dartmouth, Massachusetts, (later part of New Bedford), 1761–1803, published *Essays on Liberty and Necessity* (Boston, 1793, and New Bedford, Mass., 1795) to refute Edwards' *Freedom of the Will* (Boston, 1754).

8. Thomas Godfrey (1704–1749) conceived a vastly improved mariner's quad-

rant which was shown to John Hadley's nephew among others. Dwight asserts the prevailing American opinion that Godfrey was denied his rightful credit for this invention. According to Joseph Jackson in the *D.A.B.*, VII, 346, in fact, the Royal Academy delivered to Godfrey household goods valued at £200 as a reward when he claimed the invention. However, Robert Edward Anderson in the *D.N.B.*, VIII, 879, states unequivocally that John Hadley (1682–1744), fellow of the Royal Society and distinguished for improving the telescope, invented the reflecting quadrant first.

9. In 1778 a lottery was held to purchase for Harvard College the orrery of Joseph Pope, a watchmaker of Boston. See "A Topographical and Historical Description of Boston, 1794," M.H.S. *Collections*, 3 (1794), 265–266. Pope's orrery is preserved in Houghton Library.

10. Although David Bushnell (c. 1742–1824), Yale 1775, was ridiculed for his unsuccessful attempt to torpedo British ships with his man-operated submarine boat, he did, in fact, while a student at Yale, invent the predecessor of the modern submarine.

11. *Hudibras,* a satirical poem by Samuel Butler, published in London (1663–1678), was the model for Trumbull's *McFingal.* For detailed analysis of the writing of *McFingal* with emphasis on the changing purposes of the author, see Leon Howard, *The Connecticut Wits,* pp. 52 ff, 67, and 70–77. John Trumbull (1750–1831), Yale 1767, tutor 1772–1773, one of the Connecticut Wits and Dwight's good friend, wrote the first canto of *McFingal* in 1775, and published the completed poem at Hartford in 1782. This satire describes the misfortunes of a Tory gentleman in the American Revolution and attacks the weaknesses of the British leaders. Trumbull, who also studied law with John Adams in Boston, became a judge in Connecticut and in later years rarely wrote poetry.

12. Benjamin West (1728–1820), after studying in Philadelphia and in Italy, lived in England for fifty-seven years. He became George III's painter of historical canvasses and succeeded Reynolds as president of the Royal Academy. John Singleton Copley (1738–1815), of Boston Irish immigrant parentage, early in his career became a portrait painter, settling in England in 1775. For a time Copley's success there brought him fame and money. He, too, turned to historical painting, but experienced great reverses in the last fifteen years of his life. The Rhode Island-born portrait painter Gilbert Stuart (1755–1828) became Benjamin West's protegé in London. Stuart's ambition to paint Washington was realized in Philadelphia in 1795; the latter years of his life were spent in Boston.

13. Bede (673–735) is known for his *Ecclesiastical History of the English Nation;* William of Malmesbury (1090/6–1143?), as an historian; and Friar Roger Bacon (1214?–1294), as a philosopher. Sir John Fortescue (1394?–1476) won reputation as a judge and writer on law. The poet Geoffrey Chaucer (1340?–1400) created the *Canterbury Tales;* John Gower (1325?–1408) wrote the *Confessio Amantis.*

14. Federalist John Marshall (1755–1835), despite his wilderness upbringing and lack of institutional education, became chief justice of the United States and wrote *The Life of George Washington* (5 vols., Philadelphia, 1804–1807). For a review such as Dwight mentions, see the *Edinburgh Review,* 13 (October 1808), 149–170.

15. Born in Scarboro, Maine, Federalist Rufus King (1755–1827), Harvard 1777, after studying with Theophilus Parsons, began his political career while practicing law in Newburyport, Massachusetts. Moving to New York City in 1788 (?), he became United States senator in 1789, and minister to Great Britain from 1796 to 1803. After two unsuccessful vice-presidential campaigns, King returned to the

Senate, 1813–1825. Like his friend Dwight, he could not sympathize with the growing democracy of the nation. See also Editor's Introduction, p. xxvii.

## LETTER V

1. Dwight again quotes from the *Quarterly Review,* 2, no. IV (London, Nov. 1809), 331. The article is a review of Abiel Holmes, *American Annals; or, a Chronological History of America* . . . (2 vols., Cambridge, 1805).

2. Cicero, *De Natura Deorum,* III, xl: "on behalf of our altars and hearths . . ."

3. The reference is to famous pugilists of Dwight's time. Daniel Mendoza (1764–1836) derived his first scientific knowledge about boxing from Richard Humphries, and published *The Art of Boxing* (1789). Ironically Richard Humphries, "the gentleman boxer," lost two of three fights with his former pupil Mendoza (1788, 1789, 1790). Tom Cribb (1781–1848) was also a champion British pugilist. Tom Molineaux, an American Negro, lost to Cribb in both 1810 and 1811.

4. Dwight refers to the textbook, *The Principles of Moral and Political Philosophy* (London, 1785), written by William Paley (1743–1805), archdeacon of Carlisle, England, and author of numerous theological works. For the specific quotation, see *Works* (Boston and Newport, R.I., 1810–1812), III, 521. In instructing Yale seniors during his presidency, Dwight made this book the basis of his accommodation of utilitarianism and Edwardsian Calvinism. In this context and in relation to Dwight's rejection of the textbooks of the Scottish philosophers he had used earlier while a tutor, see Leon Howard, *The Connecticut Wits,* pp. 235, 352, 361, 364–365.

5. The series of uprisings of impoverished farmers in western Massachusetts beginning August, 1786, was climaxed by the rebellion led by Daniel Shays (c. 1747–1825) in January and February, 1787. William Shepard (1737–1817), major general of the militia of Hampshire county, stopped the attack on the arsenal in Springfield before General Benjamin Lincoln arrived with additional troops.

6. William Windham (1750–1810), English statesman, M.P. 1784–1810, and secretary of war, 1794–1801, voiced his opposition to the bill for preventing the practice of bullbaiting in a speech of April 18, 1800. *Speeches in Parliament of the Right Honourable William Windham* (ed. Thomas Amyot, London, 1812), I, 331–356.

## LETTER VI

1. Cicero, *Pro Sexto Roscio Amerino,* XXX, 84: " . . . 'cui bono' fuisset.": " 'who had profited by it?' "

## LETTER VII

1. Oliver Goldsmith, "The Deserted Village," line 264.

2. The duties of the Sabbath are given in Isaiah lviii, 13: "If thou turn away thy foot from the sabbath, from doing thy pleasure on my holy day; and call the sabbath a delight, the holy of the Lord, honourable; and shalt honour him, not doing thine own ways, nor finding thine own pleasure, nor speaking thine own words . . ."

## RELIGION OF NEW ENGLAND

### LETTER I

1. Vergil, *Aeneid,* II, 97: ". . . the first taint of ill."

2. Dwight refers to Jean Jacques Rousseau (1712–1778), philosopher and author; Jean Le Rond d'Alembert (1717?–1783), mathematician; and Denis Diderot (1713–1784), philosopher and editor of the *Encyclopédie* (17 vols., Paris, 1751–1765).

3. Trophonius is said to have built the first temple of Apollo at Delphi and was worshiped after his death at a celebrated cave in Boeotia. Inquirers went there for purification and mystic experiences giving knowledge of the future world.

4. See Dwight's early effort to inform New Englanders of the real character of Voltaire. Dwight dedicated *The Triumph of Infidelity* (Printed in the World, 1788) to "Mons. de Voltaire" with the following statement: "Your Creator endued you with shining talents and cast your lot in a field of action, where they might be most happily employed: In the progress of a long and industrious life, you devoted them to a single purpose, the elevation of your character above his. For the accomplishment of this purpose . . . you opposed truth, religion, and their authors . . . and taught . . . that the chief end of man was to slander his God, and abuse him forever. To whom could such an effort as the following be dedicated, with more propriety, than to you. . . . Accept then, as due, this tribute of acknowledgement from the WRITER OF THIS POEM."

### LETTER II

1. Edward Herbert, first Baron Herbert of Cherbury (1583–1648), an English diplomat and philosopher, is best known for *De Veritate, prout distinguitur a Revelatione, a Verisimili, a Possibili, at a falso* (Paris, 1624; 1st London ed., 1645). Among the many works of Thomas Chubb (1679–1747), an English deist, are *A Discourse concerning Reason . . .* (London, 1731); *The True Gospel of Jesus Christ asserted* (London, 1738); and *The True Gospel of Jesus Christ vindicated* (London, 1739); his most formidable critic was Jonathan Edwards. Matthew Tindal (1657–1733) was another English theological writer; Anthony Ashley Cooper, third Earl of Shaftesbury (1671–1713), an English moral philosopher; and Henry St. John, first Viscount Bolingbroke (1678–1751), an English statesman and political writer.

2. Minos, the king of Crete, had Daedalus construct a labyrinth for the confinement of the Minotaur.

3. John Milton, *Paradise Lost,* Book III, 496.

4. Dwight refers to Jakob Bohme (1575–1624), the German mystic, and Emanuel Swedenborg (1688–1772), the Swedish scientist, philosopher, and religious writer. "The limbo of vanity" is Dwight's reference to ". . . a Limbo large and broad, since call'd The Paradise of Fools, . . ." Milton, *Paradise Lost,* Book III, 495–496.

5. Maximilien François Marie Isidore de Robespierre (1758–1794), Georges Jacques Danton (1759–1794), and Jean Baptiste Carrier (1756–1794) were leaders in the French Revolution.

6. Louis XVI (1754–1793) was King of France from 1774 to 1792.

7. Dwight is here referring to *Système de la nature* or *Des loix du monde physique et du monde moral* (London, 1770) by Baron Paul Henri Thiry Baron d'Holbach (1723–1789); *Dictionnaire philosophique . . .* (London [i.e. Geneva], 1764) by François Marie Arouet de Voltaire (1694–1778); William Godwin, *An Enquiry Concerning Political Justice, and its Influence on General Virtue and Happiness* (London, 1793); and Thomas Paine, *The Age of Reason; Being an Investigation of True and Fabulous Theology* (Paris, 1794–1795).

## LETTER III

1. Horace, *Epistulae,* I, 24, "Naturam expelles furca, tamen usque recurret": "You may drive out Nature with a pitchfork, yet she will ever hurry back."

2. Alaric (370?–410) was king of the Visigoths and conqueror of Rome, while Attila (406?–453) was the infamous king of the Huns; and Genseric (d. 477), king of the Vandals, 428–477.

3. Acts xxvi, 22.

4. Vergil, *Aeneid,* II, 5–6: ". . . quaeque ipse miserrima vidi / et quorum pars magna fui . . .": ". . . the sights most piteous that I myself saw and whereof I was no small part . . ."

5. Psalm cxxiv, 2–8.

## LETTER V

1. Dwight repeats the quotation he used a few pages earlier: Acts xxvi, 22.

2. Matt. x, 8.

3. John xviii, 36; Luke xvii, 21; Romans xiv, 17.

4. Matt. xvi, 18.

5. 1 Cor. iii, 6–7: "I have planted, Apollos watered; but God gave the increase. So then neither is he that planteth any thing, neither he that watereth; but God that giveth the increase."

6. 1 Tim. v, 8.

7. Luke iv, 23.

8. Matt. x, 7–8: "And as ye go, preach, saying, the kingdom of heaven is at hand. Heal the sick, cleanse the lepers, raise the dead, cast out devils: freely ye have received, freely give."

9. Matt. x, 9–11, 14–15.

10. 1 Cor. ix, 14.

11. 1 Cor. ix, 9.

12. Dwight has integrated 2 Tim. ii, 15; 1 Tim. iv, 13; and 1 Tim. iv, 15.

13. 1 Cor. xvi, 1–2.

## LETTER VI

1. Plutarch, *Caesaris Apophthegmata,* p. 3.

## LETTER VIII

1. Matt. xviii, 15–17: "Moreover if thy brother shall trespass against thee, go and tell him his fault between thee and him alone: if he shall hear thee, thou hast gained thy brother. But if he will not hear thee, then take with thee one or two more, that in the mouth of two or three witnesses every word may be established.

And if he shall neglect to hear them, tell it unto the church: but if he neglect to hear the church, let him be unto thee as a heathen man and a publican."

2. Dwight's version has been corrected; see *Records of the Colony of Connecticut* (Hartford, 1870), V, 87.

3. 1 Tim. v, 17: "Let the elders that rule well be counted worthy of double honour, especially they who labour in the word and doctrine." Romans xii, 8: "Or he that exhorteth, on exhortation: he that giveth, let him do it with simplicity; he that ruleth, with diligence; he that sheweth mercy, with cheerfulness." 1 Cor. xii, 28: "And God hath set some in the church, first apostles, secondarily prophets, thirdly teachers, after that miracles, then gifts of healings, helps, governments, diversities of tongues."

4. "Heads of Agreement," in Williston Walker, *The Creeds and Platforms of Congregationalism* (New York, 1893), pp. 455–462, article VIII.

5. "Heads of Agreement," in Walker, *Creeds,* p. 461–462.

## LETTER IX

1. Spencer Perceval (1762–1812), prime minister of England, 1809–1812, and an ardent opponent of Catholic emancipation, was the object of attack in *The State of the Established Church. In a Series of Letters to the Right Hon. Spencer Perceval, Chancellor of the Exchequer, etc.* (2nd ed., London, 1810). A review of the publication, to which Dwight refers, is found in the *Christian Observer,* 10 (November 1811), 708–720, and (December 1811), 778–794.

2. In his awkward Latin phrase, Dwight refers to England as the country "of my forefathers and of all the ancestors from whom my race is descended."

3. Dwight is quoting from the *Christian Observer,* November 1811, pp. 709–710, which is in turn quoting from *The State of the Established Church,* pp. 20, 15, 22.

4. *Christian Observer,* November 1811, p. 710.

5. The first volume of Gilbert Burnet's (1643–1715) *History of the Reformation of the Church of England* (3 vols., London, 1679–1715) was received with enthusiasm during the popish terror, and contributed to his disfavor under Catholic James II. Burnet's support of the Revolution of 1688 won him the bishopric of Salisbury. *Bishop Burnet's History of His Own Time* (2 vols., London, 1724–1734), his most important work, was not published until after his death. *Of the Lawes of Ecclesiasticall Politie* (London, 1594–1597, 1648, 1662) by Richard Hooker (1554?–1600), Oxford-educated theologian, provided the most influential defense of the Anglican Church after the Elizabethan settlement. Hooker, who retained the friendship of moderate Puritans at Cambridge University, accepted the Calvinist doctrine of election. On his disagreement with Puritanism, see Perry Miller, *The New England Mind* (New York, 1939).

6. *Christian Observer,* November 1811, p. 713.

7. Acts xix, 2.

8. Dudley Ryder, first Earl of Harrowby (1762–1847), Cambridge 1782, a member of Parliament from 1784 until his father's death in 1803 raised him to the peerage, was particularly interested in church questions. Dwight is referring to the "Substance of the Speech of the Earl of Harrowby, delivered in the House of Lords, Monday, June 18, 1810, upon a Clause in the Appropriation Act, for granting the Sum of One Hundred Thousand Pounds, for the Relief of the poorer Clergy" (London, 1811), which was published in the *Christian Observer,* 10 (1811), pp. 380–389.

9. *Christian Observer,* November 1811, pp. 714–715, quoting *The State of the Established Church,* pp. 37–40.

10. *Christian Observer,* November 1811, p. 715.

11. Robert Hall (1764–1831), an English Baptist pastor who was primarily noted for his ministerial eloquence, published *Christianity Consistent with a Love of Freedom* (London, 1791) and other works. Dwight may also have known of him as a frequent contributor to the *Eclectic Review.* Sydney Smith (1771–1845), an Anglican clergyman and poet, was famous for his fresh and racy style of preaching. Dwight was doubtless acquainted with Smith as a founder and frequent contributor to the *Edinburgh Review* and evidently had read the review of Smith's *Two Volumes of Sermons* (London, 1809) in the *Christian Observer,* 8 (Sept. 1809), 578–598. William Cowper (1731–1800) was the author of *The Task, a Poem in Six Books* (London, 1785). Dwight's quotation is drawn from book II, "The Time-Piece," lines 399–407. The passage gives a portrait of St. Paul as the model of the moral preacher. Dwight's version, however, alters the original to make the subject plural and, interestingly, substitutes the word "peace" in the last line for Cowper's "grace."

12. John x, 5; John x, 12.

13. 1 Tim. iv, 16.

14. Heb. xiii, 17.

15. Dwight is referring to a letter in the *Christian Observer,* 8 (August 1809), 499–503, by an author who signs himself C., "To the Editor of the *Christian Observer.*" The statements which Dwight quotes in this chapter of the *Travels* come from pp. 501–503. The table to which Dwight refers can be found on p. 502 of the *Christian Observer,* and was taken from Alexander Ranken, *The Importance of Religious Establishments* (Glasgow, 1799), "and corrected by means of Morse's Geography."

16. Horace, *Satires,* I, v, 100: "Apella, the Jew, may believe it, not I."

## LETTER X

1. The Hopkinsians adopted the theological interpretations of Samuel Hopkins (1721–1803), Yale 1741, an intimate associate and follower of Jonathan Edwards, who carried the principles of the New Divinity to their logical conclusions. Hopkins' stressed the tenet that one must be willing to be damned if the glory of God required it. For the formulation of his doctrine, see *System of Doctrines contained in Divine Revelation . . .* (Boston, 1793). See also Editor's Introduction, p. xv.

2. Jacobus Arminius (1560–1609) was the Dutch theologian whose opposition to Calvinism formed the doctrinal foundation for the Remonstrant Church in Holland. Though he never achieved logical consistency in his system, Arminius resisted the rigid uniformity of his time, asserting more and more aggressively the freedom of man. Simon Episcopius (1583–1643), another Dutch theologian, studied and taught at the University of Leiden from 1600 until 1619 when at the end of the Synod of Dort he was expelled from the country for his doctrines. Episcopius developed and systematized the principles tentatively proposed by Arminius into a scheme specifically opposed to Calvinism's emphasis on abstract dogma, arguing that Christianity was practical rather than theoretical.

3. Charles Daubeny (1745–1827) was a rigidly orthodox Anglican who showed his skill in controversy in his voluminous writings. Attacking popery as vigorously as nonconformity, he published his first work *Twelve Lectures on the Church Catechism* in 1778 (London); and the more widely discussed two-volume *Appendix to the "Guide to the Church"* (London, 1799), which endeavored to prove

that any departure from the apostolically ordained Church of England was schismatic. Sir George Pretyman Tomline (1750–1827), Cambridge 1772, the appointed tutor and later private secretary to the younger Pitt, became bishop of Lincoln in 1787. A campaigner against both Calvinist doctrine and Catholic emancipation, he published the popular *Elements of Christian Theology* . . . (London, 1799), as a guide to candidates for ordination.

4. John Overton (1763–1838), Cambridge 1790, is best known as the author of *The True Churchman Ascertained, or An Apology for those of the Regular Clergy of the Establishment who Are Sometimes Called Evangelical Ministers, Occasioned by the Publications of Drs. Paley, Hey, and Croft* . . . (York, 1801), which contended that the evangelicals were the only true churchmen.

5. John Wesley (1703–1791), Oxford-educated English evangelist and organizer of Methodism, came to Georgia as a missionary, 1735–1737. After his return to England he began his life-long career as preacher to the poorer classes of British society. His eventual conclusion that bishops and priests were essentially of the same order, and that therefore priests could ordain other priests, made inevitable a separation of the Methodists from the Church of England.

6. Rom. vi, 1.

7. 2 John i, 1.

## CHARACTERISTICS OF THE MEN AND WOMEN IN NEW ENGLAND

### LETTER I

1. Johann Kaspar Riesbeck (1754–1786) published *Briefe eines reisenden Franzosen* . . . ([Zurich], 1783), which was translated into English in three volumes in 1787 and into French from the English in 1788. See Riesbeck, *Travels through Germany* . . . (Paul H. Maty, tr., London, 1787), II, 97.

2. Aeschylus (525–456 B.C.) was a Greek tragic dramatist, as was Euripides (5th century B.C.). Johann Christoph Friedrich von Schiller (1759–1805) was a German poet and playwright, and August Friedrich Ferdinand von Kotzebue (1761–1819), a German dramatist.

3. Dwight quotes from one of his favorite poets, Edward Young (1683–1765), whose *Love of Fame, The Universal Passion, In Seven Characteristical Satires* was published in London, 1725–1728. The correct lines from Satire VI are:

> What's female beauty but an air divine,
> Through which the mind's all-gentle graces shine?
> They, like the sun, irradiate all between;
> And the body charms, because the soul is seen.

### LETTER II

1. The article to which Dwight refers in the *Quarterly Review,* 2, no. IV (Nov. 1809), 319–337, especially p. 331, reviews Abiel Holmes' *American Annals.* In the same article Dwight is criticized as a poet who "has failed because he imitated bad models," p. 330.

2. Zebulon Montgomery Pike (1779–1813), a soldier and explorer, made a mad unsuccessful attempt to reach the top of the peak that bears his name. In 1810 he published *An Account of Expeditions to the Sources of the Mississippi, and through the Western Parts of Louisiana . . .* (Philadelphia).

## MANUFACTURES OF NEW ENGLAND

1. In the following pages, Dwight is summarizing Gallatin's *Report from the Secretary of the Treasury . . . on American Manufactures* (Boston, 1810), pp. 1–26. Emigrating from Geneva and settling in western Pennsylvania, the Jeffersonian Albert Gallatin (1761–1849) served his adopted country in many offices, especially as secretary of the treasury, 1801–1814. Dwight's supplementary tables pertaining to Massachusetts and Connecticut manufactures, despite variations in form and data, are in general agreement with the U.S. Treasury Department report, *A Statement of the Arts and Manufactures of the United States . . .* (prepared by Tench Coxe; Philadelphia, 1814), part IV, *A Series of Tables of . . . Every County of the Union* (1813), pp. 4–12, 22–31. Obvious numerical discrepancies have been silently corrected.

2. Samuel Slater (1768–1835), the founder of the American cotton industry, had to disguise himself to emigrate to the United States because of prohibitive English laws. In 1790 he signed a contract with William Almy, son-in-law of Moses Brown, and Smith Brown, a young relative of Moses Brown, to reproduce Arkwright's machinery for them. Slater also subsequently established mills of his own in Rhode Island, Connecticut, and New Hampshire. Sir Richard Arkwright (1732–1792), an English inventor and textile manufacturer, constructed a spinning frame for which he was granted a patent in 1769; with capital from Strutt and Need he set up his first cotton manufactory. The eventual disallowment of Arkwright's patents had little adverse effect on his prosperity and leading position in the textile industry.

3. Self-educated Anglican clergyman Thomas Scott (1747–1821), D.D. Dickinson College 1807, wrote a commentary on the Bible which was published in 174 weekly numbers, *The Holy Bible . . . with Original Notes and Practical Observations* (4 vols., London, 1788–1792). Adam Clarke (1762?–1832), a British Wesleyan divine and Biblical scholar, published *The Holy Bible . . . With a Commentary and Critical Notes* in eight volumes (London, 1810–1826).

4. Welshman Abraham Rees (1743–1825), D.D. Edinburgh 1775, a leader among the dissenting ministry of London, edited *The New Cyclopaedia . . .* (45 vols., London, 1802–1820). The first American edition of his *Cyclopaedia,* enlarged and adapted to this country. was published in forty-one volumes (Philadelphia, 1810–1824).

5. John Pinkerton (1758–1826), a Scottish poet, numismatist, and antiquarian, published various works on the history of Scotland, and a *General Collection of the Best and Most Interesting Voyages and Travels in All Parts of the World . . .* (17 vols. London, 1807–1814).

6. Oliver Evans (1755–1819), America's first steam engine builder, perfected a complete power operation for flour milling, but it was not accepted at the time by the millers. About 1802 Evans founded a business specializing in the manufacture of the high pressure engine he had designed.

## MASSACHUSETTS

### LETTER I

1. Massachusetts Constitution of 1780, Part I, Article 17.

### LETTER II

1. Massachusetts Constitution of 1780, Part I, Articles 2 and 3.

2. Dwight discusses the witchcraft episode more extensively in volume I of the *Travels,* "Journey to Berwick," Letter XLI.

## PROSPECTS OF THE UNITED STATES

### LETTER I

1. Berkeley's poem was published in *A Miscellany, Containing Several Tracts on Various Subjects* (Dublin, 1752), pp. 185–186.

2. The area of the United States in 1810 was 1,716,003 square miles.

3. Dwight's United States population figures vary slightly from the totals given in the federal censuses for those years, which are respectively: 1790, 3,921,326; 1800, 5,319,762; and 1810, 7,239,903. The figures given by the U.S. Bureau of the Census in *Historical Statistics of the United States* . . . (Washington, 1960), p. 8, vary from both Dwight and the *Censuses* published in 1791, 1801, and 1811; they are: 1790, 3,929,214; 1800, 5,308,483; and 1810, 7,239,881.

4. Dwight was not far wrong in his projection of the United States population for 1850 which was 23,191,876; his estimate for 1900 proved to be overoptimistic; the population was only 75,994,575. (U.S. Bureau of the Census, *Historical Statistics,* p. 8).

### LETTER II

1. Gen. xi, 1.

2. Matt. xxiii, 23.

3. Job x, 21.

# INDEX

THE JOHN HARVARD LIBRARY

*The intent of*
*Waldron Phoenix Belknap, Jr.,*
*as expressed in an early will, was for*
*Harvard College to use the income from a permanent trust fund he set up, for "editing and publishing rare, inaccessible, or hitherto unpublished source material of interest in connection with the history, literature, art (including minor and useful art), commerce, customs, and manners or way of life of the Colonial and Federal Periods of the United States . . . In all cases the emphasis shall be on the presentation of the basic material." A later testament broadened this statement, but Mr. Belknap's interests remained constant until his death.*

*In linking the name of the first benefactor of Harvard College with the purpose of this later, generous-minded believer in American culture the John Harvard Library seeks to emphasize the importance of Mr. Belknap's purpose. The John Harvard Library of the Belknap Press of Harvard University Press exists to make books and documents about the American past more readily available to scholars and the general reader.*

JHL